BORDERLANDS OF WESTERN CIVILIZATION

A History of
East Central Europe

By

OSCAR HALECKI

PROFESSOR OF EASTERN EUROPEAN HISTORY
GRADUATE SCHOOL OF ARTS AND SCIENCES
FORDHAM UNIVERSITY

THE RONALD PRESS COMPANY   •   NEW YORK

Library of Congress Catalog Card Number: 52–6197

PRINTED IN THE UNITED STATES OF AMERICA

To the memory of my beloved parents

PREFACE

Having studied and taught Eastern European history for many years, I had of course always tried to include the history of all the countries that lie east of Germany. But in doing this I became more and more aware that three distinct fields of study have to be treated and differentiated. Two of these, which are universally recognized, are familiar to many scholars of various lands and are covered in numerous textbooks and historical surveys. These are the history of the Byzantine Empire in the Middle Ages, which was later replaced by the Ottoman Empire, and the history of the Russian Empire, which was created by Moscow in the course of the modern period. There remains, however, the history of the numerous peoples which in both mediaeval and modern times have lived between Germany and these empires, sometimes in independent states of their own, sometimes submerged by their powerful neighbors.

The third field is equally as interesting and important as the other two because of its internal diversity. In spite of such great variety, however, it represents a clearly distinct unity which occupies a special place in the development of mankind, as I attempted to show briefly in my recent book on *The Limits and Divisions of European History*. Yet that whole region of Europe is neglected in the writing and teaching of general and European history, as well as in the interpretation of the subject matter. No textbook is available to the student which helps him to understand the past of that large area as a whole, nor is there any synthesized survey at the disposal of the reader who feels that a broad historical background is badly needed for grasping the implications of contemporary events. Therefore, it remained difficult to realize the significance of all the many peoples between Germany and Russia—peoples whose collective population exceeds that of either the Germans or even the Russians.

To fill such a gap within the compass of a single volume is no easy task for an individual historian. Obliged to make a strict selection among countless facts, he is unavoidably influenced by the chief directions of his own research work. And even in the case of those facts which are incidentally mentioned in the outlines of world history or in the histories of contiguous or neighboring regions, the task of coordinating them into a picture which is inspired by an entirely different approach naturally raises new and complex problems.

The origins of the whole story, in part prehistoric, have received special attention in some valuable recent works. This was an additional reason for treating these distant times, which remain filled with controversial issues, as briefly as possible. Detailed discussion of the Middle Ages, from the tenth century onward, and of the Renaissance, which is usually regarded as a typically Western development, proved indispensable. This was in view of the vitality of the mediaeval traditions for nations which were later to lose their freedom, and because of the cultural community which the later Middle Ages and the Renaissance created between Western Europe and what might be called—since there is no better name—East Central Europe.

The motivating ideas in describing the fairly well-known modern centuries of European history from the point of view of the victims were these: That a free East Central Europe is indispensable for any sound balance of power on the Continent, and that the temporary disappearance of that whole region created a dangerous tension between suppressed nationalisms and apparently well-established imperialisms which usually were in dangerous rivalry with one another. Seen from the point of view of the nations of East Central Europe, which were independent between the two world wars and which again lost their freedom after the second, even contemporary history must appear in a different light.

If throughout this book, which attempts to show how far Western civilization expanded in the direction of the East, political history receives special attention, it is because for students and readers at large a knowledge of the main political events is a prerequisite framework and an indispensable basis for further study in the cultural, social, or economic field.

In addition to the results of my own research, I have tried to utilize all that I owe not only to my Polish professors and colleagues but also to the leading historians of the other nations of East Central Europe. Among the latter are such scholars as N. Iorga of Rumania, E. Lukinich of Hungary, V. Novotný of Czechoslovakia, and F. Šišić of Yugoslavia, all of whom I have met at many international congresses of the interwar period. And to these should also be added the representatives of the Baltic Countries who, under the leadership of F. Balodis of Latvia, organized the first conference of Baltic historians in 1937. I also gratefully acknowledge the experience gained through long years of teaching at the universities of Cracow and Warsaw, that of my early youth in the multinational Danubian Empire, and that of ten years spent in American centers of learning where there is an ever-growing interest in all that has to do with East Central Europe.

I am very much obliged to my publishers and to their expert staff for the careful attention with which they prepared this volume for publication, especially in dealing with the maps and the genealogical chart. Although the four maps cannot, of course, take the place of a historical atlas, nevertheless they do illustrate at least some of the basic interpretations of the text. Similarly, the genealogical table could not include all members of the various dynasties, but for the first time their relationship is presented on a single chart, thus stressing those matrimonial alliances which explain the order of succession from the mediaeval origins to the threshold of modern times.

Finally, I wish to express my sincere gratitude to my wife for her helpful cooperation, particularly in preparing the index.

OSCAR HALECKI

New York City
January, 1952

CONTENTS

PART I

The Background

PART II

The Medieval Tradition

PART III

Renaissance Developments

CONTENTS

PART VI

Twenty Years of Freedom

PART VII

During and After World War II

MAPS

GENEALOGICAL CHART

NOTES ON PRONUNCIATION

In the various languages of East Central Europe, practically all vowels are pronounced much as in Italian, Spanish, or Continental Latin. The following points must, however, be kept in mind:

1. The Czech *ě* is pronounced like English *ye*.

2. Polish *ą* and *ę* are nasal sounds which correspond to the French *on* and *in*, respectively. Polish *ó* is pronounced like *oo* in *book*.

3. In Hungarian, an acute accent makes the vowel sound long and clear so that, for instance, *á* is pronounced like *a* in English *are*. A mere *a* sounds like that same letter in English *all*.

4. In Rumanian, an *i* at the beginning of a word, followed by another vowel, is pronounced like an English *y*.

For pronouncing consonants with accents or in various combinations, the following table will be helpful:

Czech	Polish	Hungarian	English	
č	*cz*	*cs, ch*	*ch*	
ch	*ch*		*h*	
j	*j*	*j*	*y*	
ř	*rz*		*rsh*	(In Polish, the sound *r* is barely heard.)
š	*sz*	*s*	*sh*	(In Hungarian, *sz* is pronounced *s*.)
ž	*ż*		*zh*	(Like the French *j*.)

In all these languages, *c* is pronounced like *ts,* so that the combination *ck,* which is frequent in Czech and Polish names, always equals *tsk.* Furthermore, in Polish, *ń* is pronounced like the Spanish *ñ,* and *ł* like the English *w*. The Polish *w* corresponds to English *v*.

For the Bulgarian, Russian, Serbo-Croatian, Ukrainian, and White-Ruthenian languages, the conventional English transcription has been used, since all these peoples except the Croats employ the Cyrillic alphabet.

PART I

THE BACKGROUND

1

THE GEOGRAPHICAL AND ETHNOGRAPHICAL
BACKGROUND

EAST CENTRAL EUROPE

The usual approach to European history is strangely limited. Very frequently Western Europe is identified with the whole continent and even in that western part only the big powers, particularly the empires, receive serious attention. It certainly made for progress when, in the study of some periods, a few eastern powers were also included. Thus the revival of interest in Byzantium, the Eastern Roman Empire, contributed to a better understanding of the Middle Ages. The rise and decline of the Ottoman Empire, although it was a power of non-European origin, had to be considered part of modern European history. And as soon as Muscovy developed into another empire, the history of that new Russia proved to be inseparable from that of Europe as a whole.

There remained, however, a vast *terra incognita* of European historiography: the eastern part of Central Europe, between Sweden, Germany, and Italy, on the one hand, and Turkey and Russia on the other. In the course of European history, a great variety of peoples in this region created their own independent states, sometimes quite large and powerful; in connection with Western Europe they developed their individual national cultures and contributed to the general progress of European civilization.

It is true that time and again some of these nations were submerged by the neighboring empires, and so was the whole group precisely at the moment when, toward the beginning of the nineteenth century, the writing of history entered its truly scientific phase. This might to a certain extent explain why the nations of East Central Europe were so badly neglected in the contemporary study and teaching of the historical sciences. And since the period of their apparent disappearance coincided with the formation of the American nation,

3

it is even more understandable that they seemed of little interest to American historiography.

The shortcomings of such a limited interpretation of Europe became evident as soon as the process of liberation and reconstruction of East Central Europe was almost completed after World War I. But even then the so-called "new" nations of that whole region, most of them very old indeed, were usually studied without sufficient consideration of their historical background. And, both in Western Europe and in America, the realization of their importance in the making and organizing of Europe had hardly started when the normal development of that crucial region was once more interrupted by World War II. In the unfinished peace settlement after the last war, all these nations were sacrificed to another wave of imperialism in one of its contemporary totalitarian forms. No permanent peace will be established before their traditional place in the European community, now enlarged as the Atlantic community, is restored.

Historical science can contribute to such a solution by promoting a better understanding of the antecedents. But as a science, history will first have to repair its own mistake in overlooking so large a territory near the very heart of the European Continent. That territory, which never has been a historical unit, in spite of so many experiences which all its peoples had in common, is not a geographical unit either. And as it has happened with all historical regions, it did not even have any permanent boundaries.

Hence the initial difficulty of giving to that part of Europe a truly fitting name. The difficulty is increased by the artificial character of all the conventional divisions of the Continent into a certain number of regions. If only two of them, Western and Eastern Europe, are distinguished, it is impossible to find a proper place for a territory which does not belong in toto to either part. If the conception of a Central Europe is added, it must be specified at once that there is an inherent dualism in that central region. Leaving aside its western, homogeneously German section, only the eastern section can be roughly identified with the "new" or "unknown" field of study which is being introduced here into the general framework and pattern of European history. For that very reason the name East Central Europe seems most appropriate.

That means, of course, a geographical division of Europe, not into two or three but into four basic regions: Western, West Central, East

Central, and Eastern. And such a division is clearly justified, so far as the main body of the Continent is concerned. But the question arises as to how the great European peninsulas fit into that division. In the case of East Central Europe, this is the question of its relationship to the Balkan Peninsula.

The Balkans are not only geographically different from the Danubian lands, but they differ even more from the great plain north of the Sudeten and Carpathian mountains. In the days of the Mediterranean community which preceded the European, the Balkan Peninsula, and particularly its Greek extension—historically the oldest section of Europe—had been an integral part of that earliest community, and eventually of the Roman Empire. That Empire advanced to the Danube and even crossed it temporarily into Dacia. But the main part of East Central Europe remained outside; it was not even touched by Roman influence, as was West Central Europe up to the Elbe, and it definitely belonged to the historically younger part of Europe which entered the European community, and history in general, not before the centuries which followed the fall of the Empire in the West. At the same time, some of the peoples of East Central Europe invaded the European territory of the Eastern Empire, that is, the Balkans. They penetrated even as far as Greece, and definitely settled in most of the main northern section of the peninsula.

A large section of the original Eastern Europe was thus associated with East Central Europe through a historical process which disregarded the geographical factor as quite frequently happens. That very factor facilitated the eastern expansion of other peoples of East Central Europe through an early process of colonization; an advance through the practically unlimited European Plain in the direction of Asia. It was only then that the large region, which geographically is Eastern Europe, was also historically connected with Europe proper. But without discussing here the highly controversial question as to what extent that colonial area in the Volga Basin ever became fully European in the historical sense, it must immediately be pointed out that it always remained different from East Central Europe. The boundary between the two regions, hardly a natural frontier, fluctuated back and forth of course. But the clear distinction between the two is a prerequisite for a correct understanding of European history.

For similar geographical reasons, there was also no natural frontier between East Central and West Central Europe, although here again the historian has to make a distinction as clearly as possible. It was only too natural, however, that whenever in the course of history the open intermediary region of East Central Europe suffered a stronger pressure from either side, it tried to move in the opposite direction. The situation became critical when the pressure came simultaneously from both sides. Sometimes a serious threat to some of the peoples of East Central Europe also came from the south, and even from the north; through the Balkans, which they never completely controlled, or across the Baltic from the Scandinavian side of the "Mediterranean of the North."

The southern danger increased tremendously when the Byzantine Empire, which usually remained on the defensive, was replaced by the aggressive Ottoman Empire. And since the Turkish onslaught started at a time when Eastern Europe was still under Tartar overlordship, East Central Europe had to face the impact of Asiatic forces on two different fronts. Its role as a bulwark of Europe as a whole, of Christendom and Western culture, can therefore hardly be overrated.

Equally important for general European history are the problems of the Baltic. But they are merely internal problems of Europe, and since neither the Normans in the Middle Ages nor Sweden at the height of her short-lived power succeeded in creating anything like a Scandinavian Empire, the dangers which threatened East Central Europe from the northern side proved to be only temporary. But it ought to be remembered that even the natural frontier of the Baltic Sea was neither an adequate protection nor a real barrier. It was crossed more than once by Scandinavian invasions which alternated with projects of cooperation between the countries on both sides of the Baltic. And not only northern but also western conquerors and colonists succeeded in cutting off from that sea, sometimes for centuries, the native populations of East Central Europe and their national states.

Nevertheless, thanks to their access to the Baltic during most of history, and thanks to an access to the Black Sea which was, it is true, even more contested by foreign invaders from the east and the south, the peoples of East Central Europe occupied a territory which geographically can be considered a wide isthmus between two seas. Furthermore, they also reached a third sea, another bay of the Mediterranean, the Adriatic, and approached the Mediterranean itself through the Balkans. But here, too, they met with serious difficulties in really controlling the coast line and the ports which were mostly in foreign hands. With rare exceptions, the East Central European nations did not develop any considerable sea power.

This is one of the reasons why they never fully took advantage of the geopolitical possibilities offered by the huge area which they inhabited and by its position in Europe. Another even more important reason was the obvious fact that their territory, so varied in its topography, consisted of quite a number of minor regions which were very difficult to unite in one body politic. At least three of these subdivisions must be distinguished. One of them is the central sector of the great European Plain, including parts of both the Baltic and the Pontic shores. The second is the Danubian Basin, with the adjacent Bohemian quadrilateral. And third come the Balkans, without any clear-cut separation from the preceding region, however, so that there are countries which might be considered partly Danubian and partly Balkan. For these and other reasons, any geographical determinism in the interpretation of East Central Europe would be even more misleading than in the case of any other territory.

SLAVS AND BALTS

Equally misleading would be any racial interpretation of East Central European history. Practically nowhere in Europe can we identify the ethnic groups which appear in history, or even in prehistory, with races in the anthropological sense. But in addition to the usual mixture of various racial elements, there always was in East Central Europe, as there is today, a particularly great variety of ethnic groups which differ in language and general culture. It is true, however, that from the dawn of history, among these groups the Slavs occupy a central and predominant position representing the vast majority of all peoples in that whole region.

The recorded history of the Slavs begins at a comparatively late moment, not before the sixth century A.D. By their earliest invasions of the Eastern Roman Empire, at the turn of the fifth century, they came for the first time into contact with the Greco-Roman world. Therefore, though ancient writers of the preceding centuries, beginning with Tacitus, Pliny, and Ptolemy, noted a few names of tribes in the unknown northeast of Europe, including some which certainly refer to Slavic peoples, more detailed information was given by Jor-

danes and Procopius, the leading historians of the sixth century. The
three peoples, Venedi, Sclaveni, and Antes, which the former dis-
tinguishes among the Slavs (the latter omits the Venedi, known to
earlier writers but not neighboring with the Byzantine Empire), seem
to correspond to the Western, Southern, and Eastern Slavs which
until the present remained the main divisions of the Slavic world. And
there is no doubt that in the sixth century they already occupied the
whole territory north of the Balkans, east of the Elbe-Saale line and
its continuation toward the Adriatic. They also reached the southern
shores of the Baltic and the Dnieper River.

The question as to when they settled in that whole area is highly
controversial. It is now universally admitted, contrary to legendary
traditions, that the original home of the Slavs was north of the Carpathians. Furthermore, the Sudeten Mountains were not crossed, and
the Elbe was not reached by compact Slavic settlements before the
great migrations of the Germanic tribes toward the West. But contrary to the opinion which, under German influence, continues to prevail in Western historiography, the original homeland of the Slavs
was not limited to the territory east of the Vistula. Recent archaeological research seems to confirm that from the end of the Neolithic
Age, about 2000 B.C., the Slavs occupied the whole basin of the Vistula and most of that of the Oder, in addition to their eastern settlements between the Pripet Marshes and the Black Sea.

It is also highly probable that during this earliest period of their
prehistory, which lasted some three or four hundred years, they lived
in close community with their northeastern neighbors, the Balts.
There is no agreement among linguists as to the existence of a common Balto-Slavic language, but in any case Slavs and Balts had closer
relations with each other than with any other group of Indo-European
peoples. Even after the final division of their community into two
branches, in the early Bronze Age, the destinies of both groups remained inseparable, and next to the Slavs the Baltic peoples were
always the most important native ethnical element in East Central
Europe.

Originally, the Balts occupied a much larger part of that region
than in modern times. It extended from the sea to which they gave its
name (*baltas* = white), taking it in turn as the usual name of their
group (the name Aistians or Aestians is very questionable), as far as
the Oka River. In addition to the Lithuanians in the center of the

group, who were most numerous, and to the Letts or Latvians in the north, the Balts also included the old Prussians who disappeared after the German conquest of the thirteenth century, losing even their name to the invaders. The historical role of all the Baltic peoples started much later than that of the Slavs, however, not before the tenth century A.D.

It is another controversial problem as to what extent the Slavs themselves, after their separation from the Balts, constituted an ethnic and linguistic community which might be called proto-Slavic. It seems that already, in the course of the various periods of their prehistory, including the probably foreign (Celtic or Illyrian?) impact of the Lusatian culture between 1500 and 1300 B.C. and the undoubtedly Slavic Pit Grave culture down to Roman times, the differentiation among the Slavs was making rapid progress. Their territorial expansion in three directions certainly contributed to it so that when the three main branches of Slavic peoples appeared in history each of them was already divided into various groups and tribes.

Out of the Western Slavs, only the ancestors of the Poles, who took their name from the tribe of the *Polanie* (field dwellers), remained in the original Slavic homeland in the Vistula and Oder basins. Another group, linked to the Poles through the Pomeranians along the Baltic Coast (*Pomorze*—the land along the sea) and consisting of the Polabian tribes (the name means *along the Elbe*) and of the Lusatian Serbs or Sorbs, advanced to the extreme western limits of Slavic expansion. South of the latter and of the Polish tribes in Silesia and the Upper Vistula region, a third group occupied Bohemia (where the tribe of the Czechs eventually gave its name to all others), Moravia and Slovakia.

It was the southern branch of the Slavs, however, which proceeded farthest, crossing the Carpathians and leaving only vague traces north of those mountains. Following the Croats and Serbs, who moved to the frontiers of the Eastern Empire and who were soon to cross these frontiers in their invasion of the Balkans, the Slovenes occupied a territory much larger than present-day Slovenia, and from the Danubian Plain penetrated deep into the Eastern Alps.

As to the Eastern Slavs, it is not so easy to determine how far they extended their settlements during the millennium which preceded their first appearance in history about 500 A.D. Some of their numerous tribes certainly crossed the Dnieper and may have reached the lower Don River in the southeast, while others slowly advanced in a northeastern direction. From the very beginning all these "Antes" seem to have been divided into a western group, in the homeland of the Slavs, and an eastern group in the area of early colonization. But it is only at a much later date that the names of the East Slavic tribes are enumerated, and the origin of their common name, *Ruś*, is as controversial as is the process of differentiation into three groups which would correspond to the Ukrainians, White Ruthenians, and Russians proper or Great Russians, of modern times.

Although very little is known about the prehistoric culture of the various Slavic peoples, the earliest references of foreign chroniclers, combined with archaeological and linguistic evidence, make us realize certain distinctive features which they all had in common with one another and also largely with the Baltic tribes. Their agriculture and cattle breeding were well developed, and such of them as occupied themselves with fishing, hunting, and the production of furs, wax, and honey had trade relations with the outside world. It is not easy to find out to what extent differences in occupation resulted in the formation of different social groups. What is certain is that the fundamental role of large familial groups or clans constituted the first community organization under their hereditary leaders.

For a long time this seems to have been their only permanent organization. Therefore, Greek writers, such as Procopius or Mauricius, speak of their "democracy" and love of freedom. Without acknowledging any supreme power, even without any special priesthood —the elders taking care of their religious ceremonies which were chiefly based upon the worship of nature—these familial communities united in larger, tribal organizations only very slowly and under the pressure of external danger. Cooperation of such tribes in even more comprehensive groups seems to have been less frequent than quarrels among the various communities. Without being on a lower cultural level than the other "barbarian" peoples outside the Empire, and having much in common, particularly with all other Indo-Europeans, the Slavs were probably inferior to most of their neighbors in the fields of military and political organization. And the same might be said about the Balts.

Under such conditions the numerous Slavic tribes could not really control the large area of their expanding settlements nor oppose the successive waves of foreign invaders which overran that territory, dominating it temporarily and crossing it in various directions, chiefly in connection with the great migrations toward the West. For that very reason the periods which are usually distinguished throughout the long transition from prehistory to history in that part of Europe are periods of its domination by Scythians, Sarmatians, Goths, Alans, Huns, and finally Avars, none of whom had anything in common with the native population.

We know very little about the resistance of the Slavs or their earliest endeavors to create states of their own. The Antes, particularly threatened on the crossroads in the steppes north of the Black Sea, seem to have been in advance of their kinsmen. The tragic end of their struggle against the Ostrogoths, when in 374 their leader, named Boz, was crucified, together with seventy other chieftains, produced such a strong impression that the record of that event came down to us as a first memorial of an agelong fight for freedom in East Central Europe. Some kind of federation of Antic tribes appears almost two hundred years later when they were again unable to stop a new conqueror, the Avars. The memory of the latter's harsh rule was to live long in the Slavic tradition, and it was in opposition to them that around 630 a man called Samo created what is supposed to have been the first Slavic state. Whether it can be considered the first Czech state is rather doubtful, since we do not even certainly know whether that short-lived power originated among Czechs and Moravians or among Slovenes, the western and southern Slavs being not yet separated from each other.

What is more significant, Samo was probably a Frankish merchant, or rather a Latinized Celt from Frankish territory, and some historians are of the opinion that the early rulers of the Antes were of Iranian origin. The very possibility of such assumption of foreign leadership in the first political movements among the Slavs shows the tremendous importance of their protohistoric relations with foreign elements. These elements came, on the one hand, from the Asiatic East through the vast intermediary region between two continents without any distinct boundary, and on the other hand from the Germanic West. Those early associations must be studied before the first contacts of the Slavs with what remained of the Greco-Roman world can be properly discussed.

2

THE SLAVS AND THEIR NEIGHBORS

THE SLAVS AND EURASIA

Eastern Europe is sometimes called Western Eurasia. This is correct, however, only with regard to the frontier region of geographical Europe which was outside the historical European community. And so far as prehistory is concerned, we may consider as Eurasian that eastern part of the great European Plain which was inhabited by non-European peoples whose closest kin were living in Asia. These peoples were the eastern neighbors of the Slavs, whose own original home, situated in the heart of Europe, could hardly be included in any Eurasia.

It is possible, however, that the Balto-Slavic homeland in East Central Europe was at a very early date partly occupied by some of the Finnish tribes which, having been gradually pushed back, remained the northeastern neighbors of both Balts and Slavs until the present. These tribes of Mongol race were in general on a lower level of culture and without any political organization. Such of them as lived nearest to the Baltic Coast became closely associated with the Indo-European Balts and developed more successfully than the others. In that region tribes of Baltic and Finnish origin are sometimes not easy to distinguish. The name *Aestii*, used by Tacitus, seems to include both of them, and while the Ests of later centuries—the ancestors of the present Estonians—definitely belong to the Finnish group, as do the Livs who gave their name to Livonia where they lived among the Baltic Letts, the question whether the Curs, after whom Curland was named, were of Finnish or Baltic origin is difficult to decide.

Larger and more numerous Finnish tribes were living not only in Finland itself, which does not appear in history before the Swedish conquest in the twelfth century when it first became and for a long time remained associated with Scandinavia, but also in the Volga

Basin and north of it as far as the geographical limits of Europe, the Arctic Ocean and the Ural Mountains. The colonization of the Volga region by tribes belonging to the eastern branch of the Slavs, which was to become so important from the eleventh century on, certainly did not start before the seventh or eighth century, and then on a very modest scale. But from the beginning it was a process of absorption and gradual Slavization of the poorly developed Finnish tribes whose names appear, however, in those of some of the earliest Slavic settlements.

Different were the relations between the Slavs and the Eurasian peoples who were living south of the Finns. Those peoples either belonged to the Mongol race, like the Finns, but to its Turkish group, or to the Iranians, that is, to the Asiatic branch of the Indo-European race. In contrast to the rather passive Finns, these peoples of an aggressive character frequently invaded and at least temporarily dominated their Slavic neighbors, even in the prehistoric period. When such invasions were repeated in the later course of history, the Slavs and the Asiatic conquerors, exclusively Turco-Tartars, are easy to distinguish from one another. On the contrary, there is a great deal of confusion with regard to the names which appear in the steppes north of the Black Sea from the Cimmerian period (1000–700 B.C.) to the establishment of the Bulgar and Khazar states in the seventh century A.D. The ethnic origin of each of these peoples is highly controversial, and since they all exercised a strong influence upon the eastern Slavs, after controlling them politically, the question has been raised whether even undoubtedly Slavic tribes were not originally under a foreign leadership which would explain some of their rather enigmatic names.

On the other hand, it seemed equally justifiable to look for Slavic elements which might have been included among the leading Eurasian peoples. It is indeed quite possible that when the Cimmerians, of Circassian (Caucasian) or Thracian origin were replaced (700–200 B.C.) as a ruling "superstructure" by the Scythians, that name covered various tribes of different ethnic stock, including Slavs in addition to the leading "Royal Scythians" who were well known to Herodotus and probably of Iranian origin. The same might be said about the Sarmatians who took the place of the Scythians from about 200 B.C. to 200 A.D. Again, most of their tribes, including the Alans, who were the last to come from Asia but who seem to have played a particularly important role in the first centuries of the Christian era, were certainly of Iranian origin. But the loose federation of these Sarmatian tribes probably included Slavic populations also, although later traditions, which saw in the Sarmatians the early ancestors of the Slavs, particularly of the Poles, are of course purely legendary.

The following invasions of the Germanic Goths and of the Mongol Huns, both of whom only temporarily occupied the Slavic territories before crossing the frontiers of the Empire, were of a different character. Better known than their predecessors, neither of these peoples had anything in common with the Slavs and they left no traces in Central or Eastern European history. But some Iranian elements seem to have survived through the Gothic (200–370 A.D.) and Hunnic period (370–454 A.D.). According to recently expressed opinions, some tribes of the Alans continued to control the Azov region where they mixed with the eastern tribes of the Slavic Antes. Even the Croats and Serbs, that is, the leading tribes of the southern branch of the Slavs, as well as their names, would have been of Iranian origin.

Turning from these highly controversial hypotheses to the historical facts of the sixth and seventh centuries, the Avar domination of the eastern and southern Slavs must be stressed as one of the most dangerous of the Asiatic invasions. Coming from Mongolia under the pressure of their Turkish neighbors, the Avars appeared at the gates of Europe, north of the Caucasian region, in 558. They soon became a serious threat to the Eastern Empire, and at the end of the eighth century they were finally defeated by Charlemagne, restorer of the Western Empire. The Slavs, however, who suffered cruelly from these conquerors, had to face another twofold pressure coming from the Eurasian East at the same time.

In the northeast a branch of the Bulgars, a Turco-Ugrian people who at the beginning of the seventh century had created a "Great Bulgarian" Empire in the Don region, established a state in the middle Volga area after the fall of that empire. These Volga Bulgars, who must be distinguished from the main body which moved in the direction of the Balkans, chiefly conquered Finnish territory but for several centuries also remained an obstacle to further Slavic expansion.

Much more important for the Slavs was the foundation of the Khazar "Kaganate" in the southeast. The Khazars were another Asiatic tribe, probably mixed ethnically, which first appeared north of the Caucasus around 570, when they were apparently under Turkish control. After breaking up Great Bulgaria, the Khazars succeeded in creating a large state for themselves. This reached from the Caucasus to the lower Volga and the lower Don and from the very beginning included some Slavic populations. Uniting peoples of various races and religions under their "Khagan," as their supreme ruler was called, they were eventually converted to the Jewish faith. The Khazars had to fight the Arabs in the Caucasian region and to face the rivalry of Byzantium in the Azov region. But almost simultaneously they also started to advance in the opposite, northwestern, direction. Here they reached the height of their expansion in the first half of the ninth century when they conquered the Slavic tribes which had crossed the Dnieper River. They even reached Kiev and demanded tribute from that area.

The Khazar domination was, however, much milder than any other which these Slavs had known, and it did not remain unchallenged by other invaders of the same territory. When the Khazars first met the opposition of Norman vikings is a moot question which must be studied in connection with the controversial antecedents of the creation of the Kievan state later in the ninth century. But even before that, the Khazars clashed in the Kiev region with the Magyars, an Ugrian (Mongolian) people who stopped there for about three hundred years on their way from the Urals to the Danubian Plain. This was another tribe, though probably less numerous, which ruled over some eastern Slavs before penetrating between the western and southern branch of the Slavic peoples, not without experiencing some Slavic influence.

That Slavic influence proved much stronger in the case of those Bulgars who, instead of moving up the Volga River to the north, proceeded southward toward the lower Danube. Long before the Bulgars crossed that river and penetrated into imperial territory, their clans absorbed so many East Slavic elements that when they settled in the Balkans—not much later than the southern Slavs, the Serbs and Croats—they were already Slavized to a large extent. The role which they played in the history of the eastern Slavs was, however, only temporary and rather limited.

In general, however, it was the eastern branch of the Slavs, first called *Antes* in the earliest sources and later known under the enigmatic name of *Ruś*, which as a natural consequence of their geographical situation had already had the closest relations with the various

Asiatic invaders of eastern Europe in the prehistoric period. These non-European influences, of whatever kind, hardly affected the two other branches of the Slavic people, except through the Avars and Magyars. The western Slavs, especially the descendants of the Venedi, were practically not touched at all.

This basic fact contributed, of course, to the growing differentiation among the three main Slavic groups. But it also created differences within the eastern group itself; between those Antes who remained in the original Slavic homeland in East Central Europe, where they constituted a numerous, native population and easily absorbed any foreign element which passed through their territory, and on the other hand, those Slavic pioneers who penetrated beyond the Dnieper Basin into the vast intermediary region which might be called Eastern Europe or Western Eurasia.

In that region the outposts of the Slavic world were colonists who were scattered among and mixed with Finno-Ugrian, Turkish, or Iranian populations whose number increased through continuous migrations and invasions from Asia. With only the exception of most of the Finnish tribes, all these Eurasian peoples were conquerors, stronger and better organized than the Slavs and therefore in a position to exercise a permanent pressure and influence upon them. The question remained open, therefore, whether that whole area, with its mixed population subject to so many different cultural trends, would ever become historically a part of Europe.

THE EARLIEST RELATIONS BETWEEN SLAVS AND TEUTONS

The Germanic or Teutonic peoples were originally divided into three groups or branches, just as were the Slavs, with the difference that, in addition to a western and an eastern, there was a northern group although no southern. More than any other European peoples, all of them had close relations with the native inhabitants of East Central Europe, the Slavs and the Balts. It was the quasi-permanent Germanic pressure exercised upon the Balto-Slavs from the West which corresponded to the Eurasian pressure from the East. A theory was even developed, according to which the Slavs would have been from time immemorial under a twofold foreign domination, either German or Turco-Tartar, with lasting consequences of that situation in the whole course of history. And even more general among German scholars is the opinion that a large part of the historical Slavic homeland in East Central Europe had been originally inhabited in prehistoric times by Germanic tribes which left that area only during the great migrations, while the Slavs followed them and took their place.

Without returning to that controversy, it must be admitted that during the earlier phase of these migrations, before they definitely became a movement from East to West, some Germanic tribes spread all over East Central Europe but only as temporary conquerors. For obvious geographical reasons these tribes were those of the East Germanic group, the group which proved particularly active in the migration period and which eventually penetrated farther than any other Teutons in a southwestern direction, only to disappear completely. In Central Eastern Europe their invasion left nothing but a tradition of ruthless domination by the Goths, who were the leading tribe among those East Germanic ones.

This tradition was particularly strong among the Baltic peoples, but for a short time, under king Ermanaric (about 350–370 A.D.), an Ostrogothic empire seems to have also included most of the Slavic peoples. Defeated in the following years by Huns and Alans, however, the Ostrogoths crossed the Danube and in the well-known battle of Adrianople (378) started their invasion of the Roman Empire which led them far away from Slavic Europe.

At the Baltic shores the Gothic occupation was soon followed by a long series of raids and invasions, equally dangerous for Balts and Slavs, which came from another branch of the Germanic peoples, the northern. Long before the Normans played their famous role in the history of Western Europe, bold expeditions of Scandinavian vikings not only crossed the Baltic but laid out the first trade routes through Eastern Europe, as far as the Caspian and Black Sea regions, where they established contacts with the Asiatic world. Arabic sources seem to indicate that the earliest of these connections were established along the Volga without touching the original Balto-Slavic territory. The opinion has also been expressed that Norsemen appeared and even created some kind of state organization in the Azov region, perhaps under the name of *Rus*, long before the *Rus* of the later ninth century followed the shortest route from Scandinavia to Greece, and formed the historical Russian state with its centers at Novgorod and Kiev.

But again, these are merely hypotheses, and the historian is on much more solid ground if before studying that momentous intervention of Scandinavian elements in the destinies of the Eastern Slavs, he turns, in the chronological order, to the first recorded contacts between the western group of the Teutonic peoples—the Germans proper— and their Slavic neighbors. These were, of course, the Western Slavs and also the western tribes of the Southern Slavs, the ancestors of the Slovenes of today. And this is precisely the most important problem of all in the relations between Slavs and Teutons, a problem which in uninterrupted continuity and increasing significance was to last until our times.

The whole issue started when the westward movement of the Germanic tribes, after reaching the extreme limit of the Atlantic Ocean, was replaced by a return drive in the opposite direction, later known as the *Drang nach Osten*. Even if at the beginning it was a re-conquest of territories which Slavic tribes had occupied during the preceding migrations, it soon turned into a systematic aggression on a long front from the mouth of the Elbe to the Alpine valleys, soon threatening the Slavs in what undoubtedly was their original territory. As long as the German tribes which first clashed with the Slavs and tried to push them back were pagans like their opponents and hardly better organized politically, the chances were almost even in spite of the more warlike character of the Germans. But the situation changed completely when, after the conquest and conversion of the Saxons by Charlemagne and the inclusion of the Duchy of Bavaria in his empire, that very Christian Empire created by the Franks became the powerful neighbor of all Slavic tribes on the whole western front.

For the entire further course of Slavic history, that new situation had far-reaching consequences. Those Slavs who lived near the western limits of their homeland now came into permanent contact with Western culture, with both Roman tradition and the Catholic church. But as the first representatives of that world, they met those Germans who themselves had only recently accepted that culture and now wanted to use its values, particularly the propagation of the Christian faith, as tools of political domination. That danger had already appeared under Charlemagne, but it became even greater when, after the division of his supranational empire in 843 and the following partitions, the Slavs had the East Frankish kingdom as an immediate neighbor. This purely German state, the Germany of the future, had its likeliest possibilities of expansion precisely in the eastern direction through the conquest of Slavic territory and its organization into German marches.

In that relentless struggle which started at the end of the eighth century, three sectors of the long German-Slavic frontier must be distinguished. There was first, in the North, the plain between the sea and the Sudeten Mountains. Here the Germans had to do with the numerous Polabian and Lusatian tribes which in the past had even crossed the Elbe-Saale line. As soon as Saxony was organized as one of the largest German duchies, the Slavs were pushed back from the mouth of the Elbe and the southeastern corner of the North Sea to the southwestern corner of the Baltic Sea. The series of marches which were supposed to protect the German territory and serve as steppingstones of further expansion, started with the Northern march which was created toward the end of the ninth century at the expense of the Obotrites, the Slavic population of what was later called Mecklenburg. The same method was tried in the whole belt east of the middle Elbe as far as Lusatia. Already under the Carolingians, in the course of that same ninth century, that area was something like a German sphere of influence, but in view of the fierce resistance of the Veletian group of the Slavs and of the Lusatian Serbs (Sorbs), the final creation of German marches had to wait until the following century, when the pressure increased under the kings of the new Saxon dynasty.

Of special importance was the next sector of the front, the central bastion of Bohemia, surrounded by mountains which stopped the German advance or made it change its usual methods. Fights with Bohemian tribes had already started in the time of Charlemagne, but on the one hand their land proved difficult to conquer, and on the other there appeared among their princes a disposition to accept the Christian faith voluntarily in order to avoid a forcible conquest. As early as 845 some of these princes came to Regensburg where they were baptized, probably recognizing a certain degree of German suzerainty. Others, however, turned at about the same time toward a first center of Slavic power which was being created by their kin, the princes of Moravia, in an area which still was beyond the reach of German invasions and in direct contact with the south-Slavic Slovenes in the Danubian Plain, where the memory of Samo's state had perhaps not entirely disappeared.

The Slovenes themselves were, however, threatened at least from the eighth century in their Alpine settlements where Bavarian colonization was in progress. Acting as overlord of the dukes of Bavaria, Charlemagne there created a first march on what was later to be the territory of Austria, chiefly as a defense against the Avars, but also in order to control the Slavic population after the fall of the Avar power. The missionary activities of the German church, especially of the bishops of Salzburg and Passau, also contributed to strengthening Bavarian influence as far as the former Roman province of Pannonia, and under Charlemagne's son Louis the authority of the empire was temporarily recognized even by the Croats, particularly after the suppression of a revolt by the Croat prince Ludevit in 822.

That German advance far into the territory of the Southern Slavs was only temporary and exceptional, but even so it resulted in a conflict with faraway Bulgaria and in a contact between Frankish and Byzantine influence. It is, therefore, against the whole background of these international relations in the Danubian region and of contemporary developments in the Balkans, that the rise and fall of the so-called Moravian Empire must be studied. But before approaching that important turning point in the history of East Central Europe, a more general consequence of the earliest relations between Slavs and Teutons ought to be emphasized.

Just because the German power was so much stronger, the growing danger forced the Slavs at last to develop their own political organization and to cooperate in larger units under native leadership. In many cases they proved quite capable of doing so in spite of many unfavorable circumstances. In opposition to foreign aggressors whose language they were unable to understand, they became conscious of their own particularity. But in contradistinction to the Eastern Slavs who had to face semibarbarian Asiatic invaders, mostly pagans like themselves, the Western Slavs had to realize that they could not resist their opponents without themselves entering the realm of that Roman culture which was the main factor of German superiority, and most important, without becoming Christians like their neighbors. Those among the Slavs who failed to do so were doomed in advance. The others had to find ways and means of doing it without an exclusively German intermediary by safeguarding their independence and by organizing on their own account the East Central European region. In the critical ninth century, one of these possible ways seemed to be cooperation with the eastern center of Christian and Greco-Roman culture, with Byzantium.

THE SLAVS AND THE BYZANTINE EMPIRE

Long before the Croats were touched by the Frankish conquest, that same South-Slavic people, together with their closest kin, the Serbs, had entered into much more stable relations with the Eastern Roman Empire and with the Eastern church which was not yet separated from Rome. These relations were, however, of an entirely different character. In this case it was the Slavs who were the invaders. After participating, from the end of the fifth century, in various raids of other "barbarian" tribes into imperial territory, they threatened Byzantium—then the only Christian Empire—even during the brilliant reign of Justinian I, who by some earlier scholars was wrongly considered to have been of Slavic origin. Through the sixth century the Slavic danger, combined with that from their Avar overlords, constantly increased. More and more frequently they penetrated far into the Balkans, until in the first half of the seventh century the Emperor Heraclius permitted some of their tribes, freed from the Avars, to settle in the devastated lands south of the Danube.

These Slavs, soon converted to the Christian faith, were under the leadership of Chrovatos whose name, probably Iranian, was taken by his people, later known as Croats, while other tribes of the same group received the name of Serbs, which according to some authorities would be derived from *servus* (slave). Definitely established in the area which they occupy today, the Serbo-Croats made the region practically independent from Byzantium, defending themselves at the same time against the Avars. Culturally, however, they came under the influence of Byzantium, which never ceased to consider their territory—the old *Illyricum*—part of the Eastern Empire. Greek influence was, of course, particularly strong among the Serbs, who moved deeper into the Balkans and remained the immediate neighbors of the Greeks. The Croats, on the other hand, who established themselves farther to the northwest, were soon exposed to Western influences. This explains the growing differentiation between the two peoples, which were of common origin and continued to speak the same language. With the ever stronger opposition between Eastern and Western Christendom, the separation between Serbs and Croats was to become also much deeper, a distinctive feature of the history of the Southern Slavs.

But already in the early days of their settlements in regions well to the south of their original homeland, another problem proved to be of lasting importance. The problem of their relations with an entirely different people who simultaneously invaded the Byzantine Empire and after crossing the lower Danube settled permanently on imperial territory in the Balkans, but east of the Serbo-Croats, not at the Adriatic but at the Black Sea coast. These were the Bulgars or Bulgarians.

The southern branch of that Turkish people, who as a whole had played such an important but rather transitory role in Eurasia and the steppes north of the Black Sea, had already mixed with the Slavic tribes of the Antes in that region. When, after participating in earlier invasions of the Eastern Empire by the Avars, as had the Slavs, they definitely crossed the Danube under their Khan or Khagan, Asparukh, in 679, a Bulgar state was established in northern Thrace in the region of present-day Bulgaria.

That state, however, which soon extended its boundaries in all directions, had a predominantly Slavic population. For in addition to the foundation of new states in the northern part of formerly imperial territory, numerous Slavic tribes had throughout the sixth and seventh century continued to raid the whole Balkan Peninsula and even Greece proper. Most of them remained there in larger or smaller groups, creating the so-called *Sclaviniae*, that is, permanent settlements which without being organized as political units changed the ethnic character of the whole empire. Some scholars have even expressed the opinion that the Greek population was completely Slavized, an obvious exaggeration, since the Slavs rarely succeeded in taking the more important cities which they besieged, but which remained Greek as did most of the Mediterranean coast. But while scattered Slavic settlers came under the influence of Greek culture even more than in Serbia, they in turn so strongly influenced the Bulgar conquerors that even their language was adopted by the latter, and already in its pagan period the new state must be considered Bulgaro-Slavic. And gradually the Turkish element was so completely submerged that Bulgaria simply became one of the South-Slavic nations.

The Byzantine Empire, which continued to have occasional troubles with its Slavic subjects and even had to move some of them as far away as Bithynia in Asia Minor, was seriously concerned with the rise of Bulgar power so near to Constantinople itself. Emperor Justinian II, after defeating Bulgars and Slavs in 690, had to ask for their assistance in order to recover his throne from a rival, and in reward he granted to Asparukh's successor, Tervel, the title of Caesar when he received him in the capital in 705. In spite of a treaty which Byzantium concluded with Bulgaria eleven years later, and which established a new boundary line north of Adrianople, there was a whole series of Greek-Bulgar wars in the course of the eighth century. In 805 Khan Krum, after contributing in cooperation with the Franks to the fall of the Avars, created a strong Bulgarian Empire on both sides of the Danube. The role of the Slavic element was increased, and until Krum's death in 814 Byzantium, which suffered a terrible defeat in 811, was seriously threatened by its northern neighbor. Constantinople itself was besieged by the Bulgars. The relations improved under the new Khan Omortag, who even assisted Emperor Michael III against a Slavic uprising and turned against the Franks, with whom he clashed in Croatia. But it was not before the reign of Boris, from 852, that the conversion of Bulgaria to the Christian faith was seriously considered. This raised entirely new issues in her relations with Byzantium.

In contradistinction to the restored Western Empire, the Eastern Roman Empire had no desire for territorial expansion. It wanted, however, to control the foreign elements which had penetrated within its boundaries and had even created their own states on imperial territory. Moreover, it was afraid of new invasions by other barbarian tribes, the first attack of Norman "Russians" against Constantinople in 860 being a serious warning. In both respects the missionary activity of the Greek church, under the authority of the Patriarch of Constantinople, closely cooperating with the Emperor, seemed to be particularly helpful in bringing under Byzantine influence the Slavic populations of the Balkans, as well as dangerous neighbors, Slavic or non-Slavic.

That missionary activity, which in general was less developed in Eastern than in Western Christendom, was greatly intensified under the famous Patriarch Photius. Through an arbitrary decision by the imperial power, in 858 he replaced the legitimate Patriarch Ignatius, and this was the origin of a protracted crisis in the religious life of Byzantium. But he proved to be one of the most prominent leaders of the Greek church, one who was particularly anxious to promote the spread of Christianity even among the faraway Khazars, the neighbors of the last Greek colonies on the northern shores of the Black Sea. It was there that Constantine and Methodius, the Greek brothers from Salonika, who were equally distinguished as theologians and as linguists, started their missions in 860 or 861. They failed to convert the Khagan, who decided in favor of Judaism, but they were soon to be sent to the Slavs of the Danubian region. And at the same time it became known that Boris of Bulgaria wanted to become a Christian.

In both cases, however, the question had to be decided as to whether the converts would be placed under the ecclesiastical authority of the Patriarchate of Constantinople or directly under Rome, a question which had both a religious and a political aspect that was to be decisive for the whole future of the Slavs. As yet there was no definite schism between the Roman and the Greek church, but already there was a growing tension which was intensified by the fact that Pope Nicholas I did not recognize the appointment of Photius and excommunicated him in 863. Today we know that even Photius' break with Rome in 867 was by no means final, but the whole ecclesiastical conflict which lasted until 880 prepared the schism of the future. And even Ignatius, who again occupied the See of Constantinople from 867 to 877, opposed Rome in the matter of the new Bulgarian church which he wanted to place under his own authority.

The Emperor, too, though eager to remain in good relations with the Papacy, was adamant in the Bulgarian problem, and finally Boris, who was baptized in 864, after trying to find out which side would grant the greater autonomy to the new Bulgarian church, decided in favor of Byzantium, a solution which obviously was also dictated by geographic conditions and by the whole past history of the territory occupied by the Bulgars. The situation was entirely different in old Pannonia, that is in the Danubian Basin north of the Serbo-Croat settlements, where during these same years Constantine and Methodius undertook their most important mission, entrusted to them by Photius on the invitation of a new Slavic power, the so-called Moravian Empire. The outcome of their activity was to be of lasting significance, not only for the relations of the various Slavic peoples with Byzantium but also for the whole future of East Central Europe.

3

TOWARD POLITICAL ORGANIZATION

THE MORAVIAN STATE AND THE APOSTLES OF THE SLAVS

The Moravian State proved a merely ephemeral creation, founded at the beginning of the ninth century and destroyed at its end. But it was the first body politic that was large and strong enough to be sometimes named an empire, though incorrectly, and it was undoubtedly established by the Slavs themselves without any foreign impact or leadership. The very name would point to present-day Moravia as its main center, but it rather seems that the real center was in the region of Nitra in Slovakia. The Moravians, close kin of the Slovaks, were of course included from the start, and the Czech tribes of Bohemia also turned toward the new Slavic state in spite of growing German pressure to which they were exposed. That pressure from the Frankish side was precisely the chief reason why the Slavs of the Danubian region, after the fall of the Avars, resuming the old tradition of Samo's time, at last tried to create an independent political organization. That organization also included the Slovenian tribes south of the Danube, northern and southern Slavs being still immediate neighbors. The Slovenes had their own leader, Pribina, who under German overlordship controlled the region of Lake Balaton in Pannonia until his son Kotzel came under the authority of the dynasty which around 830 created the Moravian State and which after its founder is called the Moymirids.

In 846 Moymir I was succeeded by his nephew Rostislav who was fully aware of a twofold danger which threatened Moravia from the East Frankish Kingdom. Politically, the Germans tried to encircle the Slavic State by an alliance with Bulgaria which had been negotiated between King Louis the German and Boris. At the same time German missionaries continued their eastward drive and had already partly converted the Moravian and Slovene peoples, bringing them under the ecclesiastical authority of German bishops and thus also serving political German interests as usual. Rostislav himself, after being baptized, had first been a vassal of Louis, but as he wanted to free his country from German domination, in 855 he defeated the king's forces. Remaining in a very critical situation, however, in 862 he decided to turn to Byzantium. Through his envoys sent to Constantinople he asked not only for diplomatic assistance in connection with the Bulgar problem, but also for missionaries who would help him to organize a Slavic church independent of German control.

Emperor Michael III and Patriarch Photius entrusted that mission to the two brothers, Constantine and Methodius, who were familiar with the Slavic dialect spoken in the region of Salonika. It was on that dialect that they based their translation of the Gospel and of the liturgical books needed for their mission, since the Byzantine church, in the case of the Slavs as in other similar cases, had admitted the use of the vernacular in their ecclesiastical life. The two Greeks, in particular Constantine (called Cyril as a monk), not only laid the foundations for the development of the language, which under the name of Old Slavonic or Church Slavonic was to remain until the present the liturgical language of most of the Orthodox Slavs, but they also invented a special alphabet, more suitable than the Greek, for expressing Slavic sounds.

That alphabet, too, is still used today by all Slavs who belong to the Eastern church, but in a somewhat modified form. For most probably Constantine himself invented the so-called Glagolitic alphabet, which is based upon the Greek cursive and possibly some Oriental characters also. Only after his death, toward the end of the century, one of his brother's disciples developed that script of limited use into the well-known "Cyrillic" alphabet, combining Greek uncials with some additional signs for specifically Slavic sounds. In any case, the Slavs thus received their own alphabet, which contributed to their literary progress but at the same time created a lasting cultural difference, to a certain extent even a barrier, between those of them who remained faithful to that tradition, and all other European peoples, including those of the Slavs who eventually decided for the Latin alphabet.

That future division of the Slavic world was, of course, based upon something more important than the mere difference of alphabet. In connection with the Oriental Schism, it was to become a profound religious difference between Greek Orthodox and Roman Catholic Slavs. It must be remembered, however, that in the days of Constantine and Methodius, who are recognized as saints by both the Greek and the Roman church, the schism was not yet accomplished, so that the two Apostles of the Slavs, as they are called by both churches, could at the same time remain loyal to Photius, to whose partisans they seem to have belonged in Byzantium, and to the popes, with whom the patriarch had occasional conflicts.

Even Photius could not possibly question that the territory where, on Rostislav's invitation, they started to work from the next year, 863, was ecclesiastically not under the Patriarchate of Constantinople but directly under Rome. It was, therefore, indispensable to secure from the popes, too, approval of the use of the Slavic language in the liturgy and a clarification of the position of the two brothers in the general organization of the church. In both respects they encountered serious difficulties which, however, resulted neither from their Greek origin nor from any Roman opposition, but from the hostility of the German clergy and also partly from insufficient support by the Moravian rulers.

Already under Rostislav, their main protector, they were opposed not only by the Bavarian missionaries who had worked among the Slavs before the arrival of the two Greeks, but particularly by the Archbishop of Salzburg and the Bishop of Passau who claimed the whole territory of the Moravian State for their dioceses. These claims were backed, of course, by the Eastern Frankish kingdom, which wanted to create there a territorial church under a metropolitan archbishop who would closely cooperate with the king and strengthen his political control over the Slavic princes. Such an approach was a challenge, however, not only to Rostislav but also to the Roman See which was alarmed by the alliance between the secular power and the local metropolitans in many European countries. In the case of the recently converted Moravian State, the Pope much preferred to see there a missionary church under his own exclusive control.

The main argument which the German clergy used in Rome was the alleged danger of replacing the universal Latin language of the Church by the vernacular of the Slavic population which they still considered semipagan, as Constantine and Methodius had done. Therefore, after five years of struggle, in 868 the two brothers found it necessary to come to Rome in person in order to obtain from Pope Hadrian II formal approval of their methods and of the establishment of a separate ecclesiastical organization for the Moravian State.

Their arguments in favor of the use of the Slavic language in the liturgy convinced the Pope, who solemnly deposited liturgical books in Slavic on the altars of several churches in Rome. Furthermore, he decided to create a new archdiocese in the Danubian region which thus would be freed from the authority of the Archbishop of Salzburg. Since the elder brother Constantine died in Rome in 869, after receiving on his death bed the highest monastic rank and the name of "Cyril," only Methodius was ordained by Hadrian II as Archbishop of Pannonia, with his see at Syrmium.

The choice of that place is significant because it was situated at the extreme southern border of the Moravian State, near the Byzantine frontier and far away from the bases of German political and ecclesiastical power. It proved, however, impossible completely to eliminate Frankish influence from the territory of Greater Moravia. Even in Slovakian Nitra, which besides Velehrad in Moravia proper remained the main center of the state of the Moymirids, a German priest, Wiching from Swabia, had to be accepted as bishop. He was, of course, under Methodius' authority, but he soon became the leader of the opposition against his archbishop, who after his return from Rome in 870 had to struggle for fifteen years against the intrigues and accusations of his enemies.

Methodius' position was now even more difficult than before because in the same year, 870, Rostislav's nephew Svatopluk rebelled, with German assistance. After arresting his uncle, he occupied the throne himself. Although he proved a skilful and energetic ruler, who soon broke with the Germans politically and by 874 restored the independence of the Moravian State, he was prepared to compromise in ecclesiastical matters. In particular, he seems to have been less interested than his predecessor in the Slavic liturgy, which continued to be the chief target of the attacks of the German clergy.

Although Methodius probably acted as papal legate to the Slavic peoples, he was tried by King Louis the German and remained in prison for three years. Not before 873 did Pope John VIII obtain his release, and in 879 the Pope again summoned him to Rome. For the second time Methodius succeeded in defending himself against all charges regarding his orthodoxy and in obtaining another papal approval of the use of the Slavic language in church. This time, however, the Pope made some reservations; for instance, he requested that at least the Gospel be first read in Latin. But in general, John VIII continued to support Methodius. He returned to his archbishopric once more, and there, amidst growing difficulties, he defended his work until his death in 885.

In that same year a new pope, Stephen V, in a letter to Svatopluk, the authenticity of which is, however, uncertain, reversed the position of the Holy See in the matter of the Slavic language, prohibiting its use in the liturgy. Svatopluk himself now sided in that matter with Wiching, and the disciples of the two Apostles of the Slavs were expelled from Moravia. They had to take refuge in Bulgaria where they greatly contributed to the lasting Christianization of that even more recently converted country and to the final adoption of the Slavic tongue by the Bulgarians. Their national assembly of 893, which confirmed Boris' son Simeon as ruler of Bulgaria, also recognized Slavic as the official language of the Bulgarian church. With the establishment of Slavic schools, that country became for the following centuries an important cultural center where Slavic letters and religious life rapidly developed.

But in the Moravian State the results of the work of Saints Constantine and Methodius did not disappear completely either. Although the so-called Pannonian Legends which glorify their activity may contain some exaggerations, it is highly probable that their missionary activity even reached the Polish tribes on the upper Vistula which were temporarily in the sphere of influence of Greater Moravia. And positive traces of the survival of the Cyrillo-Methodian tradition and of the Slavic liturgy can be pointed out in Bohemia and even in Poland.

Politically, however, the power of the Moravian State was already doomed toward the end of Svatopluk's reign. In 892 Bishop Wiching, whom he had tried to appease by making concessions in the ecclesiastical field, openly went over to the German side and became the chancellor of King Arnulf. Two years later Svatopluk died, and during the following civil war between his sons, Pope Formosus, probably at the request of Moymir II, sent a papal mission to Moravia which tried to reorganize an independent church directly under Rome. Opposed again by the Bavarian clergy, in cooperation with their king, that action failed not only because the great Apostles of the Slavs were

no longer there to support it but also in view of the complete disintegration of the Moravian State.

THE MAGYAR INVASION AND THE PROBLEM OF
RUMANIAN CONTINUITY

In spite of the predominantly Slavic character of East Central
Europe, the role of some non-Slavic peoples throughout the history
of that region could hardly be overrated. In its northern part the
Baltic tribes, already important in prehistoric times, were to influence
that history only in the later Middle Ages. The historic action of the
Magyars, the only Asiatic invaders who notwithstanding their racial
origin were included in the European community, started much
earlier. Inseparable from Slavic history, their destinies are also closely
connected with the development of another non-Slavic people of the
Danubian region, the Rumanians, whose present territory they had
to cross before occupying the Pannonian Plain. Of European race
like the Balts, the Rumanians were always proud of their descent from
Roman colonists who through all the vicissitudes of the following centuries remained in what had been the Roman province of Dacia. The
Hungarians, however, as the Magyars were called by their neighbors,
have always contested that theory of Rumanian continuity, which is
one of the most controversial problems in the history of East Central
Europe.

The Magyars themselves were one of the Ugrian tribes, closely
related to the Finns, which in the first centuries of the Christian era
migrated from the Ural region to the North-Caucasian area and from
there to the steppes north of the Black Sea. Closely associated with
the Khazars for three hundred years, and recognizing the authority
of the Khagan, the Magyar clans, though not very numerous themselves, ruled over the native tribes of that region, Slavic and Iranian.
But in spite of mutual influences, they were never Slavized, as were
the Bulgars.

While the latter moved in the direction of the lower Danube and
the Balkans, the Magyars had already extended their domination
toward the north in the eighth century. Around 840, under their
duke, Olom (Almus), they occupied Kiev, probably in agreement
with their Khazar overlords. Soon, however, the first Norman leaders
appeared in Kiev, and around 878 the Magyar rule in the Dnieper

region definitely came to an end. Under Norman pressure from the north, and defeated by the Pechenegs (Patzinaks), a new Asiatic tribe that was advancing from the east, most of the Magyars moved westward to the Carpathian Mountains.

According to the Rumanian tradition, on both sides of these mountains they found communities that had been created by descendants of Roman settlers. These survived the passage of the successive Asiatic invaders, including that of the Magyars, who penetrated through Transylvania to the Central Plain of what was to be the Hungary of the future. The Hungarians defend the opinion that it was only much later that Rumanian elements, represented by "Vlach" (Wallachian) herdsmen from the Balkans, gradually infiltrated the no man's land of both Wallachia and Transylvania, the latter having been first settled by Magyars and the closely related tribe of the Szeklers soon after their occupation of the Danubian Plain. That issue, however, was to become of historical importance only in the later Middle Ages; the traditionally admitted date of the Magyar settlement in Pannonia is 896. Under their leader Árpád, the founder of their national dynasty, they permanently occupied the plain on both sides of the middle Danube and completely replaced its Slavic population.

Becoming the immediate neighbors of the Germans who advanced from the west through the Alpine valleys, the Hungarians forever separated the Southern Slavs—Slovenes, Croats, and Serbs, as well as Slavized Bulgars—from the Northern Slavs, whether Western (Czechs and Poles) or Eastern (the ancestors of present-day Ukrainians). Furthermore, the Slavic population which remained south of the Carpathians, especially the Slovaks, came for more than a thousand years under Hungarian rule and thus were separated from their nearest kin, the Czechs.

It is hardly necessary to emphasize the consequences of these facts for the whole later course of Slavic and Central European history. At the given moment, the appearance of the Magyars and their lasting conquest finally destroyed the Moravian State, a large part of which became the Hungary of the future. The year 906 is usually regarded as the decisive date. Before and after that year, the Magyars, following the example of the Avars, raided the neighboring territories which they did not actually conquer. These included not only Moravia proper but also the southeastern marches of Germany. They even penetrated to the Italian border and far into Bavaria, and it was there that their onslaught had to be broken, first in 933, by Henry I, King of Germany, and finally in the Battle of Augsburg in 955, by Otto I, a few years before he became Roman Emperor.

It was not before the end of that same tenth century that the pagan Magyars completed the organization of their new state, and under Prince Géza, one of Árpád's successors, they were converted to the Christian faith chiefly through German missionaries. Unusual, however, was the rapidity with which that people of alien race and nomadic origin integrated itself into the Christian European community and absorbed Western culture. It was soon to become one of that culture's outposts in a region where conflicting cultural trends had met in the preceding centuries. That advance of the Latin, Catholic West in the direction of South Eastern Europe was particularly significant at a moment when Byzantine influence, rapidly vanishing in Hungary, was achieving its farthest northeastern advance by penetrating into the vast territories of another new state which foreign invaders of Teutonic race had organized in the border regions of the original Slavic homeland, a state which was to become the Russia of the future.

On land, through the Rumania of the future, and particularly across the Black Sea, the Eastern Empire, which together with the Southern Slavs was cut off from Central Europe by pagan and later Catholic Hungary, communicated in war and peace with the distant East Slavic territory which was to become an offshoot of Orthodox Christendom.

THE NORMANS IN EASTERN EUROPE

The role of the Normans in the history of Western Europe is well known and of great importance indeed. But it was in Eastern Europe that their expeditions and conquests had particularly far-reaching and lasting consequences, since the appearance of Scandinavian vikings, the so-called Varangians, is connected with the origin of what was to be in the future the largest and strongest Slavic state—Russia.

The whole story, as it is told in detail by the *Primary Russian Chronicle,* raises more controversial issues, however, than any other problem of European history. The legendary Rurik (Riurik), who was invited by the East Slavic and Finnish tribes of the Novgorod region, according to the *Chronicle,* and arrived there from Scandinavia in 862, has been identified with Roric of Jutland, a Danish lord who is mentioned in contemporary Western sources. And all that we know about him makes it highly probable that he really undertook the expedition to Novgorod, probably as early as between 854 and 856, and there organized a state which under his leadership soon expanded toward the South along the waterways "from the Varangians to the Greeks"—the Dvina and the Dnieper. But it is equally certain that, long before Rurik, Norman vikings from Sweden appeared in what is now Russia and on the Black Sea, using first a longer route which followed the Volga and the Don rivers.

Envoys of these Russians of Swedish race, returning from Constantinople, came in 839 to Ingelheim in Germany to be sent home to their Khagan (as their ruler was called on the Khazar model) by Emperor Louis I. And in 860 a Russian fleet made a first attack against the Byzantine Empire, suffering heavy losses, however, thanks to the courageous defense of the imperial city under the leadership of Photius. These are well-established facts, and it is also quite probable that this first Russian Khaganate had its center somewhere in the Azov region, possibly in Tmutorokan, on the eastern side of the Kerch Strait, where the Russians, coming first as merchants and later as conquerors, made themselves independent of the Khazar Empire early in the ninth century.

On the contrary it is very doubtful whether the name *Ruś*, which is rather misleadingly rendered by *Russia* and *Russians*, originated in that same region or in general among the Slavic or Alanic tribes of the steppes north of the Black Sea. The traditional interpretation of that name, as being derived from the name *Ruotsi* which was given to the Norman Varangians by the Finns, seems more convincing. That philological puzzle would not be so important for the historian if it were not part of the general controversy between "Normanists" and "Anti-Normanists" which started in eighteenth-century historiography and is far from being decided even today.

According to the first of these two schools, it was the Normans who, bringing even the name of *Ruś* from Scandinavia, played a decisive role in the formation of the Russian State, giving to the tribes of the Eastern Slavs their first political organization and remaining their real leaders throughout the ninth and tenth centuries. The Anti-Normanists would reduce that role to the occasional cooperation of various groups of vikings who in the course of these centuries, and perhaps even earlier, came to a Slavic country where the name *Ruś*, of local origin, was already used. That cooperation of experienced warriors might have been valuable, but the comparatively small number of these vikings, including the dynasty founded by Rurik, were soon absorbed and Slavized.

The Anti-Normanist school has certainly contributed to a constructive revision of the oversimplified account given in the *Chronicle*, which was compiled in the eleventh century. But it seems impossible to contest the Norman initiative in the creation of one or more "Russian" states and in the process of unifying the many tribes into which the Eastern Slavs were divided. The very fact that, thanks to that process, all these tribes enumerated by the chronicler received a common name can hardly be overrated, whatever the origin of that name might be.

That gradual unification under the same Norman dynasty and the use of the common name of *Ruś*, first indicating the Varangian leaders and later all the people under their rule, does not imply the disappearance of all differences, which among the tribes of the Eastern Slavs were not fewer than among the Slavs of the west or of the south. Even from the merely linguistic point of view, at least two groups, a northern and a southern, can be distinguished among these tribes. No less important must have been the difference which developed between those Eastern Slavs who remained in their original homeland and those who, simultaneously with the coming of the Normans, colonized the originally Finnish territories in the northeast, mixing with the native population. And since the names Russia and Russian are specifically applied to the nation which in later centuries was formed precisely in that northeastern colonial region, it is highly questionable to identify these names with *Ruś* and to apply them to all East-Slavic tribes, even to those who are the ancestors of the present-day Ukrainians and White Russians or Byelorussians. For the latter, the designation White Ruthenians would be more appropriate, since in the Latin sources both western groups of the Eastern Slavs are usually called Ruthenians, from the Slavic *Rusini* which is derived from *Ruś*, and clearly distinguished from Muscovite Russia (*Rossiia*). To call the latter Great Russia, and to call old Ruthenia (now the Ukraine) Little Russia, is less advisable, although it is supported by the Greek terminology of the later Middle Ages.

The tribe of the Slovenians (*Slovene*) in the Novgorod region, which first came under Rurik's control, is indeed Russian in the specific Great Russian sense and was to play a prominent part in the colonization of the Finnish neighborhood long before Moscow appeared in history. Advancing through the territory of the Krivichians, who with their branch of the Polochanians in the Polotsk region correspond to the White Ruthenians of the future, the Normans, led by two of Rurik's "boyars," Askold and Dir, went down the Dnieper River and passing between the Dregovichians and Drevlianians in the west, and the Radimichians and Viatichians in the east—all of which were tribes that were conquered only later—came into the land of the Polianians around Kiev. Probably around 858 they established their rule in that important center which still paid tribute to the Khazars and was practically controlled by a Magyar leader. Twenty years later, Oleg, who after Rurik's death ruled in the name of the minor Igor, after occupying the cities on the upper Dnieper, including Smolensk, captured Kiev by ruse. Askold and Dir were killed and the whole area from Novgorod to Kiev was united under the same Varangian leader.

The tribes of the Kiev region are undoubtedly the ancestors of the Ukrainians of today; not only the Polianians but also their western neighbors, the Dulebians in Volhynia (therefore sometimes called Volhynians), as well as the Severians east of the Dnieper River. The Drevlianians must have belonged to the same ethnic and linguistic group too, but the Dregovichians north of them may rather be associated with the later White Ruthenians, while the Radimichians, together with the Viatichians, expanding in the Volga Basin, were the main body of the future Great Russian group. *Ukraina* was not yet a proper name, attached to the area on both sides of the lower Dnieper as it was from the sixteenth century, but the common designation of any frontier region. Typical frontier men, living south of the Polianians in the steppes between them and the Black Sea, were the Ulichians and the Tivertsians, two tribes which usually are supposed to have belonged to the same group, although they must have been mixed with the populations of Asiatic origin which one after the other migrated through that gateway toward Hungary and the Balkans.

For the Kievan State it was a very vital problem indeed to secure the control of these steppes as an indispensable basis for any further advance in the direction of Constantinople by land or by sea. Already at the beginning of the tenth century, when the Magyars had left that territory to settle beyond the Carpathians, that goal seemed to have been achieved. As a matter of fact, Oleg, who soon after the occupation of Kiev had conquered the Drevlianians and also the Severians, who were formally subject to the Khazars, undertook a first campaign against Byzantium in 907. The Tivertsians, among other tribes, also participated in this campaign. The details of the siege of Constantinople are probably legendary, but the *Primary Russian Chronicle* also contains a summary of the Russo-Byzantine treaty concluded in the same year, as well as the full text of the supplementary agreement of 911. The Russians received a huge indemnity, and their commercial relations with Byzantium were facilitated through detailed stipulations that were made on the basis of full equality.

One or two years later Oleg died and was succeeded by Igor, a grandson of Rurik. He extended the Varangian raids as far as Anatolia and the Transcaucasian region. Strong enough to crush the revolt of the Drevlianians, Igor suffered serious setbacks in his audacious expeditions, however, and another Turkish people, the Pechenegs or Patzinaks, for the first time invaded the Kievan State and were soon to become a permanent threat to its security. Nevertheless, toward the end of his reign, in 944 Igor organized a campaign against the Byzantine Empire, as his predecessor had done. He even used a horde of Pechenegs as reinforcement. But he only reached the Danube, and the peace treaty of the following year, which was less favorable to the Russians in its detailed commercial clauses, included a political agreement directed against the Khazars and the Volga Bulgars. It is therefore also possible that the ruler of the Tmutorokan Russians, who was particularly interested in relations with these peoples, was among the princes who, besides "grand prince" Igor, concluded the treaty. But even the Kievan land was obviously not yet fully united under his control, and the same year he was killed by the Drevlianians from whom he wanted to extort an increased tribute.

After avenging his death, his widow, Olga, who was possibly of Slavic origin in spite of her Scandinavian name, ruled for several years in the name of their minor son Sviatoslav, the first member of the Varangian dynasty to receive a Slavic name. Olga improved the administration of the Kievan State and was the first to realize that in order to enter the community of European nations, that state had to be Christianized. In the treaty of 945, besides the pagan majority, "Christian Ruś" are already mentioned, and it was from Byzantium that since the days of Photius the Christian faith was being propagated among both the Slavic population and their Norman leaders. But Olga, probably baptized in Kiev in 955, wanted to obtain for her country an autonomous ecclesiastical organization, and for that purpose she negotiated with both Eastern and Western Christendom, just as the Bulgars had done before their conversion. And although even in the tenth century there was not yet any schism separating Rome from Byzantium, the issue was of the greatest possible importance for the future.

Olga first went to Constantinople where in 957 she was solemnly received by Emperor Constantine Porphyrogenitus. Probably, however, no agreement was reached, since two years later she sent her envoys to the German king, Otto I, asking him to send a bishop to Kiev. This was before Otto's coronation by the pope as Roman Emperor, but in any case it would have brought Russia under papal authority and under Western influence. Just as in the case of the Moravian church almost one hundred years earlier, it would have been a German influence. In this case, however, it seemed less dangerous politically because of the great distance between the two countries, which were separated by all the Western Slavs. Nevertheless, when after initial difficulties that probably resulted from that very distance, a German monk ordained as bishop eventually reached Kiev, he was not accepted there and in 962 he had to return.

At that time, when Otto I was busy with his imperial projects in Italy, Kiev was already ruled by Sviatoslav himself. The failure to establish a Catholic ecclesiastical organization there was therefore caused not only by the problem of its autonomy but also by the lack of interest of a prince who showed all the distinctive features of a pagan viking. His ambition was first directed against the East where in two expeditions, in 963 and 968, he destroyed the Khazar Empire. He was, however, unable permanently to conquer that vast territory which was now open to new invasions from Asia. After entering Tmutorokan and raiding the Volga Bulgars, he became involved in the problems of Byzantium and the Balkans between his two eastern campaigns. In spite of the Pecheneg danger threatening Kiev, he was chiefly interested in the conquest of Danubian Bulgaria where he wanted to establish his capital. Finally, however, both Bulgarians and

Greeks joined against him, and in 971, after several defeats, he had to give up his claims. The next year, on his way back to Kiev, he was killed by the Pechenegs.

The interlude of Sviatoslav's adventures delayed the conversion and definite organization of the Kievan State. The Norman element which had so greatly contributed to the foundation of that state was, however, practically absorbed by the East Slavic population, which now was ready for joining the other Slavs, Western and Southern, in entering the European community. The later tenth century is therefore the decisive transition period between the early background of the whole East Central European region and its medieval development into a group of independent Christian states at the border of both the Eastern and the restored Western Empire and of their respective spheres of influence.

PART II

THE MEDIEVAL TRADITION

4

THE HERITAGE OF THE TENTH CENTURY

THE WESTERN SLAVS

Almost all European states which formed the Christian community of the Middle Ages can be traced back to the tenth century. That is true for both Western and Eastern Christendom, which were not yet divided by any final schism. The only difference is that in the East the Byzantine Empire had a much older tradition without, however, any possibilities of political expansion, while in the West the empire, "transferred" in 962 to the German kings, was as a matter of fact a new creation serving the purposes of German imperialism.

These purposes included the domination of Italy and an eastern expansion that was chiefly directed against the Western Slavs. After the fall of the Moravian State, Germany's immediate neighbors north of the Magyars were the Czechs of Bohemia and the Slavic tribes between the Elbe-Saale and the Oder-Neisse lines. The conquest of the latter, who persisted in their paganism and failed to achieve any political unity, caused the German marches that were created on their territory to advance to the boundaries of Poland, which also was still pagan but already united under the Piast dynasty.

When Poles and Germans clashed for the first time, probably in the year following the imperial coronation of Otto I, the Přemyslid dukes who had united the Czechs had already accepted both Catholicism and German overlordship. Decisive in that respect proved the reign of St. Václav, whose murder in 929 was largely the result of an anti-German movement but did not really change the situation. On the one hand, the crown of St. Václav remained a symbol of Bohemia's national sovereignty, but on the other hand, his brother and successor Boleslav I also had to recognize the feudal supremacy of the King of Germany, so that after 962 his state naturally became part of the Holy Roman Empire. The degree of that dependence remained, however, a controversial problem that was frequently connected with the position of Poland and the projects of cooperation between the two West Slavic powers.

From the beginning Poland decided to stay outside the Empire, and in order to avoid German pressure, Duke Mieszko I in 966 voluntarily Christianized his country, after marrying the daughter of the Duke of Bohemia the preceding year. Poland's first Christian ruler tried to limit the political influence of the Empire to a tribute which he agreed to pay from part of his territory. He also wanted the first Polish bishopric, founded in 968 in Poznań, to be directly under the Holy See, while the separate bishopric, which was established in Prague in 973, remained for almost four hundred years under the German Archbishop of Mainz.

Together with Boleslav II of Bohemia, who succeeded his father in 967, Mieszko I of Poland even interfered with the internal situation in Germany after the death of the first two emperors, Otto I and Otto II. He entered into relations with some of the neighboring German margraves and married the daughter of one of them after the death of his Czech wife. But neither Poland nor Bohemia was able to support the other West Slavic tribes in their desperate resistance against German conquest, and the joint action of both countries suffered from insufficient coordination and from territorial controversies. It is uncertain which region Mieszko I took from Bohemia in the later part of his reign. Most probably it was Cracow, together with the part of Little (Southern) Poland which the Czechs had temporarily occupied. In 981, however, he lost the region east of it (what now is called Eastern Galicia), to Vladimir of Kiev. His own interest was primarily in the opposite direction. From Great Poland, the original center of the state in the region of Gniezno and Poznań, he reached the Baltic coast, uniting the closely related tribe of the Pomeranians with the Poles and making contact with the Scandinavian world.

Toward the end of his life he placed his whole realm, at the time of his conversion already described as the largest and best organized Slavic state, under the immediate authority of the papacy. That donation of Poland, from the mouth of the Oder to the borders of Baltic Prussia and Kievan Russia, was to be the best guaranty of her independence which Mieszko I probably wanted to confirm by gaining the royal crown.

His achievements were completed by his son Bolesław Chrobry (the Brave), whose brilliant reign started in 992 with a strengthening of Poland's unity and which had as its main objective the securing of a fully independent and even leading position in East Central Europe.

Bolesław first hoped to realize his plans in friendly cooperation with the young Emperor Otto III who had a truly universal, supranational conception of the Roman Empire, uniting on equal terms Italy, Gaul, Germany and *Sclavinia*. In the latter—the Slavic world—the Emperor was prepared to recognize Bolesław as his vicar (*patricius*), whose friendly collaboration would promote the missionary activities in which they were both deeply interested. Their common friend, Adalbert, the former Bishop of Prague, having been killed in 997 on a mission in Prussia, was soon afterwards canonized by Pope Sylvester II. At Easter of the year 1000, Otto III made a pilgrimage to Poland's capital, Gniezno, where Bolesław had buried the redeemed body of the martyr. At a solemn convention attended by a papal legate, Poland received a fully independent ecclesiastical organization with an archbishop in Gniezno and new bishops in Cracow, Wrocław (Breslau in Silesia), and Kołobrzeg (Kolberg in Pomerania).

The political decisions of the congress of Gniezno made Bolesław—like his father a former *tributarius* of the Empire—a real *dominus*, that is, an independent ruler to whom most probably the royal dignity was promised. Some obscure intrigues at the Roman curia delayed the planned coronation, however, and in 1002 the death of Otto III altogether changed the situation. Fully aware of the danger of German imperialism which reappeared under the new emperor, Henry II, the Polish duke decided to oppose his policy by uniting all Western Slavs in some kind of federation under Poland's leadership.

That project included two different problems. Bolesław wanted first of all to save from German domination and to include in his realm as much as possible of the Slavic territory between Germany and Poland. Therefore in 1002 he occupied Lusatia and Misnia (Meissen), where a residuum of the Slavic population was to survive until our day. Even more important was the idea of replacing German influence in Bohemia by Polish authority. Interfering with internal rivalries among the members of the Přemyslid dynasty, in the following year Bolesław entered Prague and the creation of a common Polish-Czech state seemed nearer than in any later period of history.

But Henry II reacted by declaring a war which, twice interrupted by truces, lasted sixteen years. The final peace was concluded in 1018 in Budziszyn (Bautzen), the capital of Lusatia, which definitely remained under Bolesław's full sovereignty. He did not, however, succeed in gaining any other Slavic lands between the Oder and Elbe rivers, where the strongest tribe, the Lutitians, even cooperated with the German invaders, thus preparing their final doom. There was also a German party in Bohemia which the Poles had to evacuate in 1004. Bolesław kept only Moravia, so that the state of the Přemyslids was temporarily divided between the Empire and Poland.

In 1013, in the midst of the German war, Poland was for the first time threatened by a joint action of her western and eastern neighbors, the Emperor having resumed earlier German relations with the Kievan State. That was probably one of the reasons why Bolesław, immediately after the Treaty of Budziszyn, decided to interfere with the internal struggle among the sons of Vladimir of Kiev, supporting the one who had married his daughter. When he occupied Kiev in that same year of 1018 and there established the rule of his son-in-law, Sviatopolk, it seemed that even the Eastern Slavs would be included in Bolesław's federal system. The message which he sent from Kiev to both emperors, Henry II of Germany and Basil II of Byzantium, was a clear expression of his aim to keep the whole of East Central Europe free from any imperial authority.

Bolesław's influence reached as far as the Lithuanian border, where another missionary whom he supported, his German admirer St. Bruno, was killed in 1009, and also into Hungary, although it is doubtful whether he ever united any Slovak territories with Poland. His coronation as first King of Poland which with papal approval took place shortly before his death in 1025, finally confirmed Poland's position as an independent member of the European community.

The royal tradition of Bolesław Chrobry remained alive throughout the whole course of Polish history, although already under his son and successor, Mieszko II (1025–1034), crowned immediately after his father's death, Poland lost her leading position and entered a serious internal crisis that opened the door to German intervention. Lost were also the first king's territorial acquisitions, Lusatia and Moravia, the former coming definitely under German control and the latter returning to Bohemia. In spite of a fierce but unorganized resistance, the Slavic tribes west of Poland were absorbed by the Empire, which also continued to include the state of the Přemyslids.

The balance of power between Bohemia and Poland was, however, entirely changed during and after Mieszko II's ill-fated reign. His contemporary, Břetislav I, not only conquered the Polish province of Silesia, which was to remain an object of endless controversies between the two neighboring countries, but he also tried to unite them both, this time under Czech leadership. In spite of an invasion of Poland in 1038, his plan had even less chance of success than Chrobry's political conceptions, and the first period of Western Slavic history resulted in the final establishment of two states, separated by frequent rivalries, contrary to their common interest in opposing the German pressure. They both remained, however, centers of a Slavic culture which rapidly developed in close contact with Western Christendom, including the distant Romance countries. German influence was naturally much stronger in Bohemia, where German colonization also started much earlier, while Poland, never included in the Empire, regained her freedom of action after each attempt at interference by her neighbors.

Only the Pomeranian territory along the Baltic shores, carefully controlled by Mieszko I and his son, was not yet completely united with the other Polish lands. It could not be reached by German expansion, however, so long as the closely related Slavic tribes between the Oder and Elbe were struggling for their freedom, not without temporary successes.

THE EASTERN SLAVS

The recorded history of the Kievan State in which all Eastern Slavs were united under a dynasty of Norman origin, had started well before the consolidation of Bohemia and Poland, thanks chiefly to early contacts with the Byzantine Empire. But conversion to the Christian faith—a prerequisite condition for the inclusion of any country in the European community—was delayed here much longer. Even Prince Vladimir, the son of Sviatoslav, whom he succeeded after a few years of internal trouble, started as a pagan ruler who was similar to his predecessors. It was only in 988 that he decided to be baptized together with his people. Later he became a saint of the Eastern church.

He finally converted the Russians, both his Scandinavian vikings and the East Slavic tribes known under the name of *Ruś*, when Christendom was not yet split by any final Eastern schism. Nevertheless Vladimir's decision to accept the Christian faith, not from Rome but from Constantinople—a decision dramatically described in the *Pri-*

mary Russian Chronicle and easy to explain were it only because of geographical reasons—proved of far-reaching importance. At the beginning, the influence of Byzantium, then superior to any Western center of culture, greatly contributed to the rise of Kiev but gradually deepened the division between Eastern and Western Slavs. There was no danger of any inclusion of the new Christian state in the Empire with which Russia was to be culturally associated. Far from becoming a vassal state of Byzantium, she at once received her own ecclesiastical organization, although many details regarding the origin of the metropolitan see of Kiev and its relationship with the Patriarchate of Constantinople are subject to controversial interpretation.

But notwithstanding occasional relations with Rome and the Western Empire which appear in Vladimir's policy even after his turn toward Byzantium, that policy was now dominated by the necessity of settling the various problems raised by his cooperation with Basil II, the powerful Greek emperor whose sister he received in marriage a year after being baptized in Kiev. The agreement was completed in Kherson, an old Greek colony in the Crimea which Vladimir besieged and conquered in 989. When the pressure which he thus exercised upon the emperor proved successful and the wedding with Princess Anna had taken place, Vladimir returned the city to Basil II and the Kievan State never secured any permanent stronghold on the shores of the Black Sea. It seems, however, that on that occasion Vladimir united with his realm the city of Tmutorokan, across the strait of Kerch, which had probably been an earlier political and ecclesiastical center of Russian settlers and which was to play an important role in the history of the Kievan State during the following century.

Until Vladimir's death in 1015, the early years of that century were utilized by Russia's first Christian ruler in order to strengthen the Church and to protect the southeastern frontier of the country against the invasions of the Pechenegs, who then controlled the steppes north of the Black Sea. The defense of these border regions remained a permanent problem, with one wave of Asiatic invaders replacing the other. With all other neighbors Vladimir now lived in peace, and the various parts of the Kievan State, including the colonial northeastern territory in the Volga Basin with Rostov as its oldest center, were governed by his numerous sons.

The difficulty of maintaining the unity of the Kievan State in spite of feuds among the members of the dynasty, which besides the Church was the only link between the many East Slavic tribes, appeared immediately after Vladimir's death. After the elimination and death of Sviatopolk, supported by his Polish father-in-law, the main rivals were Yaroslav, who in his father's time had ruled over Novgorod, and Mstislav of Tmutorokan. In 1024 the two brothers decided to divide Russia with the Dnieper River as frontier—a first recognition of the difference between the original territory of the state founded by Rurik's dynasty, from Novgorod in the north to Kiev in the south, and the practically unlimited area of eastern expansion. The territory of Polotsk, the center of what was to be White Russia, remained outside that arrangement under a separate branch of the dynasty.

The unity of the whole realm was temporarily restored after Mstislav's death in 1036, when Yaroslav became the sole ruler. Only a little later the ecclesiastical relations with Byzantium were definitely fixed. An uninterrupted series of metropolitans ordained by the Patriarch of Constantinople now appeared in Kiev, a city which, thanks to Yaroslav, called "The Wise," rapidly developed on the model of the imperial capital. Nevertheless his reign ended in a twofold crisis in Russo-Byzantine relations. In 1043, after a conflict in the trade relations between the two countries, Yaroslav directed a last Russian attack against the Greek Empire, which reached Constantinople but which ended in failure. And in 1051 an attempt was made to secure not only political but also ecclesiastical independence from Byzantium, when the bishops of the Kievan State elected as metropolitan a native Russian who was not recognized by the patriarch.

It is true that in the following year relations again improved in connection with another marriage between members of the two dynasties. But Yaroslav was at least equally anxious to maintain contacts with western dynasties through matrimonial ties. The marriage of his daughter Anna, who went to France in 1050 to marry King Henry I, is particularly significant in that respect. And after interfering with the internal troubles of Poland Yaroslav was in friendly relations with that West Slavic neighbor, in spite of the persistent territorial dispute over the Halich region which changed its master several times in the course of the century.

These close contacts between Kievan Russia and Western Christendom continued in the midst of the growing tension between Rome and Constantinople which in 1054, the year of Yaroslav's death, resulted in a lasting schism. Russia was not immediately affected by that fateful break. It was not before the twelfth century that Byzantine influence also proved strong enough to raise in the metropolis of Kiev a growing distrust and sometimes even hostility against the Latins. If 1054 is a turning point in Russian history, it is rather because of the implications of Yaroslav's order of succession.

In his testament he left the throne of Kiev to his eldest son, Iziaslav, but each of the other four received his own principality, it being understood that after the death of the eldest they would move from one principality to the other in the order of seniority. That system, in itself involved, was further complicated by the fact that the line ruling in Polotsk remained outside that rotation; that the descendants of a son of Yaroslav who had died before his father, created a separate, hereditary principality in Halich; and that important regions distant from the Kievan center—autonomous Novgorod, declining Tmutorokan, and, above all, the area of colonial expansion in the Volga Basin—had their own increasingly different development.

Under such conditions Iziaslav could hardly maintain his leading position, and even his cooperation with two of his younger brothers did not last longer than 1073. When he lost Kiev for the second time, and did not receive, as in 1069, the help of Poland, he tried to save his position by turning to the leading powers of Western Christendom. Having no success with Emperor Henry IV, he particularly turned to Pope Gregory VII. His son went to Rome and placed the *Regnum Russiae* under the protection of the Holy See. In his bull of 1075, the Pope accepted that donation, which would have completely changed the destinies of Kievan Russia and would have created another Catholic kingdom in East Central Europe, next to Poland. Eastern and Western Slavs would have been united in a similar policy and in their ecclesiastical allegiance. Gregory VII could not, however, give to Iziaslav any efficient support, and the whole project, having hardly any backing in Russia, left no traces in her tradition. Iziaslav himself gave it up when, thanks to the death of his main opponent, he could return to Kiev for the last two years of his life. When he fell in a battle against his nephews, the internal struggles among the numerous members of the dynasty continued without much respect for the rule of genealogical seniority.

The Kievan State, the largest in Europe, situated in a crucial position at the limits of the European community and of Christendom, therefore had no real unity which could have made one nation out of the many East Slavic tribes. Connected with the rest of Europe through two conflicting influences, occasional ties with the neighboring Catholic West and the penetration of Byzantine Orthodoxy, this earliest Russia was at the same time exposed to a permanent threat of Asiatic invasions from the South East, but rapidly enlarged her sphere of influences through a comparatively easy expansion in the Finnish territories of the North East. That intermediary position between Europe and Asia was to remain a permanent problem for the Eastern Slavs—for Russia as a whole in the sense of the old *Ruś*. And it was gradually leading to a division into various very different Russias, facilitated by the dynastic divisions into principalities which, contrary to Yaroslav's will, practically became hereditary in various lines of Rurik's descendants. Without strictly corresponding to the original tribal areas, these principalities had, in many cases, however, a different ethnic background and, in addition to it, different political interests, dependent on their geographical situation.

Already in that earliest period of their history it became evident that the Eastern Slavs, unable to control the shores of the Black Sea, would not be able to reach the Baltic either. Both Vladimir and Yaroslav made expeditions against the Lithuanian and Finnish tribes which separated the Kievan State from the sea whence the Normans had come to Russia. But even the conquests of Yaroslav did not reach farther than Yuriev, the city which he founded on the site of the later Dorpat (Tartu). It was Novgorod and Polotsk, however, which remained the permanent Slavic outposts in that direction, and the frontier between Slavic and Baltic populations remained practically unchanged.

THE FALL OF THE BULGARIAN EMPIRE AND THE RISE OF HUNGARY

The tradition of the tenth and early eleventh centuries, so important for Bohemia, Poland, and Russia, is perhaps even more significant for the two nations formed by Asiatic invaders in the Danubian and Balkan regions. For the Bulgarians, Slavized and Christianized at the end of the preceding century, it was the period of their greatest, truly imperial expansion which remained an unforgettable inspiration, although it ended in a catastrophe with lasting consequences. For the Hungarians, never assimilated by their Slavic neighbors and not converted before the end of the tenth century, their rapid integration with the Western world immediately became the starting point of a brilliant development which was to last until the end of the Middle Ages.

Boris, Bulgaria's first Christian ruler, left to his son Simeon (893–927) a well-established kingdom, with the Slavic language introduced into the life of State and Church, both of which were practically independent of Byzantium. But his successor, educated in Constantinople, had even more ambitious aims. He wanted to conquer Byzantium and to replace the Greek Empire by a Bulgarian one. Besieging Constantinople several times, he came very near to his goal, and even after concluding a treaty with Emperor Romanus Lecapenus in 924, who agreed to pay tribute to the dangerous neighbor but who stopped his invasions at a clearly determined frontier, Simeon called himself Emperor of the Romans and the Bulgarians. He also conquered the western part of the Balkan Peninsula, particularly the Serbs who had not yet achieved any definite political organization.

However, Simeon's death in 927 left Bulgaria exhausted. It became obvious that the idea of replacing the Eastern Empire as master of the Christian Orthodox world and of the whole Balkan region was an illusion, far beyond the possibilities of a young nation which had to face serious internal problems. One of them was the heretical movement started under Simeon's son and successor, Peter, by a monk named Bogomil. Based upon the conception of earlier Eastern sects as to a permanent struggle between the forces of good and evil, Bogomilism spread from Bulgaria far toward the West and its influence is even evident in the French heretical trends of the later Middle Ages. But such a movement could hardly strengthen Bulgaria's resistance against the Greek revenge which already, during the reign of Peter, dealt a first serious blow to the new power.

After invasions by Magyars and Pechenegs, the main eastern part of the country, with its brilliant capital at Preslav, became a battlefield between the Greeks and the Russian Varangians whom Byzantium under Emperor Nicephorus Phocas used against the Bulgarians, only to defeat them in 972 under John I Tsimisces. The result was the occupation of Eastern Bulgaria by the Greeks. A new leader, King Samuel, however, appeared in the western part of the country. He resumed Simeon's struggle against the empire and opposed it for more than thirty years.

That long Greek-Bulgarian war is one of the decisive events in the history of the Balkan Peninsula. It might even be interpreted as the beginning of the disintegration of Eastern Christian society, and it indeed proved the impossibility of reconciling the imperial idea with the free development of the various nations which had settled south of the Danube. In its first phase it was a defensive war of Byzantium against Samuel's invasions which reached the Adriatic and the Aegean seas. But Bulgaria paid a heavy price for these renewed imperial ambitions. Emperor Basil II, called the "killer of the Bulgarians," in 1014 finally inflicted upon them a crushing defeat, and Samuel himself died when thousands of captives were sent back to him with their eyes gouged. Such cruelty of course exasperated the Bulgarians, who continued to resist in the Balkan Mountains for four more years. But by 1018 their whole country was conquered and again made a mere province of the Greek Empire.

Byzantium was wise enough to grant the Bulgarians a fairly large degree of regional autonomy, and although they ceased to have their own patriarch, their religious life continued to develop separately under the archbishops of Okhrida. Therefore throughout the remaining part of the eleventh and most of the twelfth century, Bulgaria seemed completely controlled by the empire, and not before the fall of the Comneni dynasty in 1185 did a revolt start again, leading to what is sometimes called a second Bulgarian Empire. There remained, however, a permanent tension between Greeks and Bulgarians, with neither side able to satisfy its imperial ambitions, and always ready to cooperate against the other with any new forces which might appear in the Balkan Peninsula.

One of these forces was to be Slavic Serbia, which neither Greeks nor Bulgarians could ever completely conquer. But here, too, a strong political movement did not start before the end of the twelfth century, although already in 1077 one of the Serb chieftains, Michael, in the Zeta region—later called Montenegro—received the royal title from Pope Gregory VII. Though without lasting consequences, that fact is highly significant because it indicates that even among the Serbs the influence of the Catholic West appeared time and again throughout the Middle Ages. That influence remained predominant among their closest kin, the Croats, where, long before Gregory VII had granted a royal crown to Zvonimir (1076–1089), a Catholic kingdom had been established in 924 by Tomislav.

EAST CENTRAL AND EASTERN EUROPE BEFORE THE MONGOL INVASION, 1237–1241

▬·▬·▬·▬·	Boundaries	⎫ of the kingdoms and
		⎬ principalities of East
▬ ▬ ▬ ▬ ▬	Approximate boundaries	⎭ Central Europe

•••••••••••••••• Boundary of Poland as extended under Bolesław Chrobry († 1025)

•••••••••••••••• Boundary of Bohemia as extended under Přemysl Otakar II († 1278)

▨ Territory of the Scandinavian kingdoms

▥ Territory of the Holy Roman Empire and (in Prussia and Livonia) of German Orders of Knighthood

▧ Greek-held territories of the Eastern Roman Empire

▨ Latin-held territories of the Eastern Roman Empire

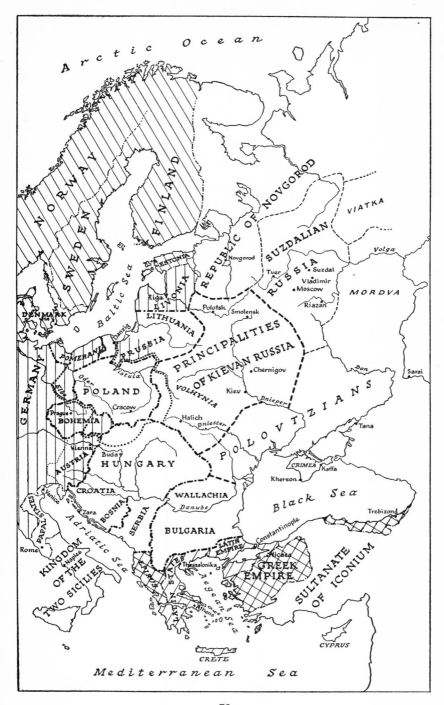

No longer threatened by the Germans as in Carolingian times, and only for a very short time under Byzantium, Croatia was, however, placed between two rising powers, one of which, the Republic of Venice, wanted to occupy her Adriatic coast in Dalmatia, while the other, Hungary, was separated from Croatia only by the Drava River. Taking advantage of Zvonimir's death and of ties of marriage with the Croat dynasty, the kings of Hungary, after a first occupation of Croatia in 1091, succeeded in establishing a permanent union of the two kingdoms under the Hungarian crown in 1102. Croatia included both Dalmatia and Slavonia, the territory between the lower Drava and Sava rivers, to which Syrmia, down to the Danube, was also added later. That whole Slavic realm, however, always remained a junior partner in the union which was to last until 1918, with Dalmatia an object of Venetian claims, while the northwestern neighbors of the Croats, the Slovenes, all came under Austrian domination.

Hungary's great success with regard to Croatia, which made her not only a Danubian but also an Adriatic power, can only be explained by her rapid rise from a pagan state which raided all neighbor countries, to a Catholic and "apostolic" kingdom, a title which in 1001 was granted by Pope Sylvester II to the son and successor of the recently converted Géza, Stephen, the future saint. His reign, which lasted until 1038, resulted in the consolidation of Hungary within natural boundaries which reached the ranges of the Carpathian Mountains. The crown of St. Stephen was to remain a symbol of Hungary's tradition and unity up to the present.

That unity included peoples of different origin, particularly the Slovaks in the northern part of the country and the largely Rumanian population of Transylvania. Stephen himself encouraged the establishment of German settlers, according to his frequently quoted statement that a country would be weak if limited to peoples of one tongue. But according to his policy, which was continued by practically all his successors, he was at the same time eager to maintain Hungary's complete independence of both Empires. Though both were her neighbors, only the Western seriously threatened that independence on various occasions. Furthermore, stressing her national unity, Hungary more and more based her political conceptions on the idea of Magyar supremacy. Identifying themselves with the nation at large, but not without absorbing many foreign elements also, the Magyars, though keeping through the ages their isolated language, were culturally Latinized very rapidly and soon considered themselves the defenders of Western culture along the Balkan border.

After St. Stephen, whose son Emeric (also canonized a few years later) died before the father, Hungary went through a serious crisis. Pagan reaction opposed a king of Venetian origin who temporarily occupied the throne, thanks to his designation by his uncle, St. Stephen. But another branch of the national Árpád dynasty soon returned to power, and even amidst these internal troubles neither Polish interference nor that of imperial Germany, which was much more dangerous, had any lasting consequences. On the contrary, at the end of the eleventh century Hungarian power had already been restored under another king who was also recognized as a saint, Ladislas I (1077–1095), and the following century was again a particularly brilliant period in the history of the country.

Among the kings of that period, Béla III (1172–1196), whose achievements have been described by a first, anonymous national chronicler, deserves special attention. He too opposed the encroachments of both German and Greek emperors successfully, and himself exercised a noteworthy influence in Balkan affairs. Under him and his successors, particularly Andrew II (1205–1235), that Hungarian influence also penetrated beyond the Carpathians into the Ruthenian principality of Halich, whose Latinized name first appeared in 1189 in a new title of the kings of Hungary: *rex Galiciae*. It was in that region that Hungarian and Polish interests clashed with each other, although the usually friendly relations between both countries were even in this controversial issue leading to attempts at cooperation toward the turn of the century.

Thus it was precisely during the elimination of Bulgarian power under Byzantine rule that Hungary succeeded in organizing the Danubian region north of the Balkans as a unified kingdom which extended the sphere of Western influence without giving up its own individuality. Such an element of stability in East Central Europe was particularly important in a period when the other countries of that part of the continent, after having made equally promising beginnings, were meeting with more and more difficulty, either through internal disintegration or under the growing pressure of the German Empire which proved so dangerous to the two West Slavic kingdoms, Bohemia and Poland. Such a situation was to last well into the thirteenth century.

5

INTERNAL DISINTEGRATION AND FOREIGN PENETRATION

In the first half of the eleventh century, the plan for creating a united West Slavic State as a check to German advance, tried first under Polish and then under Czech leadership, had ultimately failed. Alarmed by Břetislav's initiative, Germany, under Henry III, even gave some quite exceptional assistance to the son of Mieszko II, Casimir, when he restored Poland's integrity and reorganized her culturally after the crisis following his father's tragic death. But already under his son, Bolesław II (1058–1079), called "the Bold," Poland rapidly recovered the position held by Bolesław I. Siding with the Papacy in its great struggle against the Empire, Poland once more opposed German predominance in Central Europe, while Bohemia took exactly the opposite stand.

At the outset, Poland seemed to be eminently successful. Under Bolesław II she was again occupying a leading position in East Central Europe, and she at least temporarily exercised a decisive influence upon the political situation of the neighboring countries, including Kiev. Cooperating with Gregory VII, whose reforms contributed to the development of the Polish Church, Bolesław the Bold also regained the royal dignity. In 1076, shortly before Canossa, he was crowned as king, thus reaffirming Poland's complete independence of the Empire. Therefore it is hard to explain why it was precisely a conflict with one of the leaders of the hierarchy, Stanislas, Bishop of Cracow (now Poland's capital instead of Gniezno), which caused the king's fall. After the execution of the bishop, who was soon to become the nation's patron saint, Bolesław II was expelled and died in exile.

There are some indications that the opposition against the king was supported by Bohemia where Břetislav, after his initial triumphs, had already been forced by a German invasion to recognize the over-lordship of Henry III, and where his son and successor, Vratislav (1061–1092), now sided with Henry IV against the Pope. As a reward, he too, the first among Bohemia's rulers, received a royal crown in 1086, but only personally and from the Emperor, so that the connection of his country with Germany became even closer.

The Polish Piasts did not resume the royal title for more than two hundred years. After the miserable reign of Bolesław II's brother, however, who went over to the imperial camp, his nephew, another Bolesław surnamed "Wrymouth," as soon as he gained control of the whole country in 1102, fought most energetically against all German attempts to limit his sovereignty. Emperor Henry V was defeated before Wrocław (Breslau) when he invaded Silesia in 1109. During the following twenty years of his reign, Bolesław III completed the conquest and Christianization of Pomerania, restoring Poland's ac-cess to the Baltic and extending his influence as far as the island of Rügen, an old center of Slavic culture.

Thus the German advance which the pagan Slavic tribes between the Elbe and the Oder were unable to check in spite of their repeated revolts, seemed definitely halted by another Catholic power whose re-lations with the Latin West were already so well established that it was a chronicler of French origin who described the achievements of Bolesław III with due praise. Before dying in 1138 he fixed in his will an order of succession which was supposed to safeguard the unity of the country in spite of the assignment of hereditary duchies to his numerous sons. He hoped to accomplish this by deciding that Cra-cow, together with the center of the realm and with Pomerania, would always be held by the eldest member of the dynasty. As usual, such a "seniorate" proved a complete failure. A few years later Poland entered a long period of dynastic division, with ample opportunity for the Empire to interfere in her internal problems again.

The danger was so much greater, since the age of Frederick Bar-barossa was marked by a new wave of German imperialism which was not at all limited to the domination of Italy amidst a new struggle with the papacy. It was then that the conquest of all the Slavs between Germany and Poland was completed both by the Emperor himself and by his Saxon rivals of the Welf family. Western Pomerania was also lost to Poland. Bohemia, on the other hand, where dynastic troubles causing frequent interventions by Henry V had started even earlier, continued under Vladislav II (1140–1174) her policy of co-operation with the Empire. After supporting Frederick I against the Lombards, in 1158 that Czech prince again received a royal crown from the Emperor. This time it was a hereditary crown, combined with the formal right to participate in the imperial elections. But Bohemia's inclusion in the Empire, though as its foremost and most independent member, became even more evident.

A year earlier, Barbarossa, invading Poland, had also forced one of her princes to pay him homage. But that humiliation proved only temporary, and even the province of Silesia, which Bolesław IV, under German pressure, had to restore to the sons of his expelled elder brother, did not cease to be a part of Poland. That border region was, however, exposed to German influence and to the influx of German colonists more than any other of the Polish duchies. But the fateful process of German colonization had hardly started here in the later twelfth century, though in Bohemia it was already in steady progress, as was well evidenced around 1170 by the famous edict of Soběslav II. As did the other Přemyslids, he protected the settlers against any anti-German feelings of the people and granted them far-reaching privileges. They indeed contributed to the economic progress of the country, especially that of the cities, but not without seriously endangering national unity.

In these early days that danger was not yet apparent, and when in 1197, after another period of internal struggles and imperial interventions, Přemysl Otakar I, a son of Vladislav II, became king of Bohemia, the country seemed stronger than ever before and was indeed for three generations to play a prominent role in general European affairs. But that could happen only in connection with internal difficulties which affected the Empire at the turn of the century and which were skilfully utilized by Přemysl. Supporting in turn the various rival candidates for the German crown, in 1212 he finally obtained from Frederick II the so-called Golden Bull of Sicily which confirmed Bohemia's privileged position in the Empire and greatly reduced the obligations of her king. Nevertheless she entered the thirteenth century in close connection with all the vicissitudes of German policy and with an already very numerous and influential German population.

Entirely different were the contemporary developments in Poland. The rather artificial rule of the "seniorate" was definitely disregarded when the successor of Bolesław IV, his next brother, Mieszko III, called "the Old" (1173–1177), lost Cracow to the youngest son of Wrymouth, Casimir the Just. These two princes were by far the most prominent representatives of their generation. Mieszko, limited to Greater Poland, although until his death in 1202 he time and again tried to recover Cracow, was a defender of a strong monarchical power and for that very reason unpopular among the clergy and the knighthood, both of which were growing in influence. On the contrary, Casimir, who united Little Poland with Mazovia and Cuyavia, was supported by these new forces. His desire to make all his possessions, including Cracow, hereditary in his line, meant a basic change in his father's conception. Imperial and even papal confirmation of that change proved much less important than the attitude of the native hierarchy and aristocracy. At the Assembly of Łęczyca in 1180, Casimir granted a first charter of liberties to the Polish church, and the leaders of the main clans into which the Polish nobility, not yet organized as a formal class, remained traditionally divided, played an important part in all political decisions.

Proud of her royal tradition, all Poland remained one ecclesiastical province under the same dynasty, but the various lines of the Piasts came to identify their interests with those of the individual duchies more and more. All princes of any importance had the ambition of ruling in Cracow, which kept the prestige of a political center, but Casimir's line never lost that position except for very short interludes. The princes of Silesia, the eldest branch of the dynasty, and those of Greater Poland, the descendants of Mieszko III, were naturally more interested in problems of the West where the Germans were now Poland's neighbors along the whole frontier, which they tried to push back from the Oder line. Casimir the Just and his successors, ruling over the whole eastern half of the country, had to face different issues: the defense against continuous raids of the still pagan Baltic tribes in Prussia and Lithuania, and the relations with the principalities into which the Kievan State was divided. One of them, created in the originally Polish border region which had changed masters several times and now had its center in Halich, was the object of Casimir's special interest and again came to a large extent under Polish influence as well as Hungarian.

Casimir's reign was glorified in the first chronicle written by a native Pole, Master Vincentius Kadłubek, who later became bishop of Cracow. His work shows the great cultural progress which Poland had made in the last century and indicates her intimate connection with Western Europe, including France and Italy, where Vincentius had been educated. In his political philosophy he represents the ideas of a limitation of monarchical power by the nation, and of close co-operation with the church.

Both ideas are reflected in the events which followed Casimir's death. It was the support of the aristocracy which decided in favor of the succession of his young son Leszek, called "the White" (1194–1227), who continued his policy. And one of the most important decisions of the new ruler was to place Poland once more, in 1207, under the protection of the Holy See. Even under an Emperor as powerful as Frederick II, Germany did not think any longer of interfering with Polish problems or of dominating a country which, though politically divided, was a member of the state system directly controlled by Innocent III.

Poland's own power was indeed greatly reduced through a disintegration which, however, was exclusively the result of territorial divisions among the numerous branches of the national dynasty. Parallel with these divisions, a consciousness of community was growing and this frequently united even the quarreling princes in joint efforts. Therefore the prospects of the future were not so dark as they might appear at the threshold of the thirteenth century. Being an outpost of Western Latin civilization Poland, even divided, was an insurmountable obstacle to further German advance.

THE DISINTEGRATION OF THE KIEVAN STATE

The disintegration of the Kingdom of Poland, dangerous as it was, did not prove final. For various reasons an apparently similar process in the neighboring Kievan State had lasting consequences. Here the dynastic division based upon an unfortunate order of succession had started almost a hundred years earlier. It is true that after half a century of confusion which followed the death of Yaroslav the Wise, and which became particularly critical after the death of his eldest son Iziaslav in 1078, serious efforts were made to revise a situation which was leading to endless dynastic struggles. Cooperation among all the descendants of Rurik, including those who had settled in the colonial area of the northeast, was indeed urgent, since after the Pechenegs, which had at last been defeated, an even more dangerous Asiatic tribe, the Polovtsy or Cumans, penetrated into the steppes north of the Black Sea. The Kievan State was once more cut off from that sea, and the various principalities of the south suffered from repeated invasions.

It was under these circumstances that at the suggestion of Vladimir Monomach, who had defeated his rivals with the help of the Polovtsy, a conference of all the Russian princes was held in Lubech, near Kiev, in 1097. This conference changed the law of succession, which had been based upon the rule of seniority and the rotation of the various princes from one principality to another. From now on all the principalities were regarded as hereditary, but no clear decision was made with respect to the highly important issue as to who should occupy the leading position of grand prince, which remained connected with Kiev, although the title itself hardly appears in the contemporary sources.

Not even the solemn promise of keeping peace among themselves was kept by all the princes, and their next conference, held at Uvetichi in 1100, had to punish one of them who had seized and cruelly blinded his cousin. And it was only thirteen years later that Vladimir Monomach, who could claim the rank of grand prince according to the rule of primogeniture, succeeded in occupying Kiev with the consent of the others and in holding it until his death in 1125.

Under the brilliant reign of this remarkable prince, all the Eastern Slavs were united for the last time in one body politic. Without being a completely homogeneous or strongly centralized unit, it was, however, a community that was based upon the same culture and similar political principles as had prevailed under Vladimir's grandfather, Yaroslav. The code of law, the famous *Rus'ka Pravda*, compiled under the latter and developed under his successors, continued to govern relations among all classes of society from the *boyars* in the prince's *druzhina* (following) and *duma* (council), now hereditary landowners, to the various groups of peasants free and slave. The ecclesiastical organization under the Metropolitan of Kiev also continued to be an element of unity. But it was precisely under Monomach, whose very surname points to a growing Byzantine influence, that the consequences of the Greek schism also became evident in the Russian church after about sixty years. A growing prejudice against the Catholic West already appears in the *Primary Russian Chronicle*, completed by Kievan monks in 1113 at the time of Vladimir's coming into power. And in spite of repeated matrimonial ties between the Ruriks and various Catholic dynasties, including the Polish, that religious prejudice increased the political difficulties in the relations with the Western neighbors.

Nevertheless, even then the break between the two centers of European Christian civilization, Rome and Byzantium, was not yet considered final. On the other hand, the Greek Empire of the Comneni, itself in close relations with Western powers, was even less securely in a position to control the policies of Kievan Russia than it had been in the days of the Macedonian dynasty. Fully independent of any imperial authority, the Russian princes were going to participate in Greek affairs until the end of the twelfth century. Sometimes they were divided in their political sympathies, but this affected conditions in Russia only in the times of internal disintegration that followed Vladimir.

The interesting autobiographical details contained in Vladimir's will give evidence of the restless activity of a ruler who did his best both to defend the whole country against the Polovtsy, then the only real external danger, and to appease the rivalries of all those princes who remained under his supreme control. Appearances of unity continued under his son Mstislav, but after his death in 1132, and even more so after that of Mstislav's brother Yaropolk in 1139, there set in a struggle for Kiev, not only among Monomach's descendants but also between them and other lines of the dynasty, which completely destroyed old Russia's political organization.

The sack of Kiev in 1169 is usually considered the final blow, not only because the capital and its prestige never fully recovered from that first destruction in a fratricidal war, but even more so because the prince who conquered Kiev on that occasion did not care to rule there and returned to his original principality. That prince was Andrew Bogolubsky, whose father George Dolgoruky, a son of Vladimir Monomach, had controlled Kiev temporarily, but who had already been primarily interested in his hereditary possessions in the distant Volga region.

In the following three quarters of a century, Kiev changed masters so many times (more than thirty) and so obviously was no longer the real political center of even a loose federation of principalities, that usually the rise of three new centers of Russian history—Halich, Novgorod, and Suzdal—is strongly emphasized. It must be remembered, however, that until the Mongol invasion, which in 1240 interrupted the series of princes of Kiev for more than a hundred years, the importance of that original nucleus of medieval Russia did not disappear completely. There always remained the possibility that under a prominent ruler who would add his hereditary lands to Kiev, the city could again become a symbol of unity among all the Eastern Slavs.

Geographically, it would have been most natural to unite that region of the lower Dnieper with that of the upper Dnieper, which also remained a not insignificant center of Russian life. If it receives so little attention, it is because the White Russian principalities of that region used to show very little political initiative. The most important of these principalities, with its capital Polotsk on the upper Dvina, continued to be governed by a side line of the dynasty which was never seriously interested in Kiev's fate but rather in trade relations with the Baltic region. The most active of the princes of Smolensk, Monomach's great-grandson Mstislav, after failing to hold Kiev, eventually transferred his line to the distant southwestern corner of old Russia.

It was here that under his son Roman, who at the end of the twelfth century united Volhynia with Halich, a particularly important center was established in the immediate neighborhood of Poland and Hungary. At first supported by the Poles, Roman was killed in a battle against them in 1205, and the struggle for his heritage, which he left to two minor sons, led to a joint interference of both of these Catholic countries. The project of creating there a kingdom of "Galicia" (the Latinized name of the Halich region), under a Polish-Hungarian dynasty and papal overlordship, was doomed to failure, and finally Roman's son Daniel consolidated his power so that he could even claim the throne of Kiev. But in the midst of a hard fight against political conquest by the Catholic West, the cultural and social ties with that West were developed more than ever before. In the light of the local chronicle, the *boyars* who supported Roman's family appear strangely similar to the Polish knights and were gaining a similar position, limiting monarchical power.

In this new state of Halich and Volhynia, which was closely associated with the European community, as in the Kiev region the population was "Little Russian" or Ruthenian, according to the Latin sources, or Ukrainian, according to the present-day terminology. They differed from the White Russians, and even more from the ancestors of the Great Russians, the Russians in the specific sense of today. Out of the large group of East Slavic tribes whose original names were almost entirely forgotten, three distinct nations were thus being formed.

But even among the Great Russians of the North East, two entirely different centers developed as a result of the disintegration of the Kievan State. One of them originated within the limits of the original *Ruś*, in the Novgorod region where the Varangians had first appeared under Rurik. In spite of a colonial activity which soon reached the Arctic Ocean and later even the Urals, that center did not move into these distant Finnish regions but remained identified with the famous old metropolis in the original territory of the Slovene tribe. Equally important was the fact that amidst all the dynastic troubles of the Kievan State, the rich commercial city of Novgorod succeeded in gaining an exceptional autonomous position. No line of the Ruriks was ever established there. The authority of the grand prince was already limited in the days of Kiev's real power. A strange republican constitution was gradually developed, democratic in its form, oligarchic in its essence, with the bishop and the governor (*posadnik*) in the leading positions and the general assembly (*veche*) theoretically supreme. Even more than the White Russians of Polotsk, the Great Russians of Novgorod had close trade relations with the West. The danger of Latin conquest, after the establishment of German knights on the Baltic shores, created a strong political antagonism. But cultural intercourse with the Catholic West was another consequence of such a situation which also seemed to draw that section of the old *Ruś* into the European community.

Entirely different was the situation in the last center of Russian life which had been created by the colonial expansion of other Great Russian tribes that had never played an important part in their original home east of the middle Dnieper and had moved into their new, practically unlimited settlements "beyond the forests" in the basin of the upper Volga. The sparse and backward Finnish population was submerged by the Slavic colonists under the leadership of princes who here, on new and hard grounds, were never limited by boyars or popular assemblies. On the contrary, it was under the autocratic rule of Dolgoruky's and Bogolubsky's numerous descendants—the latter's son and successor, Vsevolod, was surnamed "Big Nest" because of his many children—that the new Russia centering in Suzdal, which superseded the earliest colonial outpost in Rostov, grew into a strong centralized power. Culturally, even the influence of Byzantium was hardly experienced in these remote lands, and no contact with the Western world had ever existed. Whether that colony of one of the East European peoples, Eastern Europe in the geographical sense, would ever join East Central Europe in a general European community, was a question to be decided by the political events of the thirteenth century.

THE REPERCUSSIONS OF THE FOURTH CRUSADE IN THE BALKANS

It was in the thirteenth century that the crusading movement, typical of the medieval tradition in general, reached its climax. But that same century also saw the most shocking misuses and distortions of the crusading idea which, among other things, deeply affected the relations between Western and Eastern Europe. The first example was indeed the tragic turn of the Fourth Crusade. First, in 1202 it was diverted against Catholic Hungary in order to conquer Zara, the capital of Dalmatia, for the Venetians. Eventually, in 1203–1204, it was turned against the Eastern Christian Empire. Though Greek Orthodox, the latter was prepared to discuss with Rome the possibilities of peaceful reunion and to become an indispensable ally in any real crusade against the Muslim danger.

It is well known that instead of promoting the cause of both union and crusade, as Pope Innocent III had hoped in spite of his original indignation, the conquest of Constantinople and the foundation of a Latin Empire there resulted in a struggle against the Greek Empire, which had been temporarily transferred to Nicaea in Asia Minor. This struggle absorbed the forces of the Catholic West for more than half a century, only to end in defeat, with Latins and Greeks farther apart than ever before and the imperial idea badly discredited.

For that very reason these events had important repercussions among the free nations of the Balkan Peninsula. Since the Greek Empire, in spite of the reconquest of its capital in 1261, never fully recovered from the catastrophe of 1204, and since the Latin Empire of Constantinople, with all its vassal states, was throughout its existence busy with fighting the Greeks, entirely new opportunities for the independent development of countries like Bulgaria and Serbia appeared. Furthermore, just before the Fourth Crusade, both Slavic nations had made important steps in the direction of their complete liberation and political organization.

Under Stephen Nemanya (1168–1196) the Serbs were at last united in a national state created around the Rashka region—hence called *Rascia* in the Latin sources. The Nemanyid dynasty was to rule it for two hundred years, until the Ottoman conquest. Already under Nemanya's son and successor, Stephen II, the Serbian church was placed under an autocephalous archbishop. The first of these ecclesiastical leaders was the king's brother Sava, who became the patron saint of the country. He succeeded in eliminating the former Bulgarian influence from its religious life although at the same time the Bulgarians, revolting in 1185 against Byzantine rule, regained their independence and again created a powerful kingdom under the Asenids, from Tirnovo, Bulgaria's new political and cultural center. That dynasty was of "Vlach" (Wallachian) origin, which is significant because early in the thirteenth century the Wallachians also created a first principality in what is now southern Rumania and strengthened Bulgaria by their cooperation.

It is an exaggeration to speak of a second Bulgarian Empire because the situation of the tenth century did not repeat itself. There was now no chance whatever of Bulgaria's taking the place of the empire of Constantinople. But when Latins and Greeks started fighting for that Empire, the Bulgarian neighbor state was rapidly growing in power under Asen's brother, Joannitsa, whom the Greeks called Kaloioannes (1197–1207), and it could be a welcome ally for either of the rival Empires.

The importance of both Bulgaria and Serbia was fully recognized by Pope Innocent III, who considered the withdrawal of the Greek Emperor and the Orthodox Patriarch to Nicaea an excellent opportunity to reunite these two nations with the Catholic church. Continuing, therefore, the negotiations with their rulers which had begun even before the Fourth Crusade, he offered them royal crowns as a reward for religious union and hoped to include them in the state system controlled by the Holy See. As usual, however, the results of these merely temporary unions depended on the political situation, and the Latins established in Constantinople, instead of accepting Bulgarian cooperation, made the error of resuming the policy of Byzantium and her claims of overlordship toward their northern neighbor.

The result was an unnecessary war with Kaloioannes, in which the first Latin Emperor, Baldwin of Flanders, was defeated near Adrianople in 1205 and died in prison. His brother and successor, Henry, was more successful in the protracted struggle against Bulgaria but died in 1216. These wars greatly increased the difficulties which the Latin conquerors of Constantinople had to face, since under Ivan Asen II (1218–1241) Bulgaria made an alliance against them with the Greek Empire of Nicaea, thus encircling the reduced territory of *Romania* which the Latin emperors controlled. The Bulgars also felt strong enough to fight the separate Greek state which soon after the fall of Constantinople had been created in Epirus, and thus they extended their territory through Macedonia into present-day Albania.

Bulgaria's independence was now so well established that in spite of hard struggles on practically all frontiers she survived the extinction of the Asenid dynasty in 1257 and the return of the Greeks to Constantinople under the Palaeologi four years later. But under the Terterids and Shishmanids who continued the line of her rulers, Bulgaria again became a minor power, more or less within her present frontiers.

Along with Serbia she was also threatened from the north because Hungary, after participating under King Andrew II in the Fifth Crusade (1217), became more and more interested in the Balkans and in the possibility of expansion on formerly Byzantine territory, now cut up among smaller states. Serbia proper continued to develop amidst all difficulties until Stephen Urosh II (1282–1321) made her the leading power in the Balkans, expanding in her turn toward Macedonia. But the Serbs of Bosnia could not be united with the kingdom of the Nemanyids because in that isolated mountain region the influence of Croatia and—after the Croat-Hungarian union—of Hungary continued to be predominant. Simultaneously with the rise of the Nemanyids, the Bosnian tribes had also formed an independent state under *ban* Kulin (1180–1204), but without succeeding in keeping it free from Hungarian suzerainty.

In the case of Bosnia, the decisive importance of the religious factor is particularly evident. Situated at the crossroads of Catholicism, which dominated in Croatia as well as in Hungary, and of Greek Orthodoxy, which after the brief interlude at the beginning of the century remained the national Church of Serbia and Bulgaria, Bosnia had special difficulties in deciding her ecclesiastical allegiance. The partisans of the Bogomil doctrine, who were called Patarenes in Bosnia, seemed to have a special chance under these circumstances, and indeed they made so much progress toward the middle of the thirteenth century that a crusade was directed against them under Hungarian leadership, resulting, of course, in a strengthening of Hungary's overlordship. It lasted almost a hundred years before Bosnia was able to reaffirm her autonomy, but that small intermediary region never could form a separate nation.

The fact that Serbia and Bulgaria finally remained Orthodox did not improve their relations with the restored Byzantine Empire. And the two Slavic kingdoms of the Balkans did not follow the example of Michael Palaeologus, when in order to avoid another Latin aggression planned by the Anjous of Sicily, he concluded a religious union with Rome at the Council of Lyons in 1274. Limited to the Greek Empire in spite of attempts to include the whole of South Eastern Europe, the Union of Lyons did not endure in Constantinople for more than a few years. But even Orthodox Christendom was divided in the Balkans for political reasons when at the turn of the century the rise of the Ottoman Turks suddenly became an alarming threat.

In order to understand their amazing progress in the following century, it must be remembered that in addition to the distrust and resentment between Greeks and Latins, there was in South Eastern Europe a permanent tension between the Eastern Empire, which under the Palaeologi gradually became a national Greek State, and the national states of Bulgarians and Serbs. In spite of their Orthodoxy, they claimed full autonomy even in the ecclesiastical sphere, contrary to the pretensions of the Patriarchs of Constantinople. On the other hand, because of their Orthodoxy, they could not count on the support of their Catholic neighbors in the Danubian region, which would have been badly needed to protect the Balkan countries. On the contrary, Hungary, despite many interests she had in common with them, and particularly in view of the growing Venetian pressure, was ready to seize any opportunity to include Serbia and even Bulgaria, together with Croatia and Bosnia, and soon too Wallachia, in a chain of vassal states of the Crown of St. Stephen. In this case, too, the crusading idea frequently served as a pretext for aggression against Orthodox neighbors, although it should rather have been a reason for the cooperation of all Christians against Mohammedanism, as was frequently pointed out by the Papacy.

GERMAN CRUSADERS AND COLONISTS IN
NORTH EASTERN EUROPE

A crusading action seemed more justified against the last pagan population of Europe which still survived in the Baltic region and which included both the Balts in the proper sense and the maritime tribes of Finnish race.

A first step in that direction was the conquest and conversion of Finland proper by Sweden, a comparatively easy undertaking which in the course of the twelfth century considerably enlarged that Scandinavian kingdom and for the following six hundred years extended it as far as the Gulf of Finland. South of that gulf and as far as the mouth of the Memel (Nemunas, Niemen) River, in the region which in the Middle Ages was given the general name of Livonia, Finnish tribes which included the Livs, the Ests, and probably the Curs, were mixed with purely Baltic Letts. But neither of them, ruled by *reguli*, as their chieftains are called in the contemporary sources, had succeeded in creating any political organization.

Even so, they were strong enough to resist the Russian pressure toward the Baltic Sea. But toward the end of the twelfth century German knights followed the German merchants from Lübeck who were penetrating into that region. Accompanied by missionaries who soon created a first Catholic bishopric on the shores of the Dvina which was finally established at Riga, a city founded at the mouth of that river in 1201, these Western conquerors considered themselves crusaders against both the pagan natives and the Orthodox neighbors in the east. On the initiative of the third bishop, Albert of Bremen, in 1202 they formed an order of knighthood, similar to those which supported the crusaders in the Holy Land, and called the "Knights of the Sword." It was decided that they would receive one third of all conquered lands, the rest being directly controlled by the bishops.

Such an arrangement became a permanent source of conflict between the Order and the hierarchy, especially when, soon after Albert's death in 1229, Riga was raised to an archbishopric and new bishoprics were gradually founded in the city of Dorpat, in Curland, and on the island of Osilia (Oesel). The rich and powerful city of Riga was a third partner in a rivalry which did not remain exclusively local. For the hierarchy was supported by the Holy See, who wanted to see in Livonia a purely ecclesiastical state under the exclusive authority of the Pope, while the Knights, considering Livonia something like a German colony, were looking for the protection of the Empire. The Papal legates who time and again were sent to Riga, especially William, Bishop of Modena, who played a prominent role in the Baltic region around 1230, never completely succeeded in settling all controversial problems or in protecting the native population against the oppression and exploitation of their German masters.

The resistance of these native peoples was particularly strong in the north and in the south. The northern Estonian tribes were defeated only with the assistance of the Danes, who in 1219 took the stronghold of Reval which became the capital of Estonia, a province extending to the east as far as the Narva River and which remained under Danish rule for more than a hundred years. The Baltic tribes near the southern border of Livonia, especially the fierce Semigalians, were supported by their closest kin, the Lithuanians, who at the turn of the twelfth century created a pagan state of unexpected strength and power of expansion beyond that border. After years of almost continuous fighting, the Knights of the Sword suffered a crushing defeat in 1236 at the battle of Siauliai, on Lithuanian territory, and their position in Livonia proper became highly critical. It was, therefore, in the following year that they decided to join another German order of knighthood, which was engaged in the conquest of Prussia.

The importance of that union, which made the Land Master of Livonia a vassal of the Grand Master of the Teutonic Order, the so-called Knights of the Cross, is apparent in the light of the geographical situation. Along the Baltic coast, in the region of Memel (Klaipeda) at the mouth of the river of that name, the Prussian tribes, belonging to the same ethnic groups as the Lithuanians and the Letts, almost touched the territory of Livonia. Thus, as soon as the conquest of Prussia by the Teutonic Order could be completed, an uninterrupted German-controlled territory would reach from the Vistula to the Gulf of Finland. The junction near Memel was quite narrow and precarious, however, since the Lithuanian lowland, called Samogitia, extended to the sea and formed a wedge between Prussia and Livonia. The conquest of Lithuania therefore became a common aim of both German colonies which approached her from two sides.

Before Lithuania found herself in that twin Teutonic clutch, however, the domination of the Knights of the Cross had to be well established all over Prussia. The origin of their settlement in that region, which had been very modest, resulted from a fateful decision made by one of the Polish princes, Conrad of Mazovia, the younger brother of Leszek the White. In spite of the cooperation of other Polish princes, he had difficulty in organizing the defense of his duchy against the frequent raids of the pagan Prussians and in promoting their conversion. Therefore he invited the Teutonic Order to settle in his own border district of Chełmno (Kulm) and to use it as a base for the conquest of Prussia.

The negotiations conducted with the Grand Master of the Order, Hermann von Salza, between 1226 and 1230, resulted in a series of documents, the interpretation of which is highly controversial. Without discussing the problem of the authenticity of some of these charters, it must be pointed out that the approach of either side was entirely different. The Polish prince acted under the assumption that he was simply making a grant to a religious order which would remain under his political authority, both in the Polish territory placed at its disposal and in the Prussian lands to be occupied in the future. The program of the Teutonic Knights was much more ambitious. Founded in Palestine in 1198, they soon lost their interest in the Holy Land where they could not equal the older orders of Templars and Hospitalers. After the failure of their negotiations with King Andrew II of Hungary, who hesitated to accept their conditions for a settlement at the border of Transylvania, they seized the opportunity of creating a German state at the Polish border. This was to be independent of Poland, under the authority not only of the Papacy, because of its ecclesiastical character, but also of the German Empire.

Hermann von Salza was a close collaborator and adviser of Emperor Frederick II, who even in the matter of the real crusade in Palestine was in open conflict with the Holy See. He considered the local crusading enterprise in the Baltic region to be an excellent opportunity for extending imperial influence in an entirely new direction. With all his troubles in Italy, he was not in a position to continue the eastern expansion of Germany in its original form, which had been stopped at Poland's western border. But the settlement of German knights in Prussia at her northern frontier encircled the part of Pomerania which still remained Polish with Poland's only outlet to the sea at Gdańsk (Danzig). The native princes who under Polish suzerainty governed that province—now a "corridor" between territories controlled by German powers—were the first to realize the danger. While most of the Piasts continued to cooperate with the Order without being aware of its real intentions, Prince Świętopełk of Pomerania supported the Prussians in one of their most violent insurrections against the invaders.

Both were defeated at the Sirgune River in 1236, but the conquest of one Prussian tribe after another, which started immediately after the arrival of the first Teutonic Knights in the region of Toruń in 1230, was to last until 1283. At about the same time, the warlike tribe of the Yatvegians, who belonged to the same ethnic group and together with the Lithuanians had struggled against Germans, Poles, and Russians, was finally destroyed, and their territory, the so-called Podlachia, became a bone of contention between these Christian neighbors and Lithuania.

In Prussia the German knights organized a state much more centralized than Livonia and under the exclusive control of the Order. Another important difference was the systematic colonization of the whole land from the Vistula to the Memel. This was carried out by German immigrants who settled not only in recently founded cities such as Königsberg and Marienburg (soon to become the Order's capital), but also in the countryside. There the German peasants absorbed or replaced the native Prussians, who were either exterminated in the ruthless struggle, expelled to Lithuania, or completely Germanized by the conquerors, who even took the Prussian name. The last traces of their language disappeared in the eighteenth century, while the southeastern corner of the German enclave thus formed was colonized by Poles from Mazovia.

The creation of a new, German Prussia was the most striking success of German colonization. Achieved in the thirteenth century under the pretext of a crusade, it influenced the whole political and ethnic structure of East Central Europe until the present. But it was only part of a much larger movement which without open warfare and in purely Christian lands extended German influence on a much larger scale than did the slow advance of the frontier of the March of Brandenburg which pushed Greater Poland back from the Oder. The German colonization which penetrated into practically all Polish duchies, except remote Mazovia, reached its climax in that same thirteenth century, although it never assumed the same proportions as in Bohemia.

The numerous references in the contemporary sources to settlements of towns and villages under the *ius Teutonicum* do not necessarily mean that all these places were entirely new foundations made by exclusively German people. Even urban centers of native character had existed in Poland long before they were developed according to German law, and in many cases purely Polish villages were granted the privileges of that same law. In both cases it meant a better economic organization and important franchises for the people concerned, and therefore, as in Bohemia, it was promoted by the national dynasty. But here, too, the whole process represented a foreign influence which proved particularly dangerous wherever German immigrants arrived in larger numbers, and who were soon to constitute a strong majority in most of the cities.

More than elsewhere, this became evident in the border region of Silesia, whose western part was gradually Germanized. The political disintegration of the former kingdom made the situation even more serious. It would seem that precisely in the period when the empire had ceased to threaten Poland's independence directly, a popular movement of colonization would succeed where Germany's military power had failed.

Just as in Bohemia, there appeared in Poland, in spite of her dynastic division, a national reaction against the German penetration. Polish knights would blame those princes who too obviously favored the newcomers, and also among the Polish clergy there was a growing resistance against the leading position of the German element in many monasteries and against its influence on ecclesiastical life. But that consciousness of a serious threat to Poland's development did not really manifest itself before the later part of the thirteenth century when a danger coming from the opposite direction had created conditions even more favorable to the influx of German settlers. It is an exaggeration to believe that the colonization by Poland's western neighbors was caused by her devastation through the great Mongol invasion toward the middle of the century and subsequent Tartar raids. But it is certainly true that under these conditions experienced settlers from abroad found even more opportunities than before. And it is significant that once more, not Poland alone but all freedom-loving nations in East Central Europe, found themselves under a simultaneous pressure from two sides which interfered with their normal development and seriously reduced their territories.

THE MONGOL INVASION

Soon after the German conquest of Livonia, and only a few years before the Teutonic Knights moved into Prussia, East Central Europe received a first warning that another wave of Asiatic conquerors was approaching from the East. The huge Eurasian Empire created by Jenghis Khan early in the thirteenth century was supposed to include all peoples of Mongol origin, and it therefore attacked the Polovtsy who for more than a hundred years had controlled the steppes of Eastern Europe. Although they had been a permanent plague for the Kievan State, and although the Russians were proud of their fight against them (which is described in the much discussed *Tale of the Host of Igor*), some Russian princes whom the Polovtsy asked for help in the critical year of 1223 sided with them against the Mongols, only to share in a crushing defeat at the Kalka River. Asiatic problems, and the death of Jenghis Khan four years later, delayed the revenge of the Mongols who were, however, resolved to take the place of the destroyed Polovtsy in Eastern Europe and to secure the domination of that whole region by bringing the neighboring Russian principalities under their control also.

The new colonial Russia in the Volga Basin was first invaded and conquered in 1237–1238. But instead of advancing in the direction of Novgorod, which was never taken by the Mongols, the leader of their European expedition, Jenghis Khan's grandson Batu, turned in 1240 against Kiev, which was destroyed. After also occupying the whole south of Russia, the following year he entered both Poland and Hungary. Even Western Europe was seriously alarmed when one Mongolian army defeated the Poles, first near Cracow and then at Lignica in Silesia, while another gained a great victory over the Hungarians at the Sájo River and advanced as far as the Adriatic. But again Asiatic developments, including the death of the Grand Khan, made the Mongols withdraw. They never returned to Hungary, and after being stopped at Lignica, where Prince Henry the Pious of Wrocław gave his life in defense of Christendom, they henceforth limited themselves to occasional raids into eastern Poland, sometimes forcing the Russian prince to participate in these invasions as well as in those directed against Lithuania.

On the contrary, almost all the Russian lands, with the exception of Novgorod and the White Russian principalities in the northwest where Lithuanian influence proved stronger, remained for a long period under Mongol rule. Indirectly they were under the suzerainty of the Grand Khan who resided in faraway Karakorum, in Mongolia proper. Directly they were under the Golden Horde of Kipchak, as the European part of the Mongol Empire was called. That autonomous unit founded by Batu Khan, with its capital at Sarai on the lower Volga, included both the peoples of Asiatic origin in the steppes north of the Black Sea, usually covered by the name of Tartars, and the various Russian principalities under the overlordship of the Khan of Kipchak.

That Mongol domination was indeed a major catastrophe in the history of Russia. It was that Asiatic impact that alienated her from Europe and, much more than the earlier Byzantine influence, made her different from and opposed to the West. There were, however, important differences in the position of the various parts of Russia. In general, her principalities were left to their former rulers, to the various lines of the Rurik dynasty whose members were simply made vassals of the Khan. Only in exceptional cases where no hereditary line was established, as in Kiev itself and in the lowlands of Podolia, Tartar officials were at the head of the local administration.

In such cases only the church remained as a guardian of the old tradition, and it was a metropolitan of Kiev who soon after the destruction of the glorious capital went to the Council of Lyons in 1245, asking for help from the Catholic West. Pope Innocent IV was indeed deeply concerned with the Mongol danger at the gates of Catholic Europe. He was also fully aware of the possibilities of religious reunion which any real assistance granted to Orthodox Christendom would open in Russia as well as in the Near East where he negotiated simultaneously with the Greeks of Nicaea. But absorbed by the conflict with the Western Empire, the papacy was powerless against the Mongols, who time and again were even considered possible allies against Arabs or Turks. The papal missions, sent as far as Karakorum with illusionary hopes of conversion, collected precious information about the devastated Russian lands which they had to cross, but only in the case of Halich and Volhynia did any prospects of cooperation, both religious and political, appear.

In this section of the old Kievan State which continued to have close ties with Catholic Poland and sometimes Hungary also, Tartar domination was opposed from the outset whenever it proved possible to do so, and Tartar influence remained negligible. The state of Daniel, a son of Roman, and his successors must therefore be considered an integral part of the European community, as in the past, and its role in the history of East Central Europe deserves special attention. But Daniel's earlier hopes of uniting Kiev with his patrimony no longer had any chance of success. On the contrary, the Kiev region, which during the following century of immediate Tartar control completely lost its traditional significance, was separating Daniel's realm from the eastern parts of Russia, called Great Russia in the Byzantine sources, in contradistinction to Little Russia, i.e., Halich and Volhynia.

Since the petty principalities into which the Chernigov (Severian) region was divided were of limited importance, the new Great Russian State, whose formation is the main feature of Eastern European history in the thirteenth century, was constituted by the principalities of the colonial Volga region, where Vladimir-on-the-Klazma now supplanted Suzdal as the main center.

Among the descendants of Vsevolod Big Nest, who ruled in that vast region, Yaroslav, whose brother George had been killed when fighting the Mongols in 1238, occupied after him the leading position and inaugurated a shrewd policy of appeasing the new masters of Eastern Europe. Twice he undertook the perilous and exhausting journey to the Grand Khan's Asiatic residence, only to perish on the return in 1246, as did so many other Russian princes of the Mongol period during or after such visits. It now became a rule that the Khan would decide who would occupy the position of grand prince in Russia, and after a few years of trouble that decision was taken in 1252 in favor of Yaroslav's son, the famous Alexander Nevsky. But he no longer had any pretension to claim, as his predecessors did, the ancient throne of Kiev also. On the contrary, he definitely limited his Russia to the new body politic around Vladimir.

It is true that before ruling there he had been accepted as prince by the people of Novgorod, and his very surname recalled his victory over the Swedes, gained in 1240 at the Neva River, where he defended the republic against the Scandinavian masters of Finland. Two years later he also defeated the German Knights of Livonia in another battle on frozen Lake Peipus. But since these early contacts with the Catholic West had been exclusively hostile, he turned decidedly toward the East, showed no interest in papal appeals in favor of ecclesiastical union, but on the contrary tried to strengthen his position by loyally cooperating with his Tartar overlords.

Such cooperation resulted in the privilege of collecting the heavy taxes which the Khan required from all Russian princes. It was convenient for the Tartars to receive the whole amount through the intermediation of the Grand Prince, who in turn used that rather unpleasant task for the purpose of controlling the other princes and uniting the new Russia under his own authority. After his death in 1263 such a policy was continued by Alexander's less prominent successors, the main problem being which prince would receive the supreme power connected with the possession of Vladimir in addition to his hereditary apanage. In the absence of any recognized order of succession, their rivalry could only lead to continuous Tartar interference, which was particularly evident in the longlasting struggle for supremacy between the princes of Tver and those of Moscow.

The first of these two main principalities, which seemed to have a right of seniority, succeeded in controlling Vladimir with few interruptions until 1319. But Moscow, not mentioned before 1147, which first appeared as a separate principality a hundred years later but was not really constituted as a hereditary apanage of one of the lines of the dynasty before the turn of the thirteenth century, rapidly rose to leading power under a succession of extremely efficient rulers who enlarged their territory and gradually supplanted their cousins from Tver as real masters of all dependencies of Vladimir.

That whole story, which is comparatively well known, no longer has anything in common with the history of East Central Europe. The acceptance of Mongol domination, which was to last more than two hundred years, was probably unavoidable, but in any case it decided that the new colonial Russia—Eastern Europe in the geographical sense—would develop outside the European community. Connected with an empire whose major part and basic nucleus were in Asia, it was at the same time cut off from European influence and wide open to Asiatic.

It is to the credit of the East Slavic, Great Russian settlers in that originally Finnish territory that they preserved not only their language and customs, that they not only continued to absorb various alien peoples, thanks to their cultural superiority, but also remained faithful to their religious tradition which in spite of the conflicting trends represented by pagan elements survived under extremely difficult conditions. This was to a large extent the result of an unbroken continuity of ecclesiastical organization, under the distant but respected authority of Byzantium, and particularly of the decision made around 1300 by the metropolitan of Kiev to transfer his residence to Vladimir, whence it was moved in 1326 to the promising center of Moscow.

But neither that ecclesiastical link, nor the dynastic link with the Kievan past, was sufficient to make the Muscovite State a continuation of the Kievan State with merely a shift of the center. It was a new political creation where the local autocratic tradition was reinforced by the governmental conceptions of the Mongol Empire. That empire was much more despotic than the Christian Empire of Constantinople had ever been, and at the same time much more aggressive, with an unlimited program of expansion. As soon as Muscovite Russia, trained under such an influence, felt strong enough to liberate herself from the degrading yoke of that disintegrating empire, she took over its role in Eastern Europe, later to include its Asiatic part also by means of another process of colonization.

But for that very reason Moscow under her "czars," as the grand princes later called themselves like the Tartar khans, became a threat to all free peoples of East Central Europe, who soon found themselves placed between German and Russian imperialism. The first to be threatened were those Eastern Slavs who had remained in their original settlements, in the old Russia of the Kievan *Ruś*—the Ruthenia of the Latin sources—including also the Great Russians of Novgorod, all of them soon to be claimed by the rulers of Moscow in the name of the unity of all the Russias. The question whether those peoples, particularly the ancestors of the White Russians and Ukrainians of today, would be able to save their individuality and keep in contact with their western neighbors was an issue of primary importance for the whole structure of Europe which the consequences of the Mongol invasion had already raised in the thirteenth century.

6

THE HERITAGE OF THE THIRTEENTH CENTURY

THE RISE AND FALL OF THE CATHOLIC KINGDOMS OF HALICH AND LITHUANIA

Toward the middle of the thirteenth century it seemed that the question of Europe's limits would be answered by the creation of two Catholic kingdoms placed between Poland and the German colonies on the Baltic, on the one hand, and the new Russia subjugated by the Mongols on the other. Both were established simultaneously, thanks to the far-reaching Eastern policy of Pope Innocent IV. One of them was an entirely new creation: a baptized Lithuania with which most of the White Russian principalities were being united. The other was a regenerated state of Halich and Volhynia, in religious union with Rome.

The political consolidation of the Lithuanian tribes was already in progress toward the end of the twelfth century, when their invasions into practically all neighboring countries, including the Ruthenian principalities and even Novgorod, became more and more frequent. The earliest names of their leaders are, however, purely legendary, and there is no evidence of any unified state organization. Even in 1219, when the Lithuanians made a formal agreement with the state of Volhynia and Halich, a whole series of their princes was enumerated, some of them called "seniors," and a distinction was made between Lithuania proper and Samogitia.

It is among the Lithuanian princes mentioned on that occasion that Mindaugas, or Mindove, appears for the first time. About twenty years later he already occupied a position of supremacy and had started uniting the whole country under his control. His successes, and the subsequent intensification of Lithuanian raids in all directions, provoked a coalition of his Christian neighbors and other Lithuanian princes whom he had deposed, so that toward the middle of the cen-

tury his position seemed very precarious. He fully realized that
Lithuania could survive only by becoming a Christian nation, and
therefore he accepted the proposals of the Livonian Order to assist
him in introducing the Catholic faith. In 1251 Mindaugas himself
was baptized through a Livonian intermediary, and two years later he
was crowned as a king under the auspices of the Holy See.

The *primus rex Lettovie*, as he was called, directly controlled
Lithuania proper in the basin of the upper Niemen. He claimed the
overlordship of Samogitia with her local chieftains, and he succeeded
in extending his sovereignty over most of White Russia, where relatives of Mindaugas were established in Polotsk, and also over the intermediary region between Lithuania and the Pripet marshes, divided
into petty principalities. It was there that he came into immediate
contact with Volhynia.

In that province as well as in Halich, Daniel, returning after the
Mongol invasion, was engaged in a difficult task of reconstruction and
of settling his further relation with the khans. He, too, like the princes
of Great Russia, first tried to appease them by visiting the Khan.
But with a view to escaping the humiliating Tartar domination, he
and his brother Vasilko first entered into relations with the papal
envoys who, under the leadership of Giovanni de Plano Carpini,
went through their country on their way to Mongolia, and then with
Pope Innocent IV himself.

Parallel with Rome's negotiations with Nicaea, discussions regarding a regional union with the Orthodox peoples of Daniel's realm
were started in 1247. After the recognition of the Eastern rite by the
Pope, these resulted in the agreement of 1253. Almost simultaneously
with Mindaugas, Daniel was crowned by a papal legate as a Catholic
king and hoped to receive sufficient assistance to liberate his country
from Tartar control.

It was only natural that both kings made an agreement between
Halich-Volhynia and Lithuania. In the treaty of Chełm, in 1254,
they settled their frontier problems, and a common front seemed to be
created against the Tartars whose advance in the northwestern direction was checked by Lithuania's continued expansion in Ruthenian
lands. The situation seemed the more propitious because Daniel had
friendly relations with his Polish neighbors, who favored his union
with the Catholic church as well as the conversion of Lithuania where
Polish missionaries were already active.

The various Polish duchies were, however, hardly in a position to be of much assistance, and the Pope himself could offer to that whole frontier region of the Catholic world only moral support and the usual privileges granted to crusaders. This was the main reason why Daniel, only a few years later, felt obliged to compromise with the Tartars, breaking with Rome under little known circumstances.

Even more evident were the causes of Mindaugas' apparent apostasy. Instead of really assisting him, the Knights of Livonia claimed territorial advantages, starting with the cession of minor districts and culminating in the desire to control all of Lithuania in case of the King's death. It is highly doubtful whether he ever ratified these promises, which were directed against the obvious interests of his people and of his own sons. The most extravagant of his charters are probably spurious or merely drafts that were prepared in the chancery of the Livonian Order. In any case, these German claims contributed to a growing opposition of the pagan element which was particularly strong in Samogitia, against Mindaugas' political program, and in 1260, after a crushing victory of the pagan leaders over the Germans in the battle of Durbe, the king himself felt obliged to join them.

His relations with Daniel had already deteriorated. Both kings failed to coordinate their action against the Tartars, who in 1259, probably taking advantage of territorial disputes between their opponents, forced Daniel to participate in an invasion of Lithuania as well as in the second raid into Poland. The promising but premature scheme of 1253 had broken down, and the successors of Innocent IV, deeply disappointed by the defection of Daniel and Mindaugas, could consider only Poland as the last bastion of Christendom in the East. Moreover, Daniel died in 1264, and Mindaugas was killed a year before by pagan leaders who were jealous of his power. Both Catholic kingdoms east of Poland seemed nothing but a short-lived episode.

Nevertheless that interlude had lasting consequences. There remained, first, a tradition of cooperation between the two states. In the midst of Lithuania's internal crisis after Mindaugas, his idea of a possible succession of one of Daniel's descendants was taken up by Voysielk (Vaišvilkas), the one of the sons of Lithuania's Catholic king who became a Christian of the Greek Orthodox faith. Voysielk, too, was killed soon after his father, his plan was abandoned, and Lithuania was governed for a dozen years by a pagan prince, Traidenis, who proved quite successful but who was opposed to any joint action with Christian neighbors. Yet his state already included so many Ruthenian lands with Orthodox populations liberated from Tartar control that the common interests with the Ruthenians of Volhynia and Halich were quite evident and perfectly realized by the dynasty which was founded in Lithuania toward the end of the thirteenth dynasty by a prince called Pukuveras.

On the other hand, Daniel's dynasty was far from submitting to Tartar authority as completely as the Great Russian princes of the Volga region had actually done. Volhynia and Halich were certainly in a more favorable geographical position, far away from Sarai and even more from the Asiatic center of Mongol power. But credit must also be given to Daniel's son Leo (1264–1301), and to his grandson George (1301–1308), who even used the royal title again, for their able policy which in spite of occasional collaboration with the Tartars, when it proved unavoidable, safeguarded the almost complete independence of their country. Under George, attempts were even made to have a separate metropolitan see created in Halich. His two sons, the last of Roman's line, perished around 1323 while fighting the Tartars.

Their merits in that respect were recognized in Poland, and though there were occasional conflicts between the two nations, reciprocal interferences with their internal problems and unsettled territorial claims on both sides, relations were in general rather friendly and remained close throughout the whole period. In the time of Leo, whose brother Roman was married to an Austrian princess, the house of Halich and Volhynia even participated in the typically Central European struggle for the heritage of the Babenbergs. Furthermore, the tradition of union with Rome was kept alive, and in that matter the Holy See also appealed to the last descendants of the dynasty.

The same must be said with regard to pagan Lithuania. It is true that the fight for survival which had to be conducted against the Livonian Knights—and after the conquest of Prussia against the Teutonic Order also—seemed to create a permanent hostility against the Catholic West, with frequent raids also directed against Poland. But here, too, a community of interest with a Christian neighbor became evident as soon as Poland was threatened by the Order, and in Livonia the Lithuanians took advantage of the rivalry between the archbishops of Riga and the Knights of the Sword. Occasional cooperation with the former was another opportunity for resuming plans of conversion, now no longer through the Order's intermediary and therefore with better chances of success. From the beginning of the fourteenth century, Lithuania's grand dukes returned time and again to these projects, realizing that paganism had at last to be abandoned if the country was to be admitted to the European community, instead of being considered a target of crusading expeditions.

In Lithuania as well as in the Ruthenian lands, the solution of that issue was largely dependent on developments in neighboring Poland.

POLAND'S PROGRESS IN THE THIRTEENTH CENTURY

The creation of German colonies along the Baltic, particularly in Prussia; the Mongol conquest of Russia, including the permanent danger of renewed Mongol invasions; and last but not least, the failure to establish Catholic kingdoms east of Poland, all these events deeply affected the situation of that country. Furthermore, these developments along Poland's borders occurred in the course of a century which brought the disintegration of the Polish kingdom to an alarming climax, it being divided into a rapidly growing number of petty duchies. At the same time, Cracow was losing its position as political center of the whole country, and among its rulers, as well as among the numerous members of the Piast dynasty, a leading personality qualified to reconstruct the kingdom of the eleventh century did not appear.

The only prince who seemed to have some chance of playing such a role in the earlier part of the thirteenth century was Henry the Bearded of Silesia. From his residence in Wrocław (Breslau), he exercised a strong influence over all of Poland, especially in Greater Poland, where the descendants of Mieszko the Old were quarreling among themselves. And when, in 1227, Leszek the White of Cracow, who had ruled Little Poland not without success for about thirty years, was killed by Świętopełk of Pomerania, Henry the Bearded seemed the most appropriate tutor of Leszek's minor son, Bolesław.

In claiming that function, however, which would have given him practical control of most of Poland, Henry met an obstinate rival in the person of Leszek's younger brother, Conrad of Mazovia, the same who had just made the mistake of inviting the Teutonic Knights. The Prince of Silesia, where German influence was increasing, made another mistake which did not have such far-reaching consequences, but which nevertheless troubled his otherwise truly constructive policy. In connection with his repeated disputes with the local hierarchy, he approached Emperor Frederick II in the hope of regaining Poland's royal crown with imperial support. Before these plans (which hardly had any serious chances of success) could materialize, Henry the Bearded died in 1238. His and Saint Hedwig's son, Henry the Pious, probably had the same ultimate goal. According to the Polish tradition, he tried to reach it in cooperation with the Papacy. But Henry II's promising career was interrupted by his death at the battle of Lignica in 1241.

Two years later the legitimate heir of Cracow, Bolesław, called "the Chaste," after growing up and defeating his uncle Conrad, could at last start his personal rule in Little Poland, which he governed until his death in 1279. His long reign was threatened only once, in 1273, and not too seriously, by the claims of a rival from Upper Silesia. As a whole, however, the reign was far from being a brilliant one and it could only strengthen the impression that Poland was definitely split into a few independent duchies, some of them subdivided by the local branches of the main lines of the dynasty.

These divisions went particularly far in Silesia, both in the main western part, where the branch of the two Henrys did not produce any prominent ruler for half a century, and in Upper Silesia, where the process of German colonization was much slower but the local princes equally insignificant. The situation in Greater Poland improved under two brothers, great-grandsons of Mieszko the Old, who cooperated against the aggressive policy of the margraves of Brandenburg, not without suffering minor territorial losses. Finally, the line of Conrad, who died in 1247 after a troublesome reign, was split into a Cuyavian and a Mazovian branch with many local conflicts in both provinces, inadequate defense against Lithuanian raids, and no foresight in relations with the Teutonic Order. The princes of Great Poland showed more interest in the fate of Eastern Pomerania, the only territory along the Baltic which was still free of German control. They concluded an agreement with the last native ruler of Danzig, Mestwin, which gave them the right of succession in case of his death.

It meant little change in the general picture when, after the death of Bolesław the Chaste, a prince of the Cuyavian line, Leszek the Black succeeded him, uniting his small hereditary duchy with Little Poland. It was not until Leszek's death (who had remained childless) in 1288, that almost unexpectedly the program of reuniting Poland under a crowned king made its gradual reappearance, deeply influencing the whole situation in East Central Europe. The resumption of such plans, and their final success after so long a period of political decline and confusion, can only be understood against the background of Poland's national development in the cultural field.

In that respect the thirteenth century was indeed much more satisfactory. It is fully justifiable to speak of a national development because in spite of, or rather because of, the weakness of their political organization, the Polish people were meeting the challenge of the times through a growing national consciousness. They were fully aware that the futile struggles among their princes were nothing but fratricidal wars, since members of the same clans were frequently settled in various duchies.

That clan organization of the Polish knighthood, replacing the feudal structure of Western society, was only one of the close ties which united all parts of Poland. Even more important was the ecclesiastical unity under the archbishop of Gniezno, especially as the Polish hierarchy of the thirteenth century included very prominent leaders. Among these were Archbishop Henryk Kietlicz, who introduced the reforms of Innocent III at the beginning of the century, Bishop Pełka of Cracow, who promoted at its middle the canonization of Saint Stanislas as a symbol of Poland's unity, and another Archbishop of Gniezno, Jakób Świnka, at the end of the period.

The latter was deeply impressed by the danger of German penetration into Poland, and under his inspiration the synods of the Polish clergy passed resolutions in favor of the Polish language and the independent development of the ecclesiastical life of the country. It was indeed in opposition against German influence that a genuine feeling of national community was appearing at a comparatively early date, while on the other hand, the struggle against non-Catholic and even non-Christian neighbors in the East strengthened the awareness of cultural community with the Latin West. The role of the Church was favored by the general atmosphere of the century which in Poland, no less than in Western Europe, produced a large number of men and women, including members of the dynasty, who were famous because of their saintly lives, and some of whom were eventually canonized or beatified. Greater than ever before was also the part played by religious orders. Benedictine and Cistercian monasteries were centers of cultural life, and the recently founded Franciscans and Dominicans soon became very popular in Poland and active as missionaries in her border regions.

It was the same Archbishop Świnka who supported the idea of restoring the royal dignity, and who was ready to crown the candidate in Gniezno. There was, however, a danger that if crowned in Gniezno, which remained the ecclesiastical capital of Poland, such a monarch would be regarded as King of Greater Poland only, the region specifically designated by the name of *Polonia*. The reunion of Greater Poland with Little Poland, where the political capital had been placed in the city of Cracow, was therefore particularly urgent.

With such prospects in mind, the successor of Leszek the Black as Duke of Cracow, again a Silesian Henry surnamed "Probus," before dying after a very brief reign in 1290, decreed in his will that Little Poland should be inherited by the last representative of the line ruling in Greater Poland, a very promising young prince named Przemysł II. Other dispositions of Henry's elaborate testament were supposed to promote the unification of the Silesian duchies and of these duchies with the rest of Poland. Insufficiently prepared, however, that plan of action met with serious difficulties because various other princes raised claims for the possession of Cracow. And it was particularly dangerous that one of them was a foreigner, King Václav II of Bohemia.

In all previous dynastic rivalries only members of the native Piast family appeared, and amidst all the divisions of the country no territory ever came under foreign rule. Now such a threat was the more serious because the king of Bohemia was one of the princes of the Holy Roman Empire whose rule could lead to the inclusion of Poland in that Empire, something which had been carefully avoided for so many centuries. Because of lack of unity among the Piasts, Przemysł had to recognize Václav's control of Cracow and be satisfied with Greater Poland only. But as a compensation, he united with his hereditary duchy the important province of Pomerania, where he succeeded to Mestwin in agreement with earlier negotiations. And his prestige was so great that one year later, in 1295, he was crowned as King of Poland, the first after Bolesław the Bold who had ruled more than two hundred years before.

Unfortunately he was assassinated the next year, probably at the instigation of the margraves of Brandenburg who feared the rise of a Polish kingdom with access to the Baltic Sea. And again conflicting claims of Polish princes for his succession facilitated the intervention of the King of Bohemia, who in turn was crowned as King of Poland in 1300, uniting at the same time Cracow and Gniezno.

That serious threat to Poland's independence both from Bohemia and from the Empire provoked, of course, a national reaction which was only waiting for a leader. One of the princes who had played a rather minor role in the troubles of the last decade, Władysław Łokietek of the Cuyavian line, was to satisfy these expectations very soon. But in order to understand both the temporary predominance of Bohemia and its failure, the thirteenth-century development of that country must be considered in connection with the whole Danubian region.

THE LAST ÁRPÁDS AND PŘEMYSLIDS

The fate of Bohemia was always inseparable from the history of her Danubian neighbors, Austria and Hungary. Like Bohemia, the former was part of the Empire, with a German majority, which dominated the conquered Slovenes of Carinthia, Styria, and Carniola. Hungary, on the contrary, was as independent of imperial overlordship as was Poland. In all three Danubian countries, national dynasties had been well established from the beginning. These included the Babenbergs in Austria, the Árpáds in Hungary, and the Přemyslids in Bohemia. But in 1246 the death of the last Babenberg, Frederick the Warlike, in a battle against the Hungarians, provoked a serious crisis which clearly divides the thirteenth-century history of the Danubian region into two parts.

In the first half of that century, Hungary continued to occupy the leading position. The reign of Andrew II (1205–1235), with his participation not only in the affairs of Halich but also in one of the crusades in the Holy Land, greatly increased the prestige of the kingdom which in 1222, only seven years after the English *Magna Charta*, received in the Golden Bull a similar charter of liberties for its powerful nobility, probably under the influence of the *assises* of the Kingdom of Jerusalem. The equally prosperous development of Hungary under Andrew's son Béla IV was suddenly interrupted by the Tartar invasion of 1241 which left the country as badly devastated as Poland.

With the exception of a brief passage of the Tartars through Moravia, the Bohemian Kingdom had escaped a similar destruction, and strengthened by the long and successful reign of Václav I, was therefore in a better position when both neighbors claimed the succession of the Babenbergs. After a few years of confusion, the Austrians elected Václav's son in 1251. Two years later, upon the death of his father, he also became King of Bohemia as Přemysl Otakar II. He had, however, to face the opposition of Hungary and most of the Polish dukes were also involved on both sides. The first phase of the struggle resulted in a division of the Babenberg heritage, with only Austria proper left to Bohemia. It was not before 1269, when Hungary's power was weakened under Béla's son Stephen, that Otakar extended his domination over Styria, Carinthia, and Carniola, thus uniting the Slovenian territories of Austria with his Czech kingdom also.

Such a union might have strengthened the Slavic element which was still predominant in these Austrian provinces, and it also might have re-established the contact between Northern and Southern Slavs which had been separated by German and Magyar advance. But it would be anachronistic to interpret Otakar's policy from the point of view of ethnic nationalism. Even in his Slavic kingdom he so strongly favored German colonization, as his predecessors had done, that he lost the general support of the Czechs in his decisive struggle against a third competitor, Rudolf von Habsburg, although at the decisive moment an appeal addressed by his chancery to all Polish princes raised the issue of a common defense of Slavs against Teutons.

Originally, Otakar's fight against the founder of the Habsburg dynasty had nothing to do with any national antagonism and was not motivated by the problem of the Austrian succession. During the long interregnum after the fall of the Hohenstaufen, the ambition of the King of Bohemia reached much further; he hoped to be elected King of Germany and thus gain the imperial crown with the support of the papacy. Such a solution would have made the ties uniting Bohemia and her new Austrian possession with the Holy Roman Empire of the German nation even closer than before, although under a dynasty of Slavic origin the character of the Empire could have undergone a very substantial change. Only when that plan failed and the electors preferred to choose a less powerful ruler in the person of the Count of Habsburg, Otakar had to defend at least his Austrian acquisitions

against the claims of Rudolf I who wanted to create there the hereditary domain so sorely needed by his family.

Even limited to the Austrian issue, the struggle had a lasting importance for Central Europe. Otakar's victory would have included
Austria, with her Slovene provinces, in the eastern, non-German part
of Central Europe, and the Přemyslid power would have remained
so great that the suzerainty of the Empire would have become entirely
fictitious. But when in 1278, after an undecisive treaty concluded two
years earlier, the King of Bohemia was defeated and killed in the
battle near the Morava River north of Vienna, Austria, definitely
secured by the new imperial dynasty of German origin, became a basis
not only for Habsburg influence in the Empire but also for the
dynastic policy of the German Habsburgs in East Central Europe,
even beyond the limits of the Empire and those of the Danubian
region.

These were, of course, prospects of the future. What happened immediately was a decline of Czech power, particularly during the
minority of Otakar's son, Václav II, with a corresponding growth
of German and imperial influence in that Slavic country, influence
which through Bohemia and Moravia penetrated even into Polish
Silesia more than ever before. Under the pressure of Albrecht I, the
second Habsburg on the imperial throne, his younger brother Rudolf
was even temporarily elected King of Bohemia in 1296, and only his
early death prevented serious troubles to the legitimate heir to the
crown.

The position of Václav II was of course strengthened by his successes in Poland, which in the light of the critical situation of Bohemia appear particularly important for the Přemyslid dynasty but
at the same time very precarious. Even more so was another unexpected success of the King of Bohemia and Poland, when in the year
(1301) following his coronation at Gniezno, his son became king of
Hungary.

That kingdom which had sided with Rudolf von Habsburg against
the Czech rival of the Árpáds, and which now, after 1278, was again
an immediate neighbor of a German power, entered an even more
serious period of decline under rather insignificant rulers. When
Andrew III died in 1301, as last representative of the dynasty, the
problem of succession opened a protracted crisis. The union with
Bohemia, and through her king with Poland also, could have been

a solution of the basic issues of East Central European history of much greater significance and chances of success than the abortive Austro-Bohemian union under Otakar. But it was a purely dynastic combination, insufficiently supported by Václav's personal ambition. When he died in 1305 it was doomed to failure even before his son and successor Václav III, opposed in both Hungary and Poland, was assassinated in the following year.

Now, in 1306, a crisis of succession was also opened in Bohemia, and it is no wonder that Albrecht I immediately seized that opportunity to proclaim that the Bohemian kingdom was nothing but a fief of the Empire and therefore at his disposal. This was a misinterpretation of the bull of 1212, but it was greatly facilitated by the disappearance of the national Czech dynasty. Less dangerous was the situation of Hungary, where the Empire could not raise any similar claims. But neither that country nor Bohemia was ever to have a national dynasty again, while for Poland the sudden disappearance of the last two Přemyslids was the best opportunity to liberate herself from foreign rule and from any possible imperial interference, under the rule of one of the still numerous representatives of the native Piast dynasty.

But for Poland, too, as well as for the whole of East Central Europe, it was of primary importance how the struggle for the vacant crowns of St. Václav and St. Stephen would be decided. The establishment of a German dynasty in one or both of the neighboring countries was obviously bound to threaten the friendly relations which in general had prevailed before. It was therefore very alarming that not only the Austrian Habsburgs but also the Wittelsbachs of Bavaria appeared among the various pretenders who for several years tried to gain possession of Hungary and Bohemia. And it was very favorable to Poland's interests and to the free development of the Danubian region that in Hungary, where a decision was already reached in 1308, one of the French Anjous of Naples, Charles Robert, emerged as the successful candidate. With the support of the papacy, which was equally friendly to the Polish princes, he established a dynasty there, which, although of foreign origin, continued Hungary's independent tradition and checked the possible progress of German influence.

Entirely different was the solution which two years later ended a similar crisis in Bohemia. Here it was one of the candidates of

German origin—there was practically no other—who replaced the Přemyslids. It is true that John of Luxemburg came from Germany's extreme West where French influence was considerable. But in the person of his father, Henry VII, that formerly rather modest house had reached the imperial dignity a few years before, and therefore after gaining possession of Bohemia was to connect her very closely with the Empire. Furthermore, the successor of the Přemyslids was strongly convinced that he had also inherited their claims to the crown of Poland, and he decided to continue their Silesian policy which had already brought some of the local dukes in that border province under the suzerainty of the Bohemian crown.

The near future was to show that in spite of his lifelong French sympathies, this German King of Bohemia would be one of Poland's most dangerous opponents. In intimate cooperation with the Teutonic Order, he represented the trend of German expansion toward the East. Furthermore, his successors' relations with Hungary were to lead, toward the end of the fourteenth century, to the establishment of Luxemburg rule in that country also. The simultaneous developments in both kingdoms at the beginning of that century were therefore much more than changes of dynasty. Coinciding with the rise of Moscow and with the sudden appearance of the Ottoman danger, they introduced new elements into the medieval tradition of East Central Europe and made that moment an important turning point in the history of that whole area.

7

THE NEW FORCES OF THE FOURTEENTH CENTURY

THE FIRST LUXEMBURGS IN BOHEMIA

The Luxemburg dynasty was to govern Bohemia until its extinction in 1437. But this long period is clearly divided in two parts. The death of the second Luxemburg, Charles, in 1378, a landmark in general European history along with the Great Western schism of the same year, has a special significance for Bohemia's development. A long internal crisis came soon after what is called her "Golden Age."

That brilliant era did not start immediately in 1310. On the contrary, there soon followed a rebellion of the Czech nobility against their first foreign king, who neglected their interests and proved a very poor administrator. The opposition was defeated, but John of Luxemburg hardly took advantage of his success. He preferred to play the part of a knight errant, abandoning the affairs of the kingdom to the nobles, until in 1333 his son Charles was associated with the government, and long before John's death at the Battle of Crécy in 1346, he exercised a decisive influence.

The old king's participation in the Hundred Years War of course had nothing to do with Bohemia's own problems, and when in earlier years he joined the raids of the Teutonic Knights into Lithuania, his role in these alleged crusades in distant lands touched the interests of his kingdom only indirectly as far as any joint action with the so-called Knights of the Cross was a pressure put upon Poland. It was of little practical value that one of the princes of distant Mazovia temporarily made himself a vassal of the Bohemian crown. But when John of Luxemburg received similar homage from most of the Silesian princes in 1327 and 1329, the recognition of his suzerainty by these Piasts necessarily led to the final separation of that important province from medieval Poland. It was included in the lands of the crown of St. Václav, together with Bohemia, Moravia, and parts of Lusatia which were also acquired in John's time. The recognition of that accomplished fact by the King of Poland, in the years 1335–1339, was obtained by King John by giving up the henceforth useless support of the Teutonic Knights and his own claims to the Polish crown which anyway had no chance of practical realization.

The relations with Poland which had badly deteriorated under the last Přemyslids and the first Luxemburg were gradually improved by the second, although Charles too had participated in his father's last attack against Cracow in 1344. It was not only in restoring conditions of good neighborliness with the other Slavic kingdom that Charles' policy proved much more constructive than his father's. To what an extent it was a truly Bohemian policy, however, will always remain controversial, since a few weeks before he succeeded to John in Prague he was elected Holy Roman Emperor.

That election put an end to the internal crisis of the Empire under Louis the Bavarian and restored, at least temporarily, the cooperation between Empire and papacy, with the Avignon popes consistently supporting the Luxemburgs. It was also undoubtedly a success for Bohemia, whose king reached the goal which Přemysl Otakar II had sought in vain. Her position in the Empire now became indeed a leading one, with Prague its undisputed center, but at the same time her connection with Germany became inseparable. Since it happened under a German dynasty it was hardly favorable to the national development of the Czechs.

Nevertheless, Bohemia gained so much in political influence and in cultural and economic progress that Charles IV, as he is called as emperor, is rather blamed for having neglected German interests. How difficult it is to interpret the character of his policy is particularly evident in the case of the foundation of the University of Prague in 1348. The importance of the creation of a first university north of the Alps, outside the Romance and Anglo-Saxon world, is of course evident. But while it is impossible to consider Prague as the first German university, it also is questionable whether it was founded as a Czech institution. Like all other medieval universities, it was a universal center of Western culture, open to all nations. Medieval universalism, though already in decline in the fourteenth century, is the only possible key to a genuine understanding of what the King of Bohemia, of German race but deeply influenced by French and also Italian culture, really wanted to achieve as emperor.

There can indeed be no doubt that these achievements in all spheres of life were of real advantage to the peoples of Bohemia, without distinction of origin, and particularly to the city of Prague, now the emperor's residence. And the significant fact that in 1344 Charles obtained from Pope Clement VI, his former educator, the raising of Prague to an archbishopric, is the best proof of his concern with Bohemia's independent position. Now, at last, her ecclesiastical life was no longer under the control of the German Archbishop of Mainz.

Charles' whole imperial policy, which made him twice travel to Rome—for the first time in 1353 in order to be crowned—does not of course belong to the history of East Central Europe. The same can be said of his reforms in the government of the Empire, although the famous Golden Bull of 1356, establishing permanent rules for the election of future emperors, must be mentioned here because it confirmed the privileges of the king of Bohemia as first among the lay electors. There are, however, both in his foreign relations and in his internal activities, important features directly affecting Bohemia as one of the Slavic nations of the Danubian and in general of the East Central region of the continent.

It so happened that among the rulers of that region there were several contemporaries of Charles of Luxemburg who played a prominent role, similar to his own, in their respective countries. One of them was Rudolf the Founder, first archduke of Austria, whose land was serving more and more as an intermediary between Germany proper and the non-German part of Central Europe. He was also the first of the Habsburgs who made systematic efforts to prepare the future succession of his dynasty to the thrones of Bohemia and Hungary through treaties with the Luxemburgs and the Anjous. Even Poland got involved in the intricate diplomatic game which in 1360 led to a conflict between Charles IV and Louis the Great of Hungary. Louis was offended by a derogatory statement about his mother, which was attributed to the Emperor.

Avoiding any major war, however, the two opponents settled their dispute through Polish mediation. Charles of Luxemburg, who in spite of the Czech-Polish rivalry in Silesia had made alliances with Poland in 1348 and 1356 which were apparently directed against the Teutonic Order, now went to Cracow twice. After the death of his first wife, in 1363 he there married a princess of Western Pomerania who was a granddaughter of King Casimir the Great. The following year, reconciled with Louis of Hungary, he participated with him and the kings of Denmark and Cyprus in the Cracow Congress where the problem of a new crusade was discussed and the whole situation in East Central Europe carefully reviewed.

The Emperor returned to these problems in the later part of his reign in connection with two issues which were of vital importance for his Bohemian kingdom. One of them concerned the March of Brandenburg, which after the acquisition of practically all of Lusatia had become a neighboring country. In this formerly Slavic land where, as in Lusatia, the native population had not yet entirely disappeared, Charles IV obtained the succession for his son Sigismund, after a branch of the Bavarian Wittelsbachs, old rivals of the Luxemburgs, which like their Askanian predecessors had made the march the most important German outpost in the East, particularly threatening to Poland. For the dynasty which now governed Bohemia this succession was a distinct success. Whether it would also be a check to German influences and expansion was to depend on the personality of Sigismund of Luxemburg.

However, the Emperor wanted to secure a much higher position for him, equal to that of his elder brother who received the typically Czech name Václav and was to inherit Bohemia and possibly also the imperial crown. Therefore, along with the Habsburgs, Charles of Luxemburg entered into negotiations with the last Anjou king of Hungary, his former rival Louis the Great, who had only daughters, the future heiresses of both Hungary and Poland. Almost simultaneously one of them, Mary, was betrothed to Sigismund of Luxemburg, and her younger sister Jadwiga to William of Habsburg. For the old Emperor it seemed a guaranty that Sigismund would succeed to Louis in either Poland or Hungary, and in any case this was to be a gain not only for the Luxemburg dynasty but also for Bohemia where their power would remain based.

Under Charles IV, who did not live to see the outcome of these carefully planned developments, Bohemia also made a great deal of progress in the field of administration, thanks to his codification of the law of the country. He enjoyed the full support of the hierarchy, with Arnošt of Pardubice, the first Archbishop of Prague, as his main advisor. Both not only maintained a close contact with the papacy, the Emperor in 1368 paying a visit to Urban V when he had temporarily returned to Rome from Avignon, but they also showed a real interest in missionary problems, such as the conversion of Lithuania, whose princes came to see Charles in 1358.

It was even more important that both of them realized the necessity of ecclesiastical reforms which were claimed by eloquent preachers from among the Czechs and from abroad. These were shocked by the wealth and worldly life of part of the clergy, including the richly endowed monasteries. In the days of Charles that reform movement had not yet had any heretical or distinctly anti-German character. It was a serious warning which gained in significance when in 1378 the final return of the Holy See to Rome was followed by the outbreak of the Great Western schism.

It was regrettable that the Emperor died just at the beginning of that crisis. But his death was a special loss for Bohemia, where the general problems of Christendom were to have particularly serious repercussions. The country soon lost the position, unique in its history, which it had occupied under Charles, while the close association of a Slavic people with German power, apparently successful during his lifetime, soon produced the most dangerous consequences. And none of his sons, the last Luxemburgs, proved equal to his task.

HUNGARY UNDER THE ANJOUS

That task was the more responsible because four years after the death of Charles IV the Hungarian branch of the Anjous was extinguished and the parallel development of Bohemia and Hungary under the foreign dynasties established there at the beginning of the fourteenth century came to an end. There are, however, other differences in that development. The reign of the Anjous in Hungary was much briefer than that of the Luxemburgs in Bohemia, limited as it was to two generations in the male line, and that dynasty, although of foreign origin, was not German but French.

There was, therefore, no danger whatever that the foreign rulers, the second of whom had incidentally already been born and bred in Hungary, would promote a foreign influence dangerous to the independence and national character of the country. Their French homeland was faraway, without any ambitions or possibilities of controlling or absorbing a country in East Central Europe which even the neighboring German Empire had failed to include. It is true that the Anjous who took the place of the Árpáds did not come directly from France but from Italy. Their ancestors, so long as they ruled Sicily, had shown the usual ambitions of all masters of Sicily directed toward the East. But even these aggressive aims were directed at the Byzantine Empire and its possessions in the south of the Balkan Peninsula, and since as early as in 1282 Sicily had been lost to the kings of Aragon and the Italian kingdom of the Anjous practically limited to Naples, that dynasty could hardly dream of creating an empire on both sides of the Adriatic.

In Hungary, they did, of course, spread from their brilliant court at Buda or nearby Vissegrad, a Romance culture, partly French, partly Italian, already touched by the early Renaissance movement. But this proved a real contribution to Hungary's genuine cultural life which in spite of an entirely different racial background was Latin in its character from the day of her conversion. Under the Anjous there could not possibly appear that German impact which at the equally brilliant court of the Luxemburgs in Prague, in connection with a German colonization much more important in Bohemia than in Hungary, gradually supplanted the native Slav and also the Romance elements introduced by the French contacts of the Luxemburgs and Charles IV's relations with great Italians such as Cola di Rienzi and Petrarch.

All that does not mean that the Hungarians did not resent, at least at the beginning, the establishment of foreigners at the site of their native kings. Just like the Bohemian nobles in the early years of King John, so also important factions of the Hungarian nobility, nationally more homogeneous, proud of their Golden Bull, and organized in powerful *genera* as in Poland, created opposition to Charles Robert when he arrived in 1308. But his wise policy, which enabled him to find a large group of supporters for his efficient administration, soon made him much more popular than John had ever been in Bohemia. Residing permanently in his new kingdom, he fully identified himself with its national interests, leaving those of Naples to his brother.

Even better than many of the Árpáds, Charles Robert realized the importance of a close cooperation with neighboring Poland, restored as a kingdom and always popular among the Hungarian nobles, especially in the northern counties where at the outset there had been the greatest reluctance to accept the Anjou rule. The king's marriage to

Elizabeth of Poland, the highly intelligent and ambitious daughter of Władysław Łokietek, which was contracted in 1320, the very year of the latter's coronation, was accompanied by a close alliance which was to last throughout the whole Anjou period.

That alliance made Charles Robert the natural mediator in the conflict between Poland on the one hand and Bohemia and the Teutonic Order on the other. It was therefore at Vissegrad, the Anjou residence, at a congress of the three Kings of East Central Europe held in 1335, that an arbitration suggested by Charles Robert tried to appease that conflict. While it did not put an end to the basic antagonism between the Poles and the Teutonic Knights, it prepared the rapprochement between Poland and Bohemia. Such a friendly collaboration with both Slavic kingdoms in Hungary's immediate neighborhood was in itself an advantage to that country. But as far as the relations with Poland were concerned, they opened for the King of Hungary two additional opportunities, both discussed, at a second Vissegrad meeting in 1339, with his Polish brother-in-law, King Casimir the Great.

First, there was the old Hungarian claim to Halich and even to Volhynia, expressed in the addition to their title, *rex Galiciae et Lodomeriae*. After the death of the last descendants of Roman and Daniel, around 1323, one of their Polish relatives, Bolesław of Mazovia, called George when he became the ruler of an Orthodox country, succeeded them. Facing internal troubles which were to lead to his assassination in 1340, George in turn designated his cousin King Casimir as his successor, precisely on the occasion of the second Vissegrad congress. It probably was at once anticipated that Hungary would support Poland in that matter, as she actually did in the following years, but not without serious chances of connecting, one way or another, the *regnum Russiae*, as the heritage of Daniel used to be called, with the crown of Hungary.

That issue was inseparable from an even more important one. Although the King of Poland was still quite young, discussions regarding his successor immediately started. It was decided that if he were to continue to have only daughters the Hungarian Anjous would inherit the crown of Poland, uniting both countries in a powerful confederation. If, however, these prospects, so attractive to the new Hungarian dynasty, would not materialize, the *regnum Russiae* could be redeemed by the King of Hungary.

These arrangements became final under Louis, the son of Charles Robert. He succeeded his father in 1342, two years after the beginning of the struggle for Halich and Volhynia between Poland and Lithuania. The new King of Hungary participated in this struggle on several occasions, once personally joining an expedition into distant lands. But the problem of the Polish succession, combined with Ruthenian and Lithuanian entanglements, was merely one aspect of the many-sided foreign policy of a king whom the Hungarians, proud of his achievements, called the Great. And he proved equally remarkable in his internal administration.

Like his neighbors, he also founded a university in the Hungarian city of Pécs, but that foundation of 1367 did not develop into a lasting institution. And though he contributed successfully to the country's cultural and economic progress, favoring particularly the cities and promoting their trade relations, he was chiefly interested in a better organization of the military forces needed for Hungary's territorial expansion. To the geographical unit already formed by the lands of the Crown of St. Stephen, he wanted to add a surrounding belt of vassal provinces. In the east, in addition to his Ruthenian project, he tried to bring under Hungarian suzerainty the principalities created by the Rumanian people; not only Wallachia which already had an existence of more than a hundred years, but also Moldavia, organized in his own time, where Hungarian and Polish interests had clashed from the beginning.

Even more ambitious in that respect was Louis' program of expansion toward the south, far into the Balkans. Here his prestige was at its height when in 1366 the Byzantine Emperor, John V Palaeologus, visited him in Buda to get military assistance against the Turks. In spite of papal appeals and encouragements, Louis' plans for conducting an anti-Ottoman crusade never materialized. But he extended Hungarian influence over at least part of Bulgaria, checked Serbia's expansion in the years of her greatest power, and tried to keep Bosnia under his control, marrying Elizabeth, the daughter of Stephen Kotromanich, the rival of Stephen Tvrtko, King of Serbia and Bosnia. In all these regions the advance of Hungary was also a progress of Catholic influence.

Like his predecessors, however, Louis of Anjou had as his main rival another Catholic power, the Republic of Venice. He definitely served the interests of his country when in 1358, in his first war

against Venice, he regained the maritime province of Dalmatia for
Hungary. But when he joined the coalition against the Republic
which toward the end of his reign almost destroyed Venetian power,
it was in connection with his Italian policy, in which he was deeply
interested for dynastic reasons. Louis' brother Andrew, who had
gained the Kingdom of Naples by marrying its heiress, his cousin
Joan, was murdered in 1345, not without his wife's responsibility.
Through repeated but unsuccessful expeditions into Southern Italy,
Louis wanted not only to avenge that crime but also to conquer
Naples for himself or his successors.

This was an additional reason why he regretted having no son,
and why after the birth of his three daughters in the early seventies,
one of his main objectives was to secure a third kingdom in order to
leave a royal crown to each of them. From 1370 onward he already
possessed a second kingdom in Poland where, according to the frequently confirmed earlier agreements, he succeeded the last Piast.
Even here, however, it was not without difficulty that the hereditary
rights of one of his daughters were recognized because the Poles
blamed him for neglecting their interests and for placing the province
of Halich under Hungarian administration. It also proved difficult to
determine which of the daughters, all of whom were already engaged
in their childhood to members of the leading European dynasties,
would inherit which kingdom. Since Naples was never retaken from
the Italian branch of the Anjous, and since the eldest daughter, Catherine, the fiancée of Louis of France, the future Duke of Orléans, died
before her father, the problem was reduced to Hungary and to Poland.

It was Louis' final decision that Hungary should be left to his
youngest daughter Jadwiga, and since she was engaged to William of
Habsburg, this would have resulted in a first Austro-Hungarian
union. Mary, who was supposed to rule in Poland, would have connected that country with the Brandenburg March of her fiancé Sigismund and thus with the domains of the Luxemburgs. The consequence of this intricate dynastic policy of Louis the Great and of
his matrimonial projects would have been, therefore, a wide advance
of German influence in East Central Europe, an advance which
that Hungarian king of French-Italian descent had rather opposed
throughout his life.

The artificial combinations of his last years were reversed after his
death by the strong national forces which he himself had fostered in

Hungary and never completely controlled in Poland. But when he disappeared in 1382, he left behind him the memory of a period of real greatness which Hungary had enjoyed under the last Anjou, who did his best to make her the leading power of East Central Europe, closely associated with the Latin West and yet fully independent in her national development. It soon became evident, however, that such a role was beyond the forces of Hungary alone; she was not even in a position to maintain the union with Poland and entered into a very serious internal crisis. The death of Louis of Anjou, coming only four years after the death of Charles of Luxemburg, is therefore a similar landmark in the course of the history of East Central Europe.

THE RISE AND FALL OF SERBIA, AND THE
OTTOMAN ADVANCE

The Hungarian crisis which followed the Anjou period was the more regrettable because at this very moment the Turkish onslaught was already approaching the Danubian region after conquering most of the Balkans, while the rest of the Byzantine Empire was completely isolated. Hungary was, however, not without responsibility for the main reason which made possible that sweeping advance of a new Muslim power—the lack of unity and cooperation among the Christian countries. A serious obstacle was, of course, the continuing schism between Catholics and Orthodox, but even among the Orthodox, who were supreme in the Balkan Peninsula, there was no coordination in defense against the Asiatic invaders. On the contrary, there continued, first, the agelong antagonism between the Greek Empire and the Slavic states north of its reduced territory, and secondly, the almost equally old rivalry between Bulgarians and Serbs.

In the fourteenth century it was definitely Serbia which was assuming the leading position in the Balkans. Under Stephen II's equally prominent and warlike successor, Stephen Urosh III, the kingdom of the Nemanyids had to face the joint opposition of Byzantium and Bulgaria which were temporarily allied. But the Serbs defeated both of them in 1330, when Michael Shishman, together with his Bulgarian army, was killed in the battle of Velbuzhd, and when Emperor Andronicus III had to make peace after the loss of most of Macedonia. In the following year Stephen III was replaced by his son and former co-ruler, Stephen Dushan, who ranks among the

greatest monarchs of his time and who aimed at the creation of a
Serb Empire which would take the place of the declining empire of the
Palaeologi.

His chances seemed quite favorable because Byzantium, after
losing almost all its possessions in Asia Minor to the Ottoman Turks
during the reigns of Andronicus II and Andronicus III, after the
death of the latter in 1341, entered into a period of civil war between
his son John V and a highly gifted usurper of the Cantacuzene family
who made himself a rival emperor under the name of John VI. Both
of them continued the negotiations with the papacy, which had been
started by their predecessor with a view to putting an end to the
eastern schism and joining the league against the Turks which was
promoted by the Avignon popes. But while that action was making
little progress, both emperors occasionally used Turkish auxiliaries in
the civil war. It was of little avail that in 1344 Catholic crusaders
took Smyrna from a less dangerous Turkish ruler, since about the
same time the Ottomans, under Osman's particularly aggressive successor, Urkhan, started their invasions of European territory as allies
of one or the other Greek Emperor.

In the meantime, Dushan, at the beginning, also unaware of the
supreme Ottoman danger to all Christendom, was occupying more
and more imperial territory, extending the frontier of Serbia far into
Albania and Thessaly. First crowned in 1333 as king of Serbia only,
in 1346 he celebrated another coronation in the Macedonian capital,
Skoplje, assuming the ambitious title of Emperor of Serbs and Greeks
or, as he was later called, *Imperator Rasciae et Romaniae*. During
all these years he also strengthened Serbia internally, unifying the
country under a well-organized administration, codifying the customary law, and favoring cultural relations with the West.

In addition to negotiations with Emperor John V who in 1354
finally defeated his rival, Pope Innocent VI also tried to gain Dushan
for a religious union with Rome and for an active participation in the
crusade against the Turks. The Serbian ruler now realized the urgent
necessity of stopping the Muslim invaders who inflicted upon the
Serbs a first defeat near Adrianople in 1352 and finally, in the
critical year of 1354 gained a first permanent foothold on European
soil by occupying Gallipoli. Unfortunately, Dushan's possible cooperation in a crusade which he himself wanted to lead was troubled

by the persistent hostility of the other prospective leader of the Christian forces, Louis of Hungary, the rival of the Serbs in Bosnia. Under these conditions even Dushan's better relations with Venice were of little help, and the plan of Serbia's religious union with the Catholic world, which would have been so important for the cultural unity of all Yugoslavs, was abandoned.

Another obstacle to any joint defense of the Balkans was of course Dushan's imperial ambition which made impossible any real collaboration with Byzantium. When he suddenly died in 1355, it was at the very moment when instead of marching against the Turks he was probably preparing for the conquest of Constantinople. Nevertheless his premature death was a serious blow not only for Serbia but also for the Christian peoples of the Balkans in general. The kingdom of the Nemanyids was divided among the last members of the dynasty, who proved of much less prominence, and local chieftains, among which the Balshas in the Zeta region—the future Montenegro—were most important and most interested in relations with the Catholic West. Bulgaria, too, which was divided among the last Shishmanids, could not possibly be a really helpful ally of the Byzantine Empire. When Emperor John V, in spite of his conversion to Catholicism of the Western rite and the sympathy of popes Urban V and Gregory XI, did not receive any Catholic assistance against the Turkish power, rapidly growing after Murad I's conquest of Adrianople, the Orthodox party in Constantinople, led by the Patriarch, continued to hope for efficient cooperation with the Orthodox Slavs of the Balkans. But all such prospects came to an end with the battle on the Maritsa River near Adrianople, then the Turkish capital, in 1371.

Even at this critical moment no league of Christian powers, either Catholic or Orthodox, had been concluded, and it was Serbian forces alone, under Dushan's last successors, which were crushed in that first major victory of the Turks in Europe. And it was Serbia which Murad I now wanted to destroy completely before attempting to conquer encircled Constantinople where his influence was already decisive. The final blow came in the famous battle at Kossovo Polje—"the field of the blackbirds"—where the Turks crushed the remaining forces of free Serbs in 1389. The assistance of other Balkan peoples had again proved entirely inadequate, and even one of the Serbian chieftains, Marko Kralyevich, wrongly praised in later legends, probably fought on the Turkish side. It is true that along with the Christian leader, Lazar, Murad I also lost his life, but his son and successor, Bayazid I, continued his policy of ruthless conquest.

The next victims were the now isolated Bulgarians. While some Serb elements continued to resist in the northwestern corner of the Balkan Peninsula, in the mountains of Zeta and of Bosnia where Stephen Tvrtko's kingdom disintegrated only after his death in 1391, Bulgaria, near the European center of Ottoman power, was completely subjugated in 1393 after the fall of its capital, Tirnovo. The cultural leaders who had been active in that city went into exile, and the national life of the Bulgarians was simply annihilated for almost five hundred years. There always remained, however, the tradition of Bulgaria's medieval power, just as Dushan's glory and the tragedy of Kossovo continued to inspire the Serbs not only during their last local struggles in the following century but also until their liberation in the nineteenth.

With Wallachia threatened and repeatedly raided immediately after the conquest of neighboring Bulgaria, there started, therefore, for all free peoples of the Balkan region the dark era of Turkish oppression and of the imposition of a completely alien Muslim civilization and political organization. For Christian Europe this was a serious though insufficiently realized loss. Greater was the impression created by the imminence of the conquest of Constantinople, now completely encircled and engaged in a policy of appeasement under both the old Emperor John V and, after his death in 1391, his son Manuel II. Only in connection with attempts at saving the Eastern Christian Empire, was the liberation of the Balkan Slavs also incidentally considered.

Even these attempts were, however, more difficult than before, since Constantinople was now impossible to reach except from the sea, and since, instead of ending the Eastern schism, the Great Western schism had been started, adding another element of division to the lack of unity among the Christian countries. Although the Catholic powers of East Central Europe at first remained loyal to the legitimate pope in Rome, the participation of Burgundy—the Western country most seriously concerned with the Eastern problem, but siding, like all of France, with the Pope of Avignon—excluded any papal initiative in the crusade of 1396, which seemed to have a good chance of success. That expedition ended, however, in the defeat of

Nicopolis, where the crusaders, long before reaching imperial territory, met the Turkish forces near the Danubian border between Wallachia and Bulgaria. That fateful event therefore merely strengthened in that whole region the position of the Ottoman conquerors who had even compelled Serbian forces to fight on their side.

Strangely enough, it was also an auxiliary Serb detachment which distinguished itself six years later in the battle of Angora, where Bayazid I was in turn defeated by another Asiatic conqueror, Timur the Lame, or Tamerlane, who for a short period revived the empire of Jenghis Khan. It is well known that this unexpected catastrophe of the rising Ottoman power permitted the Byzantine Empire to survive for another half century. Under the impression of his intervention in Turkish affairs, the Christian West even considered the savage Mongol leader as a possible ally. Only Venice never shared this illusion, having lost her Eastern European colony of Tana, at the mouth of the Don, in 1393, through an earlier invasion of Tamerlane in northeastern Europe.

That same invasion not only threatened Muscovite Russia, where the opposition against Mongol rule had just started, but also the new power in East Central Europe which the Venetians and other experts on the whole Eastern question rightly considered an indispensable factor in any action against the Muslim onslaught, even in the Balkans. This was the Polish-Lithuanian federation, including also the Ruthenian lands of the old Kievan State, which had been formed, thanks to the restoration of a powerful kingdom of Poland and to the stupendous expansion and eventual Christianization of the Lithuanian Grand Duchy. These two events are therefore an important part of the profound changes in the whole structure of East Central Europe which developed in the course of the fourteenth century.

THE LAST PIAST KINGS OF POLAND

The growing international role of Poland in the fourteenth century, so different from her precarious political position in the thirteenth, was the natural result of her restoration as a united kingdom. That restoration on a national basis and as a permanent factor in the European state system was the achievement of two remarkable rulers, father and son, and it came immediately after the merely temporary and territorially limited restoration of the kingdom under Przemysł II and its occupation by a foreign ruler, Václav II of Bohemia, followed for just one year by his son Václav III.

After the death of the latter in 1306, the Piast prince, Władysław Łokietek, who had become the leader of the national opposition against Czech domination, immediately succeeded in occupying Little Poland, but it took him six years before he was universally recognized in Greater Poland where he had a Silesian cousin as his rival, and eight more years before he was crowned king in 1320. Through his tireless efforts during these difficult years of transition, he emerged as the first restorer of the kingdom which, after his death in 1333, his only son Casimir could inherit without any difficulty.

It was, however, a state which included little more than the two basic provinces of Little and Greater Poland with Cracow and Gniezno as main centers, in addition to Łokietek's original patrimony, which was only a small part of Cuyavia. In that very region there remained local dukes, close relatives of the king, who recognized his authority but who also enjoyed a large degree of autonomy, while the dukes of Mazovia, the youngest line of the dynasty, were practically independent. And even before the loss of Silesia, which the numerous descendants of the eldest Piast line placed under the suzerainty of Bohemia, Łokietek suffered the equally painful loss of Polish Pomerania.

In the difficult beginning of his reign, when that province, together with the port of Danzig, was threatened by the margraves of Brandenburg, Łokietek asked the Teutonic Order, still considered a friendly neighbor and possible ally, to come to the rescue of the city. They did so, but only to occupy it for themselves after the treacherous slaughter of a large part of the Polish population. By 1309 the conquest of the whole province and its incorporation into Prussia was completed, and Poland was completely cut off from the Baltic Sea.

The king was so determined to regain Pomerania that in the very year of his coronation he submitted the dispute to the judgment of the Holy See. Pope John XXII, with whose agreement Władysław I (as he was called as king) had been crowned, appointed leading representatives of the Polish clergy as arbitrators. After a careful canonical trial, they recognized the king's claims. Their decision was of course disregarded by the Teutonic Order, and as soon as the king had added to his alliance with Hungary a similar alliance with Lithuania in 1325, threatened by the Order in her very existence, he tried to reconquer the lost province by force of arms.

In the course of these years of hard fighting, he even invaded Brandenburg, now allied with the Teutonic Knights, but the cooperation with the still pagan Lithuanians did not work, while the Order enjoyed the support of John of Luxemburg. In 1331 and 1332 Poland herself suffered invasions and devastations by the Knights of the Cross, which limited victories, like that of Płowce, could not possibly compensate, and when the king died, even his native Cuyavia was occupied by the Germans under a truce which he had been obliged to accept.

It was therefore in extremely difficult circumstances that his son Casimir took the power the next year. But his reign of thirty-seven years proved so successful that, alone among all kings of Poland, he was later called "the Great," and already in his lifetime he enjoyed an extraordinary prestige both at home and abroad.

His greatness is particularly evident in the field of internal administration, which had been rather neglected by his father. With experienced jurists as collaborators, throughout his whole reign he worked at a codification of Polish law which helped him to restore order in the whole country and to establish a sound balance of all classes of society. In his time the Polish knighthood already appears as a privileged class of nobles, but supported by faithful partisans he checked any possible abuses of turbulent aristocratic leaders, particularly in Greater Poland where a first "confederation" or league of nobles directed against his authority had been formed. He also promoted the development of the cities, which continued to enjoy the franchises of German law but under a local court of appeal established in Cracow. Finally, he became famous as protector of the peasants and also of the Jews, who having already received charters of liberties in the preceding century, now settled in Poland in rapidly growing numbers, thus escaping from persecution in the Western countries.

It is doubtful whether Casimir succeeded in having a unified code of law accepted in all Poland which would have combined his separate drafts for Great and Little Poland that had been promulgated around 1346. But great progress was achieved in the unification of the administration through the creation of central offices, and almost all local duchies were converted into provinces directly under the king whose Cuyavian cousins died out with only one exception. As to the dukes of Mazovia, they gradually recognized the king's suzerainty, and here too the extinction of various side lines of the dynasty enabled Casimir to establish his immediate rule over at least part of that province and to remove any foreign interference with its affairs.

In his foreign policy, Casimir realized the necessity of beginning with concessions made to stronger neighbors. After the unavoidable recognition of Bohemia's suzerainty over almost all the Silesian duchies, he hoped to concentrate against the Teutonic Order and tried once more to recover Pomerania peacefully through the decision of another papal court of arbitration which this time met in Warsaw in 1339 and was composed of French prelates. But once more a decision favorable to Poland was rejected by the Order, and in 1343 Casimir felt obliged to conclude the peace treaty of Kalisz, which gave only Cuyavia back to Poland, while Pomerania was left to the Teutonic Knights as a "perpetual alm."

The king never ceased to look for an occasion to reclaim it, but he was already engaged in a political action which was to be his main objective from 1340 onward and which kept him busy at the eastern borders of Poland. It was the problem of his succession in Halich and Volhynia after the death of his cousin Bolesław—a problem intimately connected with that of the Hungarian succession in Poland.

Casimir was well received by the population, though mostly Ruthenian, of that controversial border region, to which he granted full autonomy and respect of their local customs. He was, however, opposed not only by the Tartars, but particularly by the Lithuanian princes who also claimed the heritage of the former princes of Halich and Volhynia. The King of Poland, after occupying all the former state of Halich and Volhynia in 1349, had to limit himself to the province of Halich in 1352. Lwów, a recently founded but rapidly developing city, was its new capital. Finally, in 1366, he added the western section of Volhynia to it and his overlordship was recognized by the Lithuanian rulers of Podolia.

Time and again he tried to come to an understanding not only with that Podolian line but with the whole Lithuanian dynasty and to co-operate against the Knights of the Cross. He encouraged all projects of converting Lithuania to the Catholic faith. There are also some indications that he was already considering the opportunity of a Polish-

Lithuanian union, again in connection with the choice of his own successor. This choice was his permanent concern in the later part of his reign when he realized that in spite of his three marriages he would leave no male heir.

Casimir did not see any suitable candidate for the Polish crown among the surviving lines of the Piasts, and though he seems to have taken into consideration various alternatives, including the succession of a grandson, Casimir of Stettin, whom he adopted and endowed with large territories in Poland, the original idea of leaving Poland to Louis of Hungary prevailed. The relations with this nephew, so important for Casimir's policy in general European affairs, were particularly close at the time of the Congress of Cracow in 1364, when Casimir showed his unusual versatility, dealing even with Scandinavian and Balkan problems. In the very year of that memorable assembly which best evidenced the rise of Poland's power, the king also made his greatest contribution to the progress of Polish culture by founding the University of Cracow on the model of the famous Italian law schools.

When Casimir died prematurely in 1370, Louis of Hungary started the twelve years of his Polish reign in cooperation with his mother, the sister of Casimir. Supported by a strong party among the aristocracy of Little Poland, opposed by most of Greater Poland where native candidates were much more popular, he practically limited his interest in Polish affairs to the desire of having the succession of one of his daughters recognized in Poland also. He reached that goal at the price of a charter of liberties granted to the Polish nobles in 1374 at the second of three successive meetings he held with them in Kassa (Košice) in northern Hungary.

It was then that the privileged position of the *szlachta*, which had been developing throughout the preceding centuries, was legally established. The most important concession, which limited the ordinary taxes to a small merely symbolic payment, was the origin of parliamentary government in Poland, since no further taxation was henceforth possible without a vote of representatives of the nation. Equally important was the participation of the nobles in the settlement of decisive political problems. Well trained in that respect under a foreign ruler who was frequently absent, they themselves were prepared to take care of the vital interests of the country when he died in 1382, hoping in vain that the daughter whom he had chosen for Poland would rule there, together with her future German husband who had also been selected by her father.

His plan to assign Poland to Mary, who was engaged to Sigismund of Luxemburg, failed as soon as the Hungarians elected her as queen. Nobody wanted the personal union with Hungary to continue. Amidst the general confusion of an interregnum which seemed to favor the election of a Mazovian Piast, the Poles remained faithful to their obligations toward the Anjou dynasty but invited Louis' youngest daughter, Jadwiga, who in spite of her age of hardly ten was sent to Cracow in 1384 and crowned as "King" of Poland.

The choice of her husband was to have a decisive importance for all East Central Europe. She, too, had a German fiancé, William of Habsburg, but the Poles were no less opposed to him than to Sigismund of Luxemburg. They decided to choose another candidate who was himself eager to gain the Polish crown in the interest of Lithuania, his country of origin.

LITHUANIA'S EXPANSION UNDER GEDIMINAS AND HIS SONS

While two remarkable kings re-established the great medieval tradition of the Poland of the Piasts, two simultaneous generations of Lithuania's rulers succeeded in making Europe's last pagan country the largest state in East Central Europe. They did it through an almost uninterrupted struggle on two fronts: defending what remained of the free Baltic tribes against the German Knights of conquered Prussia and Livonia, and at the same time expanding in the opposite direction in spite of Tartar opposition and the growing power of Moscow, while the Ruthenian population remained practically passive.

That tremendous task, which resulted in a basic change of the map of Europe and in the creation of its largest body politic outside the German Empire, was started by the first prominent representative of Pukuveras' dynasty, his son Vytenis. But it was chiefly by his brother Gediminas, who followed him in 1315, and after the death of the latter in 1341 by his numerous sons, successfully led by two of them, that the decisive achievements were performed.

Gediminas realized even better than his predecessors, from Mindaugas onward, that he could not create a real European power nor even assure the peaceful survival of the Lithuanian peoples without converting them to the Christian faith. As early as 1321 he started negotiations with the papacy, avoiding the dangerous intermediary of the Teutonic Order and using Franciscan friars to take his letters to Avignon. Again there is some doubt as to the authenticity of the source material, and it is hard to determine whether Lithuanian hesitation or German intrigues made the whole project fail, although papal delegates arrived in Vilnius (Wilno), Gediminas' recently founded capital, and peace was concluded with his German neighbors in 1323.

A few years later, in spite of his temporary alliance with Poland, Gediminas again found himself in an extremely difficult position, while regular raids of the Teutonic Knights penetrated far into Lithuania and used her persistent paganism as a pretext for crusades which attracted participants from all Western Europe. But in addition to the permanent effort of organizing the defense of the country along the western border, the *rex Lithwinorum et multorum Ruthenorum,* as the grand duke proudly called himself, continued to extend his eastern frontier by connecting the main White Russian principalities with Lithuania. These principalities were Polotsk, where Lithuanian influence had already been established, and Vitebsk, whose prince gave his daughter in marriage to Gediminas' heir. He also incorporated minor territories, still held by the Tartars, as far as the limits of Volhynia and Kiev.

After a few years of internal crisis which followed the death of Gediminas, his most prominent sons, Algirdas and Kestutis, settled the problem of succession. In 1345 they made an agreement which put the whole state, including the duchies of their other brothers, under their joint leadership. Loyally cooperating with each other for more than thirty years, they divided the two main problems of Lithuania's foreign policy between themselves. Algirdas, the senior partner who resided in Vilnius, mainly directed the activities in the East, while Kestutis, from nearby Trakai (Troki), organized the defense against the Germans. Frequently, however, they would both join in facing that increasing danger or in invading the Teutonic Order's territories in turn. Sometimes they suffered serious defeats and saw a large border region of their country practically turned into a wilderness, but they still resisted the onslaught of what was then the strongest military power in Central Europe.

From time to time there again appeared projects for the conversion of Lithuania, including her great leaders, to the Catholic faith, possibly through imperial, Polish, or even Hungarian intermediaries. But there was another conflict with these friendlier Catholic neighbors which proved to be a serious obstacle. It was rivalry for the possession of Halich and, at least, Volhynia. This protracted struggle, which started shortly before Gediminas' death, was only part of a much bigger problem which Algirdas summarized in his ambitious statement that *omnis Russia* ought to belong to the Lithuanians.

This was first of all a challenge to the Tartars. Their European realm was disintegrating, but they still opposed the Lithuanian advance. Finally a great victory, gained by Algirdas in 1363, brought Kiev itself together with most of what was later called the Ukraine under his control, which thus approached the Black Sea. He was wise enough to leave considerable autonomy to all the Ruthenian territories, merely replacing their native princes by members of his own family. One of his sons, for instance, was established in Kiev, after a long interruption of the historic role of that city. Most of the territory of the old Kievan State being now associated with Lithuania in one way or another, it would seem that the grand duchy was a continuation of that state under Lithuanian leadership.

As a matter of fact, that leadership was purely political, since not only did the Lithuanian princes ruling in Ruthenian lands adopt the Orthodox faith, the language, and in general, the more developed culture of their new subjects, but there was also a possibility that Lithuania proper, smaller in area and population than her acquisitions in the East and the South, would come under Ruthenian influence and, threatened by the Catholic West, turn Greek Orthodox. The Lithuanians and their dynasty, had, however, an Orthodox rival also. Moscow, too, was trying to unite "all the Russias" under her leadership, and the common faith was indeed a very important asset. On the other hand, the control of Moscow, itself still under Tartar overlordship, was not yet that full liberation from the Tartar yoke which was one of the advantages of Lithuanian rule, a rule which, autocratic in the nucleus of the state, was nevertheless more respectful of local traditions than were the despotic princes of Moscow.

Therefore various principalities, even in Great Russia, sided in that conflict with the pagan Lithuanians, in spite of the indignation of the ecclesiastical authority which was headed by the metropolitan residing in Moscow. Tver, in particular, was looking for Lithuanian protection, and it was with this and other Russian allies that Algirdas, whose second wife was a princess of Tver, thrice advanced as far as Moscow, without, however, taking the city or decisively beating his eastern neighbor. Therefore various principalities, including Smolensk, were hesitating between the two hostile powers.

The situation of Lithuania, placed between two equally irreconcilable enemies in addition to the Tartars, whose invasions did not end at all, and hesitating between Western and Eastern influence, became particularly critical when Algirdas died in 1377. It now became apparent that the internal political structure of the huge realm was also rather weak and had depended exclusively on the cooperation of two unusually gifted brothers who supplemented each other well. One of Algirdas' twelve sons, Jogaila, was supposed to continue such cooperation with Kestutis, and later with the most prominent of Kestutis' sons, Vytautas. But the relations between uncle and nephew were not as harmonious as they had been in the earlier setup, and their mutual distrust, skilfully exploited by the Teutonic Order, soon led to a disastrous civil war.

First, Kestutis, the old pagan hero of so many years of struggle against the Germans, defeated Jogaila and, taking Vilnius, expelled him to Vitebsk, inherited from his mother, in 1381. But the next year he was in turn crushed by his nephew and killed in jail. His son Vytautas escaped to Prussia and tried to recover his patrimony with the support of the Knights of the Cross, to whom he abandoned the coveted province of Samogitia, the territorial link between the two Baltic colonies of the German Knights, Prussia and Livonia. Baptized as a Catholic, Vytautas, if placed on the Lithuanian throne by the Teutonic Order, would have made the rest of the country a German protectorate.

Jogaila's policy seemed undecided. He himself would negotiate with the Order, making promises similar to those of his cousin. At the same time he would consider the possibility of turning toward the East, although it proved to be a legend that at a given moment he accepted as did many of his brothers the Orthodox faith. Against Moscow he was even ready to cooperate with the Tartars, but he avoided joining them in the decisive campaign of 1380 which ended in the famous victory of Dimitry Donskoy, so called in memory of the battle of the Don. And he was fully aware that some of the Lithuanian princes, already converted to Orthodoxy, particularly his brother Andrew of Polotsk, in alliance with Moscow if not with the Germans, were ready to oppose him. In their duchies, some of which were far away from Vilnius, they could at any moment challenge the authority of the grand duke, as Vytautas had done.

Lithuania's expansion, almost unique in its rapid success, thus proved beyond the real forces of the Lithuanians alone and of a dynasty which in spite of the unusual qualities of many of its members was too divided by the petty rivalries of its various branches to guarantee a joint action under one chief. At a time when the Teutonic Order reached the height of its power under Grand Master Winrich von Kniprode (1351–81), while Moscow tried for the first time to replace the Tartar power in Eastern Europe, Lithuania, larger than either of them but composed of loosely connected territories different in race and creed, excluded from the European community because of her official paganism, was doomed to destruction or disintegration. The comparatively small group of ethnic Lithuanians would have been the main victim, but the whole of East Central Europe would have suffered from a chaotic situation amidst German, Muscovite, and possibly Tartar interference.

But in these critical years, especially in 1384 when he made a move toward appeasing the Teutonic Order after a precarious reconciliation with Vytautas, Jogaila was already conducting secret negotiations with the Poles which were to change the situation altogether. The son of Algirdas had realized that the only way to save his country and her proud tradition, as well as his personal position, was to come to an agreement with the only neighbor who could help reorganize Lithuania as a Christian nation without destroying her very identity. A union of Poland with Lithuania and her Ruthenian lands, added to those already connected with Poland, could indeed create a new great power, comprising a large and crucial section of East Central Europe and strong enough to check both German and Muscovite advance. The amazing success of a plan which would seem almost fantastic was a turning point in the history not only of that region but also of Europe. In connection with so many other changes around 1378 and the following years, it inaugurated a new historical period.

PART III

RENAISSANCE DEVELOPMENTS

8

THE TIMES OF WLADYSLAW JAGIELLO AND SIGISMUND OF LUXEMBURG

THE FOUNDATION OF THE POLISH-LITHUANIAN UNION AND QUEEN JADWIGA

It is now more and more generally admitted that in the course of European history the real Middle Ages ended toward the end of the fourteenth century and are separated from the modern period, in the proper sense, by two centuries of transition which correspond to the flowering of the Renaissance and of its political conceptions. This is, however, particularly evident in the history of East Central Europe, and here it was the creation and development of the federal system of the Jagellonians which set the pattern of these two hundred years.

It was much more than a union of Poland and Lithuania under the dynasty founded by Jogaila—in Poland called Jagiełło—a union which for two more centuries survived the extinction of that royal family in 1572. From the outset it included all Ruthenian lands—what now is called White Russia and the Ukraine—and such a body politic extending from the Baltic to the Black Sea attracted smaller neighboring territories because of the possibilities of free, autonomous development guaranteed by its structure. On the Baltic shore the Union was gradually enlarged through the inclusion of the German colonial states in Prussia and Livonia either directly or in the form of fiefs. In the Black Sea region, the Danubian principalities, particularly Moldavia, and temporarily the Crimea also, were in the Union's sphere of influence. And at the height of the power of the Jagellonians, members of that dynasty were kings of Bohemia and of Hungary. The whole of East Central Europe, as far as it was free from the German, Ottoman, and Muscovite empires, was thus united in a political system which protected that freedom.

Even more efficiently, that system promoted the progress and spread of Western culture in East Central Europe, not through German influence, now in decline, but through direct cooperation with the Latin world, which was at the same time a powerful stimulus for the development of individual, national cultures in the various parts of the whole region. As a whole, it was a bulwark of Catholicism, favoring a reunion of the Orthodox population with Rome but without enforcing it, and also being influenced by the conflicting religious trends of the Reformation. These trends, as well as those of the Renaissance, reached precisely as far as the eastern boundaries of the Jagellonian Union. Created by a dynasty, the federation was developed with the growing participation of representatives of the constituent nations and thus promoted a parliamentary form of government in between absolute powers.

When Jogaila, grand duke of Lithuania, was accepted as husband of Queen Jadwiga by her Polish advisers and by her mother, the widow of Louis of Hungary, the whole project seemed to be just one more dynastic combination, as were so many other succession treaties of the same century. But when the young queen herself agreed to give up her Austrian fiancé, it was a sacrifice inspired by her desire thus to convert the last pagan nation in Europe. The conversion not only of Jogaila and his dynasty but also of the Lithuanian people was indeed the first condition which the grand duke had to accept when on August 14, 1385, he signed the Treaty of Krewo with the Polish delegates. Furthermore, he promised to regain the territorial losses of both states—a clear reference to the conquests of the Teutonic Order —and to unite these states by what was called *terras suas Lithuaniae et Russiae Coronae Regni Poloniae perpetuo applicare.*

That brief but momentous formula is not easy to interpret. A comparison with similar contemporaneous texts indicates that it was decided that the various Lithuanian and Ruthenian duchies, which hitherto had recognized the grand duke's suzerainty, would now be fiefs of the crown of Poland which Jogaila was to obtain through his marriage. As a matter of fact, immediately after the wedding, which was celebrated in Cracow on February 18, 1386, preceded by Jogaila's baptism under the Christian name of Władysław and followed by his coronation as king of Poland, the various members of his dynasty, ruling in the constituent parts of his realm, paid formal homage to the crown, the king, and the queen of Poland.

In February, 1387, the king returned to Lithuania where the Catholic faith was now accepted without any difficulty. A bishopric was founded in Vilnius (now called *Vilna* in Latin and *Wilno* in Polish), and charters of liberties on the Polish model were granted to the Church and the knighthood of Lithuania. At the same time the queen conducted an expedition into the Halich province. With only one of the Hungarian governors trying to resist, the whole region with Lwów as its capital was restored to Poland without using force and at once received the usual privileges. And it was here that for the first time the homage of a prince of Moldavia was received, followed by a close alliance with Wallachia. While in the north, the last prince of Smolensk became another ally, and the Republic of Novgorod seemed ready to accept one of Jagiełło's brothers as ruling prince.

These successes, which completely changed the map of Europe, were of course a challenge to Poland's and Lithuania's old opponents. Moscow tried to create trouble among the Lithuanian princes in her neighborhood, but the main opposition came from the Teutonic Order. Once more it was Vytautas—called Vitold in Latin and Polish sources —who was used as an appropriate instrument. He too had signed the Treaty of Krewo and paid the requested homage, but he was deeply disappointed when the king chose one of his brothers as his lieutenant in the most important part of Lithuania instead of this brilliant and ambitious cousin. Therefore Vytautas escaped for the second time to the Teutonic Knights in the winter of 1389–1390. Hoping also for the support of Moscow, whose grand prince, Vasil I, had married his daughter, he again tried to conquer Lithuania with German assistance. Pretending that the conversion of the country was not really accomplished, the Order continued to organize crusades, even with the participation of French and English knights. But Wilno was defended with Polish help, and after two years of inconclusive fighting, the king succeeded in recalling his cousin. Both were reconciled in the Ostrow Agreement of 1392, which not only restored his patrimony to Vytautas but also entrusted him with the administration of all Lithuanian and Ruthenian lands.

He first united all these provinces under his control, removing the local princes, even those who were brothers of Jagiełło, and replacing them with his own governors. Then he started a foreign policy, rich in initiative and versatility but not always in agreement with the general interests of the federation and going beyond the possibilities of Lithuania herself. Chiefly interested in her eastern expansion, he was prepared to appease the Teutonic Order not only at the expense of

Poland, which the Knights of the Cross planned to partition through secret negotiations with the Luxemburgs and one of the Silesian princes, but also sacrificing the important Lithuanian province of Samogitia, as he had done before, and giving up promising possibilities of cooperation with the Livonian hierarchy. A separate peace which Vytautas concluded with the Order in 1398, not without hope of becoming an independent king of Lithuania, was to facilitate his interference with Tartar problems. Supporting the adversaries of Tamerlane, he expected to control all Eastern Europe.

Queen Jadwiga, who throughout these critical years had contributed to the peaceful cooperation of all members of the dynasty, was alarmed by Vytautas' ambition and predicted that his expedition against Tamerlane's lieutenants would end in failure. Indeed, Vytautas suffered a complete defeat in the battle of the Vorskla, in August 1399, in spite of the support of many Polish knights. He then had to limit himself to the defense of the prewar frontier along the Dnieper River and the Black Sea coast which he had reached in earlier campaigns. A few weeks before, on the 17th of July, the Queen of Poland died, soon after her newborn daughter. The situation was now propitious for a fair solution of the controversial problems regarding the structure of the Polish-Lithuanian Union and the personal role of Vytautas, a solution which Jadwiga had carefully prepared.

In a new agreement made with King Władysław Jagiełło at the end of 1400, Vytautas, realizing that Lithuania could not stand alone, accepted the idea that she would remain permanently under the Polish crown but as a restored unit of her various lands. Wherever feudal principalities still existed, they were now recognized as fiefs of the grand duchy, which as a whole would continue to be a fief of the kingdom of Poland, Vytautas acting as grand duke on behalf of the king. In practice such an arrangement guaranteed to Lithuania not only full autonomy but also a development in the direction of full equality. Equally important was the fact that early in 1401 the Union thus amended was confirmed in charters issued by the representatives of both nations, promising each other full support against all enemies. It was no longer a dynastic affair but a real federation.

Such a development was possible because the Lithuanians were making rapid progress not only in the participation in their country's government but also in the cultural field, benefiting in both respects from their close association with Poland. Here, again, Queen Jadwiga had made a decisive contribution which fully matured only after her death. She was not only encouraging the Christianization of Lithuania and projects of religious union with the Orthodox Ruthenians, but she also wanted to reorganize the University of Cracow, which had declined after the death of its founder, Casimir the Great, and to make it a center of Western cultural influence and missionary activities in the eastern part of the federation. After first founding a college for Lithuanians at the University of Prague, she obtained from Pope Boniface IX, with whom she frequently cooperated, permission to add a school of theology to the University of Cracow. It was as a full *studium generale*, on the model of the Sorbonne, that this university was reopened in 1400, richly endowed by the will of the queen and soon attracting many Lithuanians, one of whom was its second rector.

Queen Jadwiga was considered a saint by her contemporaries, and even from a secular point of view her achievements and her lasting significance in history can hardly be overrated. Devoted to the idea of peace, she tried to postpone the unavoidable conflict with the Teutonic Order and to arrive at some understanding with the Luxemburg dynasty, not only with Václav of Bohemia, the king of the Romans, but also with Sigismund, from whom she did not reclaim her Hungarian heritage after the death of her sister Mary, his wife. But when she herself died without leaving children, it seemed doubtful whether Jagiełło would have any hereditary rights in Poland. He was, indeed, re-elected, but when he later had children by other marriages, the problem of their succession was an additional difficulty in the settlement of the constitutional issues of the federation.

JAGIEŁŁO AND VYTAUTAS

Fortunately for both Poland and Lithuania, in the following years and for more than a quarter of a century there was loyal cooperation between King Władysław II and his cousin, a return—at last—to the friendship which had united their fathers. They both developed Jadwiga's heritage and led the united countries to unprecedented successes. Their cooperation was based upon the Covenant of 1401, which in addition to the settlement of the internal problems of the federation also provided for a common defense against the Teutonic Order. That problem, including the recovery of the territories which had been lost to the Order by Poland and Lithuania, remained the main objective of their foreign policy.

Still unprepared for a decisive struggle, both countries had to conclude a peace treaty with the Knights of the Cross in 1404. This was a first recognition of the Polish-Lithuanian Union by the Order, but otherwise it proved rather unsatisfactory. Only a small frontier district was restored to the Poles, who had to redeem it through a payment approved by a formal vote of the regional dietines—a first appearance of those assemblies that were to be basic for the development of the Polish Parliament. Samogitia, however, seemed to be definitely abandoned by Lithuania, and Vytautas turned once more to problems of eastern expansion. He secured the possession of Smolensk and with Polish assistance conducted three campaigns against his son-in-law, Vasil of Moscow, with the result that in 1408 the Ugra River was fixed as the frontier between the two powers.

But the people of Samogitia suffered so much under German rule, which tried in vain to enforce their conversion, that in 1409 they started an insurrection which Vytautas could not but support, at least unofficially. When, consequently, the Teutonic Order threatened to attack Lithuania proper once more, the Poles declared their full solidarity so that the knights preferred to invade the richer Polish territories, not without initial success. Both sides now prepared for what was to be the "great war" of the following year. Carefully planned strategically by the king and the grand duke, the campaign of 1410 was also preceded by what might be called a flow of propaganda throughout all Western Christendom, as far as France and England. In reply to the Order's charges that Lithuania was not really converted, the Poles tried to explain that the basic issue was the defense of that new Catholic nation against German aggression.

Anticipating another invasion, a strong Polish-Lithuanian army entered Prussia and on July 15th met almost equally strong and better equipped German forces between Tannenberg and Grunwald. Under the supreme command of Jagiełło, and in spite of a withdrawal of the Lithuanian wing at the beginning of the battle, it ended in a complete defeat of the Order, whose grand master, Ulrich of Jungingen, was killed in action with most of his knights. The Order never recovered from that unexpected blow, and its whole territory seemed open to its former victims.

That great victory, one of the greatest in Polish history, was, however, poorly utilized. Marienburg, the capital of the Teutonic Knights, was well defended by Heinrich von Plauen, and when the siege dragged on, while German reinforcements were approaching from Livonia, Vytautas returned to Lithuania. In spite of another Polish victory, peace had to be concluded at Toruń (Thorn) in 1411 on very disappointing conditions. Poland's gains were insignificant, and Samogitia was restored to Lithuania only for the lifetime of Jagiełło and his cousin. That ambiguous situation, as well as endless controversies regarding the indemnities which the Order promised to pay in successive instalments, made the peace very precarious from the outset. Yet the prestige of the Polish-Lithuanian federation was greatly increased, both in the West, where it was at last realized that a new great power had appeared in the state system of Catholic Europe, and in the East, where both rulers reviewed their border regions, making favorable agreements with Russian and Tartar neighbors and solidly establishing their domination as far as the Black Sea.

Another result of Grunwald was a strengthening of the Union, evidenced in a new series of charters which were issued at Horodło in 1413. At this Polish-Lithuanian convention, which was to be followed by similar meetings whenever necessary, the permanence of Lithuania's ties with the crown of Poland was once more confirmed, but at the same time her autonomy under a separate grand duke, even after the death of Vytautas, was formally guaranteed. The liberties granted to the Catholic boyars of Lithuania were extended on the pattern of the Polish constitution, and forty-seven of their leading families were adopted by so many Polish clans and permitted to use the same coats of arms in the future. That unusual gesture of symbolic fraternity was in full agreement with the principles expressed in the introductory statement of the Polish charter, which emphasized that government and politics ought to be based upon the *misterium caritatis*.

Another application of these principles was the joint action of all parts of the federation at the Council of Constance which opened one year later. It was decided to submit the whole controversy with the Teutonic Order to that international assembly through a well-chosen delegation which also participated in the main religious discussions of the council. The Polish delegates were led by the Archbishop of

Gniezno, henceforth Primate of Poland. The prominent theologian Paulus Vladimiri, rector of the University of Cracow, which closely cooperated with that of Paris, played a particularly significant part. In his treatises on papal and imperial power he developed before the council almost revolutionary ideas on national self-determination and religious tolerance, also recalling the traditional doctrine of the church in matters of war and peace. In the application of those principles he defended the rights of the Lithuanians against German imperialism, but he was immediately answered by a German Dominican, John Falkenberg, who on the instructions of the Teutonic Order branded the King of Poland as a pagan tyrant whom true Christians had the right and even the duty to put to death.

In connection with the problem of *tyrannicidium*, also raised in the dispute between France and Burgundy, that debate attracted the attention of the whole council but of course could not contribute to any solution of the Polish-Prussian conflict. The Poles did not even succeed in having Falkenberg's doctrine condemned as heretical, but they created a great impression when a special delegation from Samogitia confirmed both the charges against the Teutonic Order and the fact that Jagiełło and Vytautas were peacefully Christianizing that last pagan stronghold which German pressure had failed to convert. Scarcely less impressive was the appearance at Constance of the Metropolitan of Kiev, a Bulgarian recently elected under the influence of Vytautas, who in his address before Pope Martin V declared that he was ready for religious union with Rome. It seemed that soon after the end of the Western schism—the council's greatest success— the old Eastern schism could also be healed, thanks to the initiative of the Polish-Lithuanian federation which included so many Orthodox Ruthenians, who were also represented at Constance by numerous delegates.

After establishing diplomatic relations with France and England and making an alliance with Eric of Denmark, the ruler of all Scandinavian countries federated in the Union of Kalmar, the King of Poland and his cousin were in a better position to resume the struggle against the Teutonic Knights, which neither imperial nor papal arbitration could appease. After two abortive campaigns, the war of 1422 was ended by the Melno Treaty which slightly improved the Polish frontier and definitely attributed Samogitia to Lithuania. At the same time Jagiełło and Vytautas, at the request of the moderate wing of the Hussites who wanted one of them to accept the royal crown of Bohemia, were interfering with the internal troubles of that Slavic neighbor country which was included in the German Empire. They had to proceed very carefully, however, in order to avoid any appearance of supporting heretical revolutionaries whose reconciliation with the Catholic church proved impossible. There was, indeed, among the Poles a certain sympathy with the Hussite movement, but it was opposed by the majority which in 1424 concluded a confederation in defense of Catholicism and found a prominent leader in the Bishop of Cracow, Zbigniew Oleśnicki, whose influence was growing in the later part of Jagiełło's reign.

The aging king had just contracted a fourth marriage with a Lithuanian princess who at last gave him the long-expected sons. They had, however, no hereditary rights to the Polish crown, which became elective, although in practice everybody wanted Jagiełło's highly successful rule to be continued by his descendants. But the nobility made the formal recognition of the succession of one of the young princes, dependent on a confirmation and extension of the rights and privileges which the king had granted in a series of constitutional charters. These rights included, among others, the *neminem captivabimus*, i.e., the promise that nobody would be put in prison without trial.

Final agreement between the king and the nation was not reached before 1430, and then in the midst of a conflict with Vytautas. After thirty years of cooperation, this disagreement now threatened the very foundations of the whole political system. In the preceding years the ambitious Grand Duke of Lithuania, frequently participating in the solution of Polish problems also, had profited from the union of both countries in order to extend his influence in all Eastern Europe. Under his efficient rule, even the danger of Tartar invasions had been reduced, a friendly Khan had been established in the Crimea, and the control of the coast of the Black Sea had been made complete. Furthermore, when Vasil I of Moscow died in 1425, his minor son, Vasil II, was placed under the tutorship of his maternal grandfather, Vytautas, who thus included even Muscovite Russia in his sphere of influence. Occasional expeditions against Pskov and Novgorod created a similar situation with regard to these two republics, each of which tried to maintain an independent position between Lithuania, Moscow, and the German Knights of Livonia.

The power of Vytautas reached its climax when in 1429, in his city of Lutsk in Volhynia, he acted as host to a congress in which not only the King of Poland but also Sigismund of Luxemburg, king of the Romans, of Hungary, and Bohemia, participated, along with representatives of many other countries of Western and Eastern Europe. Similar to an earlier meeting held in Cracow in 1424, this congress was supposed to review the whole political situation of East Central Europe, and the presence of a papal legate also permitted inclusion of the religious problems. But it was precisely one of these problems, the Hussite revolution in Bohemia, which Sigismund did not want to have touched by the Polish-Lithuanian federation, now the leading power in the whole region and his and Germany's most dangerous rival. He therefore raised an unexpected question which was to disrupt that federation. He suggested that Vytautas be made an independent king of Lithuania.

The grand duke realized the danger of that diplomatic move better than Jagiełło, who at first favored it for dynastic reasons. But offended by the protest of the Poles, Vytautas was inclined to accept the royal crown offered by Sigismund, who himself was not yet crowned as Holy Roman Emperor. A compromise solution which would have made Vytautas a king under the auspices not of Sigismund but of the pope was being considered when Lithuania's greatest leader died in 1430, leaving open the controversial problems of Polish-Lithuanian relations which were involved in the whole issue.

THE EASTERN POLICY OF SIGISMUND OF LUXEMBURG

Sigismund's action during and after the Congress of Lutsk was nothing but the climax of his eastern policy, which from the beginning opposed to the Polish-Lithuanian Union the old idea of the control of all East Central Europe by a German dynasty ruling the empire.

Between the two sons of Emperor Charles IV, who one after the other succeeded him as kings of the Romans and of Bohemia, Venceslas (Václav) and Sigismund represented two different policies. The elder, who had received a Czech name, rather identified himself with his Bohemian kingdom which he governed from 1378 untl his death in 1419. Even here his achievements can hardly be compared with those of his father, and in Germany he was a complete failure. He never obtained the imperial crown, was deposed by the electors in 1400, and after a schism in the empire parallel to that in the church, was replaced in 1410 by his younger brother.

Sigismund had first been made margrave of Brandenburg by his father, and he had been engaged to Mary, one of the daughters of Louis of Hungary. They were supposed to rule Poland after Louis' death, and although Mary was elected Queen of Hungary in 1382, her German fiancé did not give up hope of also becoming King of Poland. Disappointed in this respect, he never forgave his happier rival Jagiełło, and this was one of the reasons why, in contradistinction to Venceslas who temporarily was even allied with Poland, Sigismund, in spite of repeated rapprochements, actually remained hostile to that country as long as he lived.

In Hungary, too, Sigismund was from the outset opposed as a German. Only after several years of civil war, in which the Anjou candidate, Charles of Naples, as well as Mary's mother were murdered, was the margrave of Brandenburg recognized as king in 1387. During the fifty years of his reign in Hungary, Sigismund was seriously interested in the defense of that country against the Turkish onslaught. The crusade which he organized in 1396, in cooperation with Burgundy and with the support of knights from Germany and other lands, ended in the defeat at Nicopolis and failed to check the Turkish advance in the Balkans. Nevertheless the crusading idea remained part of Sigismund's imperial ambitions, although even later, when he really was at the head of the empire, his attempts in that direction were handicapped by his persistent hostility against Venice, whose participation would have been indispensable, and by so many other. problems which absorbed Sigismund's versatility.

One of them was the rivalry with Poland, which was conducted in close contact with the Teutonic Order. After years of intrigues, which even as early as 1392 included a first plan for partitioning Poland, the King of Hungary declared war upon her in the critical moments of 1410, and after Grunwald he wanted to act as mediator between Jagiełło, Vytautas, and the Knights of the Cross. A congress held in Buda in 1412 was a first not unsuccessful step in that direction, but at the Council of Constance, where the new king of the Romans hoped to be the arbiter of all Christendom, the Polish opposition to the idea of imperial supremacy shocked him deeply and influenced his position in all Eastern affairs during the following years.

At the same council his role in the tragic fate of John Hus, the Czech reformer to whom he had given a safe conduct and who was nevertheless burned at the stake, had an even greater bearing on the whole further development of Sigismund's policy. In the preceding years it was mainly his brother Venceslas who had to deal with the reform movement in Bohemia, which had been prepared by lively discussion in the second part of the fourteenth century, encouraged and radicalized by the impact of Wycliffe's doctrines, and combined with Czech resentment against the ever-growing German influence in their country. Under the leadership of John Hus, an inspiring preacher, the movement made steady progress in the first years of the fifteenth century, and the wavering attitude of both King Venceslas and the ecclesiastical authorities made the situation even more confused.

The trial of the religious reformer, whom the Czechs also regarded as a national leader, followed the next year, 1416, by the similar fate of one of his disciples, also condemned to death at Constance, raised a storm of indignation in Bohemia. When Venceslas, who tried in vain to appease it, suddenly died in 1419 and was succeeded, as formerly in Germany, by his brother Sigismund, the Hussites refused to recognize as king the man whom they held responsible for the martyrdom of their master. Moreover, all anti-German elements in Bohemia joined the opposition movement, seeing in Sigismund a symbol of German predominance and of Bohemia's ties with the empire. And finally the radical wing of the Hussites put forward a bold program of social reforms.

In the purely religious field, too, the Hussites were divided. The moderates would have been satisfied with concessions which did not touch upon dogmatic problems, particularly the privilege of holy·communion under both species for the laity—hence their designation as *Utraquists* or *Calixtins*. Others went further than Hus himself, and even further than Wycliffe, in their attacks against the Catholic church and its basic teachings and in their utopian request for the official punishment of all sins. That division, doctrinal and social, had its repercussions on Czech policy. A tremendous majority was in agreement as to the desire to get rid of Sigismund of Luxemburg. But while the moderates and those chiefly directed by motives of nationalism wanted to replace him by a member of the Polish-Lithuanian dynasty, the extremists only created trouble for the viceroy whom Vytautas sent to Prague, and started a revolution which was at once religious, national, and social.

Sigismund was particularly afraid of a solution which would connect Bohemia with the Polish-Lithuanian federation to the detriment of his dynasty and possibly also of the empire. Furthermore, for reasons of prestige, he wished to crush the rebellion of his subjects himself. But the radical Hussites, called Taborites, since a mountain named Tabor was their strategic center, found a remarkable military leader in the person of John Žižka. Even after he was killed in action in 1424, his followers, who called themselves "orphans," continued their desperate fight against the king and his Catholic, German, and aristocratic supporters under other chiefs. Of these, Prokop the Bald became particularly famous.

The Hussite wars, ceasing to be an internal revolution in Bohemia, upset the situation in all Central Europe because, on the one hand, the Czechs were making raids far into the neighboring countries, and on the other hand, Sigismund organized a series of "crusades" which, instead of being directed against the Turks, were supposed to destroy the Hussite movement. In spite of the participation of many other German princes, these crusades, one after the other, ended in humiliating defeats and the Taborites became a real military power.

Even Catholic Poland made use of them as auxiliary forces in her struggle against "the whole German nation," which was one of the consequences of Sigismund's shrewd initiative at Lutsk. For after the death of Vytautas, the Polish-Lithuanian conflict continued under his successor Svitrigaila (Świdrygiełło), a brother of Jagiełło who was made grand duke without the constitutional agreement of the Poles. He not only resumed his predecessor's relations with Sigismund, but also, contrary to Lithuania's real interest, made an alliance with the Teutonic Order which, breaking the peace, invaded Poland. The Poles and their Lithuanian partisans opposed another grand duke to Svitrigaila, a brother of Vytautas, called Sigismund, like the Luxemburg, and in addition to the civil war in Bohemia there was now a civil war in Lithuania also, and German powers were interfering with both of them.

Along with all the other problems which threatened the peace of Europe, both issues were brought before the new ecumenical council which was inaugurated at Basle in 1431. The position of the council was, however, even more difficult than that of the Council of Constance because almost from the outset there was a conflict between the council and Pope Eugene IV in matters of ecclesiastical organization and reform. Therefore all those who wanted the support of the church for their political objectives, including Sigismund of Luxemburg who at last, in 1433, obtained the imperial crown from the Pope, were in turn applying to Basle and to the Roman Curia and playing off the council and the Pope against each other. It was only during the short periods of agreement with Eugene IV that the Council of Basle could make constructive contributions to the solution of the problems of the day, including those of East Central Europe.

The most important of these contributions was a negotiated peace with the moderate wing of the Hussites. Cardinal Cesarini, who had himself earlier conducted one of the futile crusades against them, now, as president of the Council of Basle, showed the same spirit of moderation which later made him abandon the radical opposition party at the council and remain loyal to the Holy See. After years of discussion with a Czech delegation which came to Basle, and through representatives of the council sent to Bohemia, the so-called *Compactata* were concluded at Basle in 1433 and approved at Prague the next year. They were based upon the four "articles" prepared at Prague as a minimum program of the Czech reform movement. These requests, including indeed the privilege of the chalice for all receiving communion, did not affect the Catholic doctrine and therefore could be approved by the church. They did not completely satisfy either side and in the future they were subject to controversial interpretations. In Bohemia the compromise was accepted only after the crushing defeat of the radical Hussites by the moderates in the battle of Lipany in 1434. But eventually peace was restored, Bohemia was officially reconciled with the church, and even Sigismund of Luxemburg was recognized as king.

There remained, of course, an internal tension on religious as well as on national grounds, and the Hussite tradition was to affect the whole further development of the Czech people. But without much personal contribution Sigismund at last achieved his aim of uniting the crowns of the Roman Empire, of Bohemia, and Hungary, although Hungary remained outside the empire as in the past. In any case, a large section of East Central Europe, together with West Central Europe, now seemed to be under German leadership, and when the Luxemburg Emperor died in 1437 without leaving a son, he decided to bequeath his three crowns to his son-in-law, Albrecht of Austria, who had married Sigismund's daughter Elizabeth. The political system created by the last Luxemburg would thus also include the Austrian lands of the Habsburgs, and under another German dynasty the whole Danubian region would be united and more or less intimately connected with the empire.

Albrecht was indeed elected in Germany, starting the practically uninterrupted line of Habsburg rulers of the empire. He also obtained the Hungarian succession without difficulty, and only in Bohemia did he have to face a strong opposition which again put forward a member of the Jagellonian dynasty as a national anti-German candidate. This was possible because in the meantime the renewed war between Poland and the Teutonic Order, as well as the civil war in Lithuania, both at least indirectly provoked by the Luxemburg's eastern policy, had ended in 1435 in a victory of the Jagellonian political conception. The Peace of Brześć forced the Knights of the Cross to give up their anti-Polish policy, though they again lost only a very little of their territory. A few months earlier, in the battle on the Święta River, Svitrigaila and his German allies from Livonia were decisively defeated by his rival who had confirmed the union with Poland and received Polish support.

All that happened, however, after the death of the old King, Władysław II Jagiełło in 1434. His son, Władysław III, the new King of Poland, was a minor, and the predominating influence of Bishop Zbigniew Oleśnicki was challenged by a strong opposition party, while in the Lithuanian grand duchy Svitrigaila was still supported in most of the Ruthenian provinces. Under such conditions it proved impossible to promote the candidature of the new king's younger brother Casimir to the throne of Bohemia—a project which Oleśnicki never favored, fearing Hussite influence—and on the contrary, Albrecht of Habsburg was able to resume his father-in-law's idea of playing off Lithuania against Poland.

9

THE LATER FIFTEENTH CENTURY

FROM THE UNION OF FLORENCE TO THE CRUSADE
OF VARNA

One of the reasons for the internal troubles in the grand duchy of Lithuania was the religious difference between the Catholics of Lithuania proper and the Orthodox of her Ruthenian provinces. Svitrigaila, though himself a Catholic, was taking advantage of the dissatisfaction in these provinces which did not share in the privileges of 1387 and 1413 that were reserved to Catholics only. It is true that in 1434 Svitrigaila's rival, Sigismund, issued a new charter of liberties, this time for all parts of the grand duchy without any religious discrimination, and that in the same year the privileges of Polish law and self-government were extended to the Ruthenian lands of the kingdom of Poland. Nevertheless it was obvious that a religious union between Catholics and Orthodox, as already planned by Jagiełło and Vytautas during the Council of Constance, could contribute to the cohesion of the political union and to internal peace in both parts of the federal system.

That problem was part of the larger issue of a reunion between Rome and Constantinople. It had been simultaneously studied at the Council of Basle, to which Emperor John VIII Palaeologus sent an important delegation, hoping thus to obtain much needed assistance against the Turks. In this matter too, however, the regrettable misunderstandings between Pope and council delayed any solution, while the civil war in Lithuania also created unexpected difficulties. In agreement with the Metropolitan of Kiev, Svitrigaila first declared in favor of such a religious union, but he later condemned that metropolitan to be burned at the stake because he suspected him of political treason. In 1436, when Svitrigaila had hardly any real power and while his rival did not show any interest in the union of the churches, the Patriarch of Constantinople appointed another Metropolitan of

Kiev and all the Russias in the person of the noted Greek humanist Isidor. In contradistinction to his unfortunate predecessor, he was at first recognized in Moscow also, and he immediately came there to win that country for the union with Rome which he had already favored at Basle as one of the Greek delegates.

Grand Prince Vasil II authorized him to return to the council at the head of a Russian delegation but on condition that he would not bring back anything "new" to Moscow. In the meantime the pope transferred the council to Italy, where Isidor joined the other delegates of the Eastern church who had arrived from Constantinople. First in Ferrara and later in Florence, where the union was finally concluded on July 6, 1439, the Metropolitan of Kiev greatly contributed to that success and was sent to Russia as cardinal and legate of Eugene IV in order to have the union accepted there. He obtained such a result, however, only in the dioceses which were within the borders of Poland and Lithuania, where he stopped on his way to Moscow. There he was put in jail by Vasil II who rejected all decisions of the council. After escaping from prison, Isidor once more visited the Polish-Lithuanian part of his metropolis, and then went to Rome through Hungary, never to return to Russia.

It was obvious that the Union of Florence had no chance whatever in the Great Russian State in spite of its official acceptance by the Byzantine Empire. On the contrary, when Vasil II had received information that the Greek church was now really reunited with Rome, and when he had defeated his internal opponent in a protracted civil war in which he was supported by the Russian church, in 1448 he gave another metropolitan to that Church, severing its ties with Constantinople. The conception that Moscow was to be the third and final Rome can be traced back to these events which were a further step in the separation of Muscovite Great Russia from the territories of old Kievan *Ruś*, now included in the Jagellonian federation.

The leading role of that federation in all East Central Europe became even more apparent when in 1440, the year after the death of Albrecht II of Habsburg, Władysław III of Poland was elected King of Hungary. There he received Cardinal Isidor on his way back to Rome, and in his privilege of 1443 guaranteed full equality to Catholics of the Eastern rite in the Ruthenian provinces of Poland. In the same year (1440), his brother Casimir was made grand duke of Lithuania after the assassination of Sigismund by leaders of the local aristocracy. Though there remained important controversial problems both constitutional and territorial between Poland and Lithuania, their continued union under the same dynasty was assured.

The Habsburg dynasty, however, not only remained in control of Bohemia, but also opposed Władysław of Poland in Hungary, forcing him to postpone the struggle against the growing Ottoman danger which he had promised to conduct. But when Cardinal Cesarini negotiated an agreement with Austria in 1442, the moment had arrived to make a last effort to liberate the Balkan peoples, saving what remained of the Byzantine Empire and thus securing the Union of Florence.

The first crusade which was undertaken in 1443 under the leadership of the young king and of John Hunyadi, palatine of Transylvania who had defended Hungary's southern frontier in the preceding years, was a great success. In cooperation with the despot of Serbia, George Brankovich, and with the participation of many Polish knights, the Hungarian army advanced through Bulgaria and reached the Balkan Mountains. It was too late in the year to continue in the direction of Constantinople, but the Turks were beaten in several battles and another expedition was planned for the following year, in alliance with Western rulers who on the Pope's invitation had promised to mobilize a Christian fleet and to send it to the Straits.

There were partisans of appeasement in Hungary and in Poland, particularly among those who favored the Council of Basle in its opposition to Eugene IV. Brankovich was also influenced by the peace proposals of the Turks, and in June, 1444, a Hungarian-Serb delegation was sent to Adrianople, then the Turkish capital, and it there concluded a ten-year truce with Murad II. But King Władysław faithful to his earlier engagements, refused to ratify that treaty when Turkish envoys came to Szeged in Hungary. Knowing that the Christian fleet, supplied by the Pope, Venice, Ragusa, and Burgundy, had left for the Straits, that the Turks had transferred their main forces to Asia Minor, and that the Greeks, expecting his help, were advancing from Morea, the Jagellonian undertook his second crusade which in spite of a separate peace made by Brankovich had serious chances of success.

It so happened, however, that the fleet failed to hinder the return of Murad to Europe, and the crusaders therefore met overwhelming forces when they reached Varna on the Bulgarian coast. In the battle of November 10, 1444, King Władysław was killed when he led the main attack in person; Cardinal Cesarini, who had accompanied the army, also lost his life, and the Christian army suffered a serious defeat. The last chance of saving Constantinople was lost, so that the ruin of the Byzantine Empire became unavoidable and the liberation of the Balkans out of the question. Hungary was not invaded by the Turks, and in 1448 Hunyadi again tried to fight them but was beaten at Kossovo, the place of the Serbian defeat of 1389.

That was already under the reign of Ladislas, the son born posthumously to Albrecht II of Habsburg, who after Varna was universally recognized in Hungary and until his death in 1457 ruled that kingdom along with Bohemia and his Austrian lands. Since Frederick III, a descendant of another line of the Habsburgs, was from 1440 King of the Romans and was later to be crowned as emperor, the power of that dynasty and its influence in East Central Europe were increasing in spite of the rather poor qualifications of its representatives. The short Polish-Hungarian Union had ended in the catastrophe of 1444, and only the Polish-Lithuanian Union was strengthened when Casimir succeeded his brother Władysław in Poland.

This, however, was achieved not without difficulties. In Poland, during her king's absence beyond the Carpathians, Bishop Zbigniew Oleśnicki, soon to be the first Polish cardinal, occupied a leading position and wanted Casimir to accept the conditions of election which were unfavorable to the Lithuanians. During the years when Casimir had ruled only in Lithuania, the power of the grand duchy had considerably increased and so had the influence of the local aristocracy which did not sufficiently realize that the relations with the Teutonic Order were still unsettled and that Moscow, after her internal crisis, was aiming at supremacy in Eastern Europe. The Lithuanians not only claimed full equality in a merely personal union with Poland, but also both provinces, Volhynia and Podolia, which from the beginning had been an object of controversy between the two parts of the federation.

The principle of equality, corresponding to the stage of cultural and constitutional development which Lithuania had already reached, was practically recognized at Casimir's Polish election in 1446. After being crowned the following year, he successfully prepared a compromise of the territorial issue, leaving Podolia to Poland and Volhynia to Lithuania, which controlled by far the larger part of the Ruthenian (all White Russian and most of the Ukrainian) provinces, granting them their traditional autonomy. It was therefore under favorable conditions that after years of internal crisis and after the unexpected blow of Varna, the Jagellonian federation entered a new period of its development, forming by far the largest body politic in East Central Europe—the only one which remained completely free from the influence of the neighboring powers—and next to the disintegrating Holy Roman Empire, the largest in all Europe, placed at the exposed limits of what then was the European community.

Before Casimir could begin his constructive activities aiming at an organization of the whole East Central European region, however, he had to liquidate some undertakings of the preceding years which proved beyond the forces of the Jagellonian system. Particularly hopeless was the old ambitious dream of Lithuania to control all the Russias and thus the whole of Eastern Europe. Such plans, considered in the grand duchy as late as 1448, were replaced the following year by a treaty with Moscow which tried to define the spheres of influence of both powers. Even now parts of Great Russia, opposed to Moscow's leadership, particularly the Grand Principality of Tver, were considered to be in the orbit of their traditional ally, Lithuania, which also attempted to find guaranties for the independence of the Russian republics of Novgorod and Pskov.

These possibilities were soon to appear as illusions, but what was a definite mistake was the appeasement in the religious sphere. Soon after the political agreement, the Orthodox metropolitan residing in Moscow, who had helped to negotiate the treaty, was also recognized as head of the Eastern Church in the Ruthenian provinces of the Jagellonian federation. That abandonment of the Union of Florence in the regions where it had the last chance of survival was not yet final and a better solution was discovered a few years later, but it was a serious indication of the growing pressure from the East at a time when equally serious problems had to be faced by Casimir in the West.

CASIMIR THE JAGELLONIAN, GEORGE OF PODĚBRADY, AND MATHIAS CORVINUS

King Casimir had scarcely settled the relations between Poles and Lithuanians and established some kind of *modus vivendi* with Moscow, when early in 1454 he was invited by the subjects of the Teutonic

Order in Prussia to take them under his protection. The oppressive rule of the Knights of the Cross had, indeed, first led to a conspiracy and finally to an open revolt of both the German and the Polish populations of their disintegrating state. In spite of Oleśnicki's hesitation, Casimir decided to accept a proposal which would not only restore to Poland her old Pomeranian province with the flowering port of Danzig, but also unite Prussia proper with the Polish crown, thus completely eliminating the dangerous Order.

There was also a chance for Lithuania to obtain better access to the Baltic Sea because the eastern part of the Order's possession, with the port of Memel at the mouth of the Niemen, was of course destined for the grand duchy. But the troublesome magnates who practically controlled Lithuania did not favor her participation in a war which, thanks to the energetic counteraction of the Order, both military and diplomatic, and to an initial defeat of the Polish forces was to last thirteen years. Although at the beginning almost all the castles of Prussia were occupied by the estates in revolt, and although Danzig proved particularly helpful in financially supporting the struggle, it soon became apparent that eventually the territory of the Order would be divided. In addition to Polish Pomerania, a few districts on the right bank of the Vistula, including the capital Marienburg which had been sold to the Poles in 1457 by the Order's own mercenaries, and the bishopric of Warmia (Ermeland), were definitely liberated from the rule of the Knights. But in spite of an important victory gained in 1462 by the Poles, who also started to use mercenary forces in the exhausting struggle, the eastern part of Prussia with Königsberg as a new capital was left to the Order in the peace treaty which was concluded at Toruń in 1466, through papal mediation after the failure of earlier diplomatic intervention of other powers. But the grand master was to be a vassal of the King of Poland, so that all Prussia was formally incorporated with Poland—the western part, now called Royal Prussia, as an autonomous province, the eastern part as a fief.

Such a solution was far from satisfactory, especially since the Order almost immediately started to claim a revision of the treaty which was never finally approved by either pope or emperor, the traditional protectors of the Order whose grand masters scarcely observed their feudal obligations toward Poland. Nevertheless, the recovery of free access to the Baltic shores, where Danzig was granted a privileged position, was a tremendous success for the kingdom which now reached the height of its power and extended from the Baltic to the Black Sea.

In the course of the war the king had to make new concessions to the nobility, but he succeeded in isolating the opposition of the aristocracy of Little Poland, led by Cardinal Oleśnicki, and the legislative power granted to the provincial dietines in 1454 accelerated the development of parliamentary government. In the second part of Casimir's reign, the Polish Diet (*Sejm*) was already constituted as a bicameral body composed of the King's Council, now called the Senate, and of the Chamber of Deputies elected by the dietines. Nevertheless the power of the king, who tried to preserve a sound balance among all classes of society, was still so great that almost immediately after the Prussian war he could undertake a wide diplomatic action in the interest of his dynasty.

It was, indeed, also in the interest of the Polish nation to have at least dynastic ties with the neighboring countries of Bohemia and Hungary, and it was in the interest of all East Central Europe to be united in a political system which, without being a real federation, guaranteed peace and security under a common dynasty whose members everywhere promoted free national development. The Jagellonians were therefore much more acceptable to the interested populations than were the Habsburgs who represented German penetration and the influence of the empire whose crown had been in their house since 1438.

During the long reign of Emperor Frederick III (1440–93), the power of the Holy Roman Empire was declining more rapidly than ever before. Furthermore, the last descendant of the elder line of the Habsburgs, Ladislas Posthumus, who was king of Bohemia and Hungary, died in 1457. The elections which followed in both kingdoms gave them native kings for the last time in history: George of Poděbrady, a Czech nobleman of Utraquist faith who had already been the able administrator of the country under the young Habsburg, now became King of Bohemia, while Mathias Corvinus, a son of the national hero John Hunyadi, was elected King of Hungary. Both of them hoped to found national dynasties, but not being of royal blood they encountered serious difficulties. And while the Habsburgs never gave up their pretensions to both kingdoms, Casimir Jagiello could also claim the succession, having married Elizabeth, the sister of Ladislas Posthumus. He was, however, waiting until one of his grown-up sons could be freely elected by Czechs or Hungarians or by both, and until the Prussian war would be over.

In the course of that war, in the decisive year 1462, he made an alliance with George of Poděbrady. For the king of Bohemia this was a first step toward the realization of his great design to create a league of European rulers. This league was supposed to replace, in a more efficient form, the medieval unity of Christendom under Pope and Emperor, to secure the common defense against the Turks, and also to promote the ambitious aims of George, who himself hoped to become king of the Romans if not emperor. In spite of the diplomatic action conducted by George's French adviser, Dr. Antoine Marini, of Grenoble, the whole plan, submitted to the Polish Diet, to the Republic of Venice, and to France, hardly had any real chances, and besides the Polish alliance, George succeeded only in making a treaty with Louis XI the next year. These alliances with Catholic kings were particularly valuable at a time when George had to face serious troubles in connection with his religious policy.

Still under the reign of Ladislas Posthumus, had been suppressed the last of the Taborites. What remained of the radical wing of the Hussite movement was organized by an able preacher, Peter Chelčicky, in a purely religious community called the Unity of Czech Brethren. But King George himself, together with the majority of the Czechs, was deeply attached to that moderate form of Hussitism which had been recognized by the Council of Basle but never completely reconciled with Rome. After a protracted conflict with the papacy, in the course of which Pope Pius II revoked the Compactates of Basle, George was excommunicated and deposed as a heretic by Paul II.

While the King of Poland, desirous of gaining the Bohemian crown in agreement with the Czech people themselves, refused to interfere, another neighbor was ready to become executor of the papal decree. It was the King of Hungary. Mathias Corvinus' reign was very successful in spite of the growing Turkish danger which he opposed in the long series of campaigns that followed the heroic defense of Belgrade under his predecessor. He became equally famous as a patron of Renaissance culture, which flowered at his brilliant court in Buda, particularly after his marriage with Beatrice of Aragon. And wishing to make Hungary the leading power in the whole Danubian region, he attacked George of Poděbrady in 1468, resolved to face not only Czech opposition but also the rivalry of the two dynasties of the Jagellonians and of the Habsburgs.

He seemed to be very near to his ambitious aim when a treaty concluded the next year not only gave him immediate control of all lands of St. Václav's crown outside Bohemia proper, i.e., Moravia, Silesia, and Upper Lusatia, but also promised him the succession after George of Poděbrady. But in agreement with the intentions of the latter, the Czech Estates elected Vladislav, eldest son of the King of Poland, when their own king died in 1471.

His father Casimir tried to eliminate Mathias by attacking him in Hungary where an opposition party seemed to favor the candidature of another Polish prince, Vladislav's younger brother, Casimir, the future saint. His expedition ended in failure, however, and the war between Mathias Corvinus and the Jagellonians dragged on until 1478. It ended in the compromise of Olomouc which left to Mathias the occupied provinces and even the title of King of Bohemia, although Vladislav remained the real king of that country.

At the same time, the King of Poland put an end to the cooperation of Mathias with the Teutonic Order, forcing the grand master to respect the treaty of Toruń. But neither Casimir nor his rival succeeded in coming to a lasting agreement with the third power that was interested in the Bohemian succession—the Habsburgs. In what was practically a three-cornered conflict, Emperor Frederick III, seconded toward the end of his reign by his much abler son, Maximilian, opposed both non-German powers only to see a large part of his own Austria, including Vienna, finally occupied by Hungarian forces.

Hungary's predominance in the Danubian region ended, however, with the death of Mathias in 1490. Now Habsburgs and Jagellonians openly opposed each other in claiming his succession. The Hungarians, afraid of German control, decided in favor of the Polish-Lithuanian dynasty. Unfortunately there was an additional rivalry between two sons of King Casimir. A younger one, John Albert, first supported by his father, later acting on his own account, was defeated by the much stronger partisans of his brother, Vladislas of Bohemia, who as duly elected King of Hungary united the two countries in 1491. Such a solution also ended the territorial division of the Bohemian lands, all of them being reunited with Prague, while the common ruler took up his usual residence in Buda. He was soon reconciled with his father and his brother, and Casimir's dynastic plan

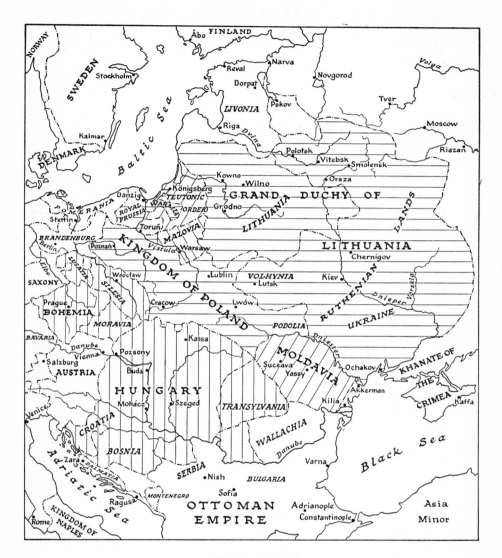

THE JAGELLONIAN STATE SYSTEM, 1492

Poland and Lithuania

Bohemia and Hungary

Vassal states

141

seemed fully achieved when the old king died in 1492, rightly alarmed by new developments in the East.

THE EASTERN QUESTIONS IN THE FIFTEENTH CENTURY

The so-called Eastern question did not originate with the decline of the Ottoman Empire but rather with its rise, and simultaneously with that development in South East Europe similar problems appeared in the northeast of the Continent. For Asiatic pressure upon Europe was never limited to the region around the Straits, but it usually proved no less dangerous in the wide plains north of the Black Sea in the zone of transition between Europe proper and Eurasia. In both cases East Central Europe, exposed to serious dangers from two sides, was the main victim.

In 1453 the Byzantine Empire, which never had been a real threat to any country beyond its original frontiers and during the last centuries of its precarious existence had given up any idea of reconquering its lost territories, was replaced by an aggressive, truly imperialistic power which after the conquest of the Balkans was trying to penetrate into the Danubian region. In the years following the fall of Constantinople the Turks not only occupied the last Greek states—the Despotate of Morea at the southern end of the Balkan Peninsula and the Empire of Trebizond in Asia Minor—but completed the annihilation of Serbia and isolated the last forces of resistance in Albania, a mountain region heroically defended by Alexander Castriota (Skanderbeg) and—like Montenegro—never completely subjugated even after his death. The Turks very soon extended their raids far into the neighboring countries. While, however, the occupation of Italian Otranto in 1480 proved to be only temporary, and though the invasions of Venetian and Austrian border regions were more of a nuisance than a real danger, Hungary and the Danubian principalities were in a very critical position.

The country of the Hunyadis was still strong enough to defend its Danube frontier, even after occasional defeats, and to keep a foothold deep in Bosnia. However, the two principalities, Wallachia and Moldavia, which in the thirteenth and fourteenth centuries had been created by the ancestors of the Rumanians but were rarely united with each other, had to look for the protection of larger Christian states in order to escape the suzerainty of the sultans. The nearest of these neighbors having the same interest in checking the Ottoman advance was indeed Hungary, which included a large Wallachian population in Transylvania. But in spite of close historical ties—the Hunyadis themselves were of Wallachian origin—there was never any real cooperation between Rumanians and Magyars who wanted to connect both Danubian principalities with the Crown of St. Stephen as vassal territories.

Vacillating between Turkish and Hungarian influence, the southern of these principalities, Wallachia, was of course the first to come under Ottoman overlordship which was already well established there at the time of the fall of Constantinople. While in Wallachia Polish influence was only occasional, in spite of the alliance concluded in 1390, Moldavia was looking for the protection of Poland against both Turkey and Hungary. The homage paid by her prince to King Jaggiełło in 1387 was frequently repeated by his successors throughout the fifteenth century. At least one of these Moldavian princes, however, Stephen the Great, succeeded during his long reign (1457–1503) in making his country practically independent of all its neighbors and in defending it rather successfully against repeated Ottoman onslaughts. It was not before the loss of his Black Sea ports, Kilia and Akkerman, in 1484, to Bayezid II, that Stephen, too, tried to obtain Polish assistance by means of homage paid to Casimir the Jagellonian. But he was disappointed because Poland herself, remembering the catastrophe of Varna, did not feel sufficiently prepared to undertake the struggle with the Ottoman Empire. When she finally did so in 1497, under Casimir's son, John Albert, a tragic misunderstanding made Poles and Moldavians turn against each other and ended in a defeat of the Polish king in the forests of the Bukovina. This was followed by the first Turkish invasions which reached far into Poland.

Poland had entered the war with a view to retaking not only the Moldavian ports from the Muslims, but also the equally important trade center of Caffa in the Crimea, a Genoese colony which in 1462 had placed itself under Polish protection but which was conquered by the Turks in 1475. The fall of Caffa was of especial significance because it also enabled the Ottoman Empire to turn the Tartar khanate of the Crimea into a vassal state which could be used against Christian neighbors at any time. Of these neighbors, Lithuania, in cooperation with Poland, had originally promoted the creation of the Crimean Khanate—a further step in the gradual disintegration of the Golden

Horde which seemed to be the most dangerous enemy. The new Crimean dynasty, the Gireys, who ruled there for almost four hundred years, was indeed an ally of the Jagellonians until the death of Hadshi Girey, the most prominent of them, in 1466. But subsequent internal troubles in the Crimea resulted in the victory of Hadshi's ambitious son, Mengli, who, after being seized by the Turks at Caffa, returned a few years later as their vassal. Through frequent raids, he not only practically cut off Lithuania and Poland from their Black Sea coast but replaced his father's alliance with King Casimir by an alliance with Ivan III of Moscow.

Mengli Girey had, indeed, a common interest with the powerful grand prince who had succeeded his father, Vasil II, in 1462. Ivan considered it one of his main objectives to liberate Moscow from the overlordship of the Golden Horde, the deadly enemy of the Crimean Khanate. But an even more important objective of Ivan III's policy was the unification under Moscow's leadership of all the Russias. After his conquest of the Republic of Novgorod in 1478, which completely upset the balance of power in Eastern Europe, and after his conquest of Tver in 1485, which liquidated the last independent state between Moscow and Lithuania, the unification of all Great Russian lands was achieved and Ivan III started raising claims to the White Russian and Ukrainian territories of Lithuania.

These claims were based upon dynastic and religious arguments since these territories of the old Kievan State had once been under the same Rurik dynasty whose Muscovite branch Ivan now represented, and because all Eastern Slavs professed the Orthodox faith. For that very reason, Casimir the Jagellonian, after trying to appease Moscow even in matters of ecclesiastical organization, had welcomed the return of his Ruthenian subjects to the Union of Florence. A metropolitan sent from Rome in 1458 was residing in Kiev and extending his authority as far as the political boundaries between Lithuania and Moscow. That separation of old Kievan *Ruś* from the metropolitans of Moscow was to become permanent, but even the metropolitans of Kiev did not safeguard the union with Rome which a few of them tried to revive in the following decades but without much success. Nevertheless the White Russian and Ukrainian lands were definitely in a cultural sphere which was completely different from that of Moscow, and they were also under a different form of government which, while respecting their autonomy, intimately connected them with the European community. East Central Europe, to which they now belonged through a political federation, was undoubtedly part of that community, while Muscovite Russia, although freeing herself from Tartar rule, developed along entirely different lines. It was Ivan III, who in 1472 through his marriage with Zoë (Sophia), the heiress of the Palaeologi dynasty, greatly contributed to the political conception of Moscow as the Third Rome. He was building up another aggressive empire and threatening all his Western neighbors from Swedish Finland in the north to Kiev in the south, which at his instigation was sacked by the Tartars of the Crimea in 1482.

Ivan used these Muslim allies against Casimir whom he did not dare attack directly, and similarly the Polish king and his successors would occasionally use the Tartars of the Golden Horde against Moscow. Through a strange reversal of alliances these Tartars were now usually on the Lithuanian side. Between Lithuania and Moscow there developed a tense situation of neither war nor peace which Ivan III utilized in order to occupy some border regions. These changes of the frontier were of limited importance but they created dangerous precedents and prepared the way for open aggression against Lithuania immediately after Casimir's death in 1492.

That fateful year was the beginning of a long series of wars which in Eastern European history had an importance similar to that of the Italian wars of the same period in the history of Western Europe. Lithuania was now under a separate grand duke, one of Casimir's numerous sons, Alexander, who closely cooperated with his brother John Albert, the new King of Poland, and even with Vladislav of Hungary and Bohemia. But he did not receive adequate assistance, and in the peace treaty of 1494 he had to make the first territorial cessions to Moscow. These did not vitally affect the position of Lithuania, and Alexander hoped to appease his dangerous neighbor by marrying Ivan's daughter Helen on the same occasion. But it was precisely that marriage which gave her father new opportunities for raising controversial issues by complaining, contrary to Helen's own assurances, that she did not enjoy the promised freedom of worship in her Orthodox faith. At the same time, modest attempts at restoring the Union of Florence were branded by Ivan as persecution of the Orthodox Church. And as soon as the Polish defeat in Moldavia had affected the prestige of the whole Jagellonian dynasty, the grand prince of Moscow launched another much more violent attack against Lithuania in 1500.

Ivan was able to keep all his initial conquests which at this time reached deep into the White Russian and Ukrainian lands almost to the gates of Smolensk and Kiev. In 1501 Alexander was also elected King of Poland, succeeding his brother, and had made alliances with the German Knights of Livonia in the north and with the last Khan of the Golden Horde in the south. In 1502 the latter was completely destroyed by Moscow's ally, the Khan of Crimea, the isolated successes on the Livonian front were of no avail, and in 1503 only a precarious armistice could be concluded. Having renewed the union between the two countries in 1501, the Lithuanians negotiated together with the Poles, and the king of Hungary and Bohemia acted as mediator. But the Jagellonians could not concentrate in the eastern direction because they had to face growing difficulties on an equally long western front, from Prussia to Buda, at the same time.

10

FROM THE FIRST CONGRESS OF VIENNA TO THE UNION OF LUBLIN

JAGELLONIANS AND HABSBURGS BEFORE AND AFTER THE FIRST CONGRESS OF VIENNA (1515)

The Habsburgs never accepted their defeat in the Hungarian election after Mathias Corvinus. They not only immediately reoccupied the lost Austrian territories, but they were resolved to realize their old plan of uniting Hungary and possibly also Bohemia with Austria. Their rivalry with the Jagellonians, who had gained both kingdoms for themselves, was therefore more acute than ever before and led to a first rapprochement between Austria and Russia, the eastern enemy of the Polish-Lithuanian dynasty. Negotiations between Vienna and Moscow which started under Emperor Frederick III in the eighties, parallel to Ivan III's negotiations with Casimir's other opponents including Mathias Corvinus, were now continued with a view to encircling the Jagellonian state system. At the same time there was a danger that the energy and versatility of the new emperor, Maximillian I, would create internal difficulties for Vladislav of Hungary, using the partisans of the Habsburgs in that country who were few in number but who belonged to some of the most powerful families.

The Jagellonians reacted by secretly discussing the possibilities of cooperation among the three brothers who ruled Poland, Lithuania, Bohemia, and Hungary, including also their two younger brothers: Frederick, who led the Polish hierarchy as primate archbishop of Gniezno, bishop of Cracow, and finally also cardinal, and Sigismund, who was growing up at the court of Buda. When, after the discussions of John Albert and Alexander at the Polish-Lithuanian border, they all met in 1496 at Levocsa, in Hungary, they were also joined by their brother-in-law, Frederick of Brandenburg. The matrimonial relations of the Jagellonians with some of the minor German dynasties seemed to become particularly valuable at a time when the Teutonic

Order, after the death of a grand master who proved loyal to Poland and who participated in the ill-fated expedition of 1497, elected as successor one of the princes of the Empire, Frederick of Saxony, who refused to pay the homage due to the Polish king according to the treaty of 1466.

That tension in the relations with the Teutonic Knights was the problem which most seriously troubled the end of John Albert's reign. Popular among the gentry, whose privileges he had extended at the Diets of 1493 and 1496 at the expense of burghers and peasants, after his defeat in Moldavia he lost much of his authority, which an Italian exile, the humanist Philip Callimachus Buonaccorsi, advised him to strengthen according to the Renaissance pattern. Such councils proved entirely impracticable in Poland, but in the field of political relations, great possibilities seemed to open up when in 1500 an alliance was concluded in Buda between the Jagellonian brothers and two Western powers, France and Venice.

Allegedly directed against the Turks, that treaty was an answer to the German-Russian encirclement of East Central Europe. It integrated the Jagellonian kingdoms into the general European state system and seemed to guarantee a valuable support against the Habsburgs and also indirectly against the Teutonic Order which the Empire continued to protect. It so happened, however, that the following year John Albert unexpectedly died at the very moment when he was preparing an energetic action against the Knights of the Cross and planning to marry a French princess. Her sister became the wife of Vladislav of Hungary and Bohemia, but the weakness of this king's rule was another reason, in addition to the Russian invasion of Alexander's grand duchy, why the high hopes of the turn of the century did not materialize.

Under such conditions, Habsburg pressure increased in Buda where in 1505 the Diet decided never again to elect a foreigner as king. Alexander, who from 1501 had also been King of Poland, made no progress in settling the Prussian problem, and his struggle against the supremacy of the senatorial families ended in the compromise of 1505. This was the famous constitution *Nihil Novi* which confirmed the legislative power of both houses of the Diet, and promised that "nothing new" would be decreed without their joint consent. But while in Hungary and Bohemia the aging Vladislav was to continue his policy of appeasement for another decade and in 1514 the constitutional privileges of the Hungarian nobility were fixed in Stephen Verböcsy's *Tripartitum,* Alexander, who died in 1506, was followed in both Lithuania and Poland by his youngest brother, Sigismund, who was to be the leading personality in all East Central Europe until his death in 1548.

A man of refinement and culture, which he acquired at the court of Buda, and trained in government as Vladislav's viceroy in Silesia, he was also anxious to solve through peaceful methods the big problems which he had to face. He tried to establish a lasting peace not only in his relations with the West but also in the East, after the failure of an attempt to regain Lithuania's territorial losses in a first war against Vasil III, the son and successor of Ivan III. There continued, however, the cooperation of Moscow and Vienna against the two closely united surviving Jagellonian brothers. At the same time Maximilian I supported the new grand master of the Teutonic Order, another prince of the Empire, Albrecht of Brandenburg, of the Hohenzollern family. He was elected in 1510 after Frederick of Saxony, and though he was a nephew of the King of Poland he decided to obtain a revision of the Toruń treaty by any means. And Vasil III, encouraged by a rebellion in Lithuania which was led by Prince Michael Gliński—an exceptional case in view of the loyalty of the tremendous majority even among the Orthodox Ruthenian population—was preparing further aggression in cooperation with that ambitious exile of Tartar origin.

In the war which Moscow started in 1512, breaking the "eternal" peace of 1508, the main attack was directed against Smolensk. When the two first sieges of that strategically important White Russian city ended in failure, Vasil persuaded the envoy of Maximilian I to conclude in Moscow a treaty which, going beyond the Emperor's intentions, pledged him to join in the struggle against Sigismund I. With Albrecht of Prussia also ready for action after the breakdown of protracted negotiations, and the Crimean Tartars as a permanent threat at the southeastern border, the situation of Poland and Lithuania indeed became critical after the fall of Smolensk in 1514. Seizing that opportunity for pressing his claims to Hungary and Bohemia, the Emperor was planning a congress on German territory where Sigismund and Vladislav would practically surrender in all controversial issues.

But only a few weeks later, in the same year, the great victory of Orsza, won by the Lithuanians under the leadership of Prince Constantine Ostrogski, the most powerful Orthodox Ruthenian magnate, assisted by Polish forces, altogether changed the situation. Welcomed even in distant Rome as a decisive victory of the Western world, that battle did not regain Smolensk, lost for almost a century, but made the Emperor decide in favor of an understanding with the Jagellonians to be negotiated at a congress which started in Pozsony (Pressburg), Hungary, where Sigismund, with his Polish and Lithuanian advisers, joined the King of Hungary and Bohemia.

That congress of 1515 can be called a first Congress of Vienna, three hundred years before the famous one, because it was concluded in the Austrian capital after Maximilian I had met his guests near the frontier. The consequences of that meeting were to prove of primary significance for the history of East Central Europe. The three monarchs, all humanists of distinction, rather liked one another upon becoming personally acquainted. The Emperor promised no longer to support either the grand prince of Moscow against Lithuania or the grand master in Prussia against Poland, but to act as a friendly mediator, advising Albrecht to pay his homage to the king and Vasil III to stop his aggressions. For these concessions made to Sigismund I, Maximilian of course expected some compensation with respect to the succession in Hungary and Bohemia. But no treaty which would guarantee that succession to the Habsburgs after the extinction of the elder branch of the Jagellonians was signed in Vienna. Only a double wedding was celebrated. Vladislav's only son, Louis, married the Emperor's granddaughter Mary, while Maximilian himself was married *per procuram* to Vladislav's daughter Ann, acting for one of his grandsons, Charles or Ferdinand.

These matrimonial alliances of course increased the influence of the Habsburgs and the chances of their succession in both kingdoms, but in 1515 it was impossible to foresee which dynasty would be extinguished first. Vladislav died the next year, and Ferdinand of Austria, who finally married his daughter, soon started to organize a pro-Habsburg party among the Hungarian magnates. But before the fate of Hungary and Bohemia was decided, Sigismund I, acting as tutor of his nephew, had an opportunity to play a rather important part in the imperial election in 1519 after the death of Maximilian I.

Poland did not want to alienate the Habsburgs once again, and she hoped that Charles V would continue the policy which his grandfather had promised to follow at the Congress of Vienna in 1515. Therefore, though neither the Prussian issue was settled nor peace with Moscow secured through Habsburg mediation, the Polish envoys at the Election Diet of Augsburg, acting jointly with the representatives of the minor King of Bohemia, managed not to side with the French candidate, Francis I. The new Emperor, whose main interests were in the West, never did turn against the Jagellonians and he continued to send missions to Moscow with peace suggestions, presented by the famous Sigismund von Herberstein. But, just like the abortive papal interventions, being dictated by illusory hopes of gaining Moscow for a religious union, these diplomatic actions never had any concrete results and hardly contributed to the armistice of 1522 which did not restore any of her losses to Lithuania. Furthermore, already in 1519 Poland had to decide for a war against the grand master, who not only refused due homage but also conspired with all her neighbors in view of a simultaneous aggression. When that war proved inconclusive, and here too a mere armistice had to be signed in 1521, it was agreed that once more the Habsburgs, together with Louis of Hungary and Bohemia, would act as mediators. But as a matter of fact, as in the past, they favored the Teutonic Order, and Ferdinand was only waiting for a change in the Hungarian situation to put forward the old claims of his dynasty. Such a change, giving a new significance to the Vienna decisions of 1515, was to occur in 1526, preceded in 1525 by an entirely unexpected turn of the Prussian issue.

THE SECULARIZATION OF PRUSSIA AND THE CONSEQUENCES OF MOHÁCS

In comparison with the Jagellonians and the Habsburgs—the two main rivals in East Central Europe—at the beginning of the sixteenth century the Hohenzollern dynasty seemed to have rather limited possibilities of action in that region. It is true that they ruled in the March of Brandenburg for about a hundred years. But that originally Slavic territory was by now almost completely Germanized except for the small group of Lusatian Sorbs at the border between Brandenburg and Saxony. Projects for gaining the Polish crown for a Hohenzollern, soon after their establishment in Berlin, had failed, and as electors they seemed to be chiefly interested in the problems of Germany. And it was in distant Franconia, near the Swabian cradle of the family, that the younger branch of the Hohenzollerns was ruling the tiny duchy of Ansbach.

It was, however, precisely a member of that side line who as grand master of the Teutonic Order transferred his activities to Prussia and revived the Order's old conflict with Poland. Gradually he had to realize that neither Pope nor Emperor was willing or able to give more than occasional moral support to the disintegrating community of the once powerful Knights of the Cross, and before the armistice of 1521 had expired, Albrecht of Hohenzollern decided to reverse his policy completely, thus revealing his real personal and dynastic ambitions. Fully aware of the progress of Lutheranism in Prussia, he himself joined the new faith, dissolved the Order, and turned its Prussian territory into a secular duchy. Of course he needed a protector against the claims of what remained of the Order in Germany, where another grand master was elected, and even more against the indignation of Rome which was shared by Charles V. Such protection he could find only in Poland. Therefore he was now ready to recognize the frontier fixed in 1466 and the suzerainty of the king, if recognized, in turn, as hereditary "Duke in Prussia."

The decision which Sigismund I had to make was a very difficult one. A devout Catholic who just had repressed a Lutheran rebellion in Danzig, he was deeply shocked by Albrecht's apostasy. But on the other hand, this seemed a unique opportunity for at last getting rid of the traditionally hostile Order and severing all ties between the part of Prussia, which was not directly subject to the authority of the king of Poland, and any foreign power. When Albrecht accepted the condition that the duchy should be hereditary only in the Ansbach line of the Hohenzollerns, and that it should return to the Polish crown after the extinction of the male descendants of himself and his three brothers, an agreement was reached. On April 15, 1525, on the market square of Cracow, the duke paid the king the homage which he had refused as grand master.

The establishment of the Hohenzollerns in East Prussia was to prove extremely dangerous for Poland. Her own province of "Royal-Prussia"—old Polish Pomerania—was now placed between the possessions of two branches of the same ambitious German dynasty. It soon became apparent that the electoral branch in Brandenburg would henceforth consider its main objective to be that of obtaining hereditary rights in "Ducal Prussia," a first step in the direction of creating a new great power at the expense of Poland and another means for effecting German penetration far into East Central Europe.

These future developments were difficult to foresee, however, at a moment when the attention of Sigismund I and of his advisers, all eager to avoid violent conflicts, was distracted by other urgent problems. Comparatively easy was the incorporation into the kingdom of that part of Mazovia, with Warsaw, where a side line of the old Piast dynasty ruled as vassals of the crown until the death of the last of them in 1526. The regional autonomy which for a certain time had to be guaranteed to that purely Polish province was no danger to the unity of the realm. But in the same year the long-feared invasion of Hungary by Suleiman the Magnificent shook the very foundations of the Jagellonian state system.

The attack had been expected since, at least, 1521, when the Turks had conquered Belgrade, the gate to Hungary. The Hungarians themselves were divided into partisans of the Habsburgs, who counted in vain on Austrian help against the Muslim, and a national party, opposed to German influence and to a decisive struggle against the sultan's overwhelming power, in which, as they anticipated, the Hungarians would be left alone. This actually happened in the critical summer of 1526 when their army, assisted only by a few Polish volunteers, was crushed in the battle of Mohács on August twenty-ninth. Like his grand uncle at Varna, young King Louis lost his life in the defense of Christendom. The elder line of the Jagellonians disappeared with him.

That defeat had far-reaching consequences for all East Central Europe. Ferdinand I of Austria, backed by the prestige of his brother Charles V who a year before had defeated the Western opponent of the Habsburgs, Francis I of France, in the battle of Pavia, immediately seized the opportunity to realize at last the old design of his dynasty to gain the crowns of both Bohemia and Hungary. Sigismund I of Poland saw no possibility of claiming the succession of his nephew. His only son, Sigismund Augustus, was a minor. This son had been born to Sigismund I in 1520 by his Italian wife, Bona Sforza, whom he had married in 1518 and who was strongly opposed to the Habsburgs. The aging king himself could hardly govern two more countries. In the East he was threatened by Moscow and the Tartars, and he had achieved no success with his plan for a French alliance. Thus the only presumptive rival practically abandoned the field to Ferdinand, who was first unanimously elected in Bohemia and a few months later in Hungary also. In the latter country, how-

ever, only by the aristocratic leaders of the pro-Habsburg party. The
opposition, which included a majority of the gentry, had already
elected a native Hungarian a few weeks earlier. This was John
Zápolya, the palatine of Transylvania.

The partisans of Zápolya were the first to realize that Habsburg
rule in Hungary as well as in Bohemia meant the end of national independence and of the rights of the Estates, a strong German penetration, and the predominance of royal authority. Criticized for their
weakness, the Jagellonian kings had never represented any similar
danger, and their replacement by Ferdinand, an event which is sometimes considered the origin of the Danubian Habsburg monarchy
of the future, ended the cooperation of both medieval kingdoms with
the Polish-Lithuanian Federation in a free East Central Europe.

In the case of Hungary, Mohács proved an even greater catastrophe. Because of the twofold election which followed the defeat in
a foreign war, before that conflict was over the country entered into
a protracted civil war. Zápolya, whose sister had been the first wife
of Sigismund I, hoped for the support of the King of Poland and
indeed enjoyed much Polish sympathy. But the Jagellonian who had
not opposed the Habsburgs even in his own interest was still less inclined to fight them in favor of Zápolya. He limited himself to a
mediation which had no chance of success and to granting Hungary's
national king an asylum on Polish soil at a critical moment of his
struggle. Even so, Poland's relations with the Habsburgs naturally
deteriorated, especially when she refused to side with them in their
war against Suleiman the Magnificent.

Such a war necessarily developed, since the sultan, eager to control
defeated Hungary himself, was not prepared to tolerate Habsburg
domination in that country. In 1529 the Turks besieged Vienna for
the first time. They had to withdraw but they continued to support
Zápolya who, finding no other ally, turned to Hungary's traditional
foe. Under these conditions Sigismund I had to observe an even
stricter neutrality. He was fully aware that Zápolya's cooperation
with the Turks would ultimately lead to their domination in most of
Hungary, a domination which for Poland would be even more dangerous than Habsburg rule on the other side of the Carpathians. At
the same time, however, he was eager to avoid an open conflict with
the Ottoman Empire which could at any time launch its Tartar vassal,
the khan of the Crimea, against Poland and Lithuania.

Even so, these Tartar neighbors in the southeast were a permanent nuisance, and some of their repeated invasions were a real threat to the normal development of the Ukraine, as the Ruthenian border regions of the Lithuanian grand duchy were called from the sixteenth century on. Through these poorly defended southern provinces of the Lithuanian state, the Tartar raids quite frequently penetrated far into the Ruthenian provinces of Poland, which in addition had to suffer from unsettled relations with Moldavia. Formerly vassals of Poland, the Moldavian princes, though more and more threatened by the Turks who controlled Wallachia, now claimed a relatively small frontier district in the Carpathian Mountains which became a source of endless trouble between the two countries. A Polish victory in 1531 brought no decisive change in that tense situation, just as the successful resistance of Austrian forces against the Turkish pressure at the Austro-Hungarian border in the following year hardly affected the chaos and anarchy south of Poland. It was therefore only natural that Sigismund I should continue a cautious external policy as well as his efforts to secure a better defense of his own country.

What might sometimes seem a policy of appeasement becomes understandable if in addition to growing dangers on all fronts, including the Russian, where Lithuania could only make short armistices, the internal problems of the Jagellonian Federation are considered. In both component parts constitutional reforms were being studied. These would give the common ruler necessary financial means for organizing a permanent defense of the frontiers. With a view to strengthening the position of the dynasty, Sigismund I, at the queen's suggestion, had his son elected grand duke of Lithuania and then also king of Poland during his own lifetime. But when this action resulted in the coronation of Sigismund Augustus, then ten years old, in 1530, his father was still far from having settled all the difficulties caused by the growing power of the Polish Diet and by the rivalries of a few leading aristocratic families in Lithuania.

THE HEIGHT OF OTTOMAN PRESSURE IN
EAST CENTRAL EUROPE

The rise of Ottoman power and the pressure which that new empire exercised upon Europe as a whole until the end of the seventeenth century was always facilitated by the lack of unity among the Christian powers. In the days of Suleiman the Magnificent, when the danger threatening Europe from a completely conquered Balkan Peninsula was greatest, both the Protestant Reformation and the hostility between the Habsburg and Valois dynasties made a common front of all Christendom quite impossible. These Western developments also deeply affected the situation in East Central Europe. The diplomacy of Francis I of France, who in 1536 had made a formal alliance with the sultan, supported all opponents of the Habsburgs in the Danubian region but proved unable to help them in their struggle for freedom from both German and Turkish predominance.

In 1538 a serious effort was made in Hungary to put an end to the disastrous civil war and to find a compromise solution. Another Turkish success in the neighboring country of Moldavia, which in that very year definitely came under the overlordship of the Ottoman Empire, as had Wallachia, was a serious warning. The advisers of John Zápolya, including Croat and Italian diplomats who knew the Turkish danger through long experience, now, after many hesitations, arrived at the conviction that an understanding with Ferdinand I was preferable. They negotiated the treaty of Nagyvárad (Grosswardein) which temporarily sanctioned the division of Hungary between the two rival kings but envisaged the unification of the country under the Habsburg after his opponent's childless death. But the next year Zápolya married Izabel, a daughter of the King of Poland, and when a son, John Sigismund, was born to him, he tried to revise the agreement. After his death in 1540 there was again a strong party among the Hungarians who opposed the unpopular Ferdinand and supported the claims of Zápolya's widow in favor of her minor child.

This was, of course, an excellent occasion for more Turkish interference. Pretending to defend the rights of John Sigismund, Suleiman once more invaded Hungary. In 1541 he occupied Buda where a Turkish pasha was to have his see for almost a century and a half. It soon became obvious that the unhappy country would henceforth be divided not only in two but in three parts: the central portion, by far the largest, under direct Ottoman control; a border region along the northern and western frontiers occupied by Austrian forces; and a semi-independent Transylvania left to the Zápolya family.

Ferdinand I tried in vain to expel the Turks, but absorbed by the problems of Germany, where he supported his brother, Charles V, against the Protestant princes, he had to make peace with Suleiman in

1547, to whom he even promised a yearly tribute from his section of Hungary. It seemed much easier for the Habsburgs to act against the Zápolyas with a view to adding at least Transylvania to their small share in the partition of Hungary. Here, however, they also met the opposition of Poland because Sigismund I, and after his death in 1548, his son and successor Sigismund Augustus, wanted to protect Izabel and her child. In full agreement with all Hungarian patriots, Sigismund I considered Transylvania the nucleus of an independent Hungary, since even the Turks found it difficult to penetrate into that isolated mountain region.

Negotiations with Ferdinand I were resumed, however, by the same diplomat, the Franciscan friar George Martinuzzi, who had been instrumental in preparing the agreement of 1538. Now, fourteen years later, a somewhat similar plan was being discussed. The Habsburg King of Hungary was once more supposed to succeed the Zápolyas, taking over Transylvania too, on condition that he would assure the defense of the country against the Turks and compensate John Sigismund and his ambitious mother in Silesia. But the Habsburgs were neither able nor willing to fulfill these conditions, and furthermore they distrusted their opponents to such an extent that Martinuzzi was murdered at the order of one of the Austrian generals.

Any agreement had thus become impossible, and Transylvania was constituted as an entirely separate body politic, first under the rule of John Sigismund Zápolya and after his death in 1571 under another family of the Hungarian aristocracy, the Báthorys. These princes of Transylvania, as well as their successors in the following century, were all eager to prepare the liberation of Hungary from both Germans and Turks. But they barely succeeded in gaining a few frontier counties of Hungary proper and had to be satisfied with creating within the limits of their principality, especially in its capital Koloszvár, a center of national life where in an atmosphere of unusual religious tolerance various Protestant and even anti-Trinitarian groups, who were also opposed to the Catholic Habsburgs, found possibilities of development.

The constitution of autonomous Transylvania was based upon the cooperation of three officially recognized "nations," out of which two, the Hungarians proper and the Széklers in the southeastern part of the country were ethnically Magyar, while the third was formed by the numerous Germans, called Saxons, particularly in the cities. The majority of the population were Wallachs, however, and being mostly composed of peasants they did not enjoy any political rights. They were indeed part of the people, now called Rumanians, who had their own principalities in Wallachia and Moldavia but had little interest in uniting with them, since these eastern neighboring countries were even more strictly controlled by the Turks.

It is true that time and again princes appeared, particularly in Moldavia, who tried to liberate themselves from Ottoman suzerainty. As in the preceding century, some of them preferred to recognize Polish overlordship, and there were, in the times of Sigismund Augustus, repeated Polish interventions in Moldavian affairs. They mainly resulted, however, not from the king's own initiative, since, like his father, he tried to avoid an open conflict with the Ottoman Empire, but rather from projects of individual magnates, sometimes acting in understanding with the Habsburgs.

In that distant region the Habsburgs used some of their Polish partisans because divided Hungary was of course unable to resume her earlier attempts at placing the Danubian principalities under her influence. But both Ferdinand I, Roman Emperor after the abdication of Charles V in 1556, and after Ferdinand's death in 1564, his successor Maximilian II, continued to oppose Suleiman the Magnificent directly in Hungary, always eager to bring the whole of it under their domination. The war of 1566 ended, however, with the loss of the important fortress of Szigetvár, whose siege became equally famous through the heroic defense of the city by Count Nicholas Zrinyi (Zrinski, a Hungarian leader of Croat origin, whom both peoples consider a national hero) and through the death of the sultan just before its conquest.

Even the decline of Turkey's power after the disappearance of the last of an interrupted line of great sultans, notable already under Suleiman's insignificant son Selim II, hardly affected the situation in Hungary. Only a league of Christian powers, persistently recommended by the Holy See, could have liberated the territories conquered by the Ottomans. Yet the only joint action which materialized in the second half of the sixteenth century was limited to the sea, where it achieved the famous victory of Lepanto in 1571. Toward the end of the century, under Emperor Rudolf II, the Habsburgs alone undertook an expedition which was supposed to reconquer Hungary. But after an initial success of the imperial forces and a Turkish victory at Keresztes in 1596, the protracted war ended with the Treaty of Zsitva Torok in 1606. Though this treaty marked the end of Ottoman advance and supremacy, it did not change the frontier but left most of the country in Turkish hands.

That Austrian effort was not at all coordinated with the simultaneous action of the most prominent prince of Wallachia, Michael the Brave, who at the same time tried to liberate all Rumanian peoples from Turkish domination and to unite them in a national state. Since he wanted to include Transylvania, which the Habsburg kings of Hungary hoped to regain for themselves, he was also obliged to fight against Austrian forces. It was precisely by them that he was killed in 1600 after clashing with Poland in Moldavia, where the Movila dynasty, supported by related Polish families, checked Turkish influence only temporarily.

Turkish rule was of course particularly severe where it was exercised directly, with no autonomous national authority protecting the conquered peoples. It is true that at the time of the greatness of the Ottoman Empire its administration was efficient and in general even tolerant. But after centuries of freedom and cultural development, the Christian population of central Hungary suffered a fate similar to that which for a much longer period deprived all the Balkan peoples of any dignified existence and active historical role, with all their resources exploited by a foreign government, and their most promising male children taken away from them to serve as Janizaries fighting for the sultan.

Hungary's position at the extreme limits of the Ottoman Empire was even worse with regard to the immediate consequences of the almost uninterrupted warfare. The devastation of war did not reach the Balkan territories, which were now well at the center of the empire. But in addition to southern Hungary, which had already been badly ruined by frequent Turkish invasions that took place before the actual conquest began, the whole belt along the dividing line between the two parts of Hungary proper was now thoroughly devastated. That area served as a defense against the Habsburgs and taxes had to be paid both to the Turks and to the local administration that was left in Hungarian hands.

Some self-government survived in the central part of Hungary, especially in large "peasant towns" where helpless people joined together to find a little more security and tolerable conditions of life.

But most regrettable was the temporary disappearance of all the old centers of national culture, including Buda itself, which had been largely destroyed, the burned palaces being replaced by Turkish barracks or mosques. And that center of the country was completely cut off, both from Transylvania and from the northern and western counties of Hungary and Croatia which escaped Turkish domination only to be controlled by the Austrian military authorities.

THE HABSBURG ADVANCE IN EAST CENTRAL EUROPE

At the very time when the area of free East Central Europe was so greatly reduced by Ottoman conquest, foreign penetration and pressure was also advancing from the West. The progress of the Catholic Habsburgs, representing the Western world, was of course something entirely different from the invasion by an Asiatic power, alien in religion and culture, which after annihilating all freedom and independence in South East Europe was starting a similar procedure in a large part of the Danubian region. But what remained of that region was also unable to develop freely on the ground of national tradition. The rule of the Habsburgs, though much less despotic and ruthless than the sultan's domination, was gradually curtailing the rights of the Estates. With German Austria as a territorial basis and with the imperial crown of Germany as a symbol, it represented a trend toward Germanization and centralization around a foreign source of authority. It would be anachronistic to identify the Habsburg regime, particularly in the age of Charles V, that King of Spain whom so many Germans opposed as a foreigner, with any German nationalism in the modern sense or to see in the cosmopolitan court of the emperors a center of German life. But in the eastern section of what Charles V, with the assistance of his brother Ferdinand, tried to merge into a universal empire, the German element was the main unifying force and the strongest support of Habsburg domination. This was rapidly developing in the direction of a more or less enlightened absolutism.

In the century which followed the elections after Mohács, a clear distinction must be made in all these respects between the two kingdoms gained by the Habsburgs, namely, Bohemia and Hungary. Of the latter, they really controlled so small a part which was in such a precarious condition of quasi-permanent war or threat of war, that their administration could hardly be considered a real test of Habsburg rule in Hungary. But even those Hungarians who definitely preferred it to the Ottoman yoke were soon to realize that here, too, they were under a foreign government which considered northern and western Hungary merely a fragment of alien territory, good only to serve as a defense for the empire.

Even that defense was so inadequate that it only exposed that "free" part of the artificially and arbitrarily divided country to devastating Turkish raids. Already under Ferdinand I and Maximilian II, but even more so under Rudolf II (1576–1612), the Hungarians complained that the German emperors who called themselves their kings sorely neglected Hungarian interests. They indeed defended the interests of Catholicism, the faith to which the majority of the Hungarians remained deeply attached. But such of them as had turned Calvinist at the time of the Reformation and were completely free in Transylvania were persecuted under the Habsburg regime, which was identified with the Counter Reformation, to an extent and in a way that was rather harmful to the Catholic church. For the cause of Hungary's freedom seemed to be intimately connected with the defense of religious liberty for the Calvinists. The protest of the Diet of 1604 was highly significant in that respect.

The Diets of which the Hungarians were so proud lost more and more of their importance because the king, who was at the same time German emperor, hardly paid much attention to the deliberations of a body which in any event could represent only a small part of historic Hungary's territory. Unable to convene in Turkish-occupied Buda, the Diets usually met in Pozsony (Pressburg), practically the capital of "free" Hungary. But even in that city which in the past had been an important cultural center, with a university founded in the brilliant period of Mathias Corvinus, these cultural activities could hardly develop since the Turkish border was now so close. All this was the more regrettable because obviously the liberation from the Turks of the other major part of Hungary could only be achieved under Habsburg leadership, with their section of the country as a basis for operations. And it was equally apparent that the conditions created in that narrow section under the Habsburg regime would then prevail in all Hungary.

In Bohemia, the election of Ferdinand I in 1526, which was free and unanimous, was not followed by any civil war or foreign invasion.

The kingdom therefore remained undivided, its peace undisturbed for almost a hundred years, and Habsburg rule well established. A first controversial problem, however, immediately appeared. It was typical of the strained relations between king and Estates. The former, as husband of Anna, the sister of the last Jagellonian ruler of Bohemia, insisted upon his hereditary rights, while the Estates considered the crown elective, as most of the Hungarians did, and were in a much better position than the latter to defend the constitution of their kingdom. Ferdinand I succeeded in having his hereditary rights recognized in the non-Bohemian lands of the crown of Saint Václav, in Moravia, Silesia, and Lusatia, where the German element was more important than in Bohemia proper. Here, in the center of the country, the opposition was much stronger, but in 1547 the Diet of Prague was forced to admit Ferdinand's interpretation that his wife had been accepted as heiress by the Estates. On the same occasion the Diet also had to pass new laws which limited its power by placing the appointment of officials and judges practically in the hands of the king alone.

Even more dangerous for Bohemia's autonomy was Ferdinand I's creation of central organs of administration for all possessions of the Habsburgs. These new bodies, the privy council and the war council, were of course located in Vienna, while Bohemia retained only her own chancellors in Prague and her own courts.

Even more than in Hungary, these limitations of political rights were connected with the religious problems of the age of the Reformation. In Bohemia the Hussite tradition was still alive, thanks to the Czech Brethren, a well-organized religious group. And while in the fifteenth century the anti-Roman movement in Bohemia had also been strongly anti-German, now in spite of national differences, there was a sympathy with German Lutheranism which contributed to the spread of the Reformation in Ferdinand's new kingdom. Since, together with his brother, Emperor Charles V, he was the main defender of Catholicism, in Bohemia as in Hungary the causes of political and religious freedom were closely tied to one another. Furthermore, since the so-called Schmalkaldic War against the Protestant princes of Germany was fought near the border of Bohemia, it had strong repercussions there where the Estates, sympathizing with the Schmalkaldic League, opposed any participation of the Bohemian army in the war against the League and even formed a similar association in Bohemia. That movement collapsed when the German Protestants were defeated at Mühlberg in 1547, and thus the war did not actually reach Bohemia. But after his victory Ferdinand I seized that opportunity for a repression that was particularly directed against the formerly so powerful cities. Some leaders of the nobility were also punished and the Czech Brethren were expelled.

Only a small number of them remained in Bohemia, under strong pressure to return to the Catholic faith. The last remnants of the Utraquists joined the Lutherans, and the "Compactates" which had once reconciled that moderate wing of the Hussite movement with Rome, completely lost their significance and were finally withdrawn at the request of the Estates. As a matter of fact there was no religious persecution in Bohemia under Ferdinand I and even less under Maximilian II who had been accepted as king in his father's lifetime. That second Habsburg who ruled in Bohemia, showed there, as in Germany, some sympathy with the Protestant movement and in 1575 he even permitted the Estates to draft a joint confession of the new denominations. But that project did not satisfy anybody and the religious situation in the country was already very tense when in the following year Rudolf II succeeded his father, having also been accepted as future king before the death of his predecessor.

Rudolf soon established his permanent residence in Prague and, thanks to his serious intellectual interests, could have again made Bohemia's capital an important cultural center if it had not been for his growing mental illness which made him neglect all public affairs not only in Bohemia but also in the empire and the other Habsburg possessions. In his ensuing conflict with his brother Mathias, Rudolf had the support of the Bohemian Estates, for which he had to pay by guaranteeing religious freedom in the "Letter of Majesty" of 1609. But since he was deposed by Mathias two years later, the confused situation in Bohemia was rapidly leading to the rebellion which was to start the Thirty Years' War.

In spite of all their troubles in Hungary and in Bohemia, the Habsburgs of the sixteenth century were not only determined to keep both crowns but planned to gain a third one, that of Poland. Such a success would have given to that German dynasty, in addition to the imperial crown, the control of all East Central Europe. On several occasions this seemed about to occur. Their expectations were based upon the fact that the last of the Jagellonians in Poland and Lithuania, Sigismund Augustus, had no children although thrice married. And since both his first wife and his last were sisters of Ferdinand I, the situation seemed similar to that which already, before Mohács, had given the Habsburg candidate a good chance to succeed to the elder line of the same Jagellonian dynasty in Bohemia and Hungary. In Poland, too, the Habsburgs tried to form a group of partisans, especially among the Catholic hierarchy and the aristocracy, and their relations with some of the leading Lithuanian magnates were to serve a similar purpose, though the alternative of abandoning the grand duchy of Lithuania to the Russian czar and claiming only Poland proper was also considered.

If, in spite of all, the Austrian candidates failed in all three elections which followed the death of Sigismund Augustus in 1572, it was for two equally important reasons. The last Jagellonian himself, disliking the imperialistic policy of his Habsburg relatives and their diplomatic intrigues at his court, opposed their plans with even greater diplomatic skill and had his own ideas as to his possible successors. On the other hand, the great majority of the Poles were determined to reject any German candidate. They particularly considered the Habsburgs, with their trend toward absolutism, a threat to the Polish constitution which had been fully developed at the time of the Renaissance and the Reformation.

RENAISSANCE AND REFORMATION IN POLAND

Though a typically Western movement, the Renaissance, in its fifteenth-century phase, had already spread all over East Central Europe, with Prague and Buda as its earliest outposts. Both of these in turn influenced Cracow, whence the trends of what might well be called a pre-Renaissance penetrated as far as the Lithuanian and Ruthenian provinces of the Jagellonian Federation. In the sixteenth century it was almost exclusively within the limits of that federation that Renaissance culture, now at its height, could successfully develop its eastern wing. In Hungary it was completely doomed by the Ottoman conquest, and even in more fortunate Bohemia the decline of national culture under foreign rule proved unfavorable to its progress. In both countries the Reformation movement now had a much stronger appeal for those who were looking for a new stimulus in their struggle for national survival.

In Poland, too, where the sixteenth century was a golden age of national civilization in close connection with the West, the flowering of the Renaissance was now inseparable from the contemporary religious crisis. This is equally true for the comparatively short period of Protestant predominance in the intellectual life of the country and for the Catholic restoration in the latter part of the century. For in Poland, which instead of a Counter Reformation enforced by foreign influence had a Catholic revival out of native sources, the result was a close connection of Catholicism and nationalism, prepared by the last Renaissance generation and leading into the specific Baroque culture of seventeenth-century Poland. That whole process stopped, of course, at the eastern frontier of the Jagellonian Federation, but within its boundaries it contributed to a spontaneous Polonization of the upper classes in both Lithuania and the Ruthenian lands where the interest in humanism and the religious controversies of the time created an intimate cultural community with the Poles. Hence, also, the repercussions of all these developments in the constitutional debates which shaped the political structure of the commonwealth.

In all these respects the reign of Sigismund I was a period of preparation for the decisive results achieved under his son. Under the old king the impact of the Reformation was rather limited. Lutheranism was soon to appear in the western provinces that were neighbors to Germany, especially in the cities and in Polish Prussia, but it never had any deep attraction for the Polish population. Sigismund I was alarmed, however, and he tried to stop the movement by means of severe but rarely enforced decrees which could not reduce the interest in ecclesiastical reform. That interest was provoked—as in other countries—by real abuses in the church, by travel and studies in foreign lands, by the spread of Protestant literature, and also, toward the end of the reign, by the first contacts with non-German reformers, including even anti-Trinitarians who appeared in Poland. Since that interest was shared by the young Sigismund Augustus, all partisans of the Reformation were eagerly waiting for his succession.

In the meantime Renaissance culture had finally established itself under his father, a patron of architecture and literature as were his most distinguished collaborators and his Italian wife, Bona Sforza, who brought to Poland many prominent Italians and also the political conceptions of the country of her origin. Truly symbolic was the reconstruction of the old royal castle on Wawel Hill in Cracow, already started before the queen's arrival and producing one of the finest Renaissance monuments in the eastern part of Europe. But the same cultural trend is also reflected in a collection of state papers, letters, and reports which cover the whole of Sigismund I's reign. It is called *Acta Tomiciana* from the name of Peter Tomicki, Bishop of Cracow and Vice-Chancellor, who represented Polish humanism at its best. But it also contains contributions of the leading writers of the period, all using a brilliant Renaissance Latin and frequently appearing as Polish diplomats at the Western courts.

In that respect the Łaski family was conspicuous for a special versatility. In the next generation it was to produce the leader of Polish Protestantism. After an important part played in the English Reformation, Johannes a Lasco—as he was called abroad—returned to Poland when the creation of a national church, separated from Rome, seemed possible under Sigismund Augustus. From the beginning of the new reign in 1548 there were, indeed, public discussions both in the diets and at synods of the various denominations. In addition to the old disputes between the clergy and the nobility in the matter of tithes and ecclesiastical jurisdiction, these discussions raised the most delicate dogmatic controversies. In 1550 the young king sided with the hierarchy in order to win its support for the recognition of his marriage with a Lithuanian, Barbara Radziwiłł. She died soon after her coronation, however, and Sigismund Augustus was never seriously inclined to stop the Protestant movement by force. On the contrary, even in Rome he seemed ready to support at least the more moderate claims of the religious reformers regarding the use of the vernacular in the liturgy and the chalice for layman, as well as the abolition of celibacy for the clergy.

Such a program was also advanced by one of the most talented writers of the time, Stanislaus Orzechowski, a priest who had married in spite of the protest of his bishop. Although he later turned into a passionate defender of Catholicism, other representatives of the rapidly developing national literature, such as the famous political writer Andrew Frycz Modrzewski or Nicolas Rey who first used the Polish language with remarkable success, remained intimately associated with the religious trends which toward the middle of the century attracted the most prominent minds of the country.

There was, however, among the partisans of the Reformation a great variety of doctrines and opinions which, just because they were all permitted to develop freely, made the triumph of any of the new denominations impossible. In Great Poland, where Lutheranism had many adherents, a rival Protestant church was established by the Czech Brethren. Expelled from Bohemia, they had their center in Leszno under the protection of the powerful Leszczyński family. That community was in sympathy with the Reformed church which had been organized by Calvinists in close contact with Switzerland, and which was predominant in Little Poland and also in Lithuania where the Radziwiłłs, leading in the whole grand duchy, were its chief patrons. While these Protestant groups differed in their teaching regarding the Eucharist, even more radical heresies, attacking the dogma of the Holy Trinity and sometimes leading to extreme rationalism, were propagated by brilliant exiles from Italy, including the two Socinis, but they were also developed by a few native Poles— hence the designation Polish Brethren. They seemed to revive the Arianism of early Christianity and at the same time they were under the influence of contemporary communist trends that came particularly from Moravian Anabaptists.

The orthodox Protestants were determined to exclude these extremists, and amidst continuous disputes among a rapidly growing number of sects they realized the necessity for coordinating and for adopting a common confession of faith in order to oppose a united front to the established Catholic church. When John Łaski returned to Poland in 1556, one year after an agreement between the Czech Brethren and the Calvinists, he favored the latter. But he also considered the possibility of a general adoption of the more moderate Confession of Augsburg which seemed to have the best chance and which was supported by Poland's mighty vassal, Duke Albrecht of Prussia, with Königsberg and its recently founded University as an important center of propaganda. But Łaski died in 1560 before any agreement was reached. Only ten years later representatives of all three Protestant denominations met at the Synod of Sandomierz. Though they were unable to agree on the Reformed Swiss Confession because of Lutheran opposition, they at least concluded a formal alliance.

Such cooperation was needed. First, because since 1565 the split between Protestants and anti-Trinitarians, whose movement soon centered at Raków, was finally completed, and secondly, because in almost the same year Catholicism was again resuming strength. At the Diet of 1562–63, the Protestants had enforced a decision that no sentences of ecclesiastical courts would be executed by the state authorities. But after the Council of Trent, whose decrees were accepted by the king when presented to him in 1564 by the papal nuncio, a spontaneous return to the Catholic church set in, chiefly through individual conversions in the formerly leading Protestant families. Aside from the nuncios, now regularly residing in Poland, the first Jesuits who came to the country greatly contributed to that change, and the Catholic hierarchy showed a new zeal under the leadership of Cardinal Stanislaus Hosius.

Under these conditions the non-Catholics wanted a constitutional guaranty that religious freedom would continue in Poland. They finally obtained it a year after the king's death, when during the interregnum the Confederation of Warsaw in 1573 decided to maintain permanent "peace among those who dissent in religious matters." That charter went further than any other "religious peace" in sixteenth-century Europe because it covered all denominations, even those radicals whom the Protestants wanted to see expelled.

Sigismund Augustus had decisively contributed both to creating such an atmosphere of tolerance and to safeguarding Poland's Catholic tradition because he rejected all suggestions to end his last, unhappy and childless marriage with Catherine of Austria by divorce. Furthermore, like his father, he proved to be an enlightened patron of Renaissance humanism which in Poland had a more lasting influence than the Reformation and which continued until the end of the century. The interest in literature shown by the king, who collected a remarkable library, was an inspiration to all writers of that brilliant generation, including the first great poet in the vernacular, Jan Kochanowski. It was also in the service of the last Jagellonian that Poland's greatest Renaissance statesman, Jan Zamoyski, a former rector of the University of Padua where so many Polish jurists were educated, prepared himself for his outstanding achievements during the following reigns.

THE UNION OF LUBLIN

The extension of Western culture in its typical expressions of Renaissance, Protestant Reformation, and Catholic Restoration to the extreme limits of East Central Europe was greatly facilitated and accelerated by the Diet of Lublin in 1569 which made the Polish-Lithuanian Union a close federation and determined its constitutional structure for more than two hundred years. On the other hand, the Union of Lublin had been prepared and made possible by a gradual penetration of Western culture far into the Lithuanian and Ruthenian lands of the grand duchy, a process which had already started in the fifteenth century but which chiefly developed from the beginning of the sixteenth.

In 1501, at the very threshold of the new century, when the election of Alexander, grand duke of Lithuania, to the throne of Poland restored the personal union of both states after nine years of interruption, new union charters were signed at Mielnik which decided that in the future there would always be a common election of the common ruler and that "common councils" would guarantee close cooperation in the field of legislation. But the Jagellonian dynasty, though always favorable to the Union in general, was opposed to the idea of a common election, which seemed to question their hereditary rights to the grand duchy. In the year 1505, when the legislative power of the Polish Diet was definitely confirmed, the Lithuanian Diet, encouraged by the king, refused the long-delayed ratification of the Mielnik agreement. Thus the settlement of the federal constitution remained in suspense for more than sixty years.

During that period of transition it appeared quite clearly, however, that the Union was based not so much upon legal formulas as upon a real community which bound together the constituent parts of the Jagellonian monarchy. In the field of foreign relations, that community was dictated, first, by the permanent danger of Tartar invasions which threatened the southeastern borderlands of both the grand duchy and the kingdom. Furthermore, though only the former, particularly its White Ruthenian and Ukrainian provinces, was directly exposed to Moscow's aggressive policy, it was obvious that this growing danger could be faced only with Polish assistance. The Lithuanian requests for such assistance, both military and financial, always had the full support of the kings. The Poles themselves became more and more aware that it was in the interest of their own security to strengthen Lithuania's resistance. Thus, when the armistice which in 1522 ended the second Russian war of Sigismund I expired in 1533 with the death of Vasil III of Moscow, and when the Lithuanians took advantage of the minority of Ivan IV to try to regain their big territorial losses, Polish auxiliary forces again contributed to the limited successes of that third war.

Under Sigismund Augustus the situation became much more serious. Ivan, later called "the Terrible," now grown up and crowned as czar in 1547, after his victories in the East which resulted in the conquest of Kazan and Astrakhan, instead of concentrating against the Tartars of the Crimea, where a cooperation with Lithuania would have been quite natural, decided for a westward expansion on two fronts with a view to encircling the grand duchy. Even before the war along the old White Ruthenian border was resumed in 1562, the czar invaded Livonia, which had placed herself under the protection of Sigismund Augustus, and now also threatened Lithuania from the north. When he took Polotsk in 1563, the loss of that fortress, which was almost as important as Smolensk, was a serious warning even for Poland. The Lithuanians were now more anxious than ever before to strengthen the union with the kingdom.

But the Polish-Lithuanian negotiations which, in spite of many interruptions and fluctuations dictated by the changing political and military situation, continued to absorb the diets of both countries during the six years before the Union of Lublin, were also a natural result of the growing assimilation of the kingdom and the grand duchy under the last two Jagellonians. Western culture came to the grand duchy through Polish intermediation and therefore contributed not only to the development of a common way of life but also to a spontaneous Polonization of the most influential upper classes.

Strangely enough, that Polonized aristocracy, led by the Radziwiłł family, was least in favor of closer political ties with Poland and defended Lithuania's autonomy because it was afraid to lose the exclusive control of the grand duchy if the more democratic Polish constitution would influence conditions there. For that very reason the lesser gentry of Lithuania claimed a more intimate connection with their "Polish brethren," especially after 1562. As did the Poles, they favored the fusion of both diets into one common parliament on the Polish pattern, with no privileges for the magnates and with a predominance of the freely elected deputies to the lower chamber. As in 1501, that idea was combined with that of a common election. This time the king, impressed by the external danger and losing the hope of leaving any descendants, made no difficulties for dynastic reasons but joined with the partisans of the Union in both countries.

In Poland the supporters of the Union were at the same time partisans of a reform program which under the modest slogan of "execution of the laws" wanted to improve the administration and the judiciary system, and to get the much needed financial resources for a permanent defense of the frontiers by having restored to the crown the royal lands which had been pledged to the most powerful families. That program was at least partially realized at the so-called "Execution Diet" of 1563–1564, while at the same time an even more important reform made the grand duchy ready for the final union with Poland.

Prepared by a land reform which greatly improved economic conditions, and combined with a new codification of Lithuanian law which in many respects remained different, that reform of 1564–1566 was to a large extent a reception of the Polish constitution, including its privileges for the whole gentry and the institution of provincial dietines as a basis for self-government and parliamentary rule. The last legal restrictions, discriminating against Greek Orthodox, were abolished on the same occasion. When at last both diets were convoked for a joint session in Lublin, near the Polish-Lithuanian border, there was hardly any legal difference between them.

In practice, however, the opposition of a few powerful families of the grand duchy, which were particularly hostile to a permanent fusion of the two diets, proved so strong that the discussions lasted for almost six months and, at the beginning of March, were even interrupted by a secession of the Lithuanian leaders. They finally yielded under a twofold pressure. First, the king decided that not only the small always contested province of Podlachia would be incorporated with the kingdom, but similarly the whole southern section of the grand duchy. The province of Volhynia, and the Ukraine, with Kiev, would be transferred to Poland with guaranties of local autonomy, including the use of Ruthenian as the official language and equal rights for the Orthodox. Sigismund Augustus chiefly wanted the Poles to share in the defense of the long eastern border. His decision also corresponded to the desires of the majority of the population which now joined the Ruthenian provinces of Poland proper.

At the same time the great majority of the Lithuanians also exercised strong pressure upon the opposition leaders. Eventually all of them, except one of the Radziwiłłs, returned to Lublin. There, directed by a member of the Chodkiewicz family, they signed the Union charters of July first. These were approved by the king a few days later and remained basically unchanged until the partitions of the commonwealth at the end of the eighteenth century.

According to that memorable covenant, the kingdom of Poland and the grand duchy of Lithuania were now merged in one "common republic" and both peoples were proclaimed one nation under one ruler, who was always to be elected in common, and with one diet where Polish and Lithuanian senators and deputies would mingle with one another. At the same time, however, the grand duchy not only retained its traditional title but also its own army, treasury, and code of law, under a separate administration, so that a Lithuanian official corresponded to every Polish one. Such a strict dualism was sometimes to create serious difficulties in the practice of government but as a whole it was a sound compromise between the claims of some Polish radicals, who wanted complete unification, and the narrow separatism of a few Lithuanian magnates.

The Diet of Lublin, which did not adjourn until the twelfth of August, also determined the constitutional position of two minor parts of the federation. The so-called Royal Prussia, i.e., Polish Pomerania, now divided into three provinces, was made an integral part of the kingdom represented in the common diet. The special privileges of the city of Danzig, however, raised some controversies which even a commission sent there the next year could not definitely settle.

The whole issue was part of the larger problem of the *Dominium maris Baltici* and so was of course the question of Livonia. Although the full possession of that country was not yet secured under Sigismund Augustus, it was decided at Lublin that Livonia, endowed with a large autonomy, would belong in common to Lithuania—its immediate neighbor—and to Poland. This solution corresponded to the desires of the Livonians who were anxious to be defended by both Jagellonian states.

The success of the Diet of 1569 was a great personal triumph for the king, who actively participated in the discussions. At Lublin he also received the homage of the prince of Moldavia and of the new duke of Prussia, Albrecht Frederick, who the year before had succeeded his father Albrecht. He was to be the last of the Prussian line of the Hohenzollerns, but their Brandenburg cousins had already been granted the right of succession, another question which is connected with the balance of power in the Baltic region.

11

THE LATER SIXTEENTH CENTURY

THE STRUGGLE FOR THE DOMINIUM MARIS BALTICI

The countries of East Central Europe never had easy access to the sea. In the south they indeed approached the Mediterranean, and in particular two of its main bays, the Adriatic and the Black Sea. But the Southern Slavs, who had reached the Adriatic through their migrations in the early Middle Ages, were soon almost entirely cut off from its shores by Venetian conquests. Croatia, in union with Hungary, retained only the port of Fiume. At the southern tip of Dalmatia, the port of Dubrovnik (Ragusa) had developed into a small, practically independent republic on the Venetian pattern. As to the Black Sea, Bulgaria, both Rumanian principalities, and the Ruthenian provinces of the Polish-Lithuanian Federation had long been in possession of important sections of its coast, but Ottoman expansion in the sixteenth century made the Black Sea a Turkish lake, since the Crimean Tartars, who were vassals of the empire, controlled the steppes from the Crimea to Moldavia, also under Turkish suzerainty.

For the Jagellonian Union, which therefore only nominally reached the Black Sea between the mouths of the Dnieper and Dniester rivers, under such conditions it was of paramount importance to have at least free and broad access to the Baltic, on the northern side of the wide isthmus which was the geographical basis of the whole federal system. In 1466 Poland had indeed regained Eastern Pomerania, together with the important port of Danzig. But Lithuania never possessed more than a small strip of the Baltic coast, with no port at all. Furthermore, these two coast sections of the federated countries were separated by East Prussia, a Polish fief, but under German administration and of dubious loyalty before and after the secularization of 1525. And even Danzig interpreted its royal charters as confirmation of its position as a free city with its own Baltic policy dictated by local trade interests.

For all these reasons the Polish-Lithuanian Commonwealth, although by far the largest Baltic power, was not at all the strongest rival in the contest for Baltic supremacy which opened with the disintegration of one of the smallest but crucially situated Baltic states, the semi-ecclesiastical German colony of Livonia. Its position was so important because Livonia had some excellent ports in Riga, Reval (Tallin), Narva, etc., and ancient trade relations with the Lithuanian and Russian hinterland. Also because that central sector of the southeastern coast of the Baltic was in close commercial and political relations with Germany proper, another Baltic power, thanks to the old Hanseatic center of Lübeck and to the coastlines of Mecklenburg and Western Pomerania. These traditional relations with the homeland of the German settlers and masters of Livonia seemed to assure them the permanent protection of the empire.

This rather theoretical protection, however, had never helped them much against the most serious danger which had threatened them since Moscow's conquest of the neighboring republics of Pskov and Novgorod. That danger was the pressure of a Russia which was now united under Moscow's leadership and anxious to gain for herself an access to the Baltic which would be larger than her small strip of coast between the Narva River and the Finnish border, with no port of any significance. That situation created some kind of solidarity between Livonia and Sweden, to which Finland, on the other side of the Gulf of Finland, had belonged from the twelfth century. In the sixteenth century Finland was made an autonomous grand duchy, but she always remained exposed to Russian invasions along her wide land border. Equally interested in the fate of Livonia was another Scandinavian country, Denmark, so powerful in the Baltic during the Middle Ages and always remembering that Estonia—the northern part of Livonia—had been a Danish province from 1219 to 1346. But Denmark, Sweden's deadly enemy since the dissolution of the Union of Kalmar in 1523, was rather prepared to cooperate with Moscow— first allied with her in 1493—with a view to establishing free navigation from the Russian-controlled mouth of the Narva River through the Danish-controlled Sound to the open ocean.

The problems of the Baltic were therefore hardly less complicated than those of the Mediterranean, so that the Baltic Sea was sometimes called the "Mediterranean of the North." The precarious balance of power system of that region was completely upset when it became apparent that Livonia was no longer in a position to defend her independence. From 1237, when the Livonian military order, the Knights of the Sword, joined the Teutonic Knights of Prussia, Livonia had always been dependent on the support of that much stronger German Order of knighthood, and the Livonian land master willingly recognized the overlordship of the grand master of Prussia. When Albrecht of Hohenzollern secularized the Order in Prussia in 1525, Livonia could hardly enjoy her complete sovereignty. Even the prominent land master of that period, Walter von Plettenberg, famous because of his victories over the Russians in 1501–1502, had serious difficulties in ruling a territory which remained divided into possessions of the Order, of the hierarchy under the powerful Archbishop of Riga, and of the rich cities. Moreover, as in Prussia, the spread of Lutheranism disorganized the ecclesiastical institutions which were supposed to maintain the body politic.

After the death of Plettenberg in 1535, the decline of Livonia made such rapid progress that all her neighbors became interested in the possibility of acquiring part or all of her territory. Even the Hohenzollern dynasty which had so easily gained Prussia, had some hope of repeating that successful experience in Livonia, since a brother of Albrecht of Prussia, Wilhelm, became first coadjutor and eventually Archbishop of Riga. Among the Livonian knights there were, however, two main parties. One of them tried to save the country through a policy of appeasing Russia, whose pressure became particularly threatening under Ivan the Terrible. The other favored some kind of agreement with the Jagellonian dynasty in order to obtain Lithuanian and possibly also Polish protection, and while Sigismund I had already shown some interest in the Livonian problem, Sigismund Augustus followed it with special attention.

In 1554 land master von Galen, a partisan of the Russian orientation, made a treaty with Ivan the Terrible for fifteen years. He promised not to enter into any understanding with Lithuania. Nevertheless, three years later, Galen's successor, Wilhelm von Fürstenberg, in conflict with the Archbishop of Riga and after a diplomatic incident with the King of Poland (the traditional protector of the archbishopric), who had mobilized strong forces at the Livonian border, made an agreement with Sigismund Augustus. The czar regarded this as a breach of the treaty of 1554, and in 1558 he invaded Livonia, taking Narva and Dorpat, and terribly devastated the country. Now the majority of the Livonians, under their new land-master, Gotthard Kettler, were convinced that only the Polish-Lithu-anian federation could save them from Muscovite conquest. They formally asked for the protection of Sigismund Augustus, first, in 1559, in a limited form which proved inadequate, and then in a formal treaty of union which was concluded in 1561. Kettler, who secular-ized the Livonian Order, was made hereditary Duke of Curland (the southern part of Livonia) under the king's suzerainty. The rest of the country was placed under Lithuanian administration with a large autonomy, including guaranties for the Protestant faith and the Ger-man language and with the prospect of being federated with both Lithuania and Poland, as really happened by the Union of Lublin. After the secularization of the archbishopric, the city of Riga joined the agreement in 1562.

But it was little more than that port and its environs which the Polish-Lithuanian forces succeeded in protecting against foreign in-vaders. Possible claims of the Hohenzollerns were eliminated when, in compensation, the electoral line in Brandenburg was granted the right of succession in East Prussia. But Ivan the Terrible continued to occupy a large part of Livonia, and at the same time both Sweden and Denmark entered the contest, thus making it a war among all Baltic powers, the first "Northern War." In spite of the traditional Danish-Russian alliance, renewed in 1563, and in spite of an obvious community of interest between Sweden and the Jagellonian Union, in the first phase of the war there seemed to be a strange reversal of alliances. Eric XIV of Sweden, who occupied Estonia and even parts of Livonia proper as early as 1560, sided with Ivan the Terrible. But the king—a ruthless tyrant like his ally—was deposed in 1568 by his brother John, the Duke of Finland, who was fully aware of the Russian danger and married to a sister of Sigismund Augustus. Now Sweden was again aligned against Russia, while with Russian support Denmark hoped to get a "Livonian Kingdom" for Magnus, a brother of her king, who actually seized the island of Oesel and some terri-tories on the mainland.

The war remained undecided, just like the struggle at the Russian-Lithuanian border. In the same year (1570), when an armistice was concluded by a joint Polish-Lithuanian mission sent to Moscow after the Union of Lublin, an international congress, without Russian participation, met in Stettin to settle the Baltic problem which began to raise a serious interest even among the Western powers, including France. No final decision was reached, especially since even the emperor wanted his suzerainty over Livonia to be recognized, though this no longer had any practical significance. But peace was restored between the Scandinavian kingdoms and the Polish-Lithuanian Commonwealth, while a precarious status quo continued in Livonia, which was soon to be troubled by another Russian invasion. It required the energetic action of a new Polish king to obtain a more durable solution.

FROM STEPHEN BÁTHORY TO SIGISMUND VASA

Since the commonwealth created by the Union of Lublin was now the only independent body politic in East Central Europe, the problem of the succession after the last Jagellonian was of general importance for the whole continent. And since no native candidate had any chance of being elected, it was easy to foresee that the Polish-Lithuanian Federation would enter in turn into a union, at least of a dynastic character, with some other European country, thus affecting the whole balance of power.

During the interregnum after the death of Sigismund Augustus, on July 7, 1572, it was decided that the common election of the king of Poland and grand duke of Lithuania, provided for in the Lublin Covenant, would be made *viritim*, i.e., through the votes of all members of the *szlachta* who would attend the election Diet at Warsaw. At the same time new limitations of the royal power were drafted in the form of articles which any candidate would have to accept in the future, in addition to special conditions which would constitute the *pacta conventa* of each individual election. Nevertheless, practically all neighbors were anxious to acquire the crown of one of the largest countries of Europe, and besides the Habsburgs, who appeared as candidates in all three Polish elections of the later sixteenth century, even Ivan the Terrible made attempts to gain, if not the whole commonwealth, at least the grand duchy of Lithuania for himself or his son, possibly leaving the kingdom of Poland to a Habsburg.

Such a solution was, of course, even less acceptable to the electors than the Austrian succession had been, and all such projects opposed by Sigismund Augustus himself when, anticipating his childless death, he was considering the future of his country. The solution which he had favored and prepared in secret negotiations appealed to most of those who participated in the election of 1573, and Henry of Valois, the younger brother of Charles IX of France, was finally chosen. Dynastic ties with France were indeed no danger to Poland's independence, and they seemed to open promising possibilities of cooperation between the leading powers of Western and East Central Europe, guaranteeing their security against Habsburg imperialism and Russian aggression. Henry accepted all conditions, including the promise of religious freedom embodied in the Warsaw Confederation, but after staying only four months in Poland he immediately returned to France when his brother died in 1574. Again the Polish throne had to be declared vacant.

The election of the following year created a dangerous division. This time the partisans of the Habsburgs chose Emperor Maximilian II himself, while the majority of the gentry under the leadership of the prominent statesman, Jan Zamoyski, formally elected Anna, a sister of the last Jagellonian, together with her prospective husband, Stefan Báthory, who after Maximilian's death in 1576 became undisputed king. His choice was rather unexpected, since he was only Prince of Transylvania. But besides Poland, that comparatively insignificant territory was the only free land in East Central Europe. Báthory, a Hungarian nobleman of great military ability, defended Transylvania against the Habsburgs with a view to liberating all Hungary from them. At the same time he was trying to reduce the suzerainty of the Ottoman Empire to a mere fiction and to secure peace with the Turks until the moment when he would be strong enough to turn against them.

In Poland he proved a remarkable ruler. He respected the constitution and completed the reforms of his predecessors by creating a supreme court of appeal, but with the loyal cooperation of Zamoyski he also strengthened the authority of the crown. At the very beginning of his reign he had to face serious troubles in Danzig. After supporting the Austrian candidate, this city wanted to seize the opportunity of internal division to enlarge the special privileges of the city. After a military victory the king was satisfied with a reasonable compromise which left Danzig an autonomous but henceforth loyal part of the commonwealth. Batory—as he was called in Poland—perfectly realized that Poland's position on the Baltic Sea, as well as her security in general, depended primarily on a solution of the conflict with Ivan the Terrible.

The czar had profited from the Danzig crisis in order to resume the hostilities interrupted in 1570. He started by again attacking that part of Livonia which remained under Polish-Lithuanian control, but Batory and Zamoyski (the latter was not only grand chancellor but also grand hetman, i.e., commander in chief of the Polish forces), answered his aggression by trying to reconquer the White Ruthenian border lands of the grand duchy which Moscow had occupied in the preceding wars. In three campaigns the Polish-Lithuanian armies, increased thanks to unusual taxes voted by the Diet, gained considerable success. In 1579 Polotsk was retaken, and that important city now became for two centuries an outpost of Western culture. Here Batory, soon after creating a university in Wilno, founded a Jesuit college. The conquest of another fortress, Wielkie Luki, which had long ago been lost, followed in 1580. In 1581 purely Russian territory was entered. A cavalry raid almost reached Moscow, and the city of Pskov was besieged.

In that critical situation Ivan the Terrible made a skillful diplomatic move. He asked for the mediation of the Holy See, making Rome believe, as his predecessors had done on several occasions, that Moscow would be prepared for a religious union with the Catholic church. Antonio Possevino, a member of the Jesuit order who was particularly interested in this project, was indeed delegated by Pope Gregory XIII as a negotiator. But he was soon to convince himself that the hopes raised by the czar were nothing but deceptive illusions. In endless theological discussions with Ivan it became apparent that there was no chance of any understanding between Rome and Moscow which in the religious sphere, just as in the political philosophy so typically represented by the first czar, was definitely outside the Western community. It therefore only remained to fix the eastern boundaries of that community, identical with those of the Polish-Lithuanian Commonwealth.

Batory, too, after an exhausting effort and with the siege of Pskov dragging on, was ready to make peace. But since Moscow refused to restore Smolensk to Lithuania, only a truce was concluded at Yam Zapolsky at the end of 1581. In addition to Polotsk, Ivan had to give up all that he had occupied in Livonia, and that province was now safely in the joint possession of Poland and Lithuania. Its administration was well organized under Batory; Riga developed, besides Danzig, into a second great Baltic port of the commonwealth; and Polish Jesuits who tried to propagate Catholicism in a region which the German upper class had made almost completely Lutheran showed a real interest in the neglected native population, the Letts and Estonians and in their languages.

Sweden, which continued to hold the main northern section of Estonia, with the ports of Reval (Tallin) and Narva, had been an ally in the war with Ivan the Terrible. Making peace with him in the following year (1582), King John III of Sweden gained that section of the coast at the lower end of the Gulf of Finland which connected Estonia and Finland, thus entirely cutting off Russia from the Baltic. The cooperation against the main enemy of both countries, and the rise of Swedish power on the Baltic, were to be important factors in determining the choice of Batory's successor.

In spite of internal difficulties toward the end of his reign, when he had to crush the opposition of the powerful Zborowski family, King Stefan Batory was considering far-reaching projects of an anti-Ottoman league, possibly in cooperation with Russia after the death of Ivan the Terrible, when he himself suddenly died two years later, in 1586, without having children. His faithful collaborator, Zamoyski again opposed the Austrian candidate to the crown, Archduke Maximilian, and the interregnum of 1587 once more resulted in a twofold election, the candidate of the majority being Sigismund, son of the King of Sweden and of Catherine, the elder sister of Sigismund Augustus.

The idea of a personal union with Sweden, where the crown was hereditary and where Sigismund III (as he was called as King of Poland) succeeded John III Vasa after his death in 1592, seemed to be in the interest of both countries. They could now join their forces in checking the Russian danger and controlling the Baltic, and finally settle their controversy over Estonia. When Zamoyski defeated Maximilian and his partisans in the Battle of Byczyna, the reign of the Vasa King, now universally recognized, began under favorable auspices. Soon, however, he disappointed both Poles and Swedes. Contrary to the expectations of Zamoyski, with whom he never established friendly relations, Sigismund III engaged in a policy of appeasing the Habsburgs. He was even suspected of clandestine negotiations with Emperor Rudolf II with a view to ceding the Polish crown to another archduke, his own interests being primarily with Sweden. But in his country of origin he was even less popular, since being a devout Catholic himself, he wanted to restore the traditional faith in a nation which long before had become almost completely Lutheran.

Sweden was definitely lost to him when he failed to gain the confidence of her people on a first visit in 1593 and when the forces loyal to the king were defeated near Stockholm five years later. His own uncle, Prince Charles of Södermanland, was the leader of the opposition, and first named regent in the place of the deposed Sigismund, he himself finally became king as Charles IX. The result was a long-lasting conflict between the two lines of the Vasas which destroyed all prospects of Polish-Swedish cooperation and led to a completely unnecessary series of wars between the two kingdoms. But before that protracted struggle started at the very turn of the century, Sigismund III who never renounced his Swedish title, had to face serious problems as King of Poland. The internal situation improved after the "inquisition" Diet of 1592, which apparently cleared the king of all suspicions, but two new issues proved of decisive importance for Poland's position in East Central Europe.

THE UNION OF BREST

A king as decidedly Catholic as Sigismund III was of course deeply interested in the problem of religious unity within the limits of the Polish-Lithuanian Commonwealth. When he was elected in 1587, Protestantism was already in retreat. Stefan Batory, though very respectful of religious freedom, had greatly contributed to the progress of a peaceful Catholic restoration. This had already started at the end of the reign of Sigismund Augustus and had found its clearest expression in the formal acceptance of the decrees of the Council of Trent by a synod of the Polish hierarchy held in Piotrków in 1579. Under Sigismund III there was also no persecution of what remained of the once powerful Protestant minority. The new king even continued to appoint some of its leaders to high office, and excesses against Protestant churches were exceptional actions of an uncontrolled populace. But the sympathies of Sigismund III were indeed with the Catholics, and he was concerned with the problem of the

Greek Orthodox who were not a small minority group but the bulk of the population in all White Ruthenian and Ukrainian lands of the commonwealth.

The temporary progress which Protestantism had made in these regions also contributed to the disintegration of the Orthodox Church which, though practically free under the Catholic rule of both Poland and Lithuania, was definitely in decline, since its head, the Patriarch of Constantinople, was under Turkish control, while the relations with Orthodox Moscow were consistently bad. On the other hand, the tradition of the Union of Florence was never entirely obliterated in these regions, and through their political union with Poland they were in permanent contact with the Catholic West.

The Polish Jesuits were the first to realize the opportunity for restoring the Union of Florence in that only section of Orthodox Christendom where such a project had any chance of success. The famous preacher, writer, and educator, Father Peter Skarga, was particularly active in that respect. In 1578, the very year when he became the first rector of the University of Wilno, he published the first edition of his treatise on "The Unity of the Church of God." Impressed by the reports of the papal nuncios in Poland, the Holy See also had become interested in that idea in the time of Batory. If foreign Catholic leaders sometimes had the illusion that such a regional reunion would eventually lead to the conversion of all Russia, they soon realized, including Possevino himself, that the only compensation which the Catholic church could possibly find for its great losses in Western Europe was a religious union supplementing the political federation in East Central Europe.

Even here, however, no lasting success was possible without the spontaneous initiative and cooperation of the Orthodox leaders themselves. As far as laymen were concerned, the most prominent of these leaders was Prince Constantine Ostrogski, palatine of Kiev and the wealthiest landowner in the Ukraine. Seriously concerned with the critical situation of the Ruthenian church, he founded an academy in his own city of Ostrog. To this institution he invited quite remarkable teachers, choosing them, however, without much discernment and even from among theologians having distinctly Calvinistic leanings. With the papal nuncios and with members of the Catholic hierarchy he had already discussed the possibility of a reunion with

Rome during Batory's reign. But it was not until 1590 that some of the Orthodox bishops also expressed themselves in favor of such a solution.

A series of meetings of these bishops followed. In these the plan of such a union was carefully worked out, although not all of them were equally sincere in their endeavors. Thus Gedeon Bałaban, the Orthodox Bishop of Lwów, a city where a Latin archbishopric had long ago been established, joined the union movement merely because of a personal conflict with the Orthodox brotherhood of the same city, one of the lay groups which tried to revive the Orthodox tradition. Much more genuine was the interest in the union shown by the Ruthenian Bishop of Lutsk, Cyril Terlecki, whose attitude was of special importance. He had been made an exarch or personal representative of the patriarchate of Constantinople when, in 1589, Patriarch Jeremiah visited the Ukraine on his way to and from Moscow where he elevated the metropolitan to the rank of patriarch. The danger of Moscow's supremacy among all the Orthodox of North East Europe was another argument in favor of union with Rome for the Eastern Church in the Ruthenian lands where Jeremiah's interference only resulted in growing confusion. Terlecki was encouraged to turn toward Rome by the Latin bishop of the same city of Lutsk, the future Cardinal Bernard Maciejowski. The decisive role was played, however, by another Orthodox, Hypatius Pociey, Bishop of Brest and of Volodymir in Volhynia, a former lay dignitary who had entered ecclesiastical life out of a profound desire to contribute to a better future for the Ruthenian church.

As soon as he became convinced that a return to the Union of Florence was the only solution, he tried to gain the support of the Metropolitan of Kiev, Michael Rahoza, who indeed joined the movement though not without some wavering, and also of Prince Ostrogski, with whom he had some interesting correspondence in 1593. It appeared, however, that the proud magnate, offended by not having been consulted from the outset of the discussions among the hierarchy, had a different approach to the problem. He wanted to combine the Union with some basic changes in the Protestant spirit, and he put forward the impossible condition of including the Orthodox churches of Moscow and Wallachia. For reasons insufficiently explained, he gradually became a violent opponent of the Union, a situation which seriously alarmed the king and the Polish authorities when at last, in 1595, the Ruthenian bishops, apparently unanimously, turned to them for official support. Their project seemed so desirable, however, that after consultations in Cracow, in which the papal nuncio participated, it was decided that Pociey and Terlecki should go to Rome at once and submit their desire for reunion to Clement VIII.

The Pope, a former legate to Poland, received them at the Vatican with great pleasure. There, on December 23, 1595, the union was concluded in an impressive ceremony. The two representatives of the Ruthenian hierarchy made a profession of faith in full conformity with the Catholic doctrine and with the decrees of the Council of Trent, while the Pope granted their request that the Ruthenian church be permitted to keep the Eastern rite, as recognized by the Council of Florence. There was general agreement, however, that the union had to be confirmed at a local synod of the Ruthenian church. This was finally convoked at Brest, near the Polish-Lithuanian frontier, early in October of the following year, 1596.

Despite the presence of three royal delegates who tried to mediate between partisans and opponents of the Union, that synod resulted in a split among the Ruthenians. The majority of their hierarchy, including the Metropolitan of Kiev, the Archbishop of Polotsk, and four bishops, declared in favor of the Union which was solemnly proclaimed in the Brest cathedral on the ninth of October. But two bishops, those of Lwów and Przemyśl, where Catholic and Polish influence should have been strongest, joined the opposition led by Prince Ostrogski. Contrary to the king's interdiction, he brought to Brest not only private armed forces but also foreigners. These included two Greeks who pretended to represent the patriarchate of Constantinople, then vacant, and who were suspected of being Turkish spies. One of them was the famous Cyril Lucaris, formerly a teacher at the Ostrog academy, later Patriarch of Constantinople.

In the seventeenth century Constantinople's and Moscow's hostility to the Union of Brest was time and again to affect Poland's foreign relations. But internal difficulties set in at once after the synod of 1596. The opposition, which held an antisynod in the home of a Unitarian at Brest, created a common front with the Protestants with whom Ostrogski had already established contact the year before, and with whom he later made a formal agreement in 1599. In the diets of the following years those Ruthenians who rejected the Union, and in contradistinction to the Uniates were called "Dis-Uniates," were supported by all "Dissidents" (the common designation of the non-Catholics) when they claimed for themselves all the rights and properties of the Eastern church. The government regarded the Uniates as the legitimate representatives of that church, but hesitated to take any action which would threaten religious peace. Contrary to the promises which had been made, the Uniate bishops were not granted seats in the senate. Thus they had great difficulty in defending their cause, even when the energetic Pociey became metropolitan after Rahoza's death in 1600.

Nevertheless the Union of Brest had two equally important, though apparently contradictory, consequences. First, a large section of the White Ruthenian and Ukrainian population of the commonwealth, gradually growing in number, were henceforth Catholics, like the Poles and the Lithuanians. Though attached to their Eastern liturgy, they were now much nearer to the Western community than before and were no longer subject to any influence coming from the Muscovite or Ottoman East. On the other hand, the cultural progress and greater vitality of the Ruthenian element, which resulted from the Union, was not limited to those who joined the movement but also stimulated those who opposed it. A rich polemical literature discussing all the controversial problems which were involved—theological, historic, and legal—soon developed as an expression of that spiritual revival, and even when criticizing the decisions made at Brest, this contributed to closer intellectual relations between the distant Ruthenian lands and the Western world, whether Catholic or Protestant.

It is, therefore, no exaggeration to consider the Union of Brest a last great achievement, not only of the spirit of federalism which the political Jagellonian Union had developed in East Central Europe but also of the humanistic Renaissance culture which through that Union had reached those border regions of the European community. But all depended on the issue as to whether the religious controversies would continue as a merely cultural problem in an atmosphere of peace, social and political, internal and external, particularly indispensable in such regions. They were, however, seriously troubled in the very year of the Union of Brest by a revolutionary movement of local origin which was to influence all conditions of life in the Ukraine,

THE ORIGINS OF THE UKRAINIAN COZACKS

Ukraina was originally the common designation for all frontier regions of old *Ruś* or Ruthenia. It gradually became a proper name, localized in the region where no frontier line was ever clearly fixed and where conditions remained unsettled. That was the case in the southeastern part of what had once been the Kievan State, in the wide steppes which separated the last permanent settlements and centers of administration from the shores of the Black Sea, and which were open to continuous invasions by Asiatic tribes.

The sparse population of that specific frontier territory was, in its great majority, Ruthenian. But only much later, not before the nineteenth century, the name of Ruthenians or Little Russians, always subject to confusion with the Great Russians or Russians proper, was gradually replaced by the name of Ukrainians and the whole area of that nation was called Ukraine. One of the reasons for such a change in terminology was the historical fact that it was in the original Ukraine, the southeastern border region, that not later than the sixteenth century a movement originated which gradually identified itself with the rise of modern Ruthenian nationalism. It was represented by the Ukrainian Cozacks.

The name Cozack, rather than Cossack, is of Turko-Tartar origin. In the fifteenth century it was already used for designating undisciplined groups of people, outside any stable political organization. These would sometimes appear as inspiring heroes, sometimes as dangerous brigands, in regions favorable to a life of bold adventure. Such a group also developed at the southeastern border of Muscovite Russia, in the Don region. There it was to create serious trouble for the Russian State until, after a whole series of revolts, these Don Cozacks came under strict government control and were turned into a well-known part of the Russian armed forces. Even more involved was the problem of the Ukrainian Cozacks in the Dnieper region, because when they emerged as an organization, Orthodox in faith and predominantly Ruthenian in ethnic composition, the Ukraine was part of the grand duchy of Lithuania, a Catholic state under Lithuanian leadership and federated with Catholic Poland.

So long as that state was firmly in control of the steppes as far as the Black Sea and in a position to check, one way or another, the neighboring Tartar Khanate of the Crimea, the southeastern provinces of the grand duchy, particularly Kiev—autonomous under local dukes until 1471—and Eastern Podolia with Bratslav, were comparatively safe and normal conditions of life prevailed. But as soon as the Tartar invasions, never completely stopped, became a regular plague, the Khanate of the Crimea being a vassal of the advancing Ottoman Empire and frequently allied with Moscow, the steppes north of the Black Sea on both sides of the lower Dnieper and beyond its famous cataracts —therefore in Ruthenian called *zaporoshe*—were practically a no man's land where the Cozack movement found a great opportunity both to supplement the inadequate defense of the country and to raid the Crimea or even Turkish possessions in turn.

The Lithuanian administration was equally aware of the services which the warlike Cozacks could render and of the danger of being involved in hostilities with Tartars or Turks through retaliatory expeditions made even in times of peace. Already under Sigismund I some of the starostas (governors) of the most exposed frontier districts south of Kiev would submit proposals for using the Cozacks as a permanent frontier guard under government control. Under Sigismund Augustus, an adventurous magnate, Prince Demetrius Wiśniowiecki, organized some Cozacks on one of the Dnieper islands and led them as far as the Caucasian region and Moldavia until he was captured and executed by the Turks.

A few years later the Ukraine proper, together with the whole provinces of Kiev and Bratslav, and with Volhynia in the background, was transferred from Lithuania to Poland by the Lublin Treaty of 1569. It was now the Polish administration which, along with the whole problem of the defense of the southeastern frontier of the commonwealth, had to deal with the Cozacks. This was, at the same time, a serious social question. While all other classes of the population in the Ruthenian provinces had already been assimilated to the social pattern of Poland, the Cozacks occupied a unique position between the gentry and the peasants. Almost immediately after the Union of Lublin, Sigismund Augustus decided to grant a limited number of Cozacks the status of a military organization with self-government under their own leader but under the control of the commander in chief of the Polish forces, while the others were supposed to be mere peasants. And it was precisely that basic conception which was also followed by the king's successors, with only the number of the so-called registered Cozacks varying in accordance with the political situation.

Stefan Batory, who needed the Cozacks in his struggle against Ivan the Terrible, developed that system but without any fundamental changes. He favored the establishment of a permanent Cozack center in the Ukraine, but one of their leaders who made an arbitrary expedition into Moldavia was executed because of Turkey's protest. At the same time the progress of systematic colonization in the Ukrainian region by landowners belonging to both the native Ruthenian and the Polish nobility reduced the territory where the Cozacks could move freely and created endless conflicts in individual cases.

The first of these conflicts, which provoked a formal revolt of Cozack lands, started in 1592 between one of their leaders of Polish origin, Christopher Kosiński, and the most prominent Orthodox Ruthenian magnate, Prince Constantine Ostrogski, whose estates were badly devastated. Much more serious was the rebellion under Łoboda and Nalevayko, which broke out in the very year of the Union of Brest, thus contributing to the tense situation in the Ruthenian lands but without having any religious motives. What increased the danger and encouraged the Cozacks, was the fact that shortly before that insurrection they had established independent relations with a foreign power, Emperor Rudolf II, thus for the first time making the Cozack question an international issue.

While Poland hesitated to join the league against the Turks planned by the Habsburgs, in 1593 the Cozacks received an Austrian envoy who was impressed by their military organization and, supported by papal diplomacy, he induced them to invade Transylvania and the Moldavian principalities the following year. This spectacular action in support of Austrian influence was not at all coordinated with Poland's official policy. Grand Chancellor Zamoyski also led armed forces into Moldavia, but in order to establish the Mohyla (Movila) family under Polish suzerainty there, and in 1595 he made a treaty with Turkey which recognized that situation.

In the same year the Cozack leaders who had cooperated with Rudolf II turned against the Polish authorities and made devastating raids as far as Volhynia and White Ruthenia. It was not before 1596 that a Polish army under Stanisław Żółkiewski forced the Cozacks to capitulate. Łoboda was killed in a struggle with an opposing faction, and Nalevayko was captured and executed. That bloody civil war was a first momentous warning that the Cozack problem was far from being solved and that the Ukraine remained a latent center of unrest. If new troubles did not break out in the following two decades, it was because the same Polish leaders who had opposed and crushed the rebellion used Cozacks in increasing numbers, far beyond the planned "register," in the foreign wars which started at the turn of the century.

The Cozacks fought, indeed, on the Polish side when in 1600 new troubles in Transylvania and Moldavia called for another Polish intervention. In the preceding year the Austrians had defeated the last descendants of the Báthory family and temporarily recognized Prince Michael the Brave of Wallachia as ruler of Transylvania. He also now wanted to conquer Moldavia. Zamoyski and Żółkiewski succeeded, however, in restoring the pro-Polish Mohylas in Moldavia.

Though the frontier where the Cozacks were usually fighting was now comparatively quiet, they soon found other occasions for satisfying their warlike spirit in Poland's campaigns against distant Sweden and Orthodox Moscow. This clearly indicates that they did not yet have any independent policy of their own or any special sympathies with their coreligionists. But as a group they indeed remained foreign to Poland's social structure and culture and much less integrated with the Western world than the other parts of the commonwealth. Although they so often proved to be an outpost defending the borders not only of Poland but of Christendom, and were to prove it again in the future, they could at any moment turn again against their official masters and create troubles in a crucial region where a transition between different civilizations was taking place. The question as to which side they would finally take was to be decisive for the future of the Ukraine and of the Ruthenian people in general, and especially for the fate of the Union of Brest in which the Cozacks originally showed little interest.

It was here in the Ukrainian steppes that Renaissance culture, after advancing so far in the eastern direction, was gradually disappearing, and it was here too that political trends, coming both from the Catholic West and from the Orthodox and Mohammedan East, were meeting and making that region near the Black Sea equally as important for the European balance of power as was the Livonian region on the Baltic. And it was precisely at the time when the Cozack wars started that even Western Europe, particularly France, began to realize that in the balance of power system the countries of East Central Europe were an indispensable element.

From the reign of Henry IV (1589–1610), French policy was also aware that Poland occupied a key position in that part of Europe. But France wanted her to cooperate with two other prospective allies against the Habsburgs, with Sweden and Turkey, and while the dynastic policy of the Vasas created a Polish-Swedish conflict instead, the Cozack problem was one of the factors which in the seventeenth century led to the long-postponed struggle between Poland and the Ottoman Empire.

PART IV

THE EASTERN WING OF THE BALANCE
OF POWER SYSTEM

12

THE FIRST HALF OF THE SEVENTEENTH CENTURY

WESTERN INTERFERENCE IN THE RUSSIAN "TIME OF TROUBLES"

When Henry IV or rather his minister, Sully, outlined an international organization of Europe, they attributed to East Central Europe, represented by Poland, an important place at the border of their Christian Republic from which not only the Ottoman Empire but also Orthodox Russia was excluded. Nevertheless the policies of both of these powers profoundly influenced the European state system and its precarious balance. France herself took advantage of it, cooperating with Turkey against the Habsburgs, from 1536 on, and the latter started their cooperation with Russia against the possible allies of France in Central Europe even earlier. Similar combinations reappeared time and again in the seventeenth century. But at its very beginning another possibility seemed to open up: the establishment of permanent political and cultural ties between East European Russia and her neighbors in Central Europe.

Such a situation developed during Russia's "time of troubles." As indicated in that very designation, it was primarily an internal crisis on apparently dynastic grounds, but also on much deeper social and constitutional grounds, which, however, at the same time offered a tempting opportunity for foreign interference. In that respect a first occasion was the appearance of the famous pretender, Demetrius, who claimed to be a son of Ivan the Terrible. He wanted to regain his father's throne, occupied since 1598 by Boris Godunov. His fascinating story started, indeed, in Poland, where that Russian exile found a haven in 1603 and succeeded in arousing the interest of both the king and the papal nuncio, since he made promises of cooperation with Poland and of religious union with Rome if assisted in realizing his objectives. He did not, however, inspire sufficient confidence to receive any official support. When he invaded Russia the following year it was only with a limited participation of individual Polish magnates, including non-Catholics and opponents of the royal government, and of a number of Ukrainian Cozacks, thrilled by that adventure and following the example of the Russian Don Cozacks who also rebelled against Moscow.

The sudden death of Boris Godunov facilitated the victory of the pretender in 1605. As czar he did not keep any promises made to Poland or to the Catholic Church, but even so, his marriage with a Polish lady, and Polish and Western influence at his court, contributed to the revolt of the following year in which he was killed without having established closer relations between Russia and her neighbors. Polish support given to another pseudo-Demetrius, an obvious impostor who pretended to be Ivan's son, was again entirely unofficial and only created trouble for King Sigismund III when in 1609 he finally decided to interfere with the chaotic situation in Russia.

The direct cause of the Polish invasion was the alliance which the new czar, Vasil Shuysky, concluded in the preceding year with Sweden. Asking for Swedish support, he had to pay a twofold price: the Swedes, entering the civil war in Russia, occupied a fairly large and important section of the country, including the city and region of Novgorod, and furthermore, Vasil in turn promised to cooperate with them against Poland. This was, of course, an open challenge to Sigismund III, because since 1600 he had been at war with his uncle, Charles IX of Sweden. The rivalry within the Vasa dynasty was now combined with the old rivalry of both countries in the Baltic lands where the Poles hoped to gain Estonia, while the Swedes, in spite of spectacular Polish-Lithuanian victories, penetrated deeply into Livonia.

Facing the Swedish-Russian alliance, the commonwealth had to choose between two different war aims and programs. Stanisław Żółkiewski, the nephew of Jan Zamoyski and continuator of his political and military activities, after defeating Shuysky's forces in the battle of Klushino in 1610 and taking him prisoner, together with his brothers, favored the idea of some kind of union between Poland and Russia in a spirit of reconciliation and cultural and constitutional assimilation. He succeeded in concluding a formal agreement with a strong party of prominent boyars, based upon the election of the king's son, Władysław, as czar of Russia. The young prince was supposed to become an Orthodox and, following the Polish example, the czarist autocracy would have been limited in favor of the boyars.

Sigismund III hesitated, however, to confirm that agreement. He did not want his son to go to Moscow or to change his religion, and tried to be accepted as czar himself. Such a personal union of both countries under a ruler known for his strong Catholic convictions had, of course, even less chance of success than Żółkiewski's initiative. It soon became apparent that the Commonwealth and the Czardom were so far apart and basically so different from each other that a repetition of the federal experiment which had succeeded so well in Polish-Lithuanian relations was out of the question. No Polish candidate was acceptable to the majority of the Russians, just as all Russian candidatures to the Polish throne had been and would be complete failures. Muscovite Russia, already a vast Eurasian power soon to reach the Pacific, could not possibly join the Polish-Lithuanian Commonwealth in the Western community to which all East Central Europe by now definitely belonged.

The concrete program of the king and his closest advisers was therefore strictly limited. He wanted to regain the borderlands which Moscow had conquered a hundred years before. In the present situation, the province of Smolensk, with the strategically important city which capitulated in 1611 after a long siege, was reclaimed by Lithuania, to join the other White Ruthenian provinces of the grand duchy. Severia with Chernigov, lost by Lithuania in 1500, would now come under the administration of the kingdom of Poland, along with the other Ukrainian lands.

That result was, indeed, achieved in the armistice finally concluded at Deulino in 1618, but not before a long struggle that was exhausting for both sides. Invited by their partisans among the Russian boyars, Polish-Lithuanian forces had entered Moscow and there defended themselves in the Kremlin for more than two years. But their very presence in Russia's capital contributed to a strong reaction of Russian nationalism which in 1613 resulted in the election of a new dynasty, the Romanovs, who united the Russian people against all foreign invaders when the native pretenders had disappeared one after the others. Władysław of Poland was not yet prepared to give up his title of czar based upon the election of 1611, but it had no more real significance than his father's Swedish title.

The appeal to Sweden, which had started foreign intervention and provoked the Polish one, also resulted in territorial losses for Russia. The Swedes evacuated purely Russian territory, but in the treaty of 1617 the new czar, Michael Romanov, had to restore to them the controversial section of Baltic coast between Estonia and Finland which Boris Godunov had regained. After such a dangerous crisis, there remained, therefore, in Russia a strong resentment against the Western powers which, one way or another, had profited from it, and Russia's new frontier continued to be a limit between two different regions of the continent. West of that line, all White Ruthenian and Ukrainian lands were now part of the Polish-Lithuanian Commonwealth again, associated with the West, and Moscow's advances in the preceding century seemed to be canceled.

Russia was, however, not prepared to accept that situation. After the rather disappointing experience with the Swedish alliance she never repeated it in spite of the continuing hostility between the two Vasa kingdoms which was so harmful to East Central Europe. The Romanovs, particularly Czar Michael's father and coruler, Philaret, who returned from Polish captivity and was now patriarch of Moscow, were rather inclined to cooperate with the Ottoman Empire against Poland, the Patriarchate of Constantinople serving as intermediary, particularly in the time of Cyril Lucaris. But when the Turkish onslaught against Poland started in 1620, Russia had not yet recovered from the "time of troubles." It was therefore not before Sigismund III's death in 1632 that she tried for the first time to take her revenge and, in particular, to retake Smolensk. But Władysław IV, who had been unanimously elected after his father, surrounded the Russian army which besieged that city, and in spite of a simultaneous Turkish attack, Poland was so successful in that new war that the peace treaty of Polanovka in 1634 simply made final the stipulations of the armistice of 1618. At last Władysław gave up his title of czar.

Polish-Russian relations now seemed stabilized, but as a matter of fact Russia was only waiting for a better occasion to repay the invasion of 1609 and to interfere in Poland's internal situation if and when, in turn, that country should enter a period of troubles. That did not occur, however, before 1648, a critical year in all European history, and it was to be a tragic result of the unsolved problem of the Ukrainian Cozacks. Until that date the Polish-Lithuanian Commonwealth enjoyed a period of prosperity which even serious losses in the

Swedish war (1621–1629) could not completely upset. That war could hardly be compared with the horrors of the contemporary Thirty Years' War in the Western part of Central Europe, a conflict which Poland fortunately avoided, but not without suffering from its repercussions.

THE EASTERN REPERCUSSIONS OF THE THIRTY YEARS' WAR

The Thirty Years' War, the main event in Europe's history during the first half of the seventeenth century, was primarily a "time of troubles" in the Holy Roman Empire which was more and more identified with Germany. The war, therefore, directly affected only the western part of Central Europe, and foreign intervention came exclusively from the Scandinavian North and from the West. But there were moments when it seemed that Poland too might become involved, and in any case her Western policy was unavoidably influenced by the events in her German neighborhood. Furthermore, the possessions of the Habsburgs outside the empire, particularly in Hungary, were drawn into the turmoil with consequences reaching as far as Transylvania and the part of Central Europe which was occupied by the Turks. Finally, it so happened that the civil war started in that part of the empire which was predominantly Slavic and traditionally associated with East Central Europe—in Bohemia. That country which in the past had enjoyed a privileged position within the empire, and which had successfully defended its autonomy throughout the first century of Habsburg rule, was to suffer most profoundly from the consequences of the war whose first phase was specifically Bohemian and which must be considered a tragic turning point in the development of the Czech nation.

The tension in Bohemia, which had been rapidly growing from the beginning of the reign of Emperor Mathias, was again, as in the Hussite period, religious, national, and constitutional at the same time—though this time hardly social. The so-called "defenestration" of May 23, 1618, i.e., the throwing out of two leading Catholic court officials from a window of the royal castle in Prague, was the signal for the outbreak of a revolution in defense of Bohemia's state rights against forceful centralization and of religious freedom for the Protestants. It was the leader of the German Protestants, the Calvinist Elector Palatine Frederick, who was chosen king of Bohemia the following year after Emperor Mathias' death and the deposition in Bohemia of his successor Ferdinand II. However, Frederick's crushing defeat in the battle of the White Mountain outside Prague, on November 8, 1620, also had disastrous consequences for Czech nationalism.

For the repression which followed not only abolished the old constitution and the privileges of the Estates, leaving them only the right to vote taxes and making the king residing in Vienna practically absolute, not only outlawed the Protestants who were exiled, but also contributed to the Germanization of the country. The German language now became official, on a footing of equality with the Czech and soon gaining actual predominance, and the composition of the nobility—the leading class under the circumstances—was completely changed. Those who were executed or exiled, and whose lands were confiscated, had been mostly Czechs attached to the national tradition, while those who replaced them as landowners and high officials were a cosmopolitan group who came from all Habsburg lands, but the majority of whom were of German origin or culture.

In addition to all that, Bohemia continued to be a badly devastated battlefield during the whole war, suffering a cultural and economic decline which particularly affected the Czech population. Its spiritual leaders, like the famous educator Jan Amos Komenský, had to live and work abroad, and during that dark age of Czech national culture which was to last until the great revival of the nineteenth century, Bohemia's history was more than ever before connected with the history of Germany and of the Habsburg dynasty. The liquidation of most of the Czech nobility in 1620, as well as the subsequent Germanization of the rest, was to affect permanently the social structure of the Czech nation so that the revolt of 1618 produced just the opposite of what was expected.

Even before that rebellion had openly started, disturbances in Silesia, mainly on religious grounds, attracted the attention of Poland, raising hopes that this formerly Polish province could be regained on that occasion. The king himself seemed to realize that opportunity when the bishop of Breslau, his brother-in-law Archduke Charles, facing a Lutheran revolt in 1616, asked for assistance by Polish troops and designated a son of Sigismund III as his successor. Later, however, the interest in Silesia was apparent rather among those

Poles who, in sympathy with the Czechs, were prepared to turn against the Habsburgs, while the king, who successively married two Austrian archduchesses, remained faithful to his pro-Habsburg orientation and rendered them a valuable service in the critical year of 1619.

It was then that the Hungarian opposition against the Habsburgs, largely Protestant as in Bohemia, tried to take advantage of the civil war there and to assist the rebels by besieging Vienna. They had a prominent leader in the person of Gabriel Bethlen who in 1613 had been made prince of Transylvania. A Calvinist, like most of his predecessors, particularly Stephen Bocskay, prominent at the beginning of the century, Bethlen was aiming at the unification of Hungary and her liberation from Austrian control. Threatened from two sides, Ferdinand II asked for Polish assistance, and while the Diet refused it, Sigismund III privately recruited mercenaries, the so-called "Lissowczyki," who with Cozack participation marched against Bethlen and forced him to lift the siege of Vienna. But since most of Hungary continued to be under the rule of the Turks, who were always hostile to the Habsburgs, while Bethlen carefully avoided any open conflict with them, even such an unofficial Polish interference drew Poland into a war with Turkey.

In spite of continuous Cozack raids against Turkish possessions, Żółkiewski had tried to avoid it, but now he decided to support the friendly prince of Moldavia whom the Turks had deposed, and the Polish army advanced as far as Cecora. Receiving no adequate Moldavian or Cozack assistance, however, Żółkiewski had to retreat and was himself killed in action in December, 1620. Although the emperor refused any help, glad to see Poland diverted from his Bohemian troubles, a rapidly mobilized Polish-Lithuanian army, this time with strong Cozack participation under Peter Konashevych, stopped the Turkish invasion under Sultan Osman II in the battle of Chocim and obtained honorable peace conditions in 1621.

But even now Poland could not take any position in the German war which soon entered its second (Danish) phase, because before Christian of Denmark invaded Germany a much greater Scandinavian warrior, Gustavus Adolphus, had launched another Swedish invasion against Poland. Already during the truce between 1618 and 1620, he had established close relations with the Hohenzollerns of Brandenburg, who since the extinction of the Ansbach line in 1618 were in possession of the Polish fief of East Prussia. And in the very days of September, 1621 when the forces of the commonwealth were halting the Turks at Chocim, the Swedes occupied Riga and most of Livonia.

Sigismund III still had illusions of regaining the Swedish crown with the aid of the Habsburgs, but precisely because the Poles did not want to get entangled in the Thirty Years' War, the Diets voted taxes only for the defense of the commonwealth. Even that defense proved extremely difficult when in 1625 Gustavus Adolphus renewed his aggression, with the connivance of the Elector of Brandenburg, and occupied not only the Duchy of East Prussia but also the whole Polish coast of Royal Prussia, with only the exception of Danzig which put up a strong resistance. In the following years, particularly in 1627 and 1629, the Polish army under Stanisław Koniecpolski, and even the young and rather small Polish navy, won important victories. Contrary to the endeavors of the emperor, who wanted the Polish-Swedish war to continue in order to prevent the intervention of Gustavus Adolphus in Germany, a six-year truce was signed at Altmark. Livonia remained, however, in the hands of the Swedes, who also continued to occupy the most important ports of both the Prussias, while some towns of Royal Prussia were held by the Elector of Brandenburg.

French mediation, with the participation of an English diplomat, Sir Thomas Roe, who was unusually interested in the affairs of Eastern Europe, contributed to the conclusion of that armistice which made possible Sweden's invasion of Germany. And it was Richelieu's France which again, in the presence of Dutch and English mediators, helped to negotiate another armistice in 1635, that of Stumsdorf. This was for a much longer period of twenty-six years and was more satisfactory to Poland, since the Swedes gave up the occupation of the Polish-Prussian ports and the control of the customs there. Such an agreement could at last appease the Polish-Swedish conflict because the death of Gustavus Adolphus in the Battle of Lützen (1632), in the same year in which his Polish cousin and opponent Sigismund III died after a reign of almost half a century, had greatly changed the situation. During the minority of Queen Christina, the last of the Swedish Vasas, Sweden had suffered setbacks in Germany and was no longer in a position to continue her imperialistic policy, while the new king of Poland, Władysław IV, after his successes in the east in the wars with Russia and Turkey, hoped to play a leading part in the negotiations which were supposed to end the war in Germany.

As a matter of fact, that war now entered its last phase. It was characterized by the intervention of France, which now tried more than ever before to have Poland on her side. Władysław IV hesitated. His first marriage in 1637 with a sister of Ferdinand III, the new emperor, resulted in such a tension of French-Polish relations that the king's brother, John Casimir, who was on his way to Spain where he planned to accept the position of admiral, was arrested in France and kept in prison for almost two years or until 1640. It was only three years later that Władysław IV again started negotiating with Mazarin. His second marriage with Princess Louise Marie de Gonzague-Nevers, who came to Poland in 1646, indicated a final turn in his policy. It could, however, hardly affect the issue of the Thirty Years' War which was approaching its end, and without breaking with the emperor, the King of Poland, in the last years of his life, concentrated on his plan for an anti-Turkish league.

This project could seem well justified, both by the increase of the Ottoman danger which Western Christendom had badly neglected during the Thirty Years' War, and by the urgent need for finding some constructive role for the Ukrainian Cozacks whose discontent could no longer be repressed.

THE GATHERING STORM

The dozen years before the crisis of 1648 seemed to be a period of peace for East Central Europe, particularly if contrasted with the situation in the West during the last phase of the Thirty Years' War. Such a lull was, however, nothing but an illusory quietness before the outbreak of a general conflagration, unusual even in the war-torn history of that region of the continent. It all started with another Cozack insurrection against the Polish administration of the Ukraine, but this time the conflict did not remain localized there, as it had been on earlier occasions. On the contrary, all neighboring countries gradually became involved, and the balance of power was deeply affected throughout the whole of Europe. Since general peace was not restored before the end of the century, it might be said that immediately after the Thirty Years' War in Western Europe, there was a less known but equally important Fifty Years' War in Eastern Europe, divided, just as the other had been, into various phases, and leading to the great Northern War at the beginning of the eighteenth century. Far from being exclusively a military and diplomatic problem, that series of wars resulted in a deep constitutional and social crisis.

For Poland, the only fully independent power which earlier crises had left in East Central Europe, the "Deluge," as the crisis following 1648 is called in the national tradition, was indeed a "time of troubles," as long and serious as that in Russia a few decades before. It was therefore easy to anticipate that Russia's long-awaited revenge for the Polish intervention in her troubles would now take place. But it was not only in Moscow that the Ukrainian Cozacks found a support which in the long run proved hardly helpful to their real interests. Even before the czar's decision to interfere openly, the revolution had been backed by an alliance with the Ukraine's traditional enemy, the Khanate of the Crimea, and such cooperation with a vassal state of the Ottoman Empire necessarily led to intervention by the Turks themselves. All this made the troubles in the Ukraine a part of the great conflict between Christian Europe and Islam which was resumed in the seventeenth century.

The new series of Muslim aggressions which in that century threatened large parts of the continent was rather unexpected. Since the death of Suleiman the Magnificent in 1566, and of his last grand vizier, Mohammed Sokolli, in 1579, the Ottoman Empire suffered from a complete lack of leadership even in the military field. But even after the Treaty of Zsitva Torek, which was concluded with Austria in 1606, the Ottoman Empire was still strong enough to keep all its earlier conquests. Nothing was changed in the desperate situation of the Christian peoples of the Balkans, where only in the isolated mountain regions of Montenegro and Albania some resistance and local self-government continued throughout the period. The reduced outposts of the still powerful Republic of Venice were neither secure nor a comfort to the Christian populations of the East who found Venetian domination hardly preferable to the Turkish, and who never looked for liberation toward Italian or German powers. The tiny Republic of Ragusa, that strange Slavic community organized on the model of Venice, was still a haven of comparative freedom but without the amazing sea power which it enjoyed in the preceding century.

There was no basic change in the situation of partitioned Hungary either. The major part, directly under Turkish rule, was in a position almost as bad as the Balkans. The western and northern border region, which the Habsburgs succeeded in keeping under their rule, was making some progress, thanks to the fact that the Counter Reformation, which, as in Bohemia, had started as a centralizing and Germanizing factor, became associated with the genuine progress of Hungarian culture. Archbishop Peter Pázmány, acting by peaceful methods, combined Catholic propaganda with a constructive reform of education. In 1635, after short-lived attempts in earlier centuries, he founded the first Hungarian university which was to survive until the present. Before that university could be transferred to Buda, liberated from the Turks, it had its headquarters in the town of Nagyszombat.

The Catholic Hungarians therefore preferred Habsburg rule to the Ottoman yoke from which only Austrian support could liberate the heart of their country. Some of their leaders, like Nicholas Esterházy who held the supreme office of palatine from 1625 to 1645, were even opposed to the continued existence of the Principality of Transylvania which could maintain its semi-independent status only by appeasing Turkey, and, which as a stronghold of Calvinism, persisted in the anti-Habsburg policy of Stephen Bocskay and Gabriel Bethlen. After the Bethlens, the Rákócsi family, one member of which had already been prince of Transylvania from 1606 to 1608, occupied the throne after 1630. That family wanted not only to defend Transylvania's freedom, but also to unite all Hungary under their leadership and to play a role in general European affairs in cooperation with Western Protestantism and with the other enemies of the Habsburgs.

It was precisely in the critical year of 1648 that George II Rákócsi succeeded his father George I. His interference with the affairs of Poland where—like Bethlen before him—he hoped to gain the royal crown, had to end in disaster. Not only Austria but also Turkey was opposed to such a rise of Transylvania in a region where the Ottoman Empire itself came to see a new field of expansion.

That Turkish policy of expansion was mainly directed by the Köprülüs, a family whose members occupied the office of grand vizier for more than half a century. While none of the sultans of the seventeenth century equaled their great predecessors, these viziers completely controlled the empire and hoped to stop its decline, not yet apparent to the outside world, by spectacular new victories. They realized, first, that the lack of unity among the Christian powers offered them a last chance of success, and they also became convinced that it would be comparatively easy to turn against Poland. Hence the repeated assaults against that country from the days of Cecora and Chocim, under Sigismund III, to the age of Jan Sobieski, Żółkiewski's great-grandson.

Poland was an immediate neighbor, not of the Ottoman Empire proper, but of its vassals in Transylvania, Moldavia, and in the Crimea, along an extended area of transition where frictions continuously occurred. An efficient resistance against the Muslims would have required the cooperation of all three Christian powers interested in that area: Austria, Poland, and Russia. The Catholic character of both Austria and Poland, as well as the lack of any real conflicts between the two countries, seemed to favor at least the cooperation of these two. That was precisely the opinion of Sigismund III and it was one of the reasons why Władysław IV also hesitated to break with the Habsburgs. But the imperialism of that dynasty, the distrust of the Polish nobility toward their policy, which was based upon German interests and an absolute form of government, the sympathy with anti-Habsburg movements in Bohemia and in Hungary, and last but not least, the desire for friendly relations with France, the chief opponent of the Habsburgs—all this made a close alliance with them completely impossible.

Władysław IV himself felt strong enough to assume the leadership of an anti-Turkish action without the Habsburgs, who had been weakened by the Thirty Years' War. And Poland was distant enough not to raise any fear of supremacy among the peoples which were to be liberated from Ottoman domination. It was therefore toward her king, bearing the name of the hero of Varna, that even the Balkan populations were looking as toward the Christian monarch who would come to free them. It was only after Władysław's death and Russia's victories over Poland that even a Catholic Croat priest, George Križanich, would turn with similar hopes toward the czar, the leader of another Slavic power. Russia now seemed to be in a better position to fight the Muslims and to help the oppressed Balkan nations which were mostly Orthodox like herself.

What these peoples of South Eastern Europe did not realize was, first, the aggressive policy of Moscow against her neighbors in the northern part of East Central Europe, and secondly, her desire to avoid any conflict with the Ottoman Empire as long as these neighbors were not defeated. On the contrary, since Poles and Lithuanians were Catholics, Orthodox Russia was rather inclined to cooperate against their commonwealth with Mohammedan Turkey in a common front sponsored by the Patriarch of Constantinople. In the time of Cyril Lucaris that program of action had been premature, but it was no accident that when his representative, the Patriarch of Jerusalem, returned from Moscow in 1620, he secretly ordained a new Orthodox metropolitan in Kiev, thus restoring the anti-Uniate hierarchy in the Ruthenian lands.

It was then that for the first time the Ukrainian Cozacks, even their otherwise loyal leader Peter Konashevych, became interested in the religious issues raised by the Union of Brest, and were used as supporters of those Ruthenians who remained Greek-Orthodox. The new king, Władysław IV, more tolerant than his father, tried to appease them immediately after his election in 1632. He divided the Ruthenian dioceses among Uniates and anti-Uniates, and besides the Uniate metropolitan he also officially recognized an Orthodox one in the person of Peter Mohyla. This prominent man was of Rumanian origin, a descendant of the family which had ruled Moldavia under Polish protection. He was himself loyal to the commonwealth and when he founded an Orthodox academy in Kiev, that first institution of higher education among the Eastern Slavs was an outpost of Western though non-Catholic culture.

Taking all this into consideration, Władysław IV also hoped that his Orthodox subjects, and particularly the Cozacks, so experienced in fighting Turks and Tartars, would willingly cooperate in his anti-Ottoman expedition and that even Moscow would possibly change her traditional policy. A Russian attack against the Crimean Tartars, from whose raids Moscow had to suffer as much as Poland, was planned as the eastern wing of a concerted action in which Venice was supposed to be the Western ally. While that republic really entered a war with Turkey in defense of her remote colony, the island of Crete, which resisted for thirty years, Russian cooperation remained an illusion. And when the king had to give up his plan, never favored by the Polish Diet, the Cozacks soon came to an understanding with the Tartars of the Crimea and that anti-Polish league was to enjoy the full support of both Russia and Turkey.

THE GREAT COZACK INSURRECTION

Neither the failure of the king's anti-Turkish scheme nor the personal wrong which Bohdan Khmelnitsky (Chmielnicki), a distinguished Cozack leader of noble origin, had suffered from another member of the gentry, can fully explain the origin of the Cozack insurrection of 1648 and even less its unusual violence. The reasons for the outbreak and for Khmelnitsky's amazing success were much deeper. The whole Cozack problem which troubled the Ukraine during the preceding half century had never found any satisfactory solution. In the latter part of the reign of Sigismund III, and again in 1638, whenever the Cozacks were not used in larger number in foreign wars, uprisings of those who were not included in the official register and who were threatened with being reduced to serfdom had taken place, and the repressions, which were particularly severe in the last instance, only created an even stronger tension. Such dissatisfaction of the Cozack masses could easily be used by an ambitious leader who would succeed in making it at the same time a religious and a national issue, thus appealing to a large section of the Orthodox Ruthenian population. Whether or not Khmelnitsky had such an intention from the outset, is difficult to determine. He pretended not to rise against the king, who was said to have encouraged the Cozacks to defend their rights, but only against the rich magnates who held the highest offices and most of the land in the Ukraine. However, the alliance which he at once concluded with the khan of the Crimea, who sent him considerable auxiliary forces, made the civil war an international problem and was a real threat to the commonwealth.

Without sufficiently realizing this, inadequate Polish forces which were sent against the rebels suffered a series of humiliating defeats. In the midst of a chaotic situation Władysław IV died, and of his two brothers, John Casimir, formerly a Jesuit and a cardinal, who seemed to be more popular among the Cozacks, was unanimously elected. In agreement with the grand chancellor, George Ossoliński, the main adviser of his predecessor, he tried a policy of appeasement, contrary to the opinion of Prince Jeremiah Wiśniowiecki who wanted to crush the insurrection with the same ruthlessness which the Cozacks themselves, with their Tartar allies, inflicted upon all opponents, particularly nobles, Jews, and Uniates. When, however, all negotiations failed in view of Khmelnitsky's claim to the complete control of the

Ukraine, the new king proved an excellent war leader and diplomat. In 1649 he moved to the rescue of the castle of Zbaraż, where a small army under Wiśniowiecki desperately defended itself against overwhelming forces, and although the battle at nearby Zborów remained undecided, John Casimir succeeded in making a separate peace with the Tartars. The result was a compromise with the Cozack leader which raised the number of registered Cozacks to forty thousand and granted them as a group, including their families, full autonomy in the three provinces of the Ukraine where the Union of Brest was to be abolished and all offices reserved for Orthodox.

While the Polish Diet refused to ratify the clause directed against the Union, Khmelnitsky realized that the Cozack masses which were not registered would turn against him if the Zborów agreement were strictly kept. And since he had already decided to create a Ukrainian state entirely free from Poland, he started looking for Russian or Turkish help. But although he placed the Ukraine under the sultan's protection in the spring of 1651, and made another alliance with the khan of the Crimea, the battle of Beresteczko in June of that year ended in a great Polish victory after three days. The peace concluded a few months later limited the number of registered Cozacks to twenty thousand and their territory to the Kiev region. This was of course even less acceptable to the revolutionary forces than the former agreement, Khmelnitsky was only waiting for an occasion to turn away from Poland and to get better conditions from another power. After a series of rather fantastic projects of cooperation with Moldavia, Transylvania, and Dissident elements inside Poland, he finally decided for Moscow.

Czar Alexius, the son and successor of Michael, the first Romanov, was closely observing the developments in the Ukraine, and the growing troubles during the year 1653 finally convinced him and his council that the situation was ripe for Russian intervention. When Poland refused his mediation in the conflict with the Cozacks, he decided to grant the latter his protection, fully aware that such a step involved a war with the commonwealth. But even before the czar invaded his western neighbor, he had to face difficulties in the negotiations with the Cozacks themselves. These were conducted by the Russian envoy Buturlin at Pereyaslav near Kiev.

The Cozacks had soon to find out that they would gain very little by transferring their allegiance. First they were told that the czar could not be expected to swear to his subjects, so that the final pact, signed on January 18, 1654, was not a bilateral treaty but a submission of the Ukraine to the czar. Furthermore, the text was so worded that it could be subject to different interpretations in the most important matter of self-government. Far from creating an independent Ukrainian state, the Pact of Pereyaslav merely defined the conditions of autonomy, not of the territory which would come under Russian rule but only of the Cozack community without, it is true, the previous discrimination between registered Cozacks and the others. Of course Khmelnitsky kept his office of "hetman," as the Cozack leaders were called, but the election of his successors would require a ratification by the czar who would also control the foreign relations of the Cozacks, particularly with Poland and Turkey.

On the other side, the decision of 1654 was an outstanding success for Moscow which for the first time extended its domination over territories which the Muscovites used to call "Little Russia" and which now were supposed to be permanently united with their own Great Russia, i.e., Russia proper in the modern sense. Since no territorial limits were defined, the question was left in suspense as to how much of the old *Ruś* or Ruthenia would come under Russian rule and, severed from the West, be connected with Eastern Europe. One thing was, however, obvious: the famous city of Kiev, developed into an important intellectual center and traditionally regarded as the mother of all Russian cities, would henceforth be under Moscow, thus increasing the prestige of the new Russia.

It was indeed equally clear that the final solution of the whole problem, deeply affecting the balance of power in Europe, would depend on the outcome of Russia's war against Poland, which started in the fall of the same year not only in the Ukraine where the czar's forces now supported the Cozacks but also in the White Ruthenian borderlands of the grand duchy of Lithuania, where Russia wanted, first of all, to reconquer Smolensk. When that fortress, after a long siege, capitulated in 1655, the Russians invaded Lithuania proper and on the eighth of August occupied and terribly sacked Wilno.

When that happened the commonwealth was already invaded by another enemy, the Swedes, and the problem of the Cozacks who had established relations with the King of Sweden and urged him to march against Poland was now part of a general crisis in East Central Europe which, provoked by Khmelnitsky's insurrection, turned into a conflict among numerous powers fighting one another and changing sides whenever convenient. So also did the Cozacks themselves, losing their hope of complete independence and facing the gradual liquidation of even their autonomy by Moscow.

When Bogdan Khmelnitsky died in 1657, after trying in vain to strengthen his position by alliances with Sweden and Transylvania, the new hetman, Ivan Wyhowski, a candidate of the party who favored the idea of again coming into an agreement with Poland, started secret negotiations with King John Casimir, broke with the czar, and on September 16, 1658, concluded the Union of Hadziacz with the Polish representatives. It was much more than another concession of autonomy for the Cozacks, this time by Poland. The dualistic structure of the Polish-Lithuanian Commonwealth was transformed by placing beside the kingdom of Poland and the grand duchy of Lithuania, a "Ruthenian duchy," on a footing of complete equality. The Cozack hetman was at the same time made palatine of Kiev and first senator of the new duchy and remained the commander in chief of a Cozack army with a peace strength of thirty thousand; the Cozacks were to be gradually admitted into the nobility. While the Orthodox received special rights in the duchy, including the admission of their hierarchy into the senate of the commonwealth, any progress of the Uniate church was forbidden on the duchy's territory. That territory included, however, not all Ruthenian lands but only the three frontier provinces, called Ukrainian and associated with the Cozack tradition.

Even so the new union, ratified at the Diet of Warsaw the following year, offered the best possible solution of the Cozack problem in its new phase of development. It could have been a constructive step forward in the organization of East Central Europe. Unfortunately it came too late and did not succeed either in restoring the old boundaries or in keeping the Ukraine associated with the West. After so many bloody struggles between Cozacks and Poles, there remained a mutual distrust whose victim was eventually Wyhowski himself. The Cozacks were far from being united in support of Poland in the decisive struggle with Moscow which, of course, wanted to keep the tremendous gains of 1654 and of the following campaign. After initial victories, with the cooperation of even the Tartars, the year 1659 ended with Wyhowski's resignation. His successor, Khmelnitsky's son George, first tried to keep the balance between Poland

and Russia but soon placed the Ukraine once more under the czar's protection.

After another victorious Polish campaign against Russia in 1660, he surrendered to the king, but opposed by the partisans of Moscow, he resigned in 1663, entered a monastery, and left the Ukraine in a desperate condition of chaos and ruin—the ultimate result of his father's ambitious policy. Among the Cozacks there now appeared a third party, led by Peter Doroshenko. He returned to the idea of choosing the protection of Turkey, and in the ensuing three-cornered conflict between Poland, Russia, and the Ottoman Empire, with Tartar raids completing the destruction of the country on whatever side they were fighting, the fate of the Cozacks, of the Ukraine, and of the Ruthenian people could only be a partition among all three or at least between two of these powers.

13

THE SECOND HALF OF THE SEVENTEENTH
CENTURY

THE GREAT SWEDISH INVASION

The countries of East Central Europe were under a permanent pressure from the west and from the east. After the conquest of the Balkans by the Turks, the remaining part of the most exposed region of Europe also had to suffer from an additional pressure coming from the south. But only on exceptional occasions did invasions from the north, from across the natural boundary of the Baltic Sea, add new dangers to the precarious position of East Central Europe. Except for the protohistoric period of the Norman raids and migrations, that happened only in the seventeenth and early eighteenth centuries when Sweden played the part of a great power.

The invasion of Livonia by Charles IX, and even the invasions of Gustavus Adolphus which reached as far as Prussia, were only preludes if compared with the conquests of Charles X Gustavus in the middle of the seventeenth century. And though they ended in failure, as did those of Charles XII later, they seemed to have more chance of success and they did have more lasting consequences for East Central Europe, as well as less disastrous results for Sweden herself, than the adventures of the last Swedish conqueror.

This time the Polish-Swedish war was no longer a dynastic dispute between two branches of the Vasa dynasty which in Sweden had been replaced by the German family of Pfalz-Zweibrücken. Neither was it a territorial conflict limited to Livonian and Prussian lands. What was at stake was the existence of Poland as an independent nation, her union with Lithuania, and all that remained of free political development in East Central Europe. The greater was the responsibility of a few traitors who encouraged the unprovoked aggression of Charles Gustavus and facilitated his advance. Even the fact that John Casimir, the last of the Vasas, continued to use the title king of Sweden, was no justification for the break of the truce of Stumdorf which had left him that title and was to expire only in 1661.

In July 1655 the Swedes first invaded Great Poland where the only forces which could be mobilized, in view of the dangerous situation in the East, capitulated before the well-trained veterans of the Thirty Years' War and recognized the protectorate of Charles Gustavus. Three months later the most powerful Lithuanian magnate, Prince Janusz Radziwiłł, signed the agreement of Kiejdany which replaced Lithuania's union with Poland by a union with Sweden. He hoped thus to obtain a leading position in the grand duchy and possibly also Swedish help against the simultaneous Russian invasion. But the majority of the Lithuanians considered his arbitrary decision just another act of treason, and under the leadership of Paul Sapieha they continued to resist in the no man's land between the advancing Swedish and Russian forces.

The commonwealth was in danger of total partition because Charles Gustavus, who had occupied most of Poland proper including Warsaw and Cracow, promised some Polish territories to Frederick William of Prussia, the "Great Elector," who, deserting the Polish suzerain of East Prussia, made that province in January, 1656, a vassal duchy of Sweden. In what would remain of Poland after the additional losses in the East, Charles Gustavus wanted to be king himself, having forced the legitimate ruler to go into exile in Silesia. Only Danzig held out against Swedes and Prussians, and so did Lwów against Cozacks, Tartars, and Russians, but the turn of the tide came with the successful defense of the monastery of Częstochowa at Christmas, 1655.

The retreat of the Swedish forces before a handful of monks and knights who refused to surrender the famous shrine of Our Lady was an inspiration to the whole country which suffered hard from the conqueror's absolute rule and which particularly resented the persecution of Catholicism by Protestant invaders. Returning to Poland, John Casimir created a general enthusiasm when he solemnly swore in Lwów to venerate the Virgin Mary who had saved the country as Queen of the Crown of Poland, and to improve the conditions of life of the peasant population.

Unfortunately the badly needed reforms regarding the peasants were neglected in the midst of a war which was to continue for several years with varying success. The whole country remained a battlefield, and in spite of a series of victories of the Polish forces under the able command of Stefan Czarniecki, Warsaw, retaken at the end of June, 1656, was reoccupied by the Swedes a month later after a battle of three days in which the invaders had the support of the Great Elector. Even after another liberation of the capital, the enemies of Poland, including the Prince of Transylvania who temporarily entered Cracow, signed a treaty at the end of the same year which was, as a matter of fact, a plan of partitioning the whole country.

Russia was, however, no part of that agreement. An armistice had been concluded with the czar, to whom the succession after John Casimir was promised in order to gain some respite on the eastern front. These negotiations were hardly taken seriously and were never ratified by the Diet. But Czar Alexius himself, who was alarmed by the Swedish advance, turned against Charles Gustavus, hoping to gain access to the Baltic for Russia. Even more alarmed were the Habsburgs, especially since Sweden had the support of all Protestant powers, including even distant England under Cromwell. The Polish-Austrian treaty of 1657 not only brought to the commonwealth some reinforcements sent by Leopold I, but also encouraged Sweden's old rival, Denmark, to join that alliance and to enter the war on land and on sea. And since France, as usual, was eager to mediate between Poland and Sweden, practically all Europe became interested and at least indirectly involved in the conflict.

Leopold I needed the voice of the Elector of Brandenburg for his forthcoming election as emperor and therefore he avoided having to fight against the Hohenzollern. But he persuaded him to pass from the Swedish to the Polish side, with Poland, however, having to pay a heavy price. By the Treaty of Wehlau, concluded on September 19, 1657, she gave up her suzerainty over the duchy of Prussia. Her former vassal, who had deserted her in the most critical phase of the war, became completely independent. East Prussia, with even some temporary gains in Polish West Prussia which separated that duchy from Brandenburg, was now an even more dangerous enclave in the commonwealth because it was completely under German control.

In the meantime George Rákocsi who with Sweden's assistance had advanced as far as Warsaw and inflicted one more occupation upon the unhappy capital had been forced to a disastrous retreat and had been practically annihilated by the Tartars before he reached his own country. But on the other hand, Charles Gustavus defeated the

Danes, who had to sign a separate peace in February, 1658, and only in the fall of that year, Polish and allied forces, after crossing the sea, were sent to Denmark. A little later almost the whole of Polish Prussia was at last reconquered from the Swedes, who lost not only the control of Poland but even their most important gains along the Baltic shores. And when after Cromwell, their own king unexpectedly died too, the Swedes were ready for the French mediation which eventually led to the Treaty of Oliwa, near Danzig, signed on May 3, 1660.

In spite of her military successes in the last years of the Swedish war, Poland had to make serious concessions because she continued to be threatened in the east. Most of Livonia, occupied by the Swedes in the time of Gustavus Adolphus, was now definitely ceded, including the port of Riga. Only the region on the upper Dvina, with the city of Dünaburg, was left to the commonwealth, and the duchy of Curland which, in spite of all the troubles of the period was able to gain colonial possessions in Africa, remained a Polish fief under the Kettler dynasty. It was much less important that the last of the Vasas finally had to give up his theoretical rights to the Swedish crown, keeping only his title for life.

Thus, after sixty years, the conflict between Sweden and Poland, harmful for both countries, seemed finally concluded. After threatening Poland's survival, the great Swedish invasion had provoked a real rebirth of the vitality of the nation which avoided disaster in spite of so many simultaneous aggressions. Poland's position on the Baltic was badly shaken, however, not so much because of the territorial losses in Livonia but particularly through the emancipation of East Prussia, a decisive step in the rise of the Hohenzollern dynasty which now, from both Berlin and Königsberg, was able to exercise a growing influence not only in the empire but also in East Central Europe. It is true that the agreement of 1657, confirmed at Oliwa, left Poland a claim to East Prussia in case of the extinction of the Hohenzollern dynasty, and some rights of interference in favor of the Prussian estates which were soon to suffer from the ruthless centralization of the new regime. But even in the most striking cases, these rights proved of no avail to the defenders of the old liberties. While avoiding an open conflict with Poland, the Great Elector could now embark on his general policy of aggrandizement. This was to cause much trouble to that same Sweden which had first helped him to gain full independence for the duchy of Prussia.

In addition to her losses on the Baltic and the terrible devastation of the whole country, Poland, in consequence of the so-called "Deluge," also had to suffer from a serious internal crisis which even after the Peace of Oliwa did not allow her to concentrate on the grave eastern problems. During the most critical years of the war, Queen Louise Marie de Gonzague, the widow of Władysław IV whose second husband was John Casimir, had played a very remarkable part in general politics. Better than anybody else she realized the necessity for strengthening the royal authority, and she was deeply concerned with the problem of succession after the death of the childless king. The plan which in her opinion was to replace the fictitious idea of a candidature of the czar was the election of a French candidate during the king's lifetime. That return to the conception of Sigismund Augustus would have replaced the Austrian alliance by a close cooperation with the queen's country of origin and was to be combined with constitutional reforms. But for these very reasons Louise Marie's action was opposed not only by the partisans of the Habsburgs but also by all those who feared an *absolutum dominium* on the French model. Therefore the Swedish invasion was followed by a civil war which prolonged the crisis of the country.

THE RUSSIAN AND TURKISH ADVANCE

Twice in the seventeenth century the basic idea of the Polish constitution, that the king had to be obeyed only as long as he respected the laws of the country, led to an armed rebellion of those who considered the reform projects of the court as being contrary to the constitution. The first of these rebellions, called *rokosz*—a designation of Hungarian origin—was directed in 1606 against Sigismund III and its consequences explain the lack of unity in Polish politics during the "time of troubles" in Russia. The *rokosz* of George Lubomirski, which openly broke out in 1664 and lasted two years, was even more dangerous. True, it ended like the first one in a defeat and humiliation of the opposition leader, but again the royal authority suffered greatly and all reform projects had to be abandoned. Furthermore, Poland, in her exposed position and with the foreign wars not yet ended, could not afford a bloody, internal crisis which, similar to the almost contemporary French Fronde, had much deeper repercussions in international relations.

Not only was the succession problem left open, inviting the intrigues of foreign powers in view of the forthcoming election after John Casimir, but the fruits of earlier victories in the war against Russia were lost, the prospects of reuniting the Ukraine within the limits of the commonwealth had no longer any chances of success, and in 1667 an armistice had to be concluded at Andruszowo which involved much greater sacrifices than the Treaty of Oliwa and more profoundly affected the balance of power in Eastern Europe.

On the Russian side, the negotiator on behalf of Czar Alexius was A. N. Ordin-Nashchokin, a skilful diplomat who sincerely aimed at a lasting betterment of the relations with Poland. But even he, of course, wanted to save for Russia most of the gains which resulted from the pact concluded with the Ukrainian Cozacks thirteen years before, and the compromise which was accepted was definitely to Russia's advantage. It is true that in the northern, White Ruthenian region only Smolensk, with its province, was definitely ceded by the commonwealth, and in the south the Ukraine was divided along the Dnieper River, which seemed to be the best possible natural boundary. But it was precisely Smolensk, which in all previous wars had proved of decisive military importance, and the eastern, left-bank Ukraine alone was much easier to absorb by Russia than the whole of it. On the other hand, in spite of large territorial cessions, Poland did not at all get rid of the troublesome Cozack problem which only changed its aspect.

One of the new features of that problem was the possibility of Russian influence and even interference in the territories on the right bank of the Dnieper, which continued to be part of Poland but retained close ties with those Cozacks who were now under Russian rule. But what was particularly dangerous was the solution of the problem of Kiev. Though situated on the western side of the dividing river, that center of the Ukraine and of the whole old *Ruś* was ceded to Russia, with its environs, for two years and it was doubtful from the outset whether it would be returned to Poland after that period. Ordin-Nashchokin was himself in favor of respecting that clause of the treaty, but his opinion did not prevail and Kiev was never given back, thus providing Russia with a strong base on the right bank.

It is therefore hardly necessary to point out the strategic weakness of the new frontier which, strangely enough, was to last longer than any other boundary line in that region of transition. It was not changed before the partitions of Poland more than a hundred years later. But this is precisely an indication that in the following period of Polish-Russian relations the main issue was no longer any question of boundaries but of Russian penetration far into Poland with a view to either controlling the whole of her territory or if necessary partitioning it with another power. That basic change in the situation did not appear immediately. Indeed there seemed to be a certain improvement in the relations between the two countries during the years after the Andruszowo truce so that it was transformed into a "permanent" peace in 1686. This improvement, however, was to last only as long as Russia had her own problems of succession, after Czar Alexius and his feeble-minded eldest son Fedor, who died in 1682. During these years of trouble within the Romanov dynasty, which this time did not lead to any foreign intervention, there still was some equality of forces between the commonwealth and Russia. Only when Peter the Great became the uncontested master of his country did its full power appear in the relations with all its neighbors.

Even before Peter's violent and rather superficial "Westernization" of Russia, there was a remarkable cultural progress in that typically East European or rather Eurasian land, and this was one more result of the annexation of Kiev and of the final transfer of that important center from Poland to Russia. Its influence, which introduced some Western elements into the life of the latter country, was not strong enough, however, to check Muscovite influence which in turn penetrated into the eastern Ukraine, leading to its gradual Russification and cutting it off from the West. There was also a parallel progress of the Polonization process in the western Ukraine so that the new frontier was just like the previous one, a clear dividing line between a reduced East Central Europe, part of the Latin world, and a different, predominantly eastern sphere of culture. At the same time this was a serious setback for the Ukrainian national movement into which the Cozack opposition against Poland had developed under Khmelnitsky's leadership.

But the Ukraine also suffered from the steady advance of Ottoman power which took advantage of the precarious situation of Poland and more and more seemed to concentrate its onslaught in that direction.

It is true that warfare was also continuing along the Turkish-Austrian border in western Hungary, but there an Austrian victory, under Montecuccoli, at the Battle of Saint Gotthard, in 1664, was followed by a twenty years' truce concluded at Vasvar, while two factors contributed to an increased pressure against Poland. These were, first, the decision of the Cozack hetman Peter Doroshenko to place the part of the Ukraine which he controlled under Ottoman protection in 1666, and two years later, the abdication of King John Casimir. Doroshenko's policy of course raised Turkish claims to just that section of the Ukraine which the agreement with Russia left to Poland. And the last of the Polish Vasas who had shown real qualities of leadership in the worst situations, but who now, pessimistic as to the future of the country, left for France, proved to be very difficult to replace.

At the election of the following year, the Poles, disgusted by foreign intrigues, particularly the rivalry of Austrian and French partisans which reflected the general situation in Western Europe, decided to choose a native candidate. But Michael Wiśniowiecki, the son of Prince Jeremiah—the hero of the earlier Cozack wars—was entirely different from his father and as king proved a great disappointment. Even his marriage to a sister of Emperor Leopold I did not contribute to his prestige, and his poor rule of four years, far from strengthening the position of the Commonwealth in Europe after all failures of the preceding reign, offered the Turks an excellent opportunity for another aggression.

The war ended with the humiliating Treaty of Buczacz in 1672, which, besides the obligation to pay a tribute to the sultan, deprived Poland not only of her part of the Ukraine but also of the province of Podolia, whose capital, the important fortress of Kamieniec, had been taken after a dramatic siege. The territorial losses in the north and in the east were now followed by a similar retreat in the south which was a retreat of Western Christendom to an artificial boundary, impossible to defend.

It was then that a great military leader, John Sobieski, saved Poland and as a matter of fact all Christendom, although his universal role was only to become evident ten years later during what might be called the last crusade in European history. Already his less spectacular victory of 1673, at Chocim, the same place where the forces of the Commonwealth had stopped the Turks in 1621, was of decisive importance. Although it did not end the war, it marked the turn of the tide. Sobieski's election as King of Poland in 1674, after the death of Michael, immediately after the Battle at Chocim, was a well-deserved reward.

At the same time it seemed a success for France and her partisans, to which party Sobieski had belonged for a long time. Thanks to his wife, Marie Casimire d'Arquien de la Grange, Poland again had a French queen, less talented but as ambitious as Louise Marie had been, and Louis XIV expected that under John III Poland would be his faithful ally. The new king was mainly known as a persistent and successful opponent of Turkey, another link in the traditional French system of alliances, and even French mediation could not finally settle the Polish-Turkish conflict. But a preliminary agreement was reached at the southern front in 1676, and Sobieski, realizing that the struggle against the Ottoman power had to be postponed, proved equally interested in the problems of the Baltic.

Here the general European situation seemed to favor an attempt at recovering East Prussia at least, since the Hohenzollerns were indeed more dangerous for France than any other German dynasty, including the Habsburgs, had ever been. After Poland's reconciliation with Sweden in 1660, cooperation with that country, another traditional French ally, against the common enemy, seemed quite possible. But Sobieski's plan to occupy East Prussia with Swedish cooperation and French support was doomed to failure because of the skilful policy of the Great Elector and the frequent shifts of alliances among the Western powers. From 1678 Frederick William, after defeating the Swedes, was himself in the French camp, and the Peace of Nimwegen, in the following year, made a necessarily isolated Polish action completely hopeless.

The Polish Diet of 1679–1680 was a turning point in Sobieski's policy which also affected the European situation. More than personal disappointments of his wife in the relations with Louis XIV, the missed opportunity on the Baltic contributed to a cooling off in John III's French sympathies. In spite of the intrigues of the French ambassador and his partisans in Warsaw, the king decided to turn again to the main task of his life, the defense against the Muslim danger. He did it with the hope that all European powers, possibly even France herself, could be gained for a joint action, and therefore he sent diplomatic missions to practically all the European courts.

And in spite of his sympathy with the Hungarian opposition against the Habsburgs, led at that moment by Emeric Thököly, he did not hesitate at a rapprochement with that dynasty, convinced that such cooperation between the two powers directly threatened by the Ottoman Empire, was indispensable. For the commonwealth it was more than a question of security. It was a unique occasion to play again a leading part in the European community.

THE BATTLE OF VIENNA AND ITS AFTERMATH

From the beginning of the year 1683 it was apparent that the Turks, under the influence of Grand Vizier Kara Mustapha, were planning a new war. It was uncertain, however, whether their main onslaught would be directed against Austria or against Poland. In any case a formal alliance between both threatened powers now became urgent, and with the papal nuncio in Warsaw acting as mediator, it was concluded there on March 31. The treaty provided that sixty thousand men would be mobilized by the emperor and forty thousand by the king of Poland, and that in case of a siege by the Turks of either Vienna or Cracow, all efforts would be made by the ruler of the other country to liberate the capital of his ally.

At that time it was already easy to foresee that Vienna, easy to reach from the Turkish-controlled part of Hungary whose other part was in open rebellion against Habsburg rule, would be the goal of that last Ottoman attempt to penetrate deep into Central Europe. Warfare also continued, however, on the Podolian front where part of the Polish forces, supported by loyal Cozacks, had to be kept during the whole campaign. Nevertheless, as soon as Sobieski was informed that the siege of Vienna had started, he rapidly moved with an army of twenty-five thousand through Silesia and Moravia to Austria's assistance, while a Polish auxiliary corps of six thousand, under Hieronymus Lubomirski, had already joined the imperial forces before the king's arrival.

The question as to who would be the commander in chief of the allied armies, which included contingents from most German states with the exception of Brandenburg-Prussia, was decided in favor of the King of Poland, since the emperor was not present in person. The main leader of the imperial forces of seventy thousand men, Charles of Lorraine, agreed to place himself under the orders of

Sobieski whose unique experience in fighting the Turks was universally recognized and particularly stressed by the papal representative, Marco d'Aviano. It was the King of Poland who, after the junction of both armies, drafted the plan of the battle which was fought before Vienna on September 12, 1683, and was to be one of the decisive battles in European history.

The Christian forces occupied the mountain range west of the city, which in spite of the heroism of its defenders under Rüdiger von Starhemberg was already in a desperate position, and from these heights they launched their attack against the Muslims. The fighting started at the left wing near the Danube, where the imperial regiments distinguished themselves, but according to all witnesses the battle was decided through a brilliant assault of the Polish cavalry at the right wing, which under the king's personal leadership penetrated into the camp of the Turks and broke their resistance.

The victory was so complete that the liberation of Vienna could be followed immediately by an advance far into Hungary. But while the population of the Austrian capital welcomed Sobieski with grateful enthusiasm, misunderstandings between the two monarchs arose at the arrival of the emperor. Leopold I resented the fact that the king had not waited for him to enter Vienna and at once he wanted to discourage Sobieski's hopes that his eldest son James, who had also fought bravely in the great battle, would receive an archduchess in marriage. In spite of his disappointment, the king, with all Polish forces, joined in the Hungarian campaign, and after a setback in the first battle of Párkány, where he himself was in mortal danger, he won another important victory near that place and also participated in the taking of Esztergom, Hungary's ecclesiastical center. Furthermore, he tried to mediate between Leopold I and the Hungarians and to make the reconquest of their whole country a real liberation.

That war was to continue for sixteen years. Though Sobieski and his army returned to Poland at the end of 1683, he remained resolved to participate in the struggle against the Ottoman Empire and to eliminate the Muslim danger to his own country and to the whole of Christendom once and for all. Therefore in 1684 he joined the so-called Holy League which included, besides Austria and Poland, the Republic of Venice, eager to regain its possessions in the Levant, and Pope Innocent XI, who from the very beginning had inspired the joint action in defense of Christendom.

Now, however, the forces of Austria and those of Poland were concentrated on two different fronts. For Leopold I, the main objective was the occupation of all Hungary. Sobieski wanted to regain Podolia with Kamieniec and, advancing in the direction of the Danube, to bring Moldavia and possibly also Wallachia under Polish suzerainty again. Unfortunately both actions were not only insufficiently coordinated but they were also troubled by a growing distrust between the Allies. The Emperor was afraid that Poland's progress in the neighborhood of Transylvania, the old stronghold of the Hungarian independence movement, would attract the sympathies of the anti-Habsburg elements on the other side of the Carpathians. If these apprehensions proved unjustified, it was mainly because the Austrian campaigns of the following years were much more successful than Sobieski's campaigns had been.

Two events were decisive in the Hungarian war. In 1686 Buda, the old capital, was retaken from the Turks who had ruled there for 145 years, a victory which produced an impression second only to the triumph before Vienna and which at last made the Habsburgs the real masters of a country which they had claimed since 1526. That success, gained by Prince Charles of Lorraine, was supplemented in 1697 by the victory of Prince Eugen of Savoy, another prominent Austrian general of foreign origin, in the battle of Zenta. Two years later the Turks were obliged to sign the Treaty of Karlowitz which was the first step in their withdrawal from conquered East Central Europe. In addition to important concessions to Venice, they had to give up all Hungary with only the exception of the banat of Temesvár at the southern border. Leopold I, whom the Diet of 1687 had already recognized as hereditary king of Hungary in the male line, also decided directly to govern Transylvania whose prince, Michael Apafy, a puppet of the Turks and opponent of the Habsburgs for almost thirty years, died in 1690. The former principality was now supposed to be merely an autonomous province of the kingdom, although a descendant of the Rákóczis, Francis II, looking for French and possibly Polish support also, was already leading a resistance movement against Austria.

The Treaty of Karlowitz also at last restored Podolia to Poland, but John Sobieski did not live to see the liberation of Kamieniec which he had simply bypassed in his Moldavian campaigns. In spite of all his efforts, including the appeasement of Russia in the Treaty of 1686, these campaigns ended in failure. Only one of them, undertaken that same year, parallel to the Austrian advance to Buda, had any chance of success. The immediate reason why the Polish forces, after advancing far into the Danubian principalities, had to retreat, as they also had to in subsequent expeditions until 1691, was the lack of support from the native Rumanian population. Even at the height of her power, Poland had failed to win their full confidence in a lasting protection against the Turks. Now, seeing their homeland turned into a battlefield once again, they were even less prepared to exchange a loosening Ottoman overlordship for the rule of the commonwealth, which in recent years had so poorly defended its southern borderlands, or for the domination of the Sobieski family.

For even in Poland there was a suspicion—one more reason for the king's failure—that he wanted to turn the conquered territories into a private domain for one of his sons, thus strengthening his own power and securing the future election of his descendants to the Polish throne. The result was, on the contrary, a growing opposition to Sobieski which disregarded all his outstanding achievements and troubled the end of his otherwise so glorious reign until his death in 1696.

It would be vain to speculate whether it would have been wiser, instead of persisting in the Danubian project which proved beyond Poland's military power, to concentrate on a better solution of the old Ukrainian problem with a view to regaining access to the Black Sea in the steppes between the Dniester and Dnieper rivers. This no man's land would have been much more difficult to defend by the declining Ottoman Empire, and nobody would have been better qualified to make an attempt in that direction than Sobieski, who to a large extent appeased the Cozacks, restored order in the borderlands torn by war and revolution, and time and again even succeeded in coming to an understanding with the Crimean Tartars.

Their invasions, which had plagued these borderlands and the commonwealth as a whole from the thirteenth century—there had been about two hundred Tartar incursions in the course of those four hundred and fifty years—ceased completely at the end of the seventeenth century, and this was only one of the lasting results of Sobieski's victories. Another was not only the disappearance of the

Turkish danger which had so frequently paralyzed Poland's policy from the days of Varna and Mohács, but also a basic change in Polish-Turkish relations. Permanent tension, if not open hostility, was replaced by bonds of common interest between two countries, formerly great powers, both now facing decline if not destruction. After the last abortive Polish endeavors to interfere with the Balkan problems, any interference with the internal situation of Poland, coming from powers which also began to threaten the Ottoman Empire, was considered contrary to Turkey's own interests.

This was particularly the case of Russia, whose cooperation in Sobieski's Turkish wars had been inadequate throughout the regency of Sophia, the elder sister of Peter the Great. Peter himself, from the outset hostile to Poland and determined to take advantage of any possibility of intervention opened by the 1686 treaty, began by attacking the important Turkish outpost of Azov which he conquered shortly before Sobieski's death. The pressure which the czar, jointly with Austria, Turkey's other opponent, exercised upon Poland in connection with the election after John III, was chiefly directed against a candidate who would have well suited the Ottoman Empire, since it was a French prince, François de Conti, supported by the policy of Louis XIV.

That policy, after the crisis in French-Polish relations during Sobieski's cooperation with the Habsburg emperor, resulted in 1692, after John III's gradual withdrawal from the Turkish war, in another plan of cooperation with France's traditional allies in the East. Sweden seeming to be powerless and Turkey suffering unprecedented defeats, Poland remained the most important of these possible allies, and the establishment there of a branch of the French dynasty would have changed the whole balance of power in Europe to the advantage of Louis XIV. But this was precisely one of the reasons why Poland's neighbors opposed such a solution which, coming soon after the rise of her prestige in 1683, could have saved her from either Russian control or partition. That they succeeded in forcing upon Poland in the first election, which was not really free, the worst possible candidate, the Elector of Saxony, was to influence the history of East Central Europe throughout the eighteenth century and must be explained by the constitutional crisis of Poland and of that whole region of Europe toward the end of the seventeenth.

THE CONSTITUTIONAL CRISIS OF EAST CENTRAL EUROPE

It is an almost universally admitted opinion that the Polish constitution, as finally developed after the extinction of the Jagellonian dynasty, was very inadequate if not simply "crazy," and that it led almost fatally to the decline and fall of the commonwealth. This interpretation requires, however, three rather important qualifications.

First, the Polish institutions, though far from being perfect, were not at all so bad, particularly if considered against the background of the period and of the neighboring countries. There was in Poland much more political freedom than in most of the other states of modern Europe. No other country except England had such a powerful legislature, based upon a long tradition of parliamentary government. And in spite of the strict limitations of the executive, the authority of the king largely depended on his own abilities and spirit of initiative. Until the middle of the seventeenth century, when unanimity rule in the Diet, the only too well-known *liberum veto* was first applied in its extreme form, the whole constitutional machinery, unique in its kind, worked fairly well.

What really was deplorable was the gradual abandonment of any ideas of constitutional reform, so seriously discussed and carried out on many occasions in the earlier periods of Polish history. Royal attempts toward a strengthening of the executive power failed one after the other, including Sobieski's rather vague projects in that direction, not without a serious responsibility of those of his predecessors who had tried to achieve their aims through court intrigue and illegal action. The stagnation of the normal evolution of political institutions, which was to last well into the second half of the eighteenth century, was indeed extremely harmful but certainly not irremediable as long as the nation was free to direct its own destinies.

Secondly, Poland's internal crisis around 1700, greatly aggravated by the political and economic consequences of so many foreign invasions, was not exclusively nor even predominantly of an institutional character connected with the form of government. Much more serious were the social and the cultural crises both of which reached their climax in the same period.

It was more than a defect of the constitution that all liberties, of which the Poles were rightly proud, remained limited to the *szlachta* which identified itself with the nation at large. It is true that this typically Polish privileged class was never limited to a small closed circle of aristocratic families, but, jealous of a truly democratic equality of rights and opportunities for all its members, constituted about one-tenth of the population. But being equally jealous of the development of the cities, so prosperous in earlier centuries, that numerous nobility reduced the burghers to an insignificant role, and worst of all, kept the peasants in conditions of serfdom which, though not worse than in most Western countries and definitely better than in Russia, badly required a basic reform which was completely neglected in spite of the promises of 1656.

What might be called Poland's hundred years war in the seventeenth century brought the general level of culture much lower than it had been in the "golden age" of the sixteenth. Even Polish literature of the period of crisis, though not so insignificant as it was for a long time supposed to have been, produced no masterpieces comparable to those of the Renaissance. The old universities, to which that of Lwów had been added in 1661, were declining, and education of all degrees, largely in the hands of the Jesuit Order, whose influence is, however, often misrepresented through a very one-sided criticism, was of course badly affected by the general conditions. And the participation in the development of Western culture was greatly reduced in spite of close intellectual ties with the France of the "grand siècle."

Nevertheless, even in these comparatively dark years, Polish culture proved strong enough to assimilate, more than even before, the non-Polish elements of the commonwealth, at least as far as the upper classes were concerned. Just as before, that gradual and spontaneous process of Polonization contributed to making the eastern boundaries of the country the cultural frontier of Europe. That fact is, however, closely connected with a third point which must be stressed. The crisis toward the end of the seventeenth century has to be considered from the point of view not only of Poland, then the only fully independent state in that region of the Continent, but of all countries and peoples of East Central Europe.

Particularly critical, indeed, was the situation of the Ruthenians, although their national consciousness developed in connection with the Cozack insurrections, not without the beginning of a differentiation between the White Ruthenians (now Byelorussians) in the north and the Ruthenians proper (sometimes misleadingly called Little Russians, now called Ukrainians) in the south.

As to the former, part of their territory, particularly the Smolensk region, after being definitely conquered by Moscow, was absorbed by and amalgamated into Great Russia, or Russia proper, and thus completely cut off from East Central Europe as part of the new Russian Empire. Most of the White Ruthenians remained in the Grand Duchy of Lithuania where, however, their cultural influence was to such an extent replaced by the Polish that the so-called *coaequatio iurium* of 1696 made Polish, instead of Ruthenian (in a form near to the White Ruthenian tongue) the official language of that grand duchy.

As a body politic, Lithuania continued to enjoy that full equality with the kingdom of Poland which was guaranteed by the Union of Lublin. In 1673 it was even decided that every third Diet of the commonwealth should meet, not in Warsaw, but in Grodno, on the territory of the grand duchy, under a Lithuanian speaker. But the Lithuanian citizens, deeply attached to the tradition and the local autonomy of the grand duchy, included peoples of various racial origin. Among those who were Lithuanians racially, only the peasants continued to use their own Lithuanian language which had not yet produced any notable literature. A Lithuanian national consciousness in the modern sense was hardly more developed than that of their Latvian kinsmen, now predominantly, together with the Finns and Estonians, under Swedish rule and German cultural influence.

Quite different was the situation of the Ruthenians who since the Union of Lublin had all been united within the limits of the kingdom of Poland, and since the Union of Brest, amidst the ardent discussions between its partisans and its opponents, went through a revival of their cultural life. The Cozack movement which started there as a social force and which soon became a political power also, was leading to the formation of a Ruthenian or Ukrainian nation which the Union of Hadziacz wanted to make another equal partner in the commonwealth, with all guaranties for the Orthodox faith. But the partition of the Ukraine between Poland and Russia, without even speaking of the temporary Turkish domination in a third part of the country, necessarily led to a progressive Polonization of the western section and to a gradual suppression of the promised autonomy, hence to Russification, in the eastern part, a situation which was to influence the Ukrainian national movement in the following centuries.

As to Ottoman rule in South Eastern Europe, it was becoming even more oppressive and degrading with the decline of the empire. Of all the peoples of the Balkans, only the Rumanians continued to enjoy a certain amount of autonomy, both in Wallachia, where a series of princes of Greek origin (called *Phanariots* because coming from Phanar, the Greek quarter of Constantinople) succeeded in establishing a greater continuity of government, and even more so in Moldavia, where Prince Demetrius Cantemir, Sobieski's opponent, also contributed to the cultural development of the country. Both Danubian principalities remained not only a battleground between the neighboring powers but also a gateway of conflicting cultural influences.

The Turkish withdrawal from the Danubian Plain at last brought almost the whole of Hungary, along with Bohemia, under Habsburg rule. That German dynasty thus realized its agelong objective, attained only in part after the battle of Mohács in 1526, to establish its hereditary rule in both kingdoms. The important section of East Central Europe, which the Jagellonians had before associated with Poland, was now connected with Austria, and the common dynasty tried to make that connection as close as possible. The constitutional and cultural crisis which in Bohemia had already reached its climax after the battle of the White Mountain in 1620, now affected the whole of Hungary also, where the main part, liberated from the Ottoman yoke, had to face the same danger which the northwestern border region had opposed, not without difficulty, for a century and a half. This was the centralizing and Germanizing trend of the Habsburg regime.

There was, however, a considerable difference between the situation in Bohemia and in Hungary. In the former country there was hardly any national resistance. The nobility, now largely of foreign origin, supported the policy of the court, showing little interest in the traditional autonomy of the kingdom within the empire and no interest at all in the preservation of the Czech language which in spite of its eloquent but isolated defense by the Jesuit Bohuslav Balbín was gradually replaced by German, particularly in the cities. The peasants suffered so much from the deteriorating conditions of serfdom that they revolted in 1680, only to be crushed and severely punished by the

Patent of the same year. The country, whose state rights were no longer defended by the Prague Diet which was completely losing its importance, seemed ripe for the unifying policy of the Habsburgs in the next century.

In Hungary, where the national nobility remained powerful and politically active in the Diet, with Latin as the official language, a prominent leader, Nicholas Zrinyi, a great-grandson of the hero of Szigetvár, had already realized the danger of unlimited Habsburg rule before the expulsion of the Turks, which he was one of the first to anticipate. But he died before that liberation, and the other Hungarian magnates, including his brother Peter, by conspiring with Louis XIV, only provoked the court's violent reaction and a temporary suspension of the constitution. A similar policy by Emeric Thököly and the rebellion of the so-called *Kurucok* (Crusaders) amidst the Turkish war created a tense situation between Leopold I and the Hungarian estates after the unification of the country under the emperor's rule. Here too, as in Bohemia, after the devastation of so many war years, many foreign colonists were settled, Austrian generals and dignitaries exercised an increasing influence, encouraging the non-Magyar elements, and although the Diet agreed to abolish the clause of the Golden Bull of 1222, which authorized resistance against any unconstitutional action of the king, an open rebellion broke out in 1697.

Its leader, Francis II Rákóczi, was not only a nephew of Nicholas Zrinyi but also a descendant of former princes of Transylvania where he found strong support. After a manifesto addressed to all peoples of Hungary he was elected "ruling prince" by the estates and amidst the War of the Spanish Succession that anti-Habsburg movement was again welcomed by Louis XIV, while England and Holland tried to mediate. Emperor Joseph I, who succeeded Leopold I in 1705, found Hungary in a state of rebellion which was typical of the internal crisis in the various countries of East Central Europe at the turn of the century.

14

THE END OF THE *ANCIEN RÉGIME*

THE NORTHERN WAR AND THE EASTERN QUESTION

In Poland the eighteenth century started with a new foreign war, only one year after the peace with Turkey and the internal pacification of the country. Frederick-Augustus, the elector of Saxony, whom Russian and German pressure had forced upon the Poles as King Augustus II, had hardly been universally recognized when, contrary to the interests of the country, which badly needed peace and internal reforms, he carried out a project of aggression against Sweden, secretly planned at a meeting with Peter the Great soon after his arrival in Poland.

In the war against young King Charles XII, the commonwealth was to regain from Sweden that part of Livonia which was ceded in 1660. But as a matter of fact, Augustus II, who from the beginning of his reign plotted with Poland's enemies with a view to establishing his absolute rule in the country, only served the interests of his powerful ally, the czar, who wanted to secure for Russia an adequate access to the Baltic. The Great Northern War which began in 1700 with unexpected Swedish victories over Denmark, and particularly over Peter the Great at the Battle of Narva, was for more than twenty years to be the main problem of Eastern Europe. After its decisive turn in favor of Peter the Great, and following the end of the Spanish War of Succession in 1713, it was also to be an object of concern for all Europe where the alarming rise of Russian power was for the first time realized. For East Central Europe, that is, for all peoples between the two empires, the old German and the new Russian Empire which was formally proclaimed in 1721, after Sweden's final defeat, that long war, largely fought on the soil of these peoples was one more step leading to their doom.

The first to take advantage of that situation was a German ruler who tried to remain neutral, though in an ever-closer understanding with Peter the Great. This was the Elector of Brandenburg who in 1701 made himself a king, not of Brandenburg, however, but of Prussia, where he was crowned in Königsberg. Since he really controlled only East Prussia, that isolated German enclave which until 1657 had been a Polish fief, while West Prussia continued to be a Polish province, that coronation was a challenge to Poland and a manifestation of German power beyond the frontiers of the empire, deep in the East Central European region.

At about the same time, Charles XII made the first of his strategic mistakes which affected the fate of East Central Europe even more than that of Sweden. After Narva, instead of advancing against Russia he turned against Augustus II, thus giving Peter the Great the necessary time for reforming his army and crushing internal troubles, while in Poland the Swedish invasion created only misery and division. For Charles XII tried to force upon the Poles a king who would be his subservient ally. Though he chose an excellent candidate, Stanisław Leszczyński, that election in 1704 was obviously illegal. A large part of the Poles, as well as an important faction in Lithuania, remained loyal to Augustus II in spite of his deplorable policy.

In addition to his unfortunate interference with internal Polish problems, the King of Sweden made another mistake when, after defeating Augustus II in his own Saxony and forcing him to renounce the crown of Poland, in 1708 he at last resumed the offensive against his most dangerous opponent, Peter the Great. Instead of moving in the direction of Moscow, he turned toward the south with a view to joining the forces of the Cozack hetman Ivan Mazepa in the Ukraine.

That Cozack leader in the eastern, Russian-controlled part of the Ukraine was indeed anxious to liberate the country from the czar's rule. But he proceeded so cautiously that at first Peter the Great refused to believe those who warned him against Mazepa. The czar even tried to use him for strengthening Russian influence in the Polish part of the Ukraine. The Cozacks themselves were left under the impression that their hetman continued to be loyal to the czar, and they were hardly prepared for a well-organized insurrection when Mazepa, after inviting the King of Sweden to come to the Ukraine, at last openly broke with Russia and led the troops which he had at his disposal to the Swedish camp.

But he, as well as Charles XII, suffered a great disappointment when the revolt failed to spread all over the Ukraine, where the Russians immediately took and destroyed Mazepa's capital. The old Cozack center, the Sich, was inclined to join the independence movement now formally launched by the hetman, but it was too late. Only a few thousand Cozacks, instead of the promised thirty thousand, compensated Charles XII for the destruction of his own Swedish reinforcements, which, hurrying southward from Livonia, were defeated in October, 1708 at the Battle of Lesna in White Ruthenia.

A much more famous battle, momentous in European history, was fought on the eighth of July of the next year before the Ukrainian city of Poltava which the Swedes besieged in vain. It was there that Charles XII and Mazepa were completely beaten by overwhelming Russian forces, but they escaped to Turkey. That victory over the experienced Swedish army and its famous leader convinced both the Russians themselves and the outside world that a new great power had risen at the border of the European community and was henceforth to influence the destinies of the Continent in a frequently decisive manner.

Except for its Polish section, the Ukraine was now definitely outside East Central Europe, and the cause of Ukrainian independence was lost for two centuries. The new hetman, Philip Orlyk, elected by the followers of Mazepa, who died a few months after his defeat, continued to work for that cause in exile and even drafted a constitution for the planned Ukrainian state. But all Orlyk's diplomatic versatility proved futile. Ivan Skoropadsky, whom Peter the Great designated as hetman after Mazepa's revolt, was nothing but a Russian puppet. What remained of Cozack autonomy was considered an internal problem of the Russian Empire until that autonomy was gradually liquidated after Skoropadsky's death in 1722. Governed by the so-called Little Russian Board, the Ukraine was turned into a Russian province where a Ukrainian national movement was not revived before the end of the eighteenth century.

The progress of Russia in the steppes north of the Black Sea greatly alarmed the Turks who in 1696 had already lost to Peter the Great a first foothold on the shores of that sea, the port of Azov. But when they declared war upon Russia soon after the Battle of Poltava, it was not in order to support the Cozacks, as Orlyk hoped, nor in favor of Leszczyński whose partisans were defending Poland's independence, but in order to check the Russian advance and possibly to gain once more part of or all the Ukraine for themselves. Therefore the Russian-Turkish rivalry which now started and was for the next two centuries to become a permanent element of the so-called Eastern question, did not directly affect the cause of the freedom of the peoples of East Central Europe, although it encouraged the liberation movement in the Balkan countries. Peter the Great entered Moldavia, but only to be encircled by Turkish forces at the Prut River, and the peace of compromise which he had to conclude in 1711 obliged him even to restore Azov to the Turks and to promise them not to interfere with the affairs of Poland and of the Polish Ukraine which the Ottoman Empire continued to covet.

However, that only setback in the czar's career did not really prevent him from taking advantage of his victory over Charles XII in order to "pacify" Poland, where Augustus II at once replaced Stanisław Leszczyński. Contrary to his formal engagements in renewed treaties with Turkey, the czar never hesitated to march Russian troops into the commonwealth. Without showing any interest in changes of the frontier or in partition projects which were several times suggested by the Saxon king of Poland himself, Peter the Great was gradually turning Poland into a Russian protectorate. As a matter of fact, this was a much greater challenge to the established balance of power in Europe than the change in the relations between Russia and Turkey. And Russia's advance toward the center of Europe—the main drive of her expansion—was creating an Eastern question more dangerous than the developments in the Ottoman Empire which are usually designated by that expression.

While Turkey's attention was distracted by new wars with the Republic of Venice and with Austria, Russia contributed to internal troubles in Poland between partisans of Augustus II and of his rival Leszczyński. Peter the Great tried to play off one side against the other and to act as arbiter between them. The Polish patriots, who were equally opposed to Saxon domination and to Russian interference, had joined in one of their "confederations" which were supposed to supplement the executive in times of crisis through voluntary association of the nobility. But after serious reverses of that poorly organized liberation movement, it was easy for the czar's envoy, Prince Gregory Dolgoruky, to play the role of a mediator and practically dictate the disastrous decisions of the so-called "Silent Diet" of 1717. It was under that Russian pressure that the worst features of the Constitution, particularly the *liberum veto*, were perpetuated; the army was reduced to eighteen thousand in Poland and to six thousand in Lithuania, leaving the commonwealth at Peter's mercy and helpless between the rising militaristic powers of Russia and Prussia.

More than these events in Poland, the progress which Russia made in the war against Sweden, when her armies, violating Poland's neutrality, appeared for the first time on German soil, seriously alarmed the Western countries. In 1719 Emperor Charles VI signed a treaty in Vienna with England which was concerned with Russia's role in the Baltic, and with Saxony, the homeland of Augustus II. In his Polish kingdom, however, an approval of the Vienna Treaty would have been necessary and it was refused by the Diet of 1720. It was understandable that the Poles wanted to avoid another war and that they distrusted their king who was mainly responsible for the critical situation. But a unique opportunity for stopping Russia, with the assistance of the West, was lost and the next year Sweden, which had continued to fight after the death of Charles XII, was obliged to sign the Peace of Nystadt.

Peter the Great successfully ended the Northern War by occupying Finland and using that autonomous province of Sweden as a basis for raids on the Swedish coast of the Baltic, even threatening Stockholm. He did not, however, claim Finland in the treaty which even so was extremely advantageous for Russia. She regained her former access to the sea in Ingria, at the Gulf of Finland where Peter had already started building his new capital of St. Petersburg in 1703, and furthermore she received from Sweden the Baltic provinces of Estonia and Livonia which Ivan the Terrible had tried in vain to conquer.

After the prosperous period of Swedish rule which had notably contributed to the cultural development of those provinces and had even slightly improved the position of the Estonian and Latvian peasant population, the long war years left the whole area completely devastated. But even under Russian domination the Baltic provinces remained Western in their general character. The Protestant faith was definitely established, and the German nobility had even strengthened its predominance.

The extension of Russia's boundaries was not only decisive for the old issue of the *dominium maris Baltici*, but also another threat, now from the north, came to the Polish-Lithuanian Commonwealth which still possessed the southeastern corner of Livonia and the duchy of Curland as a fief. Therefore, far from regaining Riga for herself, Poland, whose king had foolishly entered the war in 1700, was now, more than twenty years later, in a position much worse than at the end of the seventeenth century. The last part of the reign of Augustus II, until his death in 1733, was for the country a real "dark age." The growing opposition against the king, this time entirely justified by his desire to establish an absolute form of government and by his intrigues with Poland's neighbors, made any constructive reform plan impossible. And the commonwealth, still one of Europe's largest countries, indispensable to a real equilibrium on the Continent, could hardly have any foreign policy of its own.

TOWARD RUSSIAN-PRUSSIAN COOPERATION

Throughout the whole course of history East Central Europe had been under a dangerous pressure coming from two sides: from the western German part of Central Europe and from the East where at first Asiatic invaders and then the rising power of Moscow created a situation of permanent tension. Combined with the Turkish onslaught from the fourteenth to the seventeenth century, that pressure had reduced the area of free peoples in that region of Europe to the Polish Commonwealth, and by the end of the seventeenth century it also reduced the territory of that commonwealth to an area much smaller than in the past. At about the same time the pressure from West and East became more threatening than ever before, since the electors of Brandenburg, now the main representatives of German aggression, created the kingdom of Prussia, while Czar Peter the Great, through his victories in the Northern War combined with his internal reforms, transformed Muscovy into the modern Russian Empire.

In spite of their entirely different origin, both newcomers in the European state system had much in common. Both were militaristic powers under an absolute centralized government with a far-reaching program of territorial expansion. Both wanted to be culturally associated with Western Europe in spite of the growing German nationalism in Prussia and of the superficial character of Russia's "Europeanization," ruthlessly enforced by Peter. The policy of both of them completely upset the balance of power in Europe and had a common interest in destroying the state which separated them from each other, which also separated East Prussia from Brandenburg, and which was in the way of Russia's advance in the western direction.

Already, two hundred years before, the first Hohenzollern established in East Prussia, originally as last grand master of the Teutonic Order and then as secular, hereditary ruler, had considered the possibility of cooperating with Moscow against Poland and Lithuania. The liberation of East Prussia from Polish suzerainty had been at least indirectly facilitated by Russia's simultaneous invasion of the eastern part of the commonwealth. And it was in Königsberg that Peter the Great, visiting the elector who a few years later was to be the first king of Prussia, had planned his interference with the Polish election after Sobieski's death.

The year 1720 brought a decisive step in the development of cooperation between the kingdom of Prussia and the Russian Empire which was formally proclaimed the next year. Even before the Peace of Nystadt between Russia and Sweden, Frederick William I of Prussia took advantage of the latter's precarious position in order to obtain in a separate treaty all that the Swedes still possessed in Pomerania, including the city of Stettin which the Great Elector had in vain tried to occupy. The whole of Western Pomerania now being united with Brandenburg, the Polish province of Eastern Pomerania, with Danzig, was becoming a mere "corridor" between the two sections of the Prussian State. And the Russian armies which had defeated Sweden on so many fronts, including an appearance in Pomerania, before Stettin in 1717, had decisively contributed to that success.

It was also in 1720 that King Augustus II, disappointed by the opposition of the Polish Diet, turned from his transitory project of opposing Russia's imperialism to another scheme of dismembering his own Polish kingdom which he secretly presented in Berlin and also sent to Vienna. Strangely enough, it was Peter the Great, whose participation was of course a prerequisite condition, who rejected that partition plan and even revealed it to the Poles. He did it not only in order to give them the impression that he was Poland's loyal protector, but also chiefly because he still hoped to control all the commonwealth. For that purpose, however, he needed the cooperation of Prussia and therefore he concluded a personal treaty with King Frederick William I in which both dangerous neighbors of Poland pledged themselves for the first time to protect in common the "freedom" of that country and particularly the rights of its minorities.

Two different problems must be distinguished in that Russian-Prussian guaranty which until the complete elimination of Poland was repeated in a whole series of treaties between the two powers. It was, first, a threat directed against any reform of the Polish constitution which would do away with the abuses of individual liberties and strengthen the government of the commonwealth. It seemed to be merely a threat against the king, who was indeed quite prepared to violate any constitutional rights, but as a matter of fact it was also a check on all constructive reform projects which even in the dark years of Saxon rule were soon to appear in the writings of enlightened leaders of the nation.

On the other hand, Orthodox Russia and Protestant Prussia were equally eager to find a quasi-permanent opportunity for interfering with Poland's internal problems by acting as protectors of their co-religionists in that country. Russia had already made a first attempt in that direction by inserting clauses in favor of the Orthodox in her peace treaty concluded with Poland in 1686. In the meantime the number of these Orthodox had been greatly reduced, thanks to the fact that the Ruthenian dioceses of Lwów and Przemyśl now joined the Union of Brest, so that the synod held at Zamość in 1720 completed the reunion with the Catholic Church of almost all the Ruthenians who were still under Polish rule. There remained, indeed, a limited number of Orthodox non-Uniate peoples in the White Ruthenian diocese of Mstislav in the grand duchy of Lithuania, and in addition to Orthodox peasants, a small number of noble families also continued to adhere to that faith. Similarly, in addition to Protestant communities in various cities, there were also some nobles who from the days of the Reformation remained Lutherans or Calvinists. And it is true that Poland was no longer so tolerant in religious matters as she had been in the sixteenth century. But only the anti-Trinitarians, the so-called Arians, a group very small in number, had been expelled in 1658, being suspected of collaboration with the Swedish invaders. The restrictions of the constitutional rights of all non-

—————— Boundary of the Polish-Lithuanian Commonwealth before the first partition in 1772

------------ Boundaries separating Prussia, Austria, and
Russia after the third partition of Poland in
1795

–·–·–·–· National boundaries as established in 1815

·············· Boundaries of autonomous territories: Poland
and Finland in the Russian Empire, and
Wallachia and Moldavia in the Ottoman Empire

–··–··–·· Boundary of the German Confederation (co-
incides with several national boundaries, with
the boundary between Austria proper and
Hungary, and with the boundary of Poland
before the first partition)

Russian Empire ⎫

Prussia   ⎪
                ⎬ after 1815
Austrian Empire ⎪

Ottoman Empire ⎭

Montenegro and Free City of Cracow after 1815

NORWAY
SWEDEN
FINLAND

Christiania
Stockholm
ÅLAND ISLANDS

Baltic Sea

DENMARK
CopenHagen
Königsberg
Danzig

Berlin
Poznań
Toruń
Warsaw

Elbe
SAXONY
SILESIA
BOHEMIA
Prague
Vienna

POLAND
Cracow
GALICIA
Lwow
Tarnopol

St.Petersburg
Novgorod
Volga

ESTONIA
LIVONIA
Riga
CURLAND
Dvina
LITHUANIA
Wilno
Grodno
Niemen
Białystok
Pripet

Moscow
Smolensk
Kiev
Dnieper

Dniester
BUC
BESSARABIA
MOLDAVIA

HUNGARY
Buda
Pest
Danube
Tisza
TRANSYLVANIA

CRIMEA

Milan
Venice
Trieste
CROATIA
PAPAL STATES
Rome
Naples

Adriatic Sea
BOSNIA
SERBIA
Belgrade
MONTENEGRO
Ragusa

WALLACHIA
Bucharest
BULGARIA
Sofia
Adrianople
Constantinople
Salonika

Black Sea

ASIA MINOR

GREECE
Athens
IONIAN ISLANDS
Aegean Sea

SICILY

Tunis
MALTA

CRETE
CYPRUS

Mediterranean Sea

Catholics, voted by the Diets from 1717 onward, touched only a few noble families now excluded from office and no longer eligible as deputies.

Nevertheless, Russia and Prussia, where religious discrimination against Catholics went much further, considered the situation in Poland a real persecution, and soon found an occasion for a violent protest in which they were joined by King George I of England. In 1724, in the city of Toruń, the main center of Lutheranism in Poland, German Protestants raided the Jesuit college, desecrating the Host and holy pictures. The king, a former Protestant himself, who had become a Catholic only to gain the Polish crown, appointed a special commission which sentenced to death not only nine leaders of the assault but also the mayor of the city for not having checked the mob. Moreover, a church was taken away from the Protestants and given to a Catholic order. The sentence, unusually severe and unique in Polish history, was carried out in spite of an intervention of the papal nuncio, and it was branded by the Germans as a "trial of blood," while Augustus II confidentially explained that he was unable to control the fanaticism of the Poles.

The protest of Poland's neighbors had no serious consequences because Peter the Great died the next year. But the way had been opened to a continuous interference by Russia and Prussia under the pretext of protecting the "dissidents," as the religious minorities were then called. That process was leading directly to the crisis which preceded Poland's first partition.

In the meantime, Russian-Prussian cooperation was steadily developing in connection with the general European situation and also with the rise of German influence in the Russian Empire. Peter the Great has himself been called "a Germanized Russian," and it was in the North German states along the coast of the Baltic Sea, which he was so eager to dominate, that his efforts to establish close relations with Western countries proved most successful.

Among the marriages which he arranged between Russian princesses and German rulers, though the latter were of limited political power, that of his niece Anne with the last Duke of Curland, of the Kettler family, already concluded in 1710, was to have particularly important consequences. Curland, the southern part of old Livonia, had been a Polish fief since 1561 and formally continued to be so until the last partition in 1795. But when in 1721 the northern part of

Livonia, along with the other Baltic provinces, was ceded by Sweden to Russia, the latter's influence in Curland, favored by Anne's marriage, became predominant and played a decisive role when Anne, already a widow, was made Empress of Russia in 1730, after the short reigns of Peter's widow and grandson. A German of humble origin, Bühren, later called Biron, a favorite of the empress, was eventually made Duke of Curland, although the local nobility wanted a Saxon prince and the Polish Diet had tried in vain to incorporate Curland into the commonwealth. Furthermore, in addition to Biron, who during the ten years of Anne's reign was practically the ruler of Russia, many other Germans from the newly acquired Baltic provinces also soon occupied leading positions in the Russian army and diplomatic corps, while a German from Westphalia, A. I. Ostermann, later made a count, exercised decisive power as vice-chancellor.

It was only natural that the so-called "German party" which then directed Russian affairs favored the cooperation with Prussia, which already under her second king, Frederick-William I (1713–1740) was the strongest power in northern Germany, separated from Russian-controlled Curland only by a small strip of Lithuanian territory. On the other hand, the King of Prussia was the only monarch with whom the German-born king of Poland, Augustus II, maintained friendly relations until the end of his long and disastrous reign, contrary to the interests of the country where he wanted his son, Frederick-Augustus, to be elected after his death. He was even prepared to pay for Prussian support by territorial concessions.

It is true that in these years Russia did not favor the plan of Saxon succession in Poland. Twice, in 1726 and 1732, she made agreements with Austria in order to exclude the Wettins from the Polish throne. But both of them were even more opposed to the election of Stanisław Leszczyński, the exiled pretender whose chances were increased through the marriage of his daughter Mary, in 1725, to Louis XV of France. And since the pro-German Russian empress as well as Emperor Charles VI permitted the King of Prussia to take part in their projects, it was easy to anticipate, first, that the forthcoming Polish election would be decided, even more than the preceding one, by the joint pressure of the future partitioning powers, and secondly, that contrary to the wishes of the great majority of the Poles, disgusted with Saxon misrule, the elector of Saxony would have the best chance to succeed his father in Poland also.

France and her possible allies, the Bourbon king of Spain, and also Sweden and Turkey, were decidedly opposed to such a solution, and the Polish succession was therefore a big problem of international relations when Augustus II died in 1733. But at the same time it had ceased to be a problem which the Poles themselves could decide. Their country, which already under the first Saxon king had lost any initiative in the field of foreign policy, was to have no such independent policy at all under his son. The last free country in East Central Europe, encircled by the cooperation of Russia and Prussia, with Austria's inconsiderate participation, was under the appearance of neutrality a mere pawn in the game of power politics. This became clearly apparent during the European wars of the next generation which disturbed the precarious balance of power on the Continent until the partitions of Poland destroyed it completely.

DURING THE POLISH AND AUSTRIAN SUCCESSION WARS

The first of these European wars of the middle of the eighteenth century, after a brief period of peace which followed the War of the Spanish Succession in the West and the Great Northern War in the East, is called the War of the Polish Succession. The very name seems to indicate how important Poland's place continued to be in the European state system, and the war indeed started in consequence of the Polish election of 1733. But it developed outside Poland, without any participation of Poland as a sovereign power, and when it was concluded two years later the fate of Poland had practically ceased to be the main issue in the conflict among the other powers.

Before the election, at the so-called Convocation Diet, the Poles decided to exclude all foreign candidates and amidst great enthusiasm the primate, on September 12, proclaimed Stanisław Leszczyński king of Poland. Leszczyński had been able to reach that country by secretly crossing Germany, but his election, signed by about twelve thousand voters, was undoubtedly legal, and expecting French and Swedish assistance through the Baltic he moved to Danzig. Help was indeed badly needed because Russia, supported by Austria and with Prussia's silent approval, decided to enforce the election of Frederick Augustus of Saxony, as King Augustus III, after abandoning the extravagant idea of offering the throne of Poland to the Infante of Portugal. Under the control of the Russian army which occupied Praga, the eastern suburb of Warsaw, no more than a thousand voters signed the fake election of Augustus III who, after a short visit in Cracow, returned to Dresden where he was to spend most of his thirty years' reign in leisurely indolence.

The Poles were not at all prepared to recognize him. The nobility joined in "confederations" set up to support the lawful king, but their main leaders were defeated before they could reach Danzig with reinforcements. The city, also loyal to Leszczyński, was soon besieged by a strong Russian army under General Münnich. Besides a small group of Swedish volunteers, only two thousand French soldiers under Count Plélo, ambassador to Denmark, tried to rescue the king, but they were thrown back and their heroic commander was killed in action on May 27, 1734. To save the city from destruction, Leszczyński escaped to Königsberg where he was kept as hostage by the King of Prussia. Danzig surrendered one month later and the primate of Poland was himself among the prisoners.

The resistance movement continued both in Poland, under the Tarło family, and in Lithuania, where another confederation was formed, but it was necessarily limited to partisan warfare, with foreign support as only a possible hope. But even France, where a Polish embassy signed a pact of friendship with Cardinal Fleury, then directing the policy of Louis XV, did not take her engagements very seriously. She had declared war on Austria and Russia, together with Spain, Naples, and Sardinia, but was more interested in the situation in Italy and Western Germany. While the French attacked the Austrian forces in Italy, Russia was supposed to be checked by Sweden and Turkey. But neither country seized that opportunity for a joined action against the rising Russian power, and General Münnich's forces soon appeared in the Rhineland. It was therefore in Western Europe that the war was decided and it was there that France was looking for compensation for the setback of her policy in East Central Europe. When it became obvious that St. Petersburg would not accept the ally and father-in-law of Louis XV as king of Poland, Fleury, at the Peace of Vienna, signed on October 3, 1735, obtained for him, instead of Poland, the duchy of Lorraine from Emperor Charles VI, it being understood that after his death that province would be united with France.

Leszczyński's court at Lunéville was to be an important center where the king-in-exile educated young Poles and drafted reform projects not only for the Polish constitution but also for Europe's international organization. But his idea of a permanent peace under French leadership was no more utopian than his own return to power in Poland. His successful rival, Augustus III, recognized by the Pacification Diet of 1736, was to reign until his death, two years after that of Leszczyński, in 1763.

Soon after the end of hostilities in Western Europe, the Ottoman Empire started a belated war against Russia, whose southern border was raided by the Crimean Tartars. But it was in vain that Austria, which after a futile attempt at mediation entered that war on Russia's side, suggested to the Saxon king of Poland to join, as in the time of Sobieski, the action against Turkey, promising in reward to permit internal reforms in the commonwealth. And it was in vain, too, that Leszczyński's partisans were planning a revolt with Turkish and possibly Swedish support. Poland did not even receive any satisfaction for the violation of her territory by the Russian forces which defeated the Turks and, in spite of a separate peace made by Austria, forced the Ottoman Empire to conclude a much less satisfactory treaty with Empress Anne, in 1739. Russia did not yet reach the Black Sea, the Azov area being made neutral, but she advanced her frontier in the steppes north of that sea and close to the Polish border at the Boh River. The Ottoman Empire not only recognized Russia's control of what remained of the Ukrainian Cozacks, but did not claim this time, as in the earlier treaties of the century, any stipulation guaranteeing the territorial integrity of Poland.

Thus Russia's position in Eastern Europe was considerably strengthened and Poland's independence even more threatened when in the following year, 1740, the death of Emperor Charles VI was followed by the outbreak of another war called the War of the Austrian Succession. Charles VI was the last Habsburg in the male line but he had obtained from practically all powers a formal recognition of the Pragmatic Sanction which was to guarantee the hereditary rights of his daughter, Maria Theresa. The new king of Prussia, Frederick II, later called "the Great," was the first to violate that promise when he invaded Silesia.

That act of aggression was of vital significance for Poland. An old Polish land where, in spite of its loss four hundred years before, a large Polish population continued to live, was now being taken away from the Slavic kingdom of Bohemia and from a dynasty which was not basically hostile to Poland and conquered by one of her two most dangerous neighbors with the apparent approval of the other. Russia's own internal troubles between Anne's death in 1740 and the accession of Peter's daughter Elizabeth at the end of 1741, as well as the war declared by Sweden at that critical time, prevented Russia from at once taking a decided position in the Austrian war. But even so, Frederick II succeeded in keeping almost the whole of Silesia.

Furthermore, from the beginning of his reign he started the skilful diplomatic game which he had already prepared as crown prince, with a view to annexing Polish Prussia and maintaining the inner weakness of the commonwealth. That game was greatly facilitated by the inept policy of Poland's second Saxon king and of his favorite minister Count Brühl. Some Polish magnates, particularly Leszczyński's old adherent, Stanisław Poniatowski, the father of the future king, recognized how dangerous Frederick II was to be for Poland's integrity and Europe's peace. But while appeasing the Polish gentry whose liberties he promised to protect, the King of Prussia, through Brühl's influence, persuaded Augustus III to conclude with him a military alliance as elector of Saxony.

He promised him a strip of Silesian territory which would connect Saxony with Poland, and possibly even Moravia, but that fantastic promise was not kept. On the contrary, when, in the peace treaty of 1742, Silesia, except the two southern duchies, Troppau (Opava) and Teschen (Cieszyn), which were left to Maria Theresa, was for the first time ceded to Prussia, the two states of Augustus III were separated from each other more definitely than before and the whole of Western Poland, not only Royal Prussia, was now surrounded by Hohenzollern possessions. All those possessions which, in addition to comparatively small parts of Western Germany, constituted the state of Frederick II, now definitely a European power, had formerly been Slavic or Baltic. Thus the non-German, eastern part of Central Europe was greatly reduced by the advance of German political power which was accompanied by a steady progress of Germanization.

At the same time, however, there was a temporary decline of German influence in Russia. After putting in jail the young prince of Brunswick who had been proclaimed emperor on Anne's death, and after sending Anne's German advisers to Siberia, the new empress Elizabeth and her chancellor, A. P. Bestuzhev-Riumin, of purely Russian stock, first ended the Swedish war and then proceded to a reorientation of Russian diplomacy. Sweden, instead of regaining her losses, had to cede to Russia a first section of Finland in 1743, with the important city of Vyborg, and having thus strengthened her position in the Baltic region, Russia was looking for other allies instead of Prussia. This could bring about a change of her attitude toward Poland where the anti-Prussian party, led by the Czartoryski family, tried to obtain Russia's consent to financial reforms and to an increase of the Polish army. But Frederick II's intrigues made the Diet of 1744 a disgraceful failure and Russia proved to be much more interested in confirming her alliance with Austria and in concluding a new one with England.

Furthermore, Augustus III continued his undecided attitude, while in France the secret policy of Louis XV played with the idea of placing Prince de Conti, a grandson of the French candidate in the election of 1697, on the throne of Poland. As a matter of fact, this project had hardly more significance than the place reserved for Poland in the Austro-Russian treaty of 1746. When, according to this treaty, Russia interfered on Austria's side in the second phase of the War of the Austrian Succession, again it was by marching her troops, sent to the Rhine, back and forth through the territory of Poland, disregarding her neutrality and continuing to oppose, this time together with Austria, any constructive reform of the Polish constitution, particularly the suppression of the *liberum veto*.

The Peace of Aix-la-Chapelle in 1748 brought no real change in the general European situation. Silesia was left in the hands of Frederick II, and Russia's only gain was her growing influence in Poland which, in the days of Elizabeth as before, was treated like a Russian protectorate. But through the British ambassador in St. Petersburg, Sir Charles H. Williams, efforts were now made to bring both Augustus III and Elizabeth of Russia into the English political system. A treaty with the former had already been concluded in 1751 with a view to getting Russia's approval for the Saxon succession in Poland after the king's death, and at last, in 1756, the Russian-English alliance was signed, directed, as it seemed, against France and Prussia.

It was based upon the assumption that the Russian auxiliary forces which were supposed to secure the Hanoverian possessions of George II, would as usual march through "neutral" Polish territory. But this provision was the only one which remained in force throughout the following period. In that same year of 1756, an alliance which England concluded with Prussia made the one with Russia meaningless. It was an answer to the unexpected alliance between the traditional enemies, France and Austria, and the prelude to another European war which was also fought in the overseas colonies of the Western powers. Poland had no share in these negotiations, and as a result she had a dangerous opponent in each of the two hostile camps.

THE REPERCUSSIONS OF THE SEVEN YEARS' WAR IN EAST CENTRAL EUROPE

The "reversal of alliances" on the eve of the Seven Years' War is sometimes called the "diplomatic revolution" of the eighteenth century. But much more revolutionary were the basic changes in the structure of the European state system which became apparent at the same time and even more in the course of the war. These changes resulted from the gradual process which during the preceding century had replaced Sweden, Poland, and Turkey by Prussia and Russia as leading powers in the eastern part of Europe.

France, which had considered the former three as her natural allies against the leading power in Germany, the Habsburgs, realized at last that, first, she now needed other allies, and secondly, that the rulers of Austria were no longer supreme in the empire whose merely symbolic crown the house of Lorraine, now called Habsburg-Lorraine, continued to bear after the extinction of the Habsburgs. France was also becoming aware, much more so than England, that the rise of the Prussian Hohenzollerns to a leading position in Germany had to be checked, were it even in alliance with Austria, and for the first time she fought in cooperation with another entirely new ally in Eastern Europe, with Russia. Although Russian armies had made occasional appearances on German battlefields before, they now for the first time played a decisive role there. They could do it because Poland was no longer a barrier between Russia and the West, but rather a convenient passage. And while toward the middle of the war it seemed that, thanks to Russian assistance, Prussia would be reduced to her former modest place or even partitioned, a sudden change of Russian policy at the end of the war—another reversal of alliance, more decisive than that at the beginning, or rather a return to the traditional Russian-Prussian cooperation—saved Prussia as a great power. The

eastern wing of the balance-of-power system was now definitely composed of Prussia and Russia.

The consequences of such a turn of events for Western and West
Central Europe are well known, though sometimes underestimated.
Instead of the Ottoman Empire, which had ceased to be a danger to
the peace of the Continent; instead of Sweden, which had been such a
danger for only a short time; and instead of Poland, which had never
been a threat, the West had now to face two dynamic, aggressive
powers which were resolved to eliminate all that remained of the East
Central European region between them. A considerable part of that
region was already in their possession. Russia had annexed Latvia
and Estonia, along with a small but important part of Finland, and
was absorbing her section of the Ukraine. The Prussian kingdom had
taken its very name from a territory outside Germany, near the heart
of East Central Europe, so important strategically that the Russians,
as long as they were fighting Frederick the Great, occupied it with a
view to keeping it permanently. Furthermore, Silesia too, Frederick's
most valuable conquest, definitely secured through the outcome of
the Seven Years' War, had originally belonged to East Central
Europe.

The final loss of Silesia in 1763 directly affected the Habsburgs,
both their position in the empire and the territorial basis of their
hereditary power, a power chiefly founded on their Bohemian and
Hungarian kingdoms. The desire to connect with the Austrian center, as intimately as possible, all of the lands of the Bohemian crown
that still remained in their hands, as well as Hungary, naturally became even stronger after such a painful loss. The relative freedom of
all non-German East Central European countries which were under
Habsburg rule was therefore vanishing more and more rapidly.
These countries were merely serving to strengthen the position of the
dynasty in the struggle against the Hohenzollern rivals, a struggle
which was to be continued, though chiefly by diplomatic methods, for
the following hundred years. But always considering herself a German power, Austria, even as Prussia's opponent, was neither representing the real interests of East Central Europe nor was she a real
ally of the West against Prussian imperialism. Furthermore, the
Western powers were never quite decided which of the two German
rivals they should support against the other.

In general, Russia was to prove more skillful at that game of power politics, and Poland was the main victim, were it only because of her geographical situation. During the Seven Years' War it seemed that the danger which threatened that last island of freedom in East Central Europe was not so much partition among her neighbors but complete control by the strongest of them, that is, by Russia. That perspective is the only possible justification for those Polish magnates who amidst continuing internal quarrels made it impossible for Augustus III, invaded and humiliated by Frederick the Great in Saxony at the very beginning of the war, to gain his Polish kingdom for the great anti-Prussian coalition. The Czartoryskis were probably right when, in spite of their English sympathies, they considered a victory of that coalition and a defeat of Prussia the best possible solution for Poland. But it seems rather doubtful whether any Polish participation in the war would have restored to the commonwealth that East Prussia which Russia wanted for herself. Furthermore, the leaders of the opposition against the Saxon king could point at the continuing occupation of Polish territory by the troops of his Russian ally who never left Poland from the spring of 1757 to the end of the reign of Augustus III, a few months after the peace of 1763.

It is true that Poland also seemed to have friends on both sides of the fighting powers. But the France of Choiseul, exclusively interested in the overthrow of Prussia and England, did not want to become involved in the East by supporting any Polish claims, were it only by helping to abolish the *liberum veto*, now merely a tool for Prussian and Russian intrigues. On the contrary, even France was rather prepared to consider Russia's claim for a revision of Poland's eastern frontiers, raised during the diplomatic campaigns of the years 1759 to 1760. Strangely enough, the English cabinet also contemplated the possibility of satisfying Russia at Poland's expense, and therefore flatly rejected the proposal of a few younger Polish leaders to start, with English support, an uprising against the Russians which would relieve Britain's Prussian ally.

Frederick the Great, too, was only waiting for an opportunity to direct his policy of territorial annexations against helpless Poland. He already envisaged the connection of East Prussia with Brandenburg and Pomerania by an occupation of Polish Prussia. In the meantime he flooded Poland with false money forged in the Leipzig mints of her king, and he kidnapped Polish people to put them in his army. Finally, the changes on the Russian throne in 1762 not only decided the Seven Years' War in favor of Prussia but also opened new prospects for Frederick's eastern policy.

When, after the death of Elizabeth, the last of the Romanovs, Peter III, a German prince of Holstein-Gottorp and a blind admirer of the King of Prussia, became emperor, the first of these changes seemed to indicate that Russia would completely pass over to Prussia's side. When, a few months later, Peter III was murdered in a court plot, and succeeded by his wife Catherine II, also a German of the Anhalt-Zerbst family, Russian policy became more balanced again. But the new empress, too, decided to withdraw from the war against Prussia and to cooperate with Frederick II against Poland.

Like her husband, Catherine II first resolved to continue the policy of her Russian predecessors with regard to Curland. Already in 1762 Prince Charles of Saxony, the son of Augustus III who hoped to succeed him in Poland, had been expelled from that old fief of the commonwealth which was restored by Catherine II to the Russian puppet Biron. Furthermore, the rumors of a possible partition of Poland, which circulated during the brief reign of Peter III in connection with the secret articles of a twenty-year treaty of friendship which he concluded with Frederick II in June, 1762, seemed to find full confirmation in the first diplomatic activities of the new empress.

It is true that at the outset she rather seemed to follow the example of Peter the Great, that is, to aim at the exclusive control of all Poland, guaranteeing her frontiers and obsolete institutions. But since such a policy was a challenge to all other countries including Prussia, Catherine II also had to consider Frederick's suit for an alliance which would necessarily give him a share in the Polish spoils. Already in the spring of 1763, shortly before the Treaty of Hubertsburg ended the Seven Years' War, the empress agreed with the king of Prussia as to the future election in Poland, after the impending death of Augustus III.

In 1697 and 1733 the election of a Saxon candidate had been imposed upon the Poles by Russo-German intervention, contrary to the decision of the great majority of them. Now a continuation of Wettin rule, poor as it had proved, seemed to the Polish nobility a lesser evil than another foreign dictation. On the contrary, Russia and Prussia jointly decided that a native Pole ought to be elected instead of a member of the Saxon dynasty, but a candidate designated by them and ready to serve as their subservient puppet. For that very reason Catherine II disappointed the Czartoryskis who at the end of Augustus III's reign were ready to collaborate with Russia, and who expected that one of them would be made king and permitted to carry out the constitutional reforms, thus preparing a better future for their country. The empress decided in favor of a nephew of the Czartoryskis, Stanisław Poniatowski, a son of Leszczyński's partisan, a man of refined, Western culture, but a weak character and worst of all a former lover of Catherine, to whom he always remained personally attached. On April 11, 1764, the empress concluded a treaty with Frederick the Great who at the price of an alliance for eight years promised to support that Russian candidate and to join in the guaranty of all abuses of the Polish constitution.

Thus the election of the same year was decided in advance by the two powers which now together controlled North Eastern Europe. But on the one hand, the agreement with the king of Prussia necessarily directed Russian policy toward a partition of Poland instead of total absorption. On the other hand, that preliminary deal was made without the participation of Austria, Poland's third neighbor, whose influence had been decisive, along with the Russian, in the two preceding elections. Now Maria Theresa, so recently defeated by Prussia and abandoned by Russia in the Seven Years' War, was not prepared to cooperate with them. On the contrary, she earnestly wanted the Polish crown to remain in the allied Wettin dynasty. Austria's policy was, however, far from being coordinated with that of the other two powers which opposed the Russo-Prussian project. These powers were France and Turkey, both of which wanted Poland to remain free from the predominance of her neighbors because they themselves were alarmed. France was fearful of the ambitions of Prussia, Turkey of Russia's expansion, and both of the alliance of the two newcomers in the European state system. Finally, neither of these countries, though fully aware of the international importance of what was to be the last election of a king of Poland, made any serious effort to prevent that triumph of Catherine II and Frederick II which was, on September 7, 1764, the unanimous choice of Stanisław Poniatowski by those who attended the Election Diet.

There was, indeed, in Poland a strong opposition against the new king which soon proved an obstacle even to his genuine attempts at improving the internal as well as the external situation of the country. In France and in Turkey there was also a deep dissatisfaction with that turn of events, thus creating high hopes among the Polish patriots. However, before studying why no effective help came from either side in the critical years before the first partition of Poland, it must be explained why Austria, contrary to her own real interests, embarked on a policy which led to her participation, along with Russia and Prussia, in that dismemberment, which confirmed the consequences of the Seven Years' War for Eastern Europe. One of the factors of that policy was Austria's own role in the political development of the large section of East Central Europe which, south of Poland and north of the Ottoman Empire, remained under Habsburg rule.

BOHEMIA AND HUNGARY IN THE EIGHTEENTH CENTURY

Poland's southern neighbor was not Austria in the proper sense at all. Throughout the eighteenth century that name officially continued to designate only the German lands in the eastern Alps which from the later Middle Ages were the basic hereditary possessions of the Habsburgs. These lands also included some Italian territories and the whole area inhabited by the Slovene people, as far as the Adriatic coast and the boundaries of the Republic of Venice. Since the Slovenes were deprived of any historic role, the Austrian provinces as a whole could hardly be considered part of East Central Europe but they were most intimately connected with its history which they deeply influenced, thanks to their union with Bohemia and Hungary.

That union was originally merely dynastic through the persons of the Austrian archdukes who were at the same time the rulers of these two kingdoms. Both of these kingdoms were, however, more and more affected by the general policy of the Habsburgs. The Bohemian and Hungarian estates had not only ceased to deny the hereditary rights of their German dynasty but as early as 1720 and 1723 they accepted the Pragmatic Sanction, that is, the succession of Maria Theresa in all lands left to her by her father Charles VI, the last male representative of the Habsburg family. By that same act all Habsburg possessions were declared indivisible and pledged to mutual assistance against external aggression. The new dynasty, Habsburg-

Lorraine, which was Habsburg only in the female line, was recognized in Bohemia and Hungary as well as in the Austrian *Erbländer*.

But the empress—as Maria Theresa was called after her rather insignificant husband, Francis I of Lorraine, was elected Holy Roman Emperor in 1745—wanted to achieve even more. So, too, with much more ruthless energy, did her and Francis' son and successor, Emperor Joseph II, who after his father's death in 1765 was also his mother's coregent in Austria. They both tried to unify the kingdoms of Bohemia and Hungary with Austria under a common centralized administration and through a common culture which was to be predominantly German. The process was analogous in both kingdoms, but not without specific features in each of them which partly resulted from their different geographical situations.

In the Bohemian lands there had been a revolt against Maria Theresa, or rather a defection from her, in the first years of the War of the Austrian Succession, but not because of any religious or national reason. These lands simply had as their immediate neighbors all the enemies of the young queen in Germany. Of these, the Duke of Bavaria invaded Bohemia proper, was recognized as king by a large part of the nobility, and with French aid maintained himself until 1743 when Maria Theresa was at last crowned in Prague. She wisely avoided too severe repressions, but after careful preparation in 1749 she decided to unify the administration of her Austrian and Bohemian possessions. The Bohemian chancellery which, functioning in Prague with mostly Czech officials had symbolized the unity and autonomy of the Bohemian lands, was now abolished. Abolishing at the same time the separate Austrian chancellery in Vienna, the empress created new offices (*Directorium in publicis et cameralibus*) whose authority extended over both Austria and Bohemia but whose headquarters were in Vienna. They had a distinctly German character. The supreme court also was now common for both regions under the direct control of the crown.

It is true that during the dangerous crisis of the Seven Years' War some minor concessions had to be made, and in 1761 the new supreme office received the double name of Austro-Bohemian Chancellery (*Hofkanzlei*). But the growing influence of Joseph II, and finally his succession after Maria Theresa's death in 1780, inaugurated an era of particularly violent centralization and Germanization which in Bohemia was facilitated by the long decline of national culture and the abandonment of the native tongue by the upper classes. The emperor, a typical representative of the so-called enlightened absolutism, favorable to religious tolerance, to judicial improvements, and to the partial emancipation of the serfs, alienated even those who benefited from his decisions by enforcing the use of the German language, not for any racial reasons but in the interest of linguistic unity.

The conservative opposition, although already in contact with the early beginnings of a Czech national revival, was chiefly interested in defending the traditional state rights of Bohemia and the privileges of the estates, which indeed regained part of their historic influence during the two years of the reign of Leopold II (1790–1792), Joseph's brother and successor. But under Francis II the trend was to be reversed again so that the constitutional reforms of the closing century were, as a matter of fact, a prelude to the complete amalgamation of all Habsburg possessions into one Austrian Empire which was proclaimed in 1804.

That unification was also supposed to include Hungary, but in contradistinction to the largely Germanized lands of the Bohemian crown, which had been part of the Holy Roman Empire and whose position had suffered from the loss of almost all Silesia, the Hungarian kingdom and its nobility, attached to the national tradition, could organize a much stronger resistance. Subtler methods had to be used to reduce their spirit of independence.

That Hungarian resistance was no longer an armed insurrection, as it had been at the turn of the seventeenth century. The Peace of Szatmár in 1711, concluded between the generals of the emperor and those of Francis Rákóczi who went into exile and died in Turkey in 1735, promised a general amnesty and the respect of constitutional rights. What followed was as a matter of fact a period of comparative quiet and compromise and Maria Theresa, at the critical beginning of her reign, received the enthusiastic support of the Hungarian nobles against her foreign aggressors. She never forgot that, and she always showed much more sympathy to the Hungarians than to the Czechs.

Even in her time, however, there remained the economic and social problems of what is called the era of reconstruction after the long years of Turkish wars. In that field, too, the empress had a genuine understanding of Hungary's most urgent needs, and she gave that country direct access to the sea by attaching the Croatian port of Fiume to Hungary proper as a *corpus separatum*. But the colonization which she officially encouraged in the devastated country, establishing in 1766 a special colonization committee in Vienna, chiefly brought German settlers to Hungary and thus considerably increased the number of the German minority. At the same time the importance of the Serb and Rumanian element was also growing. The Serbs were particularly numerous in the southern frontier districts. These, which were the last to be recovered from the Turks, were placed under a military administration. As early as 1741 the Orthodox Patriarch of Ipek transferred his see to Karlowitz, now on Hungarian territory, where he became the religious and political leader of the Serb population. In Transylvania the Orthodox Rumanians concluded a religious union with the Catholic church soon after the establishing of Habsburg rule in 1700, and constituting the majority of the population in a province which remained a separate administrative unit, like the other nationality groups they could easily be played off against the Magyars by Vienna. And since the non-Magyars were chiefly a peasant population, that problem was inseparable from the general issues between landlords and peasants whose condition Maria Theresa had already tried to improve through her *Urbarium* of 1767.

This was indeed a constructive reform, but most dangerous for Hungary's state rights was the fact that ultimately all Hungarian affairs were under the control of the central authorities in Vienna. There was, it is true, a Hungarian deputy council (*consilium locumtenentiale*) in Pozsony (Pressburg) and later in Buda, presided over by the palatine and anxious to protect the traditions of self-government in the Hungarian counties. But the royal court chancellery was in Vienna where the king, or queen, was under the influence of Austrian officials. In their opposition to the trend toward absolute government, the Hungarians used to have the support of the estates of Croatia which continued to occupy an autonomous position. But here, too, the frontier districts were under a German controlled military administration, even after the final peace treaty with the Ottoman Empire which was concluded in 1739.

That treaty deprived Hungary of the temporary gains in the Balkans made in the Treaty of Passarowitz in 1718 after another victorious war and fixed the frontier along the Sava-Danube line, continued toward the east by the Carpathians of southern Transylvania. This frontier, as in general all boundaries of historic Hungary, was to remain unchanged until the Treaty of Trianon in 1918, and the geographic unity of that whole large territory was another element which made impossible a complete absorption by the centralizing policy of Vienna.

That policy entered a particularly aggressive phase, however, when Maria Theresa was succeeded by Joseph II. The new king wanted to abolish even the old county system and he decided to divide the whole country into ten districts under royal commissioners. An even greater mistake was his language decree of 1784. Latin, which had always remained the official language of Hungary, was to be replaced by German. Just as in the case of Bohemia, this was to be a radical measure for enforcing the administrative unity of all Habsburg possessions, but here, where German was much less known, the planned reform proved completely impracticable. Rather, it was a challenge to turn to the use of the Magyar language in connection with the general cultural revival of the country.

This revival was to a large extent based upon the cosmopolitan ideas of the Enlightenment and combined with a lively interest in French ideas, as represented by the foremost writer of the whole generation, George Bessenyei. But while these intellectual leaders were in sympathy with some of the liberal ideas of Joseph II, they even more strongly opposed his violations of constitutional and national rights. And when his campaign against the Turks in 1788–1789 ended in failure, shortly before his death he had to revoke all his edicts except those which guaranteed religious tolerance and the improvement of the lot of the peasants.

His successor, Leopold II, had to face such dissatisfaction in Hungary that, even more than in Bohemia, he had to make far-reaching concessions, undoing his brother's efforts. In the compromise of 1791 it was recognized that in spite of the Pragmatic Sanction Hungary was a *regnum liberum* where the king could govern only in conformity with the laws passed by the Diet. But on the other hand, alarmed by the attitude of the Magyar nobility, Vienna continued to oppose the other nationalities to the Hungarians, and the tension continued under Francis II, whose younger brother had been made palatine of Hungary in 1791.

Strangely enough, it was under the pretext of the historic rights of the medieval kings of Hungary that the Habsburgs claimed their share in the partitions of Poland. But the "Kingdom of Galicia and Lodomeria," thus acquired, was never attached to Hungary. On the contrary, thanks to that formerly Polish province, Austria was also to surround Hungary from the north, and ties of sympathy and sometimes also of active cooperation were to develop between the defenders of what remained of Hungary's freedom and those who fought for the independence of Poland after the three partitions which seemed to annihilate the last fully independent country of East Central Europe.

15

THE PARTITIONS OF POLAND AND THE EASTERN QUESTION

THE FIRST PARTITION OF POLAND

The three partitions of Poland, in 1772, 1793, and 1795, entirely eliminated one of the largest and oldest countries of Europe and completed the absorption of a whole region of Europe by neighboring empires. The western, German section of Central Europe and Russian Eastern Europe now for the first time became immediate neighbors, and the increase in power of the three partners in the dismemberment was not accompanied by any similar advance of the countries of Western Europe. Therefore that process, unique in history, completely destroyed the balance-of-power system and at the very time when the French Revolution shook the European state system in the West, the equally revolutionary action against Poland created a tension in the East which also affected the whole Continent.

It may seem, however, that all this is true only with regard to the final and total partition of 1795 and also the preceding one which two years before created a situation which could not possibly endure, since what was then left of Poland had obviously no chance to survive. The first partition, more than twenty years earlier, meant, on the contrary, only a territorial loss which, though considerable, and suffered under unprecedented conditions, seemed to leave to the remaining center of the commonwealth, still a very large country, possibilities of development, utilized in an unusually successful reform movement that was both constitutional and cultural.

Yet the difference between the two crises is more apparent than real. The national revival which made the last two partitions particularly shocking had to a large extent already started before the first one. Furthermore, the partitioning powers, at least the two responsible leaders of the whole political action, Russia and Prussia, whose interference with Polish affairs had so long delayed the execution of any reform projects and had limited it so severely in the years before the first partition, were already determined in these years to destroy Poland's independence altogether. They considered their annexations of 1772 as only a first step in that direction.

There can be no doubt that the idea of destroying Poland through a series of partitions originated in Prussia, which could not possibly envisage controlling all of Poland by herself. Such control of the whole country was, on the contrary, the original aim of Russia. It can be traced back as far as Peter the Great's reign, and it still appeared clearly in the first part of that of Catherine II when Count Nikita Panin was her main collaborator in the field of foreign relations. But Frederick the Great, taking advantage of the Prussian-Russian alliance, which in 1769 he proposed to extend until 1780, tried to find out at the same time, through Count Lynar's mission to St. Petersburg, whether Russia would not agree to a simultaneous annexation of Polish territories by all three neighbors. After a rather vague but by no means negative answer on that first occasion, Catherine II, two years later, in January 1771, receiving at her court Prince Henry of Prussia, the brother of Frederick the Great, no longer hesitated to discuss the proposed transaction in detail.

From the Russian point of view this was a change of attitude and a concession which cannot be exclusively explained by Catherine's first war with Turkey, which was still far from a successful end. Even that war was originally the consequence of a strong resistance against Russian control and interference which had at last started in Poland. It was precisely that unexpected resistance which made the empress give up the plan of an absorption of the whole commonwealth by Russia alone.

That resistance was unexpected for two different reasons. First, Catherine had hoped that her former lover, whom she had made king of Poland, would prove completely subservient. But Poniatowski, now King Stanisław II, in spite of his many shortcomings, took his new responsibilities very seriously. He even made an attempt at an independent foreign policy through a rapprochement with Austria and France, both of which had opposed his election. And he continued the efforts toward constitutional reforms, which had started during the interregnum under the leadership of his uncles, the princes Czartoryski, and which included the abolition of the *liberum veto*, beginning with majority rule in financial matters where drastic changes were particularly needed. Unfortunately for Poland and her king, even before Frederick the Great won over Catherine II for his partition project, he reached a full agreement with her in a matter which was to completely distort the whole reform movement.

While opposing the most urgent reforms of a constitution which they had decided to "guarantee," the two powerful neighbors started to enforce, through a joint interference with Poland's internal problems, the abolition of all legal restrictions which gradually had limited the civic rights of the "Dissidents." Among these religious minorities, Catherine II wanted to protect the Orthodox, and Frederick II the Protestants. Other Protestant powers, particularly Britain and Denmark, were induced to participate in their protests, although the non-Catholics of Poland enjoyed much more religious liberty than the Catholics in most of the non-Catholic states. As a matter of fact, the whole matter was nothing but a pretext for controlling Poland through the Russian ambassador, Prince Repnin, who did not hesitate to arrest and deport four members of the Polish parliament who most decidedly opposed his requests.

The king himself, strongly influenced by the ideas of the Enlightenment and fully tolerant in religious matters, would have been for a compromise and for making it acceptable to the nation, but Russia now took advantage of the profound cleavage between a foreign imposed ruler and the majority of the people. Not only the Confederations of the small group of non-Catholic nobles, but also the Confederation of Radom, in that same year of 1767, which apparently united the opposition against both Poniatowski and foreign pressure in favor of the "Dissidents," were inspired by Russia with a view to creating a state of anarchy.

But when, early in 1768, the Diet was forced to proclaim "fundamental" laws which gave the "Dissidents" full equality and at the same time made intangible the elective character of the monarchy and the unlimited use of the *liberum veto*, the answer of the Polish patriots was another confederation, this time directed against Russian control. It was concluded in Bar, a frontier town in Podolia, under the leadership of Bishop Krasiński and the Pułaski family, and must be considered the first of so many Polish struggles for national independence. That revolt in defense of faith and freedom was the other unexpected reaction which disturbed Russia's projects—unexpected because it came after the long years of apathy under Saxon rule and testified to a real national revival among the masses of the gentry.

The heroic fight of the Bar Confederates, spreading all over Poland, lasted four years but had no chance of success. First, because inspired by opponents of the king, it never came to an understanding with him. A hopeless attempt at kidnapping Poniatowski only harmed the cause of the patriots and seemed to justify the cooperation of royal troops with the Russians who were determined to crush the "rebellion." Furthermore, the hopes of the confederation to obtain foreign support against the overwhelming forces of Catherine II were disappointed to a large extent. From France, whose attitude seemed decisive, came only a small group of military advisers whose cooperation was of little help and which sometimes even contributed to the confusion in the leadership of the movement. Turkey, it is true, declared war upon Russia in the year 1768. She was alarmed by the situation along her northern border which was obviously leading to Russian predominance, but she did not do it in Poland's interest at all. That war continued for six years on various distant fronts. Indeed it diverted Russia's attention and forces, but it could not prevent the final defeat of the confederates. Among their leaders who had to go into exile, Casimir Pułaski became famous in the American Revolution, but the Polish Revolution which had preceded it only served as one more pretext for punishing a country which was in a state of civil war.

The first step in the direction of partial dismemberment was taken by a neighbor who, unlike Russia and Prussia, had no interest whatever in Poland's gradual destruction and had even seemed to the Confederates to be another prospective ally. Already in 1769 Austrian forces had occupied the cities of the Spisz region, in northern Hungary, which for three and a half centuries had belonged to Poland. Crossing the Carpathians under pretext of sanitary control, the Austrians continued to advance farther into the southern provinces of the commonwealth. These had been contemplated, as Austria's compensation for Russia's and Prussia's gains in the planned partition, if not by Maria Theresa, at least by her son, Joseph II, and her chancellor, Count Kaunitz.

The final partition treaties made by all three powers were not signed before August 5, 1772, when Częstochowa, the famous shrine defended to the last by the Confederates, had been taken by the Russians. But already on February 17 of that fateful year, the agreement between Catherine II and Frederick II was secretly concluded and the annexations of Polish territory outlined. Russia's share, which was the largest, gave her a better frontier along the upper Dvina and Dnieper rivers. No ethnic considerations whatever determined that occupation of an arbitrarily chosen part of White Ruthenian lands, together with the Polish corner of Livonia, which was important for Russia as a hinterland of the port of Riga. Strangely enough, the losses which Russia had suffered because so many of her serfs were escaping across the Polish border was given as the main justification. Even a harder blow for Poland were the Austrian annexation of Galicia, a name which was artificially given not only to the Halich region in the east, with Lwów as main center, claimed in the name of medieval rights of the Hungarian crown, but also to the western part of the new province, the south of Little Poland to the upper Vistula and to the gates of Cracow. Poland lost not only her natural frontier in the south along the Carpathian mountains, however, but also, in the north, her access to the Baltic Sea, because Prussia's smallest, but particularly precious share included, with a district of Great Poland, almost the whole of Polish Pomerania, that "Royal Prussia" which had separated East Prussia from the other Hohenzollern possession. It is true that not only Toruń but also the great port of Danzig was left to Poland, but that port was completely cut off from her remaining territory and henceforth was at Prussia's mercy.

Accepted without any protest by the other European countries in spite of a desperate appeal which Stanisław Poniatowski sent to the King of England, that first dismemberment dictated by the three partners had to be ratified by the Polish Diet. That disgraceful transaction was accomplished the next year under the strongest pressure of Russian troops which only one courageous deputy dared to challenge and in vain. Even worse was the fact that these Russian troops now remained in what was left of Poland, supporting the position of the Russian ambassador in Warsaw who pretended to be the real master of the country. It seemed, therefore, that at the price of abandoning some Polish territories to two German powers, Russia had not only gained other territories for herself but she had also realized her first objective to a large extent. This was to turn all that continued to be called Poland into her protectorate.

Why the internal development of that mutilated Poland turned during the following twenty years in the opposite direction, that must be studied in connection with the general situation in East Central Europe.

THE NEW EASTERN QUESTION

The Eastern question, even in the specific meaning of the problem of the Straits and the control of the Balkans, is as old as European history. It was a particularly urgent problem, even affecting the whole East Central European region, at the time of the rise of Ottoman power. So long as that power was solidly established on both sides of the Straits and in the whole Balkan Peninsula, there seemed to be no Eastern question in the usual sense. For several centuries that question was superseded by the much more alarming issue of defending Europe against a further Turkish advance. But when that advance turned into a gradual retreat, and when a partition of at least the European possessions of the Ottoman Empire seemed possible and even imminent, the Eastern question reappeared under that very name, and since medieval traditions are so frequently disregarded, that question is sometimes considered a practically new development in international relations that are typical of the later eighteenth and the following century.

In this interpretation the two Turkish wars of Catherine II of Russia seem to be at the very origin of the Eastern question. Indeed, they caused a momentous change in the situation of Southeastern Europe. Therefore these wars affected the balance of power in Europe as a whole, and their impact was even more fully realized in this respect than that of the simultaneous partitions of Poland. Both series of events are, however, intimately connected with each other, and were it only for that reason, these two wars, in the second of which the Habsburg monarchy also participated, largely belong to the history of East Central Europe.

They also belong to that history for another reason. They were fought by the empires which always influenced the destinies of the peoples of East Central Europe in one way or another, and one of the issues was indeed which of these peoples would be liberated or conquered, or which would change their master in consequence of these wars. That problem is perhaps even more important than the usual aspects of the so-called Eastern question if considered from the point of view of the big powers only.

The first war which Catherine II had to conduct against Turkey and which had started in 1768 in connection with her Polish policy, was chiefly fought in regions far away from Poland. When it was concluded in 1774 by the Kuchuk Kainarji Treaty, the first partition of Poland was already an accomplished fact. That fact, and more particularly the annexation of Galicia by Austria, also made it possible for the latter to claim a share in what seemed to be a first partition of Turkey, the northwestern corner of Turkish-controlled Moldavia called the Bukovina. Henceforth there were Rumanians not only under Hungarian but also under Austrian rule.

The Rumanians of Moldavia and Wallachia had expected something different: liberation from Turkish rule, which Russia's victories seemed to make possible for all the Orthodox peoples of the Balkans. Even the Greeks, far in the South, were stirred by the spectacular appearance of a Russian fleet in 1770, which after an amazing voyage all round Europe came from the Baltic Sea into the Aegean and defeated the Turkish navy off the Greek coast. But the only territorial changes which were really made in consequence of the long war were in the steppes north of the Black Sea where Russia, without yet reaching that sea directly, advanced her southern frontier and gained a new area of colonization east of the Ukraine. Her hold of the Ukraine on the left bank of the Dnieper was thus strengthened, and the final liquidation of the last traces of Cozack autonomy was accelerated. Furthermore, the Khanate of the Crimea, which had been a vassal of Turkey for three hundred years, was now declared independent, and in view of the general situation this was only a step in the direction of Russian control over that state which once had been a permanent threat to her as well as to Poland.

Most significant for the future, however, was another article of the Kuchuk-Kainarji Treaty which for the first time gave Russia the right to interfere in case of a violation of the religious freedom of the sultan's Orthodox subjects. That unilateral guaranty of their privileges by the great Orthodox Empire was a recognition of Russia's unique position in the Balkans. It confirmed these peoples in the conviction that an improvement of their situation, possibly leading to eventual liberation from the Turkish yoke, could only be achieved through Russian interference. Even before that liberation and before any change in the existing frontiers, these populations were thus becoming a pawn in the game of the big powers.

Along with the first partition of Poland and what seemed to be permanent Russian control of the rest of that country, the peace of 1774 contributed so much to Catherine's prestige that five years later she could act as mediator in the Austro-Prussian rivalry in German affairs. But her main interest seemed to be in the Eastern question which had been only temporarily settled. The annexation of the Crimea in 1783, which at last made Russia a Black Sea power also, and her obvious preparations for another conflict with Turkey, induced the Ottoman Empire to start a preventive war again in 1788.

This time the implications were even greater. While the King of Poland came in vain, and under rather humiliating conditions, to visit the empress in Kaniów, at the Dnieper border, and was not permitted to join the campaign, Emperor Joseph II, who also visited Catherine II, entered the war on her side in order to share in the spoils. His participation, however, made the growing Austro-Russian rivalry in the Balkans even more apparent. Being quite unsuccessful from the military point of view, it led to a separate peace that was concluded with Turkey long before Russia, after a series of important victories, at least partly reached her own objectives in the Peace Treaty of Yassy in 1792.

The hopes of the Balkan populations, especially of the Rumanians, were again disappointed. Although the Russian armies reached the Danube, where the fortress of Ismail was temporarily taken, this time, too, the Ottoman Empire made no territorial concessions in that region. But in addition to the Crimea, Russia obtained access to the Black Sea east and west of that peninsula, and the question as to how wide that access would be was the most controversial issue not only in the negotiations between the two conflicting powers but also in the opinion of all those who in Western Europe became concerned with Catherine's rapid progress. While nobody questioned her conquest of distant Azov, her determination to keep the port and fortress of Ochakov, which had been conquered after a long siege by Field Marshal Suvorov, almost provoked a general European crisis, although the place—not far from present-day Odessa—had been practically unknown in the West.

Once a port of the Jagellonian federation in the fifteenth century, then for a long time in Turkish hands, Ochakov indeed to a great extent controlled the Black Sea coast between the mouths of the Dnieper and Dniester rivers. Therefore William Pitt the Younger decided to make Russia's claim to that place an issue which he placed before the British Parliament in March, 1791. The majority which supported him in that matter was so small, however, that he could not risk the danger of a war against Russia and gave up his protest. That British withdrawal greatly facilitated Catherine's success at Yassy where Russia obtained a long shore line along the Black Sea, including Ochakov.

It was easy for the opposition leader, Fox, to argue that the question of Ochakov could hardly affect the balance of power in Europe, and for Edmund Burke to wonder whether the Ottoman Empire could be considered a member of the European state system at all. But though the issue as such was badly chosen, there could be no doubt that Catherine's second victorious war against Turkey, with much more important territorial gains than after the first and with new possibilities for interference with the Balkan problems, basically affected the whole Eastern question, and also indirectly the situation in the Mediterranean, in which Britain was always so deeply interested. Furthermore, Russia's advance in that direction was only part of an old process of expansion, greatly accelerated under the ambitious empress, which encircled East Central Europe from the South and from the North. Facilitated by these pincer movements, the main drive was directed through East Central Europe toward the heart of the Continent.

In the midst of her second Turkish war, Catherine II had indeed to fight a shorter and less spectacular war in the North, in the Baltic region where the change along the Black Sea had immediate repercussions. Sweden also thought it a propitious moment to start a preventive war, hoping again to reconquer the lost territory at the Finnish border. That hope failed once more, and the Treaty of Värälä in 1790 merely confirmed the status quo. For Sweden, which under the poor reign of Gustavus III and amidst a serious internal crisis was, just like Poland, threatened in her survival as an independent nation, even such a result was almost satisfactory. Were it only for geographical reasons she proved to be safer from Russian conquest and less important for the progress of Russian expansion than either Turkey or Poland. However, with Sweden eliminated as a possible member of an anti-Russian coalition, it was not only easier for Russia to force harsh peace conditions upon Turkey but the time had also arrived when Catherine II could at last concentrate all her military and diplomatic forces against Poland.

At the same time, Pitt's idea of a federal system uniting all countries of the northern part of Europe against the rising power of Russia—an idea which could have saved Poland—lost much of its chance of success and was soon abandoned altogether in view of Britain's growing concern with the much nearer problems of the French Revolution. Even the Eastern question, with all its Mediterranean implications, could now seem almost secondary, and in spite of his occasional talks with Polish diplomats, Pitt never realized that the gradual elimination of Poland would upset the balance of power much more than the decline of Turkey, or rather that it would destroy that balance completely.

It is true that during most of the breathing space granted to Poland between the first and the second partition, her diplomacy had continued to be rather passive, and that the king's attempts to obtain for his country the possibility of participating in the solution of the Eastern question were a total failure. But during all these years both Stanisław Poniatowski and the Polish nation, which now recognized him universally, made a tremendous effort to take advantage of Russia's absorption in other problems in order to at last achieve the badly needed constitutional reforms, accompanied by a remarkable revival of Polish culture.

That revival, conspicuous in the field of literature and art where the king proved to be an outstanding patron, was even more important in the field of education which is inseparable from the most urgent problems of political and social progress. The reforms accomplished by the Commission of National Education, which was created immediately after the first partition and is frequently called the first Ministry of Education in European history, changed the whole intellectual atmosphere of the country. To a large extent it explains why, on the eve of the second partition, that country was quite different from the dark years of Saxon rule. Decisive, however, was the convocation in 1788, just at the beginning of the Russian-Turkish war, of the so-called Great Diet. This remained in session for four years, gave Poland a new constitution without any break with the national tradition, and also tried to give her a new, constructive foreign policy. It was the failure of that policy, however, unavoidable in the European

situation of these years, which made all internal achievements futile
and raised another Eastern, or rather East Central European, question which, parallel to the French Revolution, inaugurated a new
period of European history.

THE SECOND AND THIRD PARTITIONS OF POLAND

If the defects of her constitution had been the real cause of Poland's
fall, she should have been saved by the comprehensive reforms of the
Four Years' Diet. The work of that assembly was praised by many
contemporaries in the Western countries because, though revolutionary in its results, it was accomplished without any violence
through well-balanced evolutionary methods. It was even more remarkable that those who carried out such a far-reaching reform program, the representatives of the nobility and gentry, did it at the
expense of their own privileged position and to the advantage of the
community and the other classes of society. Only one of the political
writers who inspired the whole movement, Stanisław Staszic, was
himself a burgher. But the personal initiative and cooperation of the
king also proved extremely helpful.

He himself had little to gain from the basic change in favor of the
monarchy which was declared hereditary in order to avoid the troubles
of "free" elections in the face of foreign interference. For it was not
the family of the childless Poniatowski, but the Saxon house which
was chosen as the hereditary dynasty to succeed after his death.
Whether this was a wise decision is questionable in view of the sad
experiences made with the two Augustuses, but it shows the desire to
assure the continuity of traditions which were merely adapted to new
conditions and not altogether rejected.

It was more important, however, that the strengthening of royal
authority, so badly needed, was skilfully combined with the modern
conception of parliamentary government based upon a clear distinction of the three powers, legislative, executive, and judicial. The total
abolition of the *liberum veto*, now replaced by majority rule, did away
with the main distortion of a parliamentary tradition of which the
nation was otherwise so rightly proud. Modernized was also the functioning of the ministries, the whole cabinet being placed under the
control of a special body called the Guard of the Laws. These central
departments were now common for both the kingdom of Poland in

the proper sense and the grand duchy of Lithuania, but that step in the direction of unification of the commonwealth was combined with a reaffirmation of the equality of both constituent parts, by now completely assimilated in their general culture and way of life.

Reaffirmed was also the respect for the traditional position of the Catholic church and for the rights of the nobles. But the former did not affect the full religious freedom of all other denominations, now guaranteed without foreign pressure, and the latter were made accessible to the burghers through a special bill in favor of the cities, which was declared part of the constitution. The representatives of the cities were now to share in the legislative power of the Diet in all matters concerning their interests, and admission into the *szlachta* was greatly facilitated. It is true that serfdom was not yet abolished, but a solemn declaration in favor of the peasants emphasized their importance for society at large, contrary to inveterate prejudices. All new settlers were promised complete freedom, and the others were placed under the protection of the law which made binding the numerous individual contracts concluded between landowners and peasants with a view to improving the situation of the latter.

After long discussions, already conducted under the majority rule —the Diet having been made a "confederation"—the new constitution was voted on May 3, 1791, with only a very small minority in opposition. It was at once solemnly sworn in a ceremony which closely associated the king and the nation, and it can be well compared with the almost contemporary American and French constitutions whose influence undoubtedly accelerated the native reform trends, making clearly apparent Poland's intimate connection with the Western world once more.

There was, however, a great difference which resulted from the obvious fact that the United States of America, though only recently liberated from foreign rule, and France, though threatened by foreign invasions amidst revolutionary excesses and émigré activities, were in a much less dangerous international situation than Poland, placed as she was between two equally hostile neighbors, Russia and Prussia. The Great Diet was fully aware of that situation, and even before adopting the new constitution it was unanimously decided to raise the armed forces of the country to the figure of a hundred thousand men, great progress if compared with the almost complete disarmament of Poland which can be traced back to the Russian intervention of 1717.

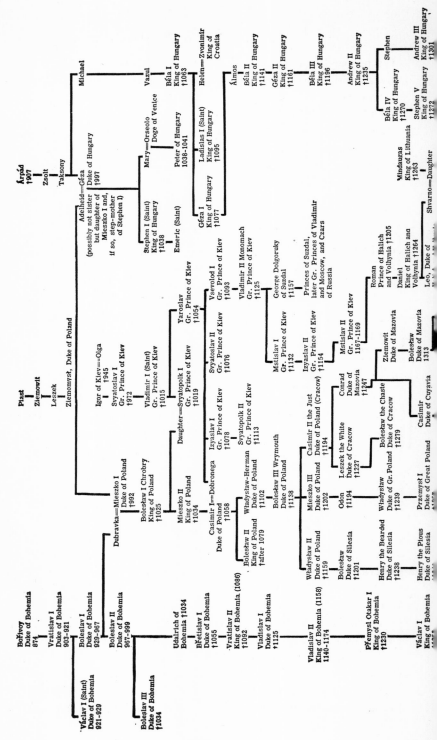

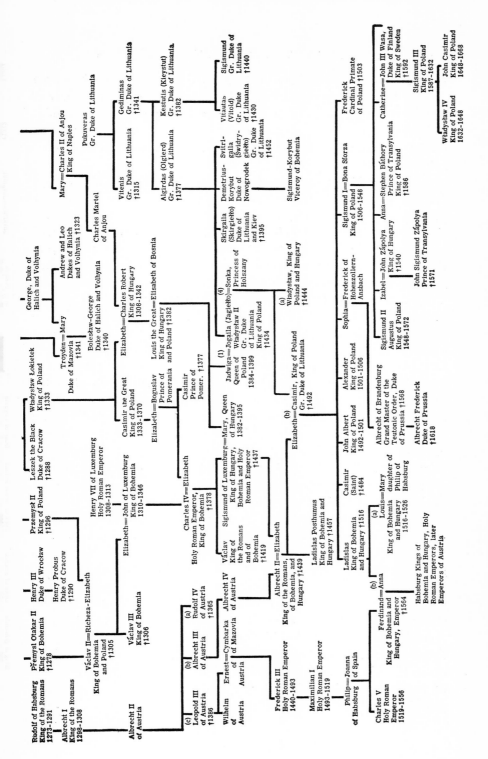

But even so the Polish army, which could not reach that increased number immediately, remained much smaller than either the Russian or even the Prussian, and it was obviously helpless against a joint action by both. There appeared, therefore, the diplomatic problem of coming to an understanding with at least one of the dangerous neighbors.

Since the king's attempts to appease Catherine II had always failed, the so-called Patriotic Party, which was chiefly responsible for the constitutional reforms, decided in favor of an alliance with Prussia. This was concluded on March 29, 1790. That alliance was indeed exclusively defensive, but even so it was of rather doubtful value from the outset because Prussia only waited for an opportunity to annex more Polish territories, beginning with the cities of Danzig and Toruń. Nobody in Poland was prepared to pay such a price, and the project of Frederick William II's minister, von Herzberg, to obtain these cities by having Galicia restored to Poland never had any serious chance of acceptance by Austria in spite of the compensations promised to Vienna. Nevertheless the treaty with Prussia seemed to be a guaranty against Russian aggression because it included Poland in the group of countries allied with Britain. For that very reason the value of the Polish-Prussian alliance was already greatly reduced when a year later the decisive turn in Pitt's policy, connected with the Eastern question, made it obvious that no British support against Russia could be expected. The real test came in 1792, however, when Catherine II, after making peace with Turkey, was ready to punish the Poles for having changed their constitution without her permission.

A small reactionary opposition against the Constitution of 1791, led by no more than three magnates who succeeded in getting only ten additional signatures for their "confederation" concluded in Targowica, offered the empress a convenient pretext for invading Poland in defense of her "freedom" against a "Jacobine" conspiracy. Even more disingenuous was the pretext invoked by the king of Prussia when he refused to honor the alliance. It had been concluded with a republic and could not bind him with respect to the monarchy established in 1791. Instead of supporting Poland, he sided with Russia in order to gain as much as possible of Poland's territory by means of another partition which had already been discussed in secret negotiations.

Under these conditions the resistance of the Polish army under Prince Joseph Poniatowski, the king's nephew, and Thaddeus Kościuszko, already famous, thanks to his participation in the American Revolution, was doomed to failure in spite of initial successes. To make things worse, the king lost his courage and joined the pro-Russian Confederation of Targowica, thus giving it the appearance of legality and making possible the cancellation of all constitutional reforms. Once more his policy of appeasement proved disastrous and could not prevent the second partition of Poland, carried out in 1793, this time without the participation of Austria, which during the whole crisis and particularly under Leopold II had been rather friendly. Again the Russian share was larger than the Prussian, extending as far as a line from the eastern tip of Curland to the Austrian border and cutting off all the White Ruthenian and Ukrainian lands that still remained to the commonwealth. In addition to Danzig and Toruń, Prussia claimed the whole western half of Great Poland.

Coming after the break of the alliance, that claim was particularly resented by the Poles so that even the Diet, convoked at Grodno after Russian-controlled elections and resigned to approve the Russian annexations, refused to ratify the Prussian contention. Terrorized by Russian forces, the deputies remained silent, but eventually that silence was interpreted as consent. Under such circumstances it was unavoidable that the rest of Poland, in its artificial boundaries, would be treated as a Russian protectorate. But for that very reason and under the influence of the internal revival that set in between the first and the second partition, immediately after the latter a strong resistance movement began which found an inspiring leader in the person of Kościuszko.

Though insufficiently prepared, his insurrection, which openly started in Cracow on March 23, 1794, seemed to develop successfully when the Russians suffered a first defeat at Racławice and both Warsaw and Wilno liberated themselves a few days later. Particularly promising was the participation in the struggle for independence of both townsmen and peasants. Kościuszko's manifesto of May 7, issued at Połaniec, was a decisive step toward the complete abolition of serfdom. Although he had practically dictatorial powers, he exercised them with great moderation, stopping occasional revolutionary excesses and taking no action against the helpless king. The situation became desperate, however, when the Prussians proved more interested in easy gains in the East than in fighting in the West against the French Revolution, which disappointed the Polish hopes for support and cooperation but which indirectly profited by the diversion of Prussian forces.

These forces decided the battle of Szczekociny and besieged Warsaw until Kościuszko suffered a final defeat at Maciejowice and the Russians under Suvorov stormed Praga. Terrified by the massacre in that suburb, the capital surrendered, and the whole insurrection, after spreading far into Prussian Poland under General Dąbrowski, as well as to the eastern border of the commonwealth, ended in failure and served as an excuse for the total dismemberment of the country.

This time, too, Austria, whose sympathy Kościuszko had tried to gain, again claimed her share. She was afraid of the progress of the two other powers. After long negotiations, that share was reduced to the triangle between the Pilica and Bug rivers, a rather artificial addition to Galicia, which, however, included Cracow and almost reached Warsaw. Prussia, which tried in vain to annex the former city, after taking away the royal insignia, obtained the capital and reached the Niemen River, thus creating a new province of South-East Prussia. Russia took almost all that remained of the Grand Duchy of Lithuania, including Curland, and the territories east of the Bug. Although most of the peasant population in the provinces annexed by Catherine II was White Ruthenian and Ukrainian, in addition to the Lithuanians, no ethnic considerations whatever determined the drawing of the new frontiers which arbitrarily divided a body politic that had existed for many centuries. An additional secret convention held in 1797 decided to eliminate forever the very name of Poland whose last king, forced to abdicate, died as an exile in St. Petersburg.

The consequences of that dismemberment, unique in history, affected not only Poland and the peoples of the former commonwealth. The balance of power in Europe was deeply disturbed, although the Western powers, in conflict among themselves, were rather slow to realize it. Since the last country which in the course of modern history had remained free and independent in East Central Europe now disappeared, that whole region of the Continent simply ceased to exist. The German part of Central Europe now became the immediate neighbor of East European Russia, with only two possible alternatives: a

German-Russian domination of Europe or a German-Russian conflict, impossible to localize. Which of these possibilities would prevail, this was to be the big issue of the following period of about a hundred and twenty years, decisive not only from the point of view of power politics but also for the fate of all the peoples of East Central Europe which after a proud medieval tradition now seemed to be completely submerged.

PART V

NATIONALISM VERSUS IMPERIALISM

16

THE NAPOLEONIC PERIOD

THE RISE OF NATIONAL CONSCIOUSNESS IN
EAST CENTRAL EUROPE

The nineteenth century, with its aftermath until 1914, is certainly one of the best-known periods of European history. It is also the first in which the whole eastern half of the Continent, including the Balkans and the Russian Empire, receives full attention and is studied as an integral part of Europe as a whole and in close connection with the West.

Nevertheless, as far as the peoples of East Central Europe are concerned, their treatment in the conventional presentation of general history continues to be quite unsatisfactory. The usual identification of state and nation, largely justified in the history of Western Europe, leads to a disregard of the basic fact that in the region between Germany and Russia, one nation after the other had lost its political independence and therefore its statehood, while some peoples had never fully succeeded in constituting their own states. Yet even the latter were by no means peoples without any history at all or without political aspirations. The others continued to remember their historic past and to be inspired by their national traditions, even if they had to look back as far as the Middle Ages. Therefore, in addition to the history of the empires which at the end of the eighteenth century completely controlled East Central Europe, there is a history of the stateless nations and of peoples aiming at full nationhood—both rather misleadingly called nationalities—which is indispensable for a genuine understanding of the tensions in nineteenth-century Europe and the crisis which followed that apparently peaceful period.

That crisis was foreshadowed and the superficial peace was quite frequently disturbed by revolutionary movements among the millions kept under foreign rule. These national movements were usually connected with revolutionary trends of a constitutional and social character—that other source of European unrest throughout the nineteenth century. In the Balkans these insurrections resulted in a gradual liberation of most of the oppressed peoples. But even the development of their new or restored states is usually studied rather from the point of view of the imperialistic rivalries of the great powers, and not without some prejudice against the so-called "Balkanization" of Europe through the multiplication of small political units. Similar and even more one-sided is the approach to those independence movements of the nineteenth century which ended in failure.

In all of them, however, there was a natural vitality which was to find a clear expression during the First World War and which is not difficult to explain. First, the submerged peoples of East Central Europe were never reconciled with their fate. The longer foreign domination lasted, the stronger was the reaction as soon as the decline of their master's power seemed to give them a chance of liberation. Furthermore, the final elimination of all political freedom in the whole region, through the partition of Poland, struck a nation with such a long and uninterrupted tradition of independence that the divided Polish territories remained throughout the following century a permanent center of unrest. The Polish people became natural leaders in a struggle which they conducted, according to a well-known slogan, "for your freedom and ours." They were interested in all similar movements, and in many cases they actively participated in them.

The Polish reaction against what happened in 1795 was so immediate, strong, and persistent because in Poland national culture not only had an old tradition but it had also reached a new climax of development on the very eve of the partitions. The national consciousness of the Poles was therefore fully developed and ready for normal progress in spite of the most unfavorable conditions. Moreover, that national consciousness, formerly limited in Poland to the upper strata of society, was also penetrating into the lower classes just at the time of the partitions, thanks to the reforms which had been started and thanks to the repercussions of the simultaneous French Revolution.

These repercussions were, of course, not limited to Poland, where they found a propitious ground in view of the close traditional relations between the two countries. French influence is rightly considered one of the main factors which at the turn of the century contributed to the vogue of nationalism everywhere, giving to that trend its modern form of expression. It is true that the revolutionary movement in France, where no problems of nationalities troubled the homogeneous state, was aiming at constitutional and social reforms in the name of the rights of men and citizens. But wherever human rights and liberties were endangered by foreign rule, the claim for freedom was to include, of course, national freedom from such alien domination. This was precisely the case of all East Central European peoples.

In addition to these political challenges, the intellectual stimuli of the Enlightenment, which spread from France as far as Eastern Europe, promoted a revival of cultural traditions. In connection with the progress of education, this encouraged an interest in native languages, folklore, and customs. The resulting growth of national consciousness was also favored by the democratic trends of the period, since in many cases only the masses of the people had remained faithful to their tongue and way of life.

The Western influences working in that direction among the people of Eastern Europe did not always come directly or exclusively from France. The role of Johann Gottfried von Herder, his interest in national cultures and his interpretation of history, is rightly emphasized in the same connection. It is well known that this highly original German writer was unusually objective with regard to the Slavs and fully aware of their historic role and future possibilities. Far from identifying Slavdom with the rising power of the Russian Empire, he was particularly interested in the smaller Slavic peoples. It is indeed their progress in national consciousness which was to prove typical of the development of nationalism in East Central Europe. The so-called national renaissance among the peoples of that region was, however, not at all limited to the Slavs. Herder himself, a resident of Riga, studied and also encouraged the national cultures of the Latvian and Estonian natives of the Baltic provinces. And just as in a better past, the development of the Lithuanians, Hungarians, Rumanians, and Greeks was to prove inseparable from the destinies of their Slavic neighbors. That their very neighborhood and reciprocal connections also frequently led to clashes of conflicting nationalisms is of course another question. What all these revived nationalisms had in common, however, was first of all the progress of national culture and later the desire for political freedom in a national state. Hence the basic opposition to the empires which ruled the East Central

European peoples from the outside and tried to absorb them politically and even culturally into their own strongly centralized state systems.

While the opposition of local nationalism to big-power imperialism was a general phenomenon throughout the whole region, there was of course much difference in the degree of development of the national consciousness of the individual peoples. In that respect the Hungarians came immediately after the Poles, although for almost three centuries they had been deprived of a fully independent national government. They had suffered from partition and from the influence of foreign rulers, western and eastern, and the Magyar nobility, which identified itself with the nation at large, continued to consider Latin the official language of the country. It was not before 1791 that the Magyar language was made an optional subject in school, and the next year a regular one, and in 1805 Magyar was permitted to be used in the Diet along with Latin. In the same generation a trend toward the revival of Magyar literature also appeared. The tendency toward democratic reforms greatly strengthened Hungarian nationalism which had hitherto been mainly evidenced in the defense of Hungary's state rights by the estates.

Within the limits of historic Hungary, Magyar nationalism, opposed to German influence, was already finding rivals in the non-Magyar nationalities. While the estates of Croatia also struggled against the centralism and absolutism of the Habsburgs, and although their leader, Nicholas Skerlecz, stressed the ties of an autonomous Croatia with Hungary, the first beginnings of a joint national revival of all Southern Slavs had already appeared. They found clear expression in the first history of all these Slavic peoples, published by Jovan Rajich in Vienna (1794–1795), and were inspired by the fight against Turkish rule which at that very moment started in Serbia, not without repercussions among the Serbs of Hungary. On the other hand it was in Hungarian-controlled Transylvania that, thanks to the Uniate Bishop Samuel Micu (Klein), the Rumanian national revival, based upon the consciousness of close ties with the Latin West, developed even earlier than in the autonomous Danubian principalities. There, under the Phanariote princes, anti-Greek feelings were combined with a common interest of Rumanian and Greek elements in French culture of the revolutionary period.

That same French influence which in Bulgaria was preceded by a first attempt to revive national culture, made by the monk-historian

Paisi as early as 1762, was chiefly responsible for the rebirth of Hellenism under the leadership of prominent writers such as Rhigas and the great poet Adamantios Korays. In general, however, the decisive rise of nationalism in the Balkans did not come until the first successes in the liberation of individual nations from Ottoman rule.

Less political in its early beginnings but particularly striking in the cultural field was the rebirth of Czech national consciousness which had comparatively little in common with the defense of Bohemia's state rights by her estates. It started toward the end of the eighteenth century with the literary activities of two prominent scholars, Josef Dobrovský and Josef Jungmann. Dobrovský still wrote in Latin or German while Jungmann, through his dictionary and translations laid the foundations for the development of modern Czech literature. Both started the outstanding Czech contribution to Slavic studies which was to be typical of the development of Czech culture in the following century and to influence the political outlook of the Czech people, whose national life had been endangered only by German influence and which never suffered from any other Slavs.

In that respect, the position of the Ukrainians, whose national revival was a reaction against Polonization and Russification, was entirely different. After the partition of Poland, that small part of the Ruthenians which came under Austrian rule in eastern Galicia had better chances for free development, were it only due to the favorable situation of the Uniate church under the Habsburgs. It was in the Ukraine proper, however, now entirely under Russia, that the cultural revival started in 1798 when Ivan Kotlyarevsky published his travesty of Virgil's *Aeneid* in the dialect of the province of Poltava, comparing the Trojans with the homeless Cozacks who had been expelled from their old center by the Russian government. In his comedies, Kotlyarevsky also stressed the difference between Ukrainian Ruthenians and Muscovite Russians, and giving his people a modern literary language, he greatly facilitated the national movement of the nineteenth century.

Nothing similar happened during these years among the White Ruthenians. Nor were the Lithuanians, who together with the White Ruthenians came under Russian domination after the partition of Poland, as yet opposing to the recent tradition of the Polish-Lithuanian Commonwealth any Lithuanian national movement on ethnic or linguistic grounds. It was among the Polonized nobility of the former grand duchy, where among other possibilities of liberation the reconstitution of that grand duchy was also being considered, but only as a first step toward restoring the old commonwealth whose purely Polish part was mostly under the rule of German powers.

National revival among the Latvians and Estonians, though earlier than the Lithuanian movement, had only a very modest beginning at the end of the eighteenth century. This was limited to a new interest in their language and customs. And as for the beginning of Finnish nationalism, it was naturally directed against Swedish influence as long as the grand duchy was connected with Sweden. Here, as in so many other cases, the basic change was to come in the Napoleonic period.

NAPOLEON AS A LIBERATOR

Whenever the nineteenth century is called a period of relative peace, without at least general European wars, an exception has to be made, of course, for the first fifteen years, which together with the last years of the eighteenth century were dominated by the overpowering personality of Napoleon. Thanks to him, these were years of almost uninterrupted wars which on several occasions involved almost all the European countries. And since the political aspirations of those European peoples which were dissatisfied with their position had the best if not the only chance of being realized through a general upheaval of the Continent, the Napoleonic wars were for some of them a great opportunity. Therefore, though Bonaparte, especially in his later phase, was a typical representative of imperialism, it is no paradox to say that in a certain number of cases he played the role of liberator.

This was obviously not the case in countries of Western Europe which were in the neighborhood of France whose territory and sphere of influence was extended at the expense of other peoples and their freedom. For the western, German part of Central Europe, the emperor of the French was simply a foreign conqueror and the reaction against him a war of liberation. More involved was the Italian situation, where the interference of Bonaparte, himself of Italian descent, in several cases replaced other completely alien foreign masters and in general seemed to be a step in the direction of national unification. But it was in East Central Europe that Napoleon was really welcomed as a liberator by many of those who were dominated by foreign powers.

The first to look upon him from such a point of view were exiles from the most recently conquered country, Poles, under the leadership of General Dąbrowski, already prominent in Kościuszko's insurrection. After the third partition they wanted to resume the struggle for independence which had set in after the second. Once more disappointed by the political authorities in France, in 1797 these Poles succeeded in being accepted by General Bonaparte as a Polish legion fighting under his command. They distinguished themselves in his Italian campaign, with the hope that his struggle against a coalition which included Austria and Russia would weaken these partitioning powers and eventually lead to a situation where they would be forced to give up part of or all their Polish acquisitions.

For almost ten years these hopes were disappointed by one after the other of the temporary peace treaties concluded by Napoleon. He used these Polish forces wherever he wanted to, even in faraway San Domingo, but he had no interest at all in raising the Polish question. There were, therefore, other Poles who expected more favorable results from cooperation with Czar Alexander I, who seemed to start his reign with generous, liberal ideas and in 1804 even made the Polish prince, Adam Czartoryski, a nephew of the last king, his foreign minister. As such, and at the same time as a close friend of the czar, Czartoryski worked out a remarkable project for a reorganization of Europe, based upon justice for all nations and including the restoration of Poland under Alexander, in personal union with Russia. The concrete proposals which the czar made to the British Government in 1804 through his envoy Novosiltsov, were, however, drafted in a more realistic sense and even so were hardly taken into consideration. Alexander I himself, frequently changing his policy and probably never quite sincere in dealing with the Poles, decided in 1805 for the traditional Russian-Prussian cooperation. This was a blow to Czartoryski's program which led to his resignation as foreign minister. In spite of Napoleon's victory over the emperors of Austria and Russia at Austerlitz, the latter continued the war in alliance with Prussia during the following two years.

Now at last Napoleon's armies appeared on Polish soil, fighting against the two chief enemies of the Poles and looking for their support. Prussia's crushing defeats resulted in the liberation of a large part of her share in the dismemberments, and the participation of considerable Polish forces in the campaign was accompanied by projects of political reorganization. Such a decision was really made by the Treaty of Tilsit in 1807, but trying to appease Alexander I, Napoleon limited the new body politic which was created in the very heart of East Central Europe to Prussia's share in the second and third partition and called it not Poland but the Duchy of Warsaw. Danzig was made a free city and the district of Białystok was ceded to Russia.

Even so the duchy, though under strict French control, was generally considered to be a first step in undoing the work of the partitions and reopening the whole problem of Poland's freedom. And the choice of the Duke of Warsaw in the person of Napoleon's ally, King Frederick of Saxony, seemed to be in agreement with the decision of the Polish Constitution of 1791 which was replaced, however, by a new constitution on the French model. The army of the duchy, placed under the command of Prince Joseph Poniatowski, was supposed to reinforce the French position in East Central Europe. Indeed it served as a useful diversion in the war against Austria in 1809.

This war against another power which had annexed Polish territory was, however, conducted in formal alliance with Alexander I. The Tilsit agreement between the two emperors amounted to a partition of all Europe in their respective spheres of influence. As a matter of fact, this scheme facilitated further aggrandizements of Russia in East Central Europe. One of them, the conquest of Finland, followed immediately and was confirmed the next year by Sweden's formal cession of that grand duchy to Russia. In spite of the large autonomy granted to Finland, to which even the Vyborg region was restored, that country, so long connected with the Scandinavian world, now came under eastern influence, which apparently tolerated the rise of Finnish nationalism but included a serious danger of Russification in the future. After Tilsit, Russia was also free to continue a new war against Turkey, started a few years earlier, which was to end in 1812 with the annexation of Bessarabia. That part of Moldavia between the Dniester and Prut rivers now became a Russian province, while Moldavia itself, as well as Wallachia, only temporarily occupied, remained under Ottoman suzerainty.

In the meantime a momentous change developed in the relations between Alexander and Napoleon which not only affected the fate of the Poles but also of all the Central European nations. Austria, again defeated in 1809, had to make great territorial cessions. Those in the southwestern part of the Austrian Empire, which had been proclaimed in 1804 in anticipation of the dissolution of the Holy Roman Empire in 1806, were no real liberation because the so-called Illyrian provinces were annexed by the French Empire, along with the old Republic of Ragusa which had lost its independence in 1805. But during the few years of French administration under Marshal Marmont, the national movement of the Croats and Slovenes was encouraged and developed in the direction of at least a cultural community of all Southern Slavs. In the north the Polish participation in the war was rewarded by adding Austria's share in the third partition, including Cracow, to the duchy of Warsaw. But Russia also received a small compensation—the district of Tarnopol, cut off from the remaining part of Austrian Galicia—for her rather fictitious role in the campaign of 1809.

Nevertheless Alexander I was so alarmed by the mere possibility of a restoration of Poland that in 1810 he requested Napoleon to give him a solemn promise that this would never happen. The disagreement of the two emperors in the drafting of such a statement was typical of their growing antagonism, and the Polish question must be considered one of the main reasons for their break in 1812 and for a war which Napoleon called his second Polish campaign. The Poles themselves were deeply convinced of their approaching total liberation, which was proclaimed in advance by a confederation created in Warsaw but discussed in very vague terms with the Polish representative in Wilno by Napoleon. In the former grand duchy of Lithuania a few partisans of cooperation with Alexander still remained, but there a great majority also hailed the emperor of the French as a liberator who would restore the Polish-Lithuanian Commonwealth. Hopes of liberation from Russian rule also appeared in the Ukraine where those faithful to the Cozack tradition were ready to join the *grande armée* which they wanted to have advanced through these southern regions of the Russian Empire.

Napoleon avoided the mistake of Charles XII, but even so, and in spite of spectacular successes to which the Polish forces under Poniatowski, almost a hundred thousand strong, greatly contributed, his campaign of 1812 ended in the well-known catastrophe. The duchy of Warsaw, the only concrete result of Napoleon's action in favor of Poland, was soon occupied by the Russians and threatened by a new partition when another Russian Prussian agreement was signed at Kalisz in 1813. Eager to achieve the old Russian project of controlling all of Poland, Alexander I tried to win over the more prominent Polish leaders. But in contradistinction to Czartoryski, who never sided with Napoleon, Joseph Poniatowski decided to save at least Poland's honor, remaining faithful to France until the end. He was killed in action in the battle of Leipzig in 1813, and there were Poles with Napoleon even in the desperate struggle of 1814, in Elba, and during the Hundred Days.

While for the other submerged peoples of East Central Europe the Napoleonic period, after so many territorial changes and diverse expectations, had few if any lasting consequences except the Russian advance in Finland and Bessarabia and the forming of a better acquaintance with French ideas, the Poles, who had made the greatest sacrifices and suffered the greatest disappointments, remained under the spell of the Napoleonic legend perhaps even more so than the French. They were not only thrilled by a heroic romantic experience, but they also rightly appreciated that thanks to Napoleon, though he fully realized Poland's importance only in his meditations at St. Helena, the Polish question had been reopened immediately after the final partition of 1795. The artificial boundaries then established were already modified twelve years later and again in 1809.

The Poles remained convinced that another European war would again bring a chance for liberation. They believed this so much the more because the peacemaking after the Napoleonic wars, in spite of an unavoidable re-examination of the Polish problem, did not succeed in solving it. This was, however, only one of the failures of the Congress of Vienna with regard to East Central Europe.

THE FAILURES OF THE CONGRESS OF VIENNA

The congress which met in Vienna in 1814, and after Napoleon's brief reappearance and final defeat at Waterloo adjourned in 1815, was supposed to reconstruct the whole of Europe after the revolutionary changes of the preceding quarter of a century. To a certain extent this tremendous task was successfully accomplished, and in particular the moderation shown in the treatment of France, hardly responsible for Bonaparte's imperialism and soon admitted into the European concert, resulted in a long-lasting stabilization of conditions in Western Europe. However, the main difficulties of the peacemaking did not result from the relations with the former enemy but from those with the most powerful ally in the anti-French coalition, Russia.

The idea of legitimacy and restoration upon which the whole work of the Congress was allegedly based would have required a return to that traditional order in East Central Europe which the partitions of Poland had so obviously violated. And it was indeed the Polish question which almost unexpectedly occupied a prominent place in the deliberations, with lip service paid by almost all the leading statesmen to the desirability of a complete restoration of the old kingdom. But at the same time all of them were soon to agree that such a restoration was practically impossible.

The reasons for these two apparently contradictory attitudes are easy to discover. On the one hand, the reconstruction of an independent Poland was not only a question of justice but also a necessary guaranty of any sound balance of power and of Europe's security against Russian imperialism which all other powers rightly considered to be the main danger to the peace of the Continent after Napoleon's fall. On the other hand, such a reparation of the partitions would have required great territorial concessions, not only by Russia but also by Prussia and Austria, both of which, in spite of their substantial gains in the West, were not at all prepared to make such a sacrifice in the East, and rather reclaimed part of if not all their Polish territories lost to the duchy of Warsaw. Under these conditions even Castlereagh, the British representative who theoretically declared himself with eloquence in favor of Poland's freedom, really favored a return to the frontiers, not before but after the three partitions of that country.

It was an illusion, however, to believe that Russia, after her recent victories, would be satisfied with these frontiers. As a matter of fact, it was hardly of decisive importance whether her western boundary would be at the Bug, at the Vistula, or even somewhat farther in the direction of Berlin. That boundary was in any case to be a common frontier with the two leading German powers without any buffer state in between. A compromise was therefore not so difficult to reach in spite of an anti-Russian alliance of Britain, Austria, and France which was drafted at the most critical moment of the Congress of Vienna. Prussia, always inclined to her traditional cooperation with Russia, so dangerous for all the other powers, was satisfied with again receiving the western corner of the duchy of Warsaw, the province of Poznań, and also the free city of Danzig. All projects of restoring something like an island of freedom in East Central Europe were reduced to the symbolic gesture of making Cracow and its environs a free city, proudly called a "republic," but practically placed under the control of the three big neighbors.

Little more than a symbolic gesture was the decision to call the remaining part of the duchy of Warsaw, ceded to Alexander I, a "Kingdom of Poland." The name of Poland which in 1795, and even more so in 1797, was supposed to disappear forever, was now misleadingly given to a small, artificially delimited part of Polish territory— almost exactly Prussia's and Austria's share in the third partition— which the Congress of Vienna, in what might be called a fourth partition, transferred to the Czar of Russia. True, the new kingdom received a rather liberal constitution with a Polish administration, Diet, and army, but with the czar as king and permanently united with Russia. Such a personal union of a petty, constitutional monarchy with the largest and strongest autocracy of the world was necessarily to prove a failure.

The Congress itself was aware that such a fictitious restoration of the former kingdom was no complete solution. Reference was made to the possibility of enlarging the new creation by adding to it some of if not all the territories which Russia had annexed in the three partitions of the eighteenth century. Furthermore, some recognition of the natural unity of the whole formerly Polish area, as it had been before 1772, was given through a provision of the final treaties, signed on May 3, 1815, that there should be free navigation on all rivers of that area. But most significant was the promise that all Poles, whether subjects of Russia, Prussia, or Austria, would obtain "a representation and national institutions regulated according to the degree of political consideration that each of the governments to which they belong shall judge expedient and proper to grant them."

The carefully worded reservation at the end of this article made its rather vague promises quite uncertain. Nevertheless, the very idea here expressed was something like a first recognition of minority rights, strictly speaking a recognition of the difference between state and nation so typical of the conditions which had developed in East Central Europe throughout the centuries. In the Polish case, even the Congress of Vienna, inspired by big-power imperialism and unconcerned with the rise of modern nationalism, had to recognize that new trend. In all lands of the partitioned commonwealth the national consciousness of the Poles had indeed such deep-seated roots that even those who violated the people's aspirations could not disregard them completely.

It is well known that in all other cases the Congress of Vienna showed a complete disregard of any kind of nationalism. This is usually stressed in the German and the Italian case, but in both of these it was only a trend, not yet fully developed, toward political unification on national grounds that was neglected by the peacemakers. The German people had, indeed, the least reason to complain, since the various political units among which they remained divided and whose individual frontiers were the exclusive concern of the Congress were associated with each other in a German Confederation hardly looser than the old empire had been. And nowhere were German populations placed under foreign rule, while so many Poles were placed under the rule of the German kingdom of Prussia and even more non-German nationalities than before were included in the German-controlled empire of Austria. The Austrian lands of the Habsburgs, where in the past the Italian minority had been small, were now enlarged by the annexation of Venetia and Lombardy. But with this exception, the Italians also, though like the Germans they remained divided into various states, some of them under dynasties of alien origin, were not incorporated into any foreign state as happened to the East Central European peoples of the Habsburg monarchy.

In its new form, the Austrian Empire which was proclaimed in 1804 and definitely established in its new boundaries at the Congress of Vienna, was so completely centralized that even the old kingdoms of Bohemia and Hungary finally seemed to lose their state rights. The lands of the former, together with those of Austria proper, were even included in the German Confederation, and though the lands of the crown of St. Stephen, as well as Galicia and Bukovina and also Dalmatia, remained outside that specifically German body politic, they were under the absolute rule not only of a German dynasty but also of a German administration directed from Vienna. In spite of their growing national consciousness, all these non-German populations, even the Magyars so proud of their national tradition, had remained loyal during all the wars against the French conqueror and had raised no specific claims at the time of the peace settlement at the Congress of

Vienna, where the unofficial activities of the Poles, particularly of Prince Czartoryski, were so intense. Nevertheless the position of inferiority in which all non-Germans were placed proved a source of unrest in the future, not because of any German nationalism of the Habsburg regime but because that regime considered German language and culture as the strongest unifying force of the multi-national empire.

If that internal tension and its dangerous consequences did not immediately appear, it was simply because the European settlement of 1815 did not give the dissatisfied nationalities of the Danubian monarchy any chance to look for outside support or for better conditions under another regime. With the exception of the Italians, they had no independent states of their kin outside the Austrian frontiers and even the Poles of Galicia could hardly look upon the "Congress Kingdom," tied as it was with Russia, as upon a free Poland. Russian nationalism, which together with Orthodoxy and autocracy was the basis of czarist imperialism, was from the outset critical of any concessions made to the Poles, whether in the "Kingdom" or in the annexed eastern provinces of the former commonwealth. And as to the other non-Russian nationalities of the empire, their very existence was simply ignored officially, with only the exception of autonomous Finland. In the whole political conception which Alexander I tried to embody in the vague phrases of the Holy Alliance, that philosophical comment on the treaties signed in Vienna, there was no place for the rights of nationalities deprived of political or even cultural freedom in spite of the invocation of Christian principles.

The Congress of Vienna can hardly be blamed for not having included in its reconstruction program that large section of East Central Europe which still remained under Turkish domination. It was easy to establish a British protectorate in the Ionian Islands off the western coast of the Balkans where the Greek population had been under the rule of Venice and recently under that of Napoleonic France. But the Balkan Peninsula itself was still part of the Ottoman Empire, a neutral power not represented in Vienna and whose integrity could not be touched, although for the Christian peoples of that empire conditions continued to be even worse than for the nationalities under German or Russian control. Therefore the rise of nationalism in the Balkans, in reaction against centuries of oppression, was one more contributing factor in the failure of the peacemaking in 1815. And it was the first source of alarm to appear in the years which followed the famous Congress.

17

REVOLUTIONARY MOVEMENTS UNTIL 1848

THE INDEPENDENCE WARS OF SERBS AND GREEKS

The independence wars of the Balkan nations started in Serbia where the fierce struggle against Ottoman rule was going on throughout almost the whole Napoleonic period and where the situation was so critical at the time of the Congress of Vienna that a Serb delegation appeared there asking for help but without receiving any attention.

It was only natural that the Serbs were the first to rise. Those of them who were living in the mountains of Montenegro had, as a matter of fact, never been completely conquered, and their independence under the prince-bishops of the Petrovich-Njegoch family, residing at Cetinje, was formally recognized by Turkey in 1799. This was of course an encouragement to Serbia proper, which after the liberation of Hungary found herself at the extreme northern border of the Ottoman Empire and had her main center at Belgrade, the strategically important city which the Turks had twice temporarily lost to the Habsburgs in the eighteenth century. At the end of that century Belgrade became an important center of Serb nationalism under a strong cultural influence coming from southern Hungary where the Orthodox Serb minority had its metropolitan at Karlowitz and where the first prominent Serb writer, Dositej Obradovich, educated in Austria, Germany, and England, started his activity.

It is highly significant that Obradovich was later made minister of education in the free Serb government created by the revolutionary leader, George Petrovich, who became known under the name of Kara (Black) George and founded the Karageorgevich dynasty. Kara George took advantage of the resistance which in the frontier regions of the declining Ottoman Empire had been provoked, first, by the abuses of the Turkish janissaries, but which also soon turned against the sultan himself. The organized revolt began in 1804 in the region between the Morava and Drina rivers and seemed to have serious chances of success when another Russo-Turkish war broke out two years later. The courageous struggle of the warlike Serb peasants proved indeed a useful diversion for the Russian forces which advanced, however, through the Danubian principalities into Bulgaria, never made contact with the Serbs, and practically abandoned them to their fate when the Peace of Bucharest was concluded in 1812. Kara George himself had to take refuge in Hungary.

In spite of a violent Turkish repression which followed, and because of the lack of any outside assistance, the fight for freedom was resumed in the very year of the Congress of Vienna under a new national leader, Milosh Obrenovich. That former collaborator of Kara George now became his competitor in the liberation movement, and his descendants, the Obrenovich, were to be for almost one hundred years the rivals of the Karageorgevich, not without harmful consequences for the common cause. Milosh fully realized that under the given circumstances the ultimate goal of full independence could not be reached at once, and supplementing his inadequate military forces by a skilful diplomacy, he tried to gain gradual concessions from Turkey. A first step in the direction of at least local autonomy was made in 1817 when Obrenovich received from the sultan the title Prince of Serbia, but of a Serbia limited to the district of Belgrade and therefore much smaller than the ethnic territory of the Serb people. To enlarge that nucleus of a restored Serb state and also to increase the very limited power granted to its ruler was to be the program of Serbia's policy for the next century.

Unfortunately, in the same year of 1817 Milosh's complicity in the assassination of his rival, Kara George, wrongly accused of having abandoned the national cause, made final the break between the two families at a time when unity was so badly needed. Nevertheless, full advantage was taken of the Russo-Turkish War of 1828–1829, although the main military action again took place in the eastern Balkans, far away from Serbia. This time the peace treaty included a promise of autonomy for Serbia, and the next year (1830) Milosh was recognized by the sultan as hereditary ruler, with a slight enlargement of Serbia's territory, from which the Turkish troops were almost completely withdrawn. This success was followed in 1831 by the establishment of a Serb metropolitan at Belgrade, an important implementation of political autonomy by ecclesiastical autonomy and

part of the prince's serious efforts to promote the cultural development of the restored country. With regard to the Serbs who remained
under Habsburg rule in Hungary, the situation was now reversed.
Those of Serbia proper, no longer under Turkish oppression, now had,
in spite of the sultan's rather theoretical suzerainty, more freedom and
opportunity for national development than their kin on the other side
of the Danube. At the same time Serbia was freed from Greek control
in the ecclesiastical field, a control which during the whole period of
Ottoman domination all Christian populations of the empire had to
suffer in addition to political oppression by the Turks.

For that very reason the problem of Greek nationalism is somewhat different from the story of the other Christian peoples of the
Balkan Peninsula. On the one hand, no other nation had an older
and prouder tradition than the Greeks, and in general, during all the
centuries of Turkish rule, their position was more favorable than that
of Serbs or Bulgars. But on the other hand, a clear distinction must be
made between two Greek traditions. In Constantinople the Greek
Empire was indeed replaced by the Ottoman, but the patriarchate
continued to play an extremely important role, sometimes humiliated
and used as a political tool by the Sultans but always recognized as
spiritual leader of all the Orthodox without distinction of nationality.
In that connection, as well as in trade relations, the Greek language
was always widely used in the whole empire, in whose diplomatic
service many Greeks achieved distinction. There also survived, however, the purely Hellenic tradition which already toward the end of the
Byzantine Empire had assumed a clearly national character and now
when the Ottoman Empire was in turn declining developed along with
the other modern national movements. Inspired by the monuments of
ancient Greece, that new-Hellenic movement had no imperial ambitions, but, similar to the others, wanted to liberate the national territory, practically identified with old Hellas, from the degrading
Turkish yoke and create an independent state there.

In view of its specific character as a revival of ancient Greece, that
movement had a strong appeal in Western Europe, were it only among
enthusiastic romanticists like Lord Byron, who was to give his life for
the Greek cause. But also from a political point of view there was a
special interest in the aspirations of the Greeks, a Mediterranean nation whose territory, including the islands of the Aegean Sea, had
great strategic significance for all other Mediterranean powers and

particularly for Great Britain. The Greeks, much better known to the
Western world than the other peoples of the Balkans, had for all these
reasons a much better chance to find outside support for both their
cultural and their political program, represented by the Philohellenic
Society (*Philiké Hetairea*), which was definitely established in the
very year of the Congress of Vienna with branches outside the Ottoman Empire. For the same reasons, however, the Greek patriarchate
in Constantinople was less enthusiastic toward a revolutionary movement influenced by French ideas, which seemed a threat to the position of the Orthodox church in the whole empire and would reduce the
Greek problem to one of the national issues amidst the empire's
disintegration.

This peculiar situation, and also the connection between the Greek
and the other national movements, may explain why the open fight for
Greek freedom started in 1821 in distant Moldavia. There Prince
Alexander Ypsilanti, a member of a noted Phanariote family which
had temporarily occupied the throne of that country, raised a rebellion against Turkish suzerainty, as leader of the Greek *Hetairea*.
In Moldavia the movement was rapidly crushed and merely resulted
in the replacement of the Phanariote princes by native rulers in both
Rumanian principalities. But almost simultaneously a genuine Greek
insurrection started in the Morea, the very center of Greek nationalism, and soon spread over northern Greece and the islands. Alarmed
by that outbreak, the sultan made the great mistake of having the
Patriarch of Constantinople publicly hanged, although he was not at
all responsible, and his ordeal shocked not only all Greeks and Orthodox but also general public opinion even in America.

It was most important, however, that the Greek independence war,
coming only six years after the Congress of Vienna, divided the leading powers of the European concert. They all had to realize that there
was a region of Europe where the general peace, established in 1815,
was extremely precarious. But though Metternich considered the
Greek movement just one of the wanton rebellions against the European order which had to be crushed, like the abortive revolutions in
Western countries, Alexander I at once seized the opportunity to
interfere in favor of the Orthodox populations of Turkey, according
to the right granted to Russia in her treaties with the Ottoman Empire. The sultan rejected the czar's request that Turkish troops be
withdrawn from the Danubian principalities and that an amnesty be

granted to the Greeks, but the progress made by the latter, who convoked a national assembly at Epidaurus in 1822, definitely made their cause an international issue.

At the same time, however, it became part of an intricate game of power politics, as the whole nationalities problem in the Balkans was to remain for the rest of the century. In the case of the Greeks, this interference of the great powers, not only of Russia but also of Britain and even of France, whose squadrons participated in the naval battle of Navarino where in 1827 the Turkish-Egyptian fleet was annihilated, greatly accelerated the achievement of the ultimate goal of the national movement—full independence. Instead of merely an autonomous status, recommended by the Western powers and rejected by Turkey in the earlier phase of the conflict, the independence of Greece had to be recognized by the Ottoman Empire in the Treaty of Adrianople, after its defeats in the Russo-Turkish war of 1828–1829. The next year, in 1830, an international protocol declared Greece an independent monarchy and there was again at least one completely free country in the intermediary zone between the empires of Central and Eastern Europe. From that moment the modern history of Greece, identified in the Middle Ages with that of one of the empires, with Byzantium, became an inseparable part of the history of the smaller nations of East Central Europe.

The Treaty of Adrianople once more confirmed the autonomous position of the Danubian principalities, which remained for five years under Russian occupation, and for the first time internationally recognized the autonomy of Serbia, so patiently prepared by Milosh Obrenovich. That country had to wait for half a century before reaching full independence, and at this early stage the boundaries of neither Greece nor Serbia included the whole area inhabited by the Greek and Serb peoples. But in both national states serious efforts in the field of internal organization at once set in.

In both cases these efforts had to meet with serious difficulties, particularly with regard to the constitutional problems, and this again is typical of the history of all liberated Balkan nations. But these difficulties are fully understandable in view of the long interruption of any normal historical development in the Balkans, of similar constitutional crises in the Western countries, and of continuous interference by the great powers, rivaling for influence in the reorganized Balkan region.

In Greece after three years of confusion before the final establishment of the monarchy, which was opposed by strong republican forces, the rule of her first king, Otto of Bavaria, was to last from 1832 until 1862 when he was forced to abdicate and a new dynasty, this time of Danish origin, took his place after another year of crisis. But already in 1843 a military revolt forced the king to dismiss his Bavarian advisers and to accept a constitution, with a responsible cabinet and a two-chamber parliament composed of a senate nominated by the king and a house of deputies elected by universal suffrage.

In Serbia, in spite of Milosh's autocratic tendencies, a parliament called *Skupshtina* was created and a first constitution drafted in 1835. Three years later a decree of the sultan instituted a council of state and a cabinet of ministers. After Milosh's abdication in 1839, the death of his eldest son and the exile of the second in 1842, the Skupshtina elected the son of Kara George, Alexander, under whom, in spite of his rather poor qualifications, a great deal of progress was achieved in the fields of both culture and administration. Language and literature developed in the direction of unity with the Croats, but the center of the Yugoslav movement was in Montenegro where from 1830 to 1851 the throne was occupied by a distinguished leader of that movement, Petar Petrovich Njegosh, the last prince who was at the same time the Orthodox bishop.

Thus nationalism was successfully growing in the Balkans, while the whole northern part of East Central Europe continued to be subject to the Austrian and Russian empires and to Prussia. And the situation in that whole region was particularly unfavorable to any national movement, since the strongest of them, the Polish, had suffered a crushing defeat at the very moment when Greece and Serbia were liberated in the Balkans and when the successful Belgian revolution forced the powers to revise the settlement of the Congress of Vienna in Western Europe.

THE ORIGIN AND BACKGROUND OF THE NOVEMBER INSURRECTION IN POLAND

The Polish insurrection which broke out in Warsaw on November 29, 1830, is sometimes called a Polish-Russian war. It was indeed a conflict between the kingdom of Poland, which was supposed to exist again after the Congress of Vienna, and the Russian Empire, to which that separated body politic was attached by a personal union only. But long before the Polish army rebelled against the czar's brother, Grand Duke Constantine, who had been made its commander in chief, and before the Polish Diet on January 25, 1831, formally dethroned the Romanov dynasty, the whole conception of 1815 proved a fiction which could not possibly endure.

During the fifteen years between the Congress and the Revolution, no little progress had been made in the kingdom, particularly in the cultural and economic fields. A Polish university was opened in Warsaw in 1817, and the most prominent member of the Polish government, Prince Xavier Lubecki, achieved a great deal as minister of finance. But already under Czar Alexander, solemnly crowned in Warsaw as king of Poland, even those Poles who had accepted the Vienna decisions as a basis for constructive activities were deeply disappointed. Alexander's vague promises that the eastern provinces of the former commonwealth would be reunited with the kingdom proved impossible of fulfilment, even if they were sincere. Although under Russian rule Polish culture continued to flourish there, particularly in the former grand duchy of Lithuania where the University of Wilno was a more brilliant center of Polish learning and literature than ever before, the Russians considered those "West-Russian" lands an integral part of the empire which the czar had no right to alienate. Already in 1823 Prince Adam Czartoryski was removed from his position as "curator" of the University of Wilno, where severe repressions against the Polish youth organizations started at once. The Russian senator N. N. Novosiltsov, chiefly responsible for these measures, was at the same time interfering with the administration of the kingdom where instead of Czartoryski the insignificant General Zajączek was appointed viceroy. Novosiltsov's role was of course contrary to the apparently liberal constitution which Czartoryski had helped to draft. The leading patriots in the Diet tried in vain to defend Poland's constitutional rights on legal grounds, while those who realized the futility of such loyal opposition engaged in conspiracies which even the most severe police control proved unable to check.

The tension rapidly increased when Alexander I died in 1825. After the abortive December revolution in St. Petersburg, whose leaders seemed to favor the Polish claims, he was succeeded by his brother Nicholas I. He too was crowned as king of Poland a few years later. But without even the appearance of liberalism which had

been shown by Alexander, he considered the parliamentary regime of
the kingdom as being completely incompatible with the autocratic
form of government which he so fully developed in Russia. Hence the
Polish radicals, under the leadership of young infantry cadets, rose in
defense of their constitution. Public opinion was alarmed by the news
that the Polish army would be used by the czar as a vanguard for
crushing the revolutionary movements which in 1830 had broken out
in France and Belgium and which received Polish sympathy.

Even the moderate leaders who were surprised by the plot of the
cadets and who considered the insurrection as having been insufficiently prepared, joined it in a spirit of national unity, though much
time was lost through the hesitation of those who still hoped to appease the czar and to arrive at some compromise. Among these was
General Chłopicki, who was entrusted with practically dictatorial
powers. Even later, the changing leadership of the Polish army, which
for nine months opposed the overwhelming Russian forces, proved
rather undecided and inadequate so that even initial successes and bold
strategic conceptions of the general staff were not sufficiently utilized.
Therefore the struggle ended in a victory of the Russian Field Marshal Paskevich, a veteran of the war against Turkey, and on September 7, 1831, after a siege of three weeks, Warsaw was taken by storm.

Two aspects of that greatest Polish insurrection of the nineteenth
century are of general interest, one with regard to the problem of nationalities in East Central Europe, the other from the point of view of
international relations in Europe as a whole. The uprising which had
started in Warsaw as an action of the so-called "Congress Kingdom,"
had immediate repercussions east of the Bug River, in the Lithuanian
and Ruthenian provinces of the historic commonwealth. Particularly
in the former grand duchy of Lithuania there was a strong participation in the revolutionary movement against Russian rule, not only
among the Polonized nobility but also among the gentry and the
peasants of purely Lithuanian stock. And though there were social
controversies in connection with the promised abolition of serfdom,
there was no Lithuanian separatism on ethnic grounds but a common
desire to restore the traditional Polish-Lithuanian Union in full independence from Russia. Regular Polish forces came from the territory
of the kingdom, and the movement spread as far as the Livonian
border but was unable to liberate the main cities and broke down with
the doom of the insurrection in Poland proper.

The leaders of the revolution also hoped to obtain the support of the Ukrainian lands. Here, too, they appealed not only to the Polish and Polonized nobles and to the idea of Polish-Lithuanian-Ruthenian cooperation in some tripartite federation of the future, but also to the peasant masses which, however, remained distrustful and passive. The young Taras Shevchenko, who was soon to become the first great Ukrainian poet, had contacts with some of the Polish leaders. But he was not won over, and later he made the significant statement that "Poland fell and crushed us too." For the czarist government, after the defeat of the Poles, started a ruthless Russification not only in the Congress kingdom but also in all Lithuanian and Ruthenian lands where not only the Poles and the supporters of the Polish cause, but all non-Russian elements, were also the victims—a situation which greatly contributed to the rise of Lithuanian and Ukrainian nationalism.

While these indirect consequences of the November insurrection appeared only later, the diplomatic repercussions in general European politics were simultaneous. All Poles realized that their fight for freedom could have notable chances for success only if supported by other powers. Therefore, turning exclusively against Russia, which controlled by far the largest part of Poland's historic territory in one form or another, they hoped for the complacence of Austria and even for some sympathy among the liberals in Germany. Decisive, however, seemed the attitude of the Western powers, France and Britain. Well realized by Polish public opinion in general, the necessity to find outside assistance was the main concern of Prince Adam Czartoryski, Poland's greatest statesman of the nineteenth century. After years of endeavor toward a reconciliation with Russia he now recognized the hopelessness of such a policy and for the remaining thirty years of his life was to be Russia's most persistent opponent.

Although Czartoryski never was popular among the leftists led by the famous historian Joachim Lelewel, his authority was so great that he was placed at the head of the national government. As such he made every effort to make the revolution an international issue, and he sent diplomatic representatives abroad, particularly to Paris and London. After the dethronement of Nicholas I as king of Poland, even the election of another king was considered. In order to interest Vienna in the Polish cause, the candidature of an Austrian archduke or of the Duke of Reichstadt, Napoleon's son who was kept at the

Austrian court, was put forward, as well as that of the Prince of Orange or of a member of the British royal family. More realistic was the conviction that all signatories of the 1815 treaties ought to be interested in the violation of the promises then made to the Poles, and that they would therefore intercede in their behalf.

But all the diplomatic skill of Czartoryski and his collaborators proved to be of no avail. Even statesmen who seemed favorable to the Poles, such as Talleyrand and Sebastiani in France or Palmerston in England, wanted them first to gain substantial victories through their own forces. Prospects of a joint French-British mediation, with the possible participation of Austria, vanished when the Belgian problem created a tension between the two western powers, while Austria showed some interest in Poland's fate only at the last moment when the defeated Polish regiments had already crossed over into Galicia, only to be disarmed there like those who crossed the Prussian border.

As a matter of fact the Polish insurrection had saved France and Belgium from Russian intervention, thus giving evidence that a really independent Poland would be a protection against czarist imperialism, as in the past. Therefore Czartoryski, who after participating as a volunteer in the last fights went into exile for the rest of his life, hoped that the complete conquest of Congress Poland by Russia would again raise those fears of Russian expansion which were so general in 1815 in Vienna. In Paris he tried to convince old Talleyrand that at least a restoration of the autonomous kingdom ought to be requested from the czar, but Sebastiani made the famous statement that "order reigned in Warsaw," and in London, where the prince made many friends for Poland, he heard the objection that "unfortunately the Polish question was contrary to the interests of all other powers."

To convince the world that this was not so was Czartoryski's main objective after his final establishment at the Hotel Lambert in Paris from 1833 on. He tried to accomplish his ends by connecting the Polish cause with that of all oppressed nations. Therefore that "uncrowned king of Poland," with his diplomatic agents in almost all European capitals, was working for the liberation of the whole of East Central Europe. In the belief that the fate of Poland was part of a much larger problem, the whole Polish emigration, concentrated in France and inspired by great poets including Adam Mickiewicz, was united in spite of differences of method between the right and the left. The latter, eager to join revolutionary movements anywhere, was also eager to organize new conspiracies in the oppressed country at once, with another insurrection as ultimate goal, without sufficiently realizing that there was not the slightest chance of success under the regime established by the victorious czar in all his Polish possessions.

In addition to the ruthless persecution of everything that was Polish or connected with Poland in the eastern provinces where the University of Wilno and the Uniate church were the main victims, a period of reaction also started in the so-called kingdom under Paskevich as general governor. Considering that the Poles through their rebellion had forfeited all rights granted them at the Congress of Vienna, in 1832 Nicholas I replaced the constitution of the kingdom by an "Organic Statute" which liquidated its autonomy and made it practically a Russian province, subject to systematic Russification particularly in the educational field. The fiction of a restoration of Poland in union with Russia was now abandoned and the czarist empire advanced to the very boundaries of Prussian and Austrian Poland.

Under these circumstances the other two partitioning powers became convinced that close cooperation with Russia was indispensable. A secret agreement was therefore concluded in 1833 by the three monarchs, who guaranteed one another their Polish possessions and promised mutual assistance in case of a new revolution. Jointly, they also militarily occupied (without however annexing it) the Free City of Cracow where the November insurrection had found numerous partisans. The settlement made at the Congress of Vienna was thus revised in East Central Europe in favor of the imperialistic powers, and it became even more intolerable for the submerged nationalities. For the reaction directed against the Poles, whom Metternich considered the typical revolutionaries, was accompanied, both in the Habsburg Empire which he fully controlled and in the Russia of his ally Nicholas I, by oppressive measures against all other peoples who were dissatisfied with their fate.

THE NATIONALITIES POLICY OF NICHOLAS I AND METTERNICH

In both the Russian Empire of Nicholas I and the Austrian Empire of the Metternich era, the government policy with regard to the non-Russian and non-German nationalities was only part of a program of administration based upon absolutism and centralism. But a clear distinction must be made between conditions in Russia and in Austria.

Under Nicholas I it was officially proclaimed that czarist Russia had three traditional pillars, and one of them, in addition to autocracy and Orthodox religion, was Russian nationalism. The process of Russification which had already set in under the predecessors of Nicholas I, but which in his reign was developed systematically, was therefore not only a tool of czarist imperialism which facilitated the unification of the whole realm but also an attempt toward making the empire, one and indivisible, the national state of the Great Russian people. In the Habsburg Empire, on the contrary, there was no Austrian nationalism, and the nationalists among the German-speaking subjects of the emperor were interested in their unity with all other Germans outside Austria rather than in the impossible task of Germanizing the non-German majority in the whole Danubian monarchy. The growing nationalism of these non-German peoples was in conflict with the German Austrians only in those provinces which had a mixed population. But everywhere that nationalism was in conflict with, and repressed by, the imperialism of a central administration which could be but German in language and culture.

In Russia the biggest nationality problem, and as a matter of fact the only one which was openly recognized as such, was indeed the Polish question. And among the Poles alone there was a nationalism which had complete political liberation in a restored national state as its immediate objective. Hence the persecutions which followed the November Insurrection and continued throughout the following twenty-five years of the reign of Nicholas I. The most numerous among the non-Russian nationalities of the empire, however, were the Ukrainians, officially called Little Russians and considered part of one Russian nation, just as were the Great Russians, while their language was supposed to be merely a dialect of Russian.

For that very reason it was important that at the very same time when Russian literature was so brilliantly developing, Ukrainian literature, following Kotlyarewsky's earlier initiative, also continued to make slow but significant progress in the first half of the nineteenth century. While Russia's first great poet, Alexander Pushkin, declared that all the Slavic rivers had to flow into the Russian sea, the somewhat younger Ukrainian poet, Taras Shevchenko, glorified the Ukraine as a separate country which was faithful to the Cozack tradition. The Ukrainian movement, too, was influenced by the rising ideology of Pan-Slavism, but this was interpreted in the spirit of romantic idealism, with equal chances of free development for all Slavic nations and without any identification with some kind of imperial Pan-Russianism. But what the Ukrainian leaders, still few in number, claimed in these early days was not yet full independence but cultural freedom and autonomy in a Slavic federation in which Russia might even play a leading role.

Such ideas, supported by scholarly and literary activities, found a natural center in the University of Kiev where the former Polish University of Wilno was transferred in 1832, of course as a Russian institution but with some distinguished professors of Ukrainian origin or interested in the Ukrainian tradition which was studied there by a special archaeological commission. In addition to Shevchenko, who on his return from St. Petersburg was attached to that commission, the historians N. Kostomarov and P. Kulish were particularly prominent. They belonged to the group that founded the "Brotherhood" or Society of Saints Cyril and Methodius, probably in 1846. The name of that association indicates its ideas of Slavic solidarity on religious grounds and its mainly cultural character. But it was of course also dedicated to the idea of national freedom for the Ukrainians, inseparable from social and constitutional liberties which men like Shevchenko, originally a serf himself, along with the liberal elements among the Russians, claimed for all peoples of the empire.

It was, however, precisely that connection between nationalism and liberalism which alarmed the Russian authorities. When denounced to the czar, the society was closed at his order in 1847 and its leaders were arrested and sentenced to imprisonment or exile. Shevchenko was treated with special severity, being condemned to serve as a private in a disciplinary battalion in Central Asia, "with a prohibition of writing and painting," as Nicholas I added with his own hand. For Shevchenko's poetic evocation of the Ukraine's past seemed so dangerous that it was decided to suppress Ukrainian nationalism completely.

No similar action was needed in the other non-Russian parts of the empire, but the situation in the Baltic region, that small but important section of East Central Europe now annexed by Russia, deserves special attention. Both in the so-called Baltic provinces, corresponding to present-day Latvia and Estonia, and in the grand duchy of Finland, the coexistence of different national groups, opposed to one another, greatly reduced the challenge to Russian imperialism and nationalism.

In the Baltic provinces, which without enjoying the full autonomy of Finland continued to have some local self-government, these privileges were exclusively in favor of a small but rich and highly cultivated German upper class, whether landowners—the Baltic "barons" —or intellectuals and merchants in the old and prosperous cities. Their German nationalism was purely cultural and combined with complete political loyalty toward the Russian czardom, which many representatives of the German-Baltic aristocracy continued to serve in diplomacy and the army. Socially and linguistically there was a clear-cut separation between these German Balts and the Latvian and Estonian peasant population, but among both non-German ethnic groups a cultural revival set in during the first half of the nineteenth century. This was facilitated by the abolition of serfdom which was here accomplished much earlier (1816–1819) than in the other parts of the empire.

In both cases the movement, still entirely non-political, started with the study of folklore, the collecting of folk songs, and the appearance of the first newspapers in the native tongues. The University of Dorpat (*Tartu* in Estonian), reorganized in 1802 with German as the language of instruction, soon became a center of local studies with the participation of many students of Latvian and Estonian origin. The foundation of the Estonian Learned Society in 1838 proved an important landmark. But it was not before the second half of the century that progress in that direction was accelerated and that a real Latvian and Estonian nationalism can be discovered.

Much earlier were the origins of Finnish nationalism which can be traced back to the time of Swedish domination, and which also in the earlier period of Russian rule, when the autonomy of the grand duchy was respected by the czars, was rather directed against the cultural supremacy of the Swedish-speaking minority in Finland. But even then prominent Finnish leaders, such as the poet and journalist A. I. Arwidson, were aware of the danger of ultimate Russification. This was inherent in the union with the colossal empire and for that very reason they wanted to eliminate the internal cleavage between the Swedish and the Finnish group. And thanks to another poet, Elias Lönnrot, Finnish nationalism received its decisive inspiration when at the middle of the reign of Nicholas I (1835–1849) he published the famous national epic *Kalevala,* compiled out of old folk poetry.

The same scale, from purely cultural to distinctly political nationalism, can be found among the nationalities of the Austrian Empire. Metternich, more than the emperors themselves, Francis I and after his death in 1835, Ferdinand I, who were rather weak and insignificant rulers, represented the idea of absolute government. He was hardly afraid of the cultural revival of the Czechs in spite of its steady progress. The foundation of the Museum of the Bohemian Kingdom in 1818 was indeed rather an expression of interest in regional studies. But when in 1830 the *Matice česká* (literally "Czech mother") was attached to it, that society also started encouraging the use of the Czech language. And it was obvious that the publication of František Palacký's *History of Bohemia* (though first in German), covering the period of independence before Habsburg rule, would revive a national tradition in complete opposition to all that Metternich was standing for.

Some of the most prominent Czech writers, like the poet Jan Kollár and the historian P. J. Šafařík, were of Slovak origin and interested in the past and the culture of all Slavic peoples. They contributed on the one hand to a feeling of Slavic solidarity in the Habsburg Empire, long before that movement was exploited by Russian imperialism, and on the other hand to a national revival even of those Slavs who never had created independent states, like the Slovenes and the Slovaks themselves. Though very close to the Czechs, the Slovaks under the leadership of Ludovít Štúr decided to use their own language in literature, thus reacting against the backward conditions in which they were left under Hungarian rule.

Trying to play off the various nationalities against one another, the Metternich regime, for instance, would use officials of Czech origin as tools of Germanization in Polish Galicia, and would welcome the growing antagonism between the Magyars and the other groups in Hungary. In that kingdom, whose state rights even Metternich could not completely disregard, Hungarian nationalism was making rapid progress, particularly in the cultural and economic field, thanks chiefly to Count Széchenyi, called "the greatest Hungarian," who in 1825 founded the Hungarian Academy of Sciences. The Diet, which continued to function though with greatly reduced power, was slow to carry out the democratic reforms advocated by Széchenyi, but in its session of 1843–1844 it at last decided to replace Latin by Magyar as the official language.

At the same time the Hungarian Diet also decided to prescribe instruction in the Magyar language in the schools of Croatia where, therefore, Croat nationalism was more alarmed by the inconsiderate pressure coming from Budapest than by the centralization of the whole empire being promoted in Vienna. Furthermore, under these conditions, the idea of Yugoslav unity, in spite of the old antagonism between Serbs and Croats, was also becoming popular among the latter where the gifted writer and politician Ljudevit Gaj (1809–1872) propagated the "Illyrian" movement and also influenced the Slovenes in a similar sense.

Even in its rather modest beginnings, that movement was dangerous for the unity of the monarchy because it could not find full satisfaction within its existing boundaries. And such was also the case of Polish and Italian nationalism, as well as of the Ruthenian and Rumanian aspirations. The former clashed in eastern Galicia with Polish supremacy, and the latter in Transylvania with Magyar supremacy, while cultural ties were at least established with the Ruthenians or Ukrainians of the Russian Empire, and with the Rumanians in the Danubian principalities. But even more than these international implications, the two big national problems which affected the Austrian Empire alone, the Czech and the Magyar, were a growing source of tension because in these cases modern nationalism found strong support in the historic tradition of two medieval kingdoms. The Pan-Slavic trend among the Czechs was ready to use the Habsburg monarchy as a basis of action, and the Hungarian program did not exclude a dynastic union with Austria. But even so they were directed against the very foundations of Metternich's system and could not be represented by the chancellor's police measures.

FROM THE CRISIS OF 1846 TO THE REVOLUTIONS OF 1848

The revolutionary crisis of the middle of the nineteenth century which shattered most of the European countries in protest against the political system established by the Congress of Vienna is usually associated with the memorable year of 1848, with the so-called "spring of the peoples." It was indeed in the spring of that year that the movement started in Western Europe and in the western, German part of

Central Europe. In East Central Europe, however, where the tension was deepest and the claims for national freedom even stronger than those for constitutional reforms, the crisis started exactly two years earlier, in the spring of 1846.

It started with the utopian project of a Polish insurrection which would be directed against all three partitioning powers at the same time. From the outset it proved impossible to include any direct action against Russia, which dominated by far the largest part of Polish lands and where the oppression was most violent. For Nicholas I who in the thirties had already crushed all conspiratorial activities of the Poles, now succeeded, and even in the decisive year of 1848, in stopping all revolutionary movements at the border of his empire. It was therefore Prussian Poland which was selected as a basis for the new struggle for freedom. Here the prospective leader, Ludwik Mierosławski, had already appeared in 1845. The reasons for such a decision must be explained against the background of the general situation in Prussia.

As far as her policy toward the Polish population was concerned, earlier attempts at reconciliation, in agreement with the promises of 1815, had been followed by the systematic repressions of Edward Flottwell who in 1830 replaced the Polish prince, Anton Radziwiłł, as governor of the grand duchy of Poznań. On the other hand, not only in that purely Polish province but also in West Prussia and Silesia all government efforts toward Germanization met with strong resistance. This was not at all limited to the Catholic clergy and to the nobility, who were considered the main representatives of Polish nationalism, but it was also organized by a Polish middle class which had been formed in these western lands earlier than in any other part of Poland. It was there that the most advanced cultural, social, and economic progress had been made by the Polish people, while such progress was entirely impossible under the regimes of Metternich and Nicholas I. Even under Frederick William IV, new king of Prussia since 1840, who recalled Flottwell, only the methods of anti-Polish policy were changed. But the apparently anti-Russian attitude of the government, and some sympathy displayed by Prussian liberals, created the illusion that eventually the planned Polish action would find Prussian support.

What really happened was, on the contrary, the arrest of Mieros-lawski and his collaborators in February, 1846, when their conspiracy was discovered and all attempts to liberate Prussian Poland failed completely. At the same time, however, a real tragedy took place in Austrian Galicia. Alarmed by preparations for a Polish insurrection which had also started there, the Austrian administration incited the peasants to rise against the noble landowners in some districts of western Galicia, promising rewards for the killing or capturing of any of them. The peasants were told by the Austrian bureaucracy that the nobles wanted to restore old Poland only to enslave them, while the emperor was ready to abolish serfdom completely. As a matter of fact it was precisely the leaders of the insurrection who, though of noble origin, like the eminently prominent Edward Dembowski, had the most advanced ideas of social reform. Their radicalism was best evidenced when at the end of February they seized power in the free city of Cracow, where Jan Tyssowski, later an exile in the United States, was proclaimed dictator. But his inadequate forces were defeated by the Austrians, Dembowski was killed, and after a brief Russian occupation the republic of Cracow was annexed by the Austrian Empire.

Even that obvious violation of the treaties of 1815 was accepted by the Western powers which in spite of the aroused public opinion in France and England limited themselves to weak diplomatic protests. And a new wave of violent repressions set in, both in Galicia where the new governor, Count Stadion, tried to play off the Ruthenians against the Poles, and in Prussia, where in December, 1847, Mierosławski and seven of his associates, after a long imprisonment, were sentenced to death. But before they could be executed, the outbreak of the 1848 revolution opened entirely new prospects not only for the Poles but for all the submerged nationalities of East Central Europe.

As a matter of fact there were several revolutions in 1848, not only in different countries but with different objectives. In the French February Revolution, the issues were exclusively constitutional and social, but just as in the case of the great Revolution of 1789, the general ideas of liberty which were spreading from Paris all over Europe had a special appeal for those peoples who were deprived not only of constitutional freedom—and this in a degree much greater than under Louis Philippe's French monarchy—but also of their national rights. Hence the growing excitement in various foreign-dominated parts of Italy and particularly in the non-German parts of Prussia and Austria. Not later than in March there appeared in both monarchies a rather confusing combination of nationalist movements and general revolts against autocratic regimes.

In Prussia, in spite of the disappointments of 1846, the situation of that year seemed to repeat itself so far as the Polish question was concerned. The liberation of Mierosławski and his friends by German crowds in Berlin was very significant in that respect. Returning to Poznań, the Polish leader also returned to the plan of a war against czarist Russia with the support of a liberalized Prussia, whose new minister of foreign affairs, Baron H. von Arnim, was in favor of such a conception. The latter was also supported by Prince Adam Czartoryski who came from Paris to Berlin. But all these plans were doomed to failure for two different reasons.

First of all, a war against Russia was seriously considered in Prussia only so long as there was fear of Russian armed intervention in the German revolution and a prospect of the active cooperation of other powers. But Nicholas I, well advised by his ambassador in Berlin, remained passive, while the ambassadors of Britain and even of revolutionary France made it quite clear that the Western powers did not desire a conflict with the czar any more than Austria, who was involved in her own troubles. On the other hand, the impossibility of Polish-Prussian cooperation became obvious as soon as the "national reorganization" of at least the province of Poznań was considered. Contrary to the initial promises of the government, any administrative reform in favor of the Poles who hoped for complete separation from Prussia was opposed by the German minority. A compromise negotiated by General Willisen, as royal commissioner, was rejected by both sides, and after a decree which announced the division of the grand duchy into a Polish and a German part, open fighting started with the result that on May 9, 1848, the insurrectionary Polish forces had to capitulate.

There followed a violent anti-Polish reaction under the new commissioner, General Pfuel, who was even ready to cede to Russia a part of the Poznań province. Finally such drastic changes were abandoned, but even the Frankfurt Parliament, where a few liberals had spoken in favor of the Poles and the reconstruction of their country, fully approved Prussia's policy in the name of a "healthy national egoism." Such an attitude was in agreement with the general program of German nationalism which in 1848 claimed the unification of all German states in one empire, whether under Prussian or Austrian leadership, but which also wanted to include many non-German populations that were under the control of both these powers.

In the case of the Habsburg monarchy, such an approach had implications of a much larger scope, affecting at least all those possessions of the dynasty which in the past had belonged to the Holy Roman Empire and which since 1815 had been included in the German Confederation. For that very reason the Bohemian lands were invited to send representatives to the Frankfurt Parliament, a claim which was rejected in the name of the Czechs by the historian Palacký, who now became the political leader of the nation. Nevertheless, when in March, 1848, almost simultaneously with the revolution in Berlin, a similar movement broke out in Vienna, here too at the beginning there seemed to be a possibility of cooperation among all those who, irrespective of nationality, had suffered under the Metternich regime. This cooperation was to include Austrian Germans, who were chiefly interested in constitutional reforms and other peoples who hoped that under a liberal constitution their national rights would also receive consideration.

In Austria, too, the Polish question, which had received such a harsh blow two years before, was immediately reopened, and in Galicia, as in Prussian Poland, concessions were made at the beginning of the revolution. These included the creation of national committees in Cracow and Lwów, and the raising of hopes for a reconstruction of Poland in connection with the Habsburg monarchy. But there was even less chance of cooperation against the Russian czardom —the main obstacle to such a reconstruction—than in Prussia. On the contrary, on April 26 Cracow had already been bombarded by the Austrian commander, and when Polish activity was transferred to the eastern part of Galicia, the Austrian government favored the claim of the Ruthenians. This was to cut off that part of Galicia as a separate province with a Ruthenian majority. In November drastic anti-Polish measures also set in there. Lwów, too, was bombarded. The first Pole, Wacław Zaleski, who had been made governor of Galicia, was recalled, and although the partition of Galicia did not materialize, the whole province was again subject to efforts of Germanization and to strict control by the central authorities.

Here, however, the analogy with the fate of Prussian Poland ends. In the multinational Austrian Empire the Poles did not limit themselves to another abortive uprising in their section of the monarchy, but took an active and sometimes a leading part in all other revolutionary movements, including even that of the Viennese population. A first important step was the Polish participation in the Slavic congress which was opened in Prague on June 2. Like the whole earlier purely cultural phase of Pan-Slavism, that congress, naturally under Czech leadership, had nothing in common with the later development of that trend which was sponsored by Russia. Except for the isolated extremist Bakunin, who hoped in vain to use Bohemia as a basis for a communist revolution, the Russians were conspicuously absent from the congress. There was indeed in Prague a difference between conservative partly aristocratic leaders who were defending traditional regionalism, and a liberal, even radical, majority. There were also individual delegates from outside the Habsburg monarchy. But all of them represented those Slavic peoples who, crushed between German and Russian imperialism, hoped that a reorganization of that monarchy on democratic principles would give them a chance for free development.

In spite of such a positive attitude toward Austria, whose existence even Palacký considered indispensable in that phase of his activity, the imperial authorities were suspicious. In Prague, as in the two Polish cities, the end was a bombardment, the congress being dispersed. In addition to that hostility of the military and bureaucratic elements in the central government, however, there was another difficulty which made the Slavic congress and its whole program end in failure. It had already appeared during the deliberations that the Slavs, though a majority in the Habsburg monarchy, were not the only non-German group which had to be taken into consideration in any reform project. Besides the Italian and Rumanian question of a rather special character, there was the big issue of Hungary with her Magyar leaders and her own nationalities problems.

SLAVS AND MAGYARS IN THE HUNGARIAN
INDEPENDENCE WAR

In spite of the failure of the various revolutionary movements in Austria in the spring of 1848, the Metternich regime could not be maintained. A constituent assembly or preliminary parliament had to be convoked by Emperor Ferdinand I even before he abdicated, on

December 2, in favor of his nephew, Francis Joseph I. That assembly, meeting first in Vienna and later in Kroměříž (Kremsier) in Moravia, had to prepare a constitution for the Habsburg monarchy which would not only establish a parliamentary government and introduce social reforms but also give satisfaction to the claims of the various nationalities. Under a Polish speaker, Francis Smolka, both German and Slav deputies made a serious effort to solve these two problems. The latter, particularly the Czechs, wanted a real federalization of the empire which Palacký, in his plan of January 13, 1849, proposed to divide into eight entirely new provinces corresponding to the main ethnic groups. In order to avoid too drastic changes of the existing boundaries and the breaking up of the various historic units, the final draft of the new constitution, of March 1, attempted a compromise. Self-government was provided for each of the historic lands of the monarchy, but those which had a mixed population were to be subdivided into autonomous districts (*Kreise*) for each nationality. This constructive idea was never to materialize, however, and the whole "Kremsier Constitution" was abandoned when the new prime minister, Prince Felix Schwarzenberg, dissolved the assembly and returned to an absolute and centralistic form of government under German leadership.

One of the reasons for that final defeat of the Austrian revolution, even in its moderate expression, was indeed the military strength of the imperial regime. The Austrian army under Field Marshal Radetzky twice defeated the only foreign power which interfered with the internal troubles of the monarchy. This was the kingdom of Sardinia which, aiming at the unification of Italy, tried in vain to liberate the Italian populations still under Habsburg rule. But for the history of East Central Europe the second reason for the temporary victory of imperialism and absolutism is even more significant. It was not only difficult in general to reconcile the frequently conflicting claims of the various nationalities—for instance, the claims of Italians and "Illyrians" (Slovenes and Croats in the maritime provinces or the claims of Poles and Ruthenians in Galicia) but any federal transformation of the empire, following ethnic lines, found an almost insurmountable obstacle in the basic opposition between the historic conception of the kingdom of Hungary and the aspirations of the non-Magyar nationalities of that kingdom which Vienna was able to play off against Budapest.

In that respect failure to arrive at an agreement was the more regrettable because the Magyars represented by far the strongest force of opposition against the central regime. Realizing this, Ferdinand I, the fourth as king of Hungary, accepted the demands of the bloodless revolution which also broke out in Hungary's capital in the middle of March, 1848. Count Louis Batthyány became the first Hungarian prime minister and the liberal bills voted by the Hungarian Diet were approved. But the delicate issue of the relations between the new democratic kingdom and Austria, which was left in suspense, alarmed both the reactionaries in Vienna and the non-Magyar peoples of Hungary. The latter were afraid of the nationalism of the most influential Magyar leader, Louis Kossuth, a man who was favorable to social reforms but who was unprepared to recognize the equal rights of all nationalities.

Most of these were Slavs, including the Slovaks of northern Hungary—close kin of the Czechs in the Austrian part of the empire—and the Serb minority in southern Hungary looking toward the autonomous principality of Serbia on the other side of the border. But more than any other Slavs and more than the Rumanians of Transylvania, who at once protested against the incorporation of that province with Hungary and who were influenced by the rising Rumanian nationalism in the Danubian principalities, the Croats were to prove the most dangerous opponents of the Hungarian revolution. Fearing for the traditional autonomy of their kingdom if the ties with a free Hungary were to be made closer, they hoped to best serve their own national interests by siding with the imperial government in Vienna. It was therefore the Croat army, under Baron Joseph Jellachich, appointed ban of Croatia by the emperor and also ready to cooperate with the Orthodox Serbs, which was used by Austria to crush the Magyars.

Jellachich's army was defeated when it entered Hungary in September, 1848. Even the occupation of Pest, early in 1849, by the same Prince Windisch-Graetz who had stopped the Slavic movement in Prague, and in October, 1848, another uprising in Vienna which was favorable to the Hungarians, did not put an end to the fierce resistance of the Magyars. On the contrary, equally opposed to the projects of the Kroměříž Assembly and to the centralized empire which was supposed to replace them, the Magyars, fearing that their kingdom would be made a mere province of Austria, with Transylvania and even the

Serb territory (Voivodina) being separated, decided to dethrone the Habsburg dynasty, and on April 14, 1849, at Debrecen, they approved a declaration of independence which was partly drafted on the American model. At the same time the parliament named Kossuth "Governing President."

He also had to conduct the war in defense of the new republic whose establishment seemed to be a turning point in the history of East Central Europe, a first step in the direction of the complete liberation of all nations placed under foreign rule. As such it was particularly welcomed by the Poles whose friendship with the Hungarians was traditional. But in spite of that friendship the Polish leaders were fully aware of the fateful mistake which the defenders of Hungarian nationalism were making by disregarding the nationalism of the non-Magyar peoples. A reconciliation between Magyars on the one hand and Slavs and Rumanians on the other, was strongly encouraged both by Prince Czartoryski, who continued to conduct Polish diplomacy from Paris and who established relations even with Sardinia and Serbia, and by the Polish generals who participated in the Hungarian independence war.

One of them, Henryk Dembiński, was for a certain time even commander in chief of the Hungarian forces. Another, Josef Bem, a better strategist and more popular in Hungary, particularly distinguished himself in the defense of Transylvania where he tried in vain to better the relations between Magyars and Rumanians. He had to fight not only against the Austrians but also against the Russians, because after the defeat of Windisch-Graetz the emperor had asked for aid from Czar Nicholas I who had been able to prevent any revolutionary outbreak in his own realm and had stopped a liberal revolt in Rumania. The czar now was ready to offer his assistance in crushing the last and most alarming insurrection in East Central Europe.

The Polish participation in that revolution was for him a special reason for interfering since he was afraid that a Hungarian victory would also encourage the Poles to resume their struggle for independence, possibly under the same generals, and with the revolutionary movement eventually spreading from Austrian to Russian Poland. On his way to Hungary the Russian field marshal Paskevich, the same who had crushed the Polish insurrection in 1831 and now governed the former "kingdom," took his auxiliary army through Galicia which was still restless after the troubles of 1848. The first

Hungarian territory which he entered was the Ruthenian region south of the Carpathians, where among close kin of the czar's "Little Russians" or Ukrainians—another national minority rather neglected by the Magyars—a feeling of solidarity with Russia was created on that occasion.

Attacked from two sides by superior forces, the exhausted Hungarian army, in spite of the courageous efforts of its last commander, General Arthur Görgey, had to capitulate. This took place at Világos near Arad on August 13, 1849, and all fighting ended in October when General George Klapka had to surrender the fortress of Komárom. This was at the same time the end of the whole revolutionary movement in the Habsburg Empire, and although even the Russians suggested an amnesty, the long resistance of the Hungarians was now ruthlessly punished. The victorious Austrian commander, General Julius Haynau, instituted a regime of terror which culminated in the execution of the former prime minister, Batthyány, and thirteen high officers. Kossuth had to go into exile and it was in America that he was received with special enthusiasm in 1851. But in general the Hungarian emigration was no more successful than the Polish in getting Western support for the oppressed peoples of East Central Europe.

Moreover, it was not only the Magyars who had to suffer from the new era of reaction. This was similar to the Metternich regime in its twofold trend of centralization and Germanization, which after the end of the military operations lasted for about ten years in the whole Habsburg monarchy under prime minister Alexander von Bach. After fighting on the Austrian side, even Croatia lost her former autonomy and separate diet, and the non-Magyar nationalities of Hungary proper, including the Saxons of Transylvania, were equally disappointed, the new Serb *voivodina* being placed under military administration.

In the Austrian part of the monarchy, all administrative and judicial reforms which had to be undertaken under pressure of the barely suppressed revolution were also aimed at a complete unification of the empire through a German bureaucracy. Contrary to the promises which had been made in March, 1849, the Bach administration, instead of a parliament, merely created a "council of state" which was composed of officials and which proved hostile to any kind of provincial self-government and particularly to the claims of all non-

German nationalities. Only in Galicia was some progress made by the Poles, when after General Hammerstein's military regime, one of them, Count Agenor Gołuchowski, was made governor or viceroy of the undivided province. But even that prominent statesman was to find greater possibilities of action only in the reform period ten years later.

Immediately after the revolutionary crisis of 1848, which in East Central Europe began two years earlier and lasted one year longer than in the West, that whole region returned to a condition similar to that which prevailed after the Congress of Vienna. In the case of the Poles, that situation was even worse as far as Russian Poland and Cracow were concerned, and all stateless nationalities resented their oppression much more than ever before because of the continuous progress of their national consciousness and the high hopes which the various revolutions had raised. These revolutions having failed, it seemed that only a European war could improve their lot, especially if Western Europe would show a real interest in the freedom of all nations in opposition to the autocratic empires in the eastern part of the Continent. Nobody expressed that idea better than the Polish poet, Adam Mickiewicz, who, turning from literature to political action, had tried in 1848 to create a Polish legion in Italy, as in the days of Bonaparte. He was now ready to welcome another Napoleon as a liberator and the Crimean War as an occasion for reorganizing Europe on a basis of national rights.

18

FROM THE CRIMEAN WAR TO THE
CONGRESS OF BERLIN

EAST CENTRAL EUROPE DURING AND AFTER THE
CRIMEAN WAR

In addition to various revolutions and localized wars between individual countries, there was in the comparatively peaceful century from 1815 to 1914 at least one war which might be called European. Although it started in 1853 as one more armed conflict between Turkey and Russia, the next year France and Britain joined the Turkish side; so, too, did Sardinia in 1855, thus preparing the great power role of the future kingdom of Italy. Austria's position could hardly be called neutral, and even the policy of Prussia was at least indirectly affected. Under such conditions it could be expected that during the war or at the peace table the unsolved problems of East Central Europe would also be raised.

These problems had little to do with the outbreak of the war. The real issue was indeed whether or not Russia would be permitted to take exclusive advantage of the decline and gradual disintegration of the Ottoman Empire. And the main reason why the Western powers entered the war was the desire to protect their interests in the Mediterranean region. But the French-Russian rivalry in the matter of protecting the Christians in the Ottoman Empire, particularly in the Holy Land, was connected with the problem of the liberation of the Balkan peoples. And to prevent another Russian penetration into the Danubian principalities, Austria, in spite of her debt of gratitude for Russia's help in 1849, decided to occupy these vassal states of Turkey herself. However, the real fighting took place in territories far away from East Central Europe, in the Crimea and in the Caucasus. Naval activities remained limited to the Black Sea, while plans of extending them to the Baltic did not materialize.

319

Therefore the war, in which Russia was not attacked in any place where she was really vulnerable, never reached or even approached Polish territories. Yet, at least the Poles, who tried to organize voluntary forces for fighting on the side of Turkey and who intensified the anti-Russian diplomatic activities directed by Prince Czartoryski from Paris, considered Russia's defeat an opportunity for reopening their own problem. And in general, Napoleon III was regarded as a champion of all nationalities which were deprived of their freedom. His prestige was indeed considerably increased. It seemed possible that the peace conference of 1856, this time held in Paris, would attempt, like that of Vienna in 1815, a reconstruction of Europe or at least with the support of Napoleon III restore to the Poles what had been granted to them even after the fall of Napoleon I.

As a matter of fact, France approached Britain with a view to claiming from Russia a restoration of the Kingdom of Poland which was created by the Congress of Vienna. But the British answer was negative. At the Congress of Paris neither the Polish question nor any problem of nationalities was mentioned at all, the only exception being the case of the Rumanians. It so happened, however, that after the Crimean War, defeated Russia proved less weakened than the Ottoman Empire. Therefore not all of Bessarabia, which Czar Alexander I had annexed in 1812, but only a little more than the small district at the mouth of the Danube which had been gained by Russia in 1829, was now restored to Moldavia, while the sultan had to enlarge the autonomy of both Rumanian principalities. As a whole, although the Crimean War was one of the rare setbacks of Russia's advance, it changed so little in the European situation that this bloody and costly conflict was practically fought in vain. At any rate, the domination of the peoples of East Central Europe by a few big powers seemed to be merely confirmed, with Russia and Prussia in traditionally friendly relations, the Russian-Austrian tension without deeper consequences, and the liberation of the Balkans from Turkish control rather delayed.

Delayed was even the unification of the two autonomous Danubian principalities, which was the first aim of Rumanian nationalism and seemed a prerequisite condition for the creation of a fully independent Rumanian state. Even when in 1858 both Moldavia and Wallachia received the right to choose their own princes, it was expressly provided that they should not be united, and only the choice of the same prince, Alexander Cuza, by both of them practically ended their separation the next year. It was not before an intervention of Napoleon III, however, that the other powers in 1862 at last recognized not only that personal union but also the fusion of both parliaments. But even then the new Rumania—the result of the agelong aspirations of Moldavian and Wallachian leaders—was far from including all Rumanian populations which partly remained under Austrian and Russian rule, while the united principality remained under Ottoman suzerainty, just as did Serbia.

As to the latter, which had been neutral during the Crimean War, the Congress of Paris merely replaced the Russian guaranty of Serbia's autonomous status by a joint protection of all great powers. It was in vain that the chief adviser of Prince Alexander Karageorgevich, Ilya Garashanin, was planning a union of all Yugoslavs. Serbia herself was going through a dangerous crisis because of the old feud of the two dynasties, of which the Obrenovich returned to power after Alexander's abdication in 1858. Even so, marked progress in administration and cultural development was being made, particularly under Michael Obrenovich who succeeded his father Milosh in 1860 and resumed the idea of cooperation with the other Balkan peoples in order to achieve full independence for all of them. In spite of his assassination in 1868 by partisans of the Karageorgevich, this policy was continued by his nephew Milan. But it had to wait for another foreign intervention in the Balkan problems, and so too did the independence movement in Bulgaria, whose modest beginnings can also be traced back to the time of the Crimean War.

After that war the policy of Napoleon III, in spite of his friendly interest in the fate of the Rumanians—the Latins of the Balkans—turned chiefly to Western problems and his effective patronage of national unification movements was limited to the case of Italy. Even so the successes of Italian nationalism in the war of 1859 and in the events of the following year were an encouragement to similar trends in East Central Europe. There was, however, an important difference. In the case of the Italians, the issue was mainly the unification of their various states, and only the cession of Lombardy by Austria in the Treaty of 1859 was at the same time a liberation from foreign rule. On the contrary, Austria's rule seemed to remain well established not only in her remaining Italian possessions, including Venetia, but also in all the other non-German parts of the Habsburg Empire. And that

Austrian rule was resented as foreign because it continued to be exercised not only by a German dynasty but also by a predominantly German bureaucracy which, together with German language and culture, was the strongest centralizing force in the monarchy.

Such a situation could prove particularly dangerous for the non-German nationalities at a time when German nationalism was rapidly growing in the non-Austrian parts of the German Confederation, especially in Prussia. That second German power, Austria's old rival, was becoming, like Sardinia in Italy, a center of unification in one national state, a unification which for the Germans, even more than for the Italians, was the main goal of their specific nationalism. That German nationalism, under the leadership and inspiration of Bismarck's Prussia, can be called specific because, under the spell of the imperial tradition of the Middle Ages, it included a program of domination over those non-Germans who were supposed to be in the German sphere of influence, political, economic, or cultural, and among whom German minorities were scattered.

The first of the cases where the programs of national unification and imperial expansion were intimately connected was the question of Schleswig-Holstein, where German nationalism had already tried not only to liberate a small number of Germans from Danish rule in 1848 but also to conquer the Danish population of the northern part of Schleswig. By means of the war of 1864 that twofold aim was achieved by Prussia, allied on that occasion with Austria, which was to share in the administration of the annexed duchies although she had no interest whatever in that region. But the troubles which arose from that joint administration were not the only reason for the growing tension between the two leading German powers which in 1866 made Prussia fight against Austria in alliance with Italy. In the new German Empire which Prussia was trying to create there was no place for even part of the Habsburg Empire which in the years following the defeat of 1859 was going through a far-reaching constitutional transformation that altered its whole character.

That basic reform of the Danubian monarchy was caused by an awareness that the absolute centralistic regime could not be continued without endangering the very existence of a power which was in a very difficult international situation. Even more important than the long overdue establishment of some kind of parliamentary government was the solution of the problem of nationalities. Nowhere was that problem more intricate than in a rather artificially unified empire which extended over a large section of East Central Europe where the medieval tradition of various national states was well alive, and where even those peoples which never had achieved full independence were rapidly developing their national consciousness. These divergent claims could not receive any lasting satisfaction so long as the idea of German predominance prevailed in the government, nor was the indispensable federalization of the monarchy compatible with the participation of some of the Habsburg lands in a German federation which under Prussia's pressure was turning into a more and more unified power of a purely German nationalistic character.

The German character of Prussia herself was stressed at the same time by more and more systematic efforts to Germanize her Polish provinces. With the exception of the part of Silesia which had remained ethnically Polish, these provinces, whether acquired through the partitions of Poland or even before, as was the case of East Prussia, had never been included in the German Confederation. Now, however, they were supposed to be a part of the planned German Empire, so that not only Prussia but the new unified Germany would be the immediate neighbor of the equally unified Russian Empire.

While, therefore, in the southern part of East Central Europe, both in the Balkans and in the Danubian region, the cause of the submerged nationalities was in progress, that same cause was threatened more than ever before in the northern part and seemed to receive a final blow through the failure of another Polish insurrection against a Russia supported by Prussia's sympathy and cooperation. That insurrection and the following repressions were clear evidence that as far as the fate of the non-Russian nationalities was concerned, the apparent liberalization of the czarist regime under Alexander II, who succeeded his father Nicholas I in the last year of the Crimean War, did not justify any "dreams" as the new czar had warned the Poles at the very beginning of his reign.

THE JANUARY INSURRECTION AND ITS CONSEQUENCES

The second of the two great Polish insurrections against Russia, which were the most striking manifestations of the struggle for national freedom in East Central Europe during the nineteenth century, broke out in Warsaw on January 22, 1863, and is therefore called the January Insurrection. From the military point of view there is an obvious contrast between that hopeless uprising and the November Insurrection of 1830. This time it was no longer a regular Polish-Russian war, conducted by the army of the autonomous kingdom of Poland against the czarist empire, not without some chance of success. The guerilla warfare which dragged on for many months, in some regions even into 1864, was little more than a humiliating and irritating nuisance for Russia and was even by many Poles regarded as a heroic but tragic act of despair. The details of the fighting are therefore of limited importance for general history. Nevertheless there are also instructive analogies between the two revolutions which illustrate the real significance of the events of 1863.

This time the armed struggle was again preceded by a serious attempt at appeasement in Polish-Russian relations. Without returning to the conception of 1815, Alexander II began by removing at least the most shocking abuses of the Russian administration in the former kingdom of Poland. There Paskevich, who died in 1856, was replaced as governor general by the more conciliatory Prince Nicholas Gorchakov, a brother of Alexander the chancellor. In the following year the foundation of the Polish Agricultural Society was permitted, which under the presidency of the conservative leader, Count Andrew Zamoyski, contributed to economic progress and studied the vital agrarian problem. Those who hoped for real concessions in the political or at least in the cultural field were, however, so completely disappointed that as early as 1860 patriotic demonstrations, followed by military repressions, created such a tense situation in Warsaw that in March, 1861, the czar decided upon a basic reform, using the services of Marquis Alexander Wielopolski, the only Polish leader who favored full cooperation with Russia.

That highly talented but unpopular statesman at once received important positions in the newly created Council of State which was to consider the Polish claims and reform the educational system. In June, 1862, after another series of violent demonstrations which temporarily forced him to resign, Wielopolski was made head of the civil government of Russian Poland, with a brother of the czar as viceroy. Real concessions remained limited to education, however, including the development of the so-called "principal school" into a Polish university, while even the rightists of the Agricultural Society requested a truly autonomous national government not only for the "Kingdom," but also for the Lithuanian and Ruthenian lands. The "Reds," as the radical left of the independence movement were called, at once created a Central National Committee in addition to the Revolutionary Committee of General Mierosławski, the veteran of 1846–1848, who decided to arm the peasants in view of the planned uprising.

Wielopolski considered the revolutionary youth of the cities even more dangerous, and in the night of January 14, 1863, he reacted by ordering a levy of recruits that was limited to the towns. That provocation merely hastened the outbreak of the insurrection on the twenty-second of the same month, along with the proclamation of complete emancipation of the peasants and revolts of the Polish soldiers within the Russian army. In spite of the radical character of the movement, the "Whites" joined it, just as the conservative elements had done in 1830, and made it a general truly national insurrection. There was even less unity of leadership, however, than in the previous one. Mierosławski was replaced as "dictator," first by Marian Langiewicz and later by Romuald Traugutt, a native of the former grand duchy of Lithuania, where, again as in 1831, the insurrection found strong support while it proved impossible to win the peasantry of the Ukraine for the common cause.

The analogy with the situation of 1831 is even more striking with regard to the problem of foreign assistance, this time particularly indispensable. It was again the Right which realized the necessity for at least diplomatic intervention of the powers in favor of the Poles, and since Prince Adam Czartoryski had died two years before it was now his son Władysław who directed the diplomatic efforts which the National Government (formally proclaimed on May 10, 1863) was making chiefly in Paris and London. While Prussia immediately took Russia's side and in the Alvensleben Convention of the eighth of February promised full cooperation in checking the revolutionary movement, even Austria, the third partitioning power, was rather sympathetic toward the Poles. Already in February and March both the French and the British governments, recognizing the international character of the Polish question, urged the czar to restore the rights guaranteed to the Poles at the Congress of Vienna, and on the tenth of April Austria, along with another protest of the two Western powers, sent a similar note to St. Petersburg. Russia knew, however, that not even Napoleon III, who personally addressed the czar in that matter, would militarily back up such diplomatic interventions, which were once more repeated in June. Chancellor Gorchakov's replies were therefore purely negative, referring first to an amnesty promised by the czar and finally declaring that before there could be any discussions with the Poles, their insurrection would have to be crushed.

That was done indeed with the utmost ruthlessness, not only by Russia's military might but also by the new administration in both the Congress Kingdom, where a German Balt, Theodore Berg, was made governor general, and in the former grand duchy of Lithuania, where General M. N. Muravyew distinguished himself by acts of special cruelty. Cooperating with them, Nicholas Miliutin tried to win the Polish peasantry for the czar, making them believe that the Polish gentry was their real enemy, although nobody had been more eager to achieve a progressive land reform than the leaders of the insurrection.

These leaders and all their followers were now severely punished, with the public hanging of Romuald Traugutt and four of his collaborators as a final climax. When that happened in Warsaw, on August 5, 1864, the mass repressions in all parts of the former commonwealth were already in full swing. The "Vistula Land," as the kingdom of Poland was now called, lost the last traces of its autonomy and was turned into just another Russian province, with Russian as the official language in the administration, courts, and schools. Even more complete was the elimination of everything Polish in historic Lithuania, where even the use of the Polish language in public places was forbidden, and the landed property of most of the Poles confiscated, as in the White Ruthenian and Ukrainian lands.

Once more, however, the systematic Russification process in the eastern provinces of the former commonwealth was not exclusively directed against the Poles. Even the Ukrainians, who had taken no part in the January Insurrection, were considered a dangerous element which had to be completely absorbed by the Great Russians. It was precisely in 1863 that the Russian minister of the interior, Count Valuyev, made the famous statement that there never was, there is not, and there never will be a separate "Little Russian" language since it was only a peasant dialect of Great Russian. And when, nevertheless, some scientific and literary activities of Ukrainian societies continued in Kiev, the decree of May 18, 1876, prohibited the importation of books printed abroad in that Little Russian dialect and also the printing and publishing of original works and translations in the empire, except historical documents and specially authorized works in belles-lettres in the generally accepted Russian orthography.

But ethnographic Lithuania also was now considered a purely Russian land, and since the Lithuanians, who were active in the struggle for the restoration of the old Polish-Lithuanian federation, had also started to use the Lithuanian language in some of their proclamations and underground manifestos, the Russians decided to stop the national renaissance movement among the Lithuanians by forcing them to use the Russian alphabet instead of the Latin. Already orally announced by Muravyev, this order was published by his successor, Governor General Kaufmann on September 6, 1865, and in the following year Valuyev made it valid within the limits of the whole Russian Empire.

Lithuanian publications in the Latin alphabet, the only one suitable and appropriate to the cultural tradition of the country, therefore had to be printed abroad henceforth. Most of them appeared in the Lithuanian-speaking part of East Prussia, a small border region called *Lithuania minor*, from which they had to be smuggled into the Russian controlled territory. Thus it happened that Lithuanian nationalism developed to a certain extent under the rule of Prussia, which did not consider her insignificant Lithuanian minority sufficiently important and dangerous to apply strict methods of Germanization or to cooperate with Russia in measures of repression.

The Poles, on the contrary, had no similar opportunities under Bismarck's regime, which was as hostile to them as was the Russian, but instead they found possibilities for free cultural progress and even for self-government in Austria, thanks to the constitutional reform of the Habsburg Empire which coincided with the worst years of Russian persecution after the abortive insurrection. And in spite of the Polish predominance in Galicia, the Ruthenian population of that Austrian province, close kin of the Ukrainians in Russia whose name most of them finally adopted, also found in the reorganized Danubian monarchy conditions that were favorable to national development—a compensation for the refusal of any rights to their much more numerous brethren on the other side of the border.

That new role of Galicia as something like a Piedmont, that is, a basis for the national movement of both Poles and Ukrainians, had a special significance in the religious sphere. In the Orthodox Russian empire, Catholicism, which was considered inseparable from Polish and Lithuanian nationalism, also had to suffer seriously. Catholicism of the Eastern rite, the so-called Uniate Church, which was to a large extent associated with Ukrainian nationalism, was not even tolerated. On the contrary, it was also liquidated (1876) in the Chełm region of the former kingdom of Poland. Under the Habsburg dynasty, Catholicism of both rites was officially promoted. This was another advantage for the Austrian Poles in contradistinction to the fate of those in either Russia or Protestant Prussia, and it was a unique chance for the Ruthenian Uniate Church which could survive only in Galicia. But the situation in that province, in sharp contrast with the situation in Russia after 1863, can be understood only as part of the general problem of Austria's internal reconstruction.

CONSTITUTIONAL REFORMS IN THE HABSBURG MONARCHY

The reorganization of the Austrian Empire is usually connected with the year 1867, the date of the "Compromise" with Hungary and of the basic laws which determined the constitution of the Austrian part of what was now a dual monarchy. These events were indeed the decisive climax of a development which, however, started immediately after the defeat of 1859, was accelerated by another defeat in the war of 1866, and was not completed before the occupation of Bosnia and Herzegovina in 1878. Since such a large part of East Central Europe and so many of its peoples—fragments, at least, of almost all of them—were included in the Habsburg monarchy, the evolution of its structure and character was one of the most important events in the nineteenth-century history of that whole region.

It was, at the same time, one of the most promising changes. Accomplished without another revolution, it was a return to the constructive ideas of 1848, which this time to a large extent materialized. For the Danubian monarchy it was a chance of survival in spite of all difficulties which that heterogeneous body politic had to face, and for its various peoples it opened possibilities of free national development which could even affect the fate of their kinsmen outside the borders of the Habsburg domains. From a German-controlled, centralized, and absolutistic empire, that realm, one of the largest in Europe, seemed to evolve into a federation with equal rights for all nationalities. Why all these hopes did not come true, this is one of the most vital questions of East Central European history and even of general European history.

It is to the credit of Emperor Francis Joseph I, born in the Metternich era and confirmed on his throne by the victory of the forces of reaction over the revolution of 1848–1849, that he realized the necessity for a twofold change in his methods of government. Though deeply attached to the imperial tradition of the past, he gradually made voluntary concessions to the modern claims for constitutional rights and social progress. And though he always considered himself a German prince, he admitted the consequences of the fact that he had to rule over a multinational state in which non-Germans constituted about three-quarters of the population and all had conserved or reached a high degree of national consciousness. That he did not always succeed in satisfying all of them, and that he did not completely liberate his internal and external policy from the influence of the German minority, which was anxious to retain its privileged position and unifying role, this is, of course, another question.

The emperor's hesitation between these two different trends is clearly apparent from the beginning of his reform program. It was a Pole, Count Agenor Gołuchowski, the former viceroy of Galicia, who was made imperial minister of the interior in 1859 and minister of state—practically premier—in 1860, whom Francis Joseph first entrusted with the task of reorganizing the monarchy and whose ideas he approved in the "October Diploma" dated October 20, 1860. Gołuchowski was a decided federalist who wanted equal rights for all nationalities, their languages, and cultures. He also wanted to extend the self-government of the historic provinces, but he was prepared to leave a limited number of common questions to the competence of the *Reichsrat* (Council of the Realm), which in spite of its hardly democratic composition could develop into a real parliament. He antagonized the Magyars, however, since Hungary was not considered a separate state but a group of autonomous lands like Austria. Even stronger was the opposition of almost all Germans, because precisely the liberals among them, who were favorable to constitutional government, wanted it to remain strictly centralized.

Under their influence, on February 26, 1861, the emperor replaced the "October Diploma" of the preceding year by the "February Patent" drafted by a new minister of state, Anton von Schmerling, a representative of the German bureaucracy. There remained the conception of a parliament composed of delegates from the local diets, but the competence of the latter was greatly reduced in favor of the central organ, and the viceroys or governors of the individual lands were made completely independent of the diets and subordinate to the ministry in Vienna. No more than Gołuchowski's could Schmerling's system satisfy the Magyars. Hungary proper, Croatia, and Transylvania were supposed to send a determined number of representatives to the central parliament, while the Hungarian Diet, with Francis Deák as leader of the opposition against Vienna, continued to claim a return to the constitution of 1848, recognizing only a personal union of the historic kingdom with Austria. The Poles were now equally dissatisfied, since two successive Germans were appointed viceroys of Galicia. Even more dissatisfied were the Czechs, who wanted for the lands of "the crown of St. Václav" a position similar to that claimed by Hungary. Even now, however, their leader Palacký defended "the idea of the Austrian state" on the condition that it would be a truly federal state with equal justice for all.

Once more that idea seemed to have chances of realization when in 1865 Schmerling was replaced by Count Belcredi. After the disastrous war of 1866 against Prussia and Italy, when one more Italian province, Venetia, was lost and Austria was excluded from the German Confederation, he seriously tried to federalize the Habsburg monarchy. He appeased the Poles by again making Gołuchowski viceroy of Galicia, where the Diet voted an address to the emperor which attributed to Austria the mission of defending Western civilization and the rights of nationalities. But already Belcredi, who was opposed by the German centralists, and even more his successor, the Saxon Baron (later Count) F. Beust, were inclined to an intermediary solution, fully satisfactory only to the Magyars. That solution, also promoted by Empress Elizabeth, was embodied in the "Compromise" of 1867 which was ratified by the Hungarian Diet on the eighth of June.

In her historic boundaries Hungary was formally recognized as an independent kingdom with its own constitution, parliament, and government, whose first prime minister was Count Julius Andrássy, prominent in the long negotiations before the signing of the Compromise. In addition to the person of the common ruler who was to be crowned as king of Hungary, the ties with Austria, where that same

ruler would continue to be an emperor, were reduced to the creation
of three "joint ministries" : for foreign affairs, for war, and for common financial affairs. The budget of common affairs was to be fixed
by the "Delegations" of the two parliaments, sitting once a year alter-
natively in Vienna and Budapest but meeting only for a vote when
three exchanges of correspondence proved to be inadequate. The
shares of both partners in these common expenses were to be determined for periods of ten years.

That elaborate system restored Hungary's freedom under very
favorable conditions so that among the Magyars only the faithful
adherents of Kossuth, later organized as an "independence party"
under a son of the famous exile, continued to be in opposition. But
much less satisfactory was the situation of the other nationalities of
Hungary. Only the Croats received guaranties of autonomy in an
additional "compromise" between Croatia and Hungary, concluded
in 1868. The Kingdom of Croatia and Slavonia was to be governed
by a *ban*, responsible to the Hungarian government, and a provincial
diet at Zagreb would be competent in matters of internal administration, justice, and education, while twenty-nine Croat members would
sit in the Hungarian Parliament to discuss common problems of
finance and defense. There remained in Croatia, however, an opposition to that agreement, inspired by Bishop J. Strossmayer, the leader
of the movement in favor of Yugoslav unity. Furthermore, some
Yugoslavs, mostly Serbs, were left within the boundaries of Hungary proper. There they were in a situation similar to that of the
Rumanians in completely incorporated Transylvania, and of the
Slovaks and Ruthenians in the northern counties of the kingdom.
Neither of these groups had any autonomous rights or even guaranties of free cultural development, in spite of an apparently liberal law
of 1868 which regulated the use of the various languages.

A much larger number of Yugoslavs, viz., part of the Croats (particularly those in Dalmatia) and all the Slovenes, together with some
Italians, all the Czechs, the Poles and the Ukrainians of Galicia, and
some Rumanians in the Bukovina, remained in the Austrian part of
the monarchy which was officially called "the kingdoms and lands
represented in the Council of the Realm." In that parliament, meeting in Vienna, all these "Crownlands" were at first represented by
delegates of their local diets and later, from 1873, by directly elected

deputies. That last change was again a step toward greater centralization and it was therefore resented by the non-German nationalities which were already disappointed by the fact that in 1867–1868, in contradistinction to Hungary, the other parts of the monarchy only received new guaranties of provincial autonomy, with equal rights for all languages in local administration, the courts, and the schools. Even the Poles, who at once accepted the solution of 1873, had to give up the so-called "Galician Resolution" of 1868, repeated several times, which requested a real "national self-government." They could only gradually develop the autonomy of Galicia and not without continuous disputes with the Ukrainians who were favored by the central government.

Particularly opposed to the settlement of 1867 were, of course, the Czechs, who had reason to hope that the state rights of Bohemia would receive recognition similar to that granted to Hungary. Such recognition, at least by a coronation oath of the emperor as king of Bohemia, was promised to them by Francis Joseph I in 1871. At the same time the Bohemian Diet was encouraged by the pro-Slav Hohenwarth ministry to formulate the national demands of the Czechs in the so-called "Fundamental Articles." All these hopes were frustrated under German and Hungarian influence, and the Czechs, who for several years boycotted the parliament in Vienna, had to face the opposition of a powerful German minority even in the local diets of Bohemia and Moravia. Under these conditions the leadership of the Czech national movement passed from the moderate Old Czechs, directed by Palacký's son-in-law, F. L. Rieger, to the radical Young Czechs, and Palacký gave up his belief in a revitalized Austria.

The main reason for Palacký's disappointment was the fact that in her foreign policy the Habsburg monarchy was gradually coming under Prussian "protection," forgetful of the humiliation suffered in 1866 and contrary to the interests and desires of all her peoples except part of the Germans and Magyars. In spite of the incomplete character of the federalization of the empire, the shortcomings inherent in its dualism, and the limitations of parliamentary government, the reforms of the sixties would have marked notable progress and an important step in the right direction if internal conditions had not suffered from a basically wrong foreign policy, already evidenced in 1873 when Francis Joseph I went to Berlin to meet the emperors of Germany and Russia.

THE LIBERATION OF BULGARIA AND THE CRISIS OF 1878

The Danubian monarchy, a great power as far as its tradition, area, and population were concerned, was of such a composition and had such a structure that in view of the conflicting national interests and aspirations of the federated peoples, a peaceful cautious policy of neutrality was the only possible method of conducting Austria-Hungary's foreign affairs. Instead of this, the agreements of 1873, leading to the so-called "League of the Three Emperors," tied up the foreign policy of the Habsburg monarchy with that of two imperialistic powers which represented German and Russian aggressive nationalism. After the triumph of 1871, which was facilitated by Austria-Hungary's attitude, Bismarck's new German Empire had of course no hostile intentions against the latter but wanted the Danubian monarchy to remain under German control and to convert it into a subservient ally of the Reich. The Russian Empire, now the official supporter of a Pan-Slav movement under Russian inspiration, considered the reorganized Habsburg monarchy a rival in the struggle for influence among the Slavs and more particularly in the Balkan Peninsula. Francis Joseph I, therefore, had little if any common interests with the other two emperors and the rapprochement with them could only involve his realm in dangerous political crises.

In the Balkans such a crisis was once more approaching in connection with the independence movement which at last also set in among the Bulgarians and gave Russia an opportunity to resume her policy of interference, interrupted after the disastrous Crimean War. In the same year of 1870 in which, taking advantage of the Franco-Prussian War, Russia unilaterally repudiated her obligation of 1856 not to keep a navy in the Black Sea, her ambassador in Constantinople, General N. P. Ignatiev, a supporter of Pan-Slavism, helped the Bulgarians to establish a national church organization—a first step in the direction of political liberation. When, a few years later, in 1876, the Turks cruelly repressed a revolt in Bulgaria which broke out soon after similar troubles in Herzegovina, not only did Serbia and Montenegro declare war upon the Ottoman Empire but Russia also decided to enter the conflict. Before doing so, however, she made a secret agreement with Austria-Hungary which was negotiated by Chancellor Gorchakov and Count Andrássy, the foreign minister of the dual monarchy. In case of a Russian victory over Turkey, the whole

Balkan Peninsula was to be divided into autonomous states, without, however, creating one large Slavic power, and Austria-Hungary was to receive compensation in Bosnia and Herzegovina. Early in 1877 a secret military convention with Russia specified the right of the Habsburg monarchy to occupy these two provinces.

Russia's war against Turkey, already imminent at that moment, broke out three months later. After almost a year of hard fighting both in the Balkans and on the Caucasian front, the conflict ended in a complete victory for Russia and brought the czarist forces, allied with all Balkan nations including Rumania, to the gates of Constantinople. In the Peace Treaty of San Stefano, signed on March 3, 1878, Russia satisfied herself with small though not unimportant gains in Transcaucasia and at the mouth of the Danube where she recovered most of her loss of 1856. Yet not only were Rumania, Serbia, and Montenegro declared fully independent, but contrary to the promises made to Austria-Hungary, a large Bulgarian state was created. Besides Bulgaria proper, this state also comprised Thrace as far as the Aegean Sea and the whole of Macedonia. It was obvious that such a Greater Bulgaria, though nominally a vassal principality under the sultan, would be a Russian protectorate and would extend Russia's sphere of influence to the Mediterranean region as far as Greece and Albania.

The frontiers of San Stefano were to remain the goal of Bulgarian nationalism, conflicting with the aspirations of other Balkan peoples, and the prospect of indirect Russian control over practically the whole peninsula was hardly favorable to the free development of any of these peoples, including the Bulgarians themselves. It is true that the alarm of the other European powers almost immediately changed the situation, reducing Russia's predominant position, but at the same time making the Balkan countries, barely liberated from Ottoman rule, mere pawns in a game of power politics and extremely dangerous to a real pacification of the whole region.

That game took place at an international congress held in Berlin, where the Peace of San Stefano was completely revised and replaced by the Treaty of July 13, 1878. The place of the meeting and Bismarck's role as mediator were evidence of the rising prestige of the German Empire and of its desire to exercise a decisive influence even in those parts of East Central Europe in which Germany, according to her chancellor himself, had no direct interest. But on the other hand, it seems doubtful whether the decisions of the congress were really such a blow to Russia's prestige as the Pan-Slavist leaders pretended them to be. In spite of all protests, including that of Rumania, nothing was changed with regard to the extensions of Russia's own frontiers, and the disappointment inflicted upon the Bulgarians made them even more convinced that Russia was their only friend and protector. Furthermore, the occupation of Bosnia and Herzegovina by Austria-Hungary, authorized by the Congress of Berlin, was nothing but a confirmation of the promise already made secretly by Russia and was to have the worst consequences for the Habsburg monarchy. Both problems were to affect conditions in the Balkans until World War I and to endanger at once the barely established peace settlement.

The boundaries of the autonomous principality of Bulgaria, as fixed in Berlin, excluded not only Thrace and Macedonia, which simply remained Turkish provinces, but also the Bulgarian territory south of the Balkans. This region, known as Eastern Rumelia, was granted administrative autonomy under a Turkish governor. In the principality whose constitution was drafted in 1879 in the historic center of Tirnovo, replaced as the capital by Sofia, Alexander of Battenberg, of German origin but a nephew of Czar Alexander II, was chosen as first prince. He had to face the difficult task of satisfying both his Russian protectors, who even wanted to direct the administration of the country, and the liberal opposition which worked for real independence and for the union of Eastern Rumelia with Bulgaria.

When that union was achieved in 1885, with the support of the other European powers and Prince Alexander's consent, Russia resented his independent action and after a kidnapping incident forced him to abdicate. His replacement by Ferdinand of Saxe-Coburg in 1887, which was not recognized by Russia before 1896, strengthened German and Austro-Hungarian influence in Bulgaria and was part of a persistent action of these empires in the Balkans which contributed to making the whole peninsula a field of dangerous big-power rivalry.

For the Habsburg monarchy, the basis for that action was Bosnia-Herzegovina which was occupied after crushing the unexpected resistance of a large part of the population and organized as a joint possession of both Austria and Hungary under the administration of their common minister of finance. That costly and unnecessary acquisition of a backward territory which formally remained part of the Ottoman Empire made the involved structure of the monarchy even more complicated, introduced almost two million Orthodox and Muslims into a body politic in which Catholicism was one of the most important elements of unity, and created very serious problems of foreign policy.

Independent Serbia, which hoped to gain these provinces with their predominantly Serbian population for herself, was permanently antagonized. The introduction of Austro-Hungarian garrisons into strategically important places of another Turkish province, the Sanjak of Novibazar which separated Serbia from Montenegro, seemed to be another obstacle to any unity of all Serbian populations in the future and a threat of expansion in the direction of highly controversial Macedonia. Nevertheless, in the years immediately following the crisis of 1878, Serbia pursued a pro-Austrian policy under Prince Milan Obrenovich who, with Austrian support, proclaimed himself king in 1882. When he declared an unnecessary war upon Bulgaria three years later in order to get some compensation for her union with Rumelia, Serbia was defeated and thanks only to Austria's intervention could she make peace upon the basis of the status quo. But like the other Balkan nations, Serbia remained hesitant to make a choice between following the policies of either Austria-Hungary or Russia, policies which could at any time clash in that crucial and troublesome region.

Under such conditions it may seem astonishing that both empires participated in the League of the Three Emperors, now consolidated in a treaty of alliance among Austria-Hungary, Russia, and Germany, signed in Berlin on June 18, 1881, for three years and renewed in 1884 for three years more. That agreement was a result of Bismarck's shrewd diplomacy. Afraid of a Russian-French rapprochement after the Congress of Berlin, in 1879 the German chancellor succeeded in making an alliance with Austria-Hungary and at the same time he arranged a meeting between Wilhelm I and Alexander II for the purpose of restoring the traditional Prussian-Russian friendship. That friendship did not even suffer from the change on the Russian throne when Alexander II, assassinated in 1881, was succeeded by his son, Alexander III, who was strongly influenced by anti-German Pan-Slavism, nor from the conclusion in the following year of the Triple Alliance in which Italy joined the two Central European empires. And even in 1887 the "Reinsurance Treaty" which Bismarck concluded with Russia, secretly guaranteeing her freedom of action with regard to the Straits, confirmed the old idea of German-Russian co-operation, while the relations between Russia and the Habsburg monarchy were so obviously deteriorating in connection with the Balkan situation that the League of the Three Emperors could no longer be continued.

These well-known facts of general European politics lead to an obvious conclusion concerning East Central Europe. After her internal reorganization Austria-Hungary missed the opportunity of becoming a real support for the various peoples of that region, now largely living within her boundaries, by following a foreign policy strongly influenced by the Prussian-controlled German Empire, a policy which made her enter into artificial agreements with powers opposed to her interests and which did not even favor her dangerous ambitions in the Balkans. Without gaining anything from her stronger German partner, the Habsburg monarchy not only remained exposed to Italian claims to a revision of its southwestern frontier, but also—and this was a much greater threat—to Russia's persistent hostility.

Like Germany, Russia too was much stronger than Austria-Hungary but she had a serious inner weakness in her own nationalities problems which she proved entirely unable to solve, while the Habsburg monarchy continued to make some progress in that respect. This progress could have saved her, if it had not been for the useless entanglements in power politics which led to a conflict in connection with the only superficially settled Balkan situation.

19

TOWARD WORLD WAR I

THE NATIONALITIES PROBLEM IN RUSSIA AND THE
REVOLUTION OF 1905

It was not before the Revolution of 1905 that the outside world realized the importance of the nationalities problem in the Russian Empire. Before that internal crisis, aggravated by simultaneous defeats in the war with Japan, that empire seemed so powerful that the dissatisfaction of its minority groups appeared not to be too serious. Furthermore, in contradistinction to the Habsburg monarchy, where no nationality constituted an absolute majority, in the empire of the czars the Russian majority seemed the more overwhelming because, according to the official interpretation which was accepted by Western scholarship, the Little Russians, as the Ukrainians continued to be called, and the White Russians were not really nationalities that differed from the Great Russians.

However, at least the former of these two, by far the largest non-Russian group, were making steady progress in their national consciousness which already toward the end of the nineteenth century created a serious revolutionary movement. Furthermore, together with the Byelorussians, the Ukrainians were living in that same western section of European Russia—the most advanced of the whole empire—where several other nationalities, clearly distinct from the Russians, were forming a belt of foreign elements along the whole western frontier. This situation in the large part of East Central Europe which Russia had annexed in the eighteenth and early nineteenth century, but never succeeded in absorbing, was therefore a much greater threat to the unity of the empire than the ethnic problems of its Asiatic part or even those of the Caucasian frontier region.

But Russian nationalism which was at its height under Alexander III and during the first part of the reign of Nicholas II, and which was strongly supported by their autocratic regimes succeeded in keeping even the most fully developed nationalities at the western border under a strict control, intensifying all methods of Russification. Therefore for forty years even the Poles had to interrupt their armed struggle for independence, and though always in close cultural community with their kinsmen in Prussia and Austria, they had to postpone their hopes for liberation and political unification, making instead a great effort in the field of economic and social progress. That so-called "organic labor," taking advantage of a beginning industrialization of Russian Poland, contributed to a rapid democratization of Polish society in the Western sense. This was promoted by two political parties that were founded toward the end of the century, the National Democratic Party under Roman Dmowski and the Polish Socialist Party with Joseph Piłsudski as its most prominent leader, both with branches in the other sections of partitioned Poland. Both had national independence as their ultimate goal. This, however, seemed very distant, even to the friends whom the Poles continued to have in the Western countries.

In these countries, besides the Poles, only one of the submerged nationalities of the Russian Empire was sufficiently known to meet with sympathetic understanding. These were the Finns, whose autonomy, after being respected by the czars almost throughout the nineteenth century, was severely restricted under Nicholas II. The Finns, who had never revolted before, reacted by killing General Bobrikov, who as governor of Finland from 1898 on consistently violated their rights, but this assassination made the situation only worse. The Finnish Diet lost its constitutional powers, and Russian officials as well as the Russian language were penetrating into the grand duchy. Both the Finnish majority of the population and the small but culturally important Swedish group were, however, so determined to defend their tradition, so deeply attached to their democratic way of life, and in such well-established contact with the Western world through Scandinavia, that Russian oppression simply created another center of resistance there.

The Estonians on the other side of the Gulf of Finland, though racially close kin of the Finns and influenced by their cultural revival, continued to develop, along with the Latvians, in opposition to both Russification and German social supremacy in the Baltic provinces. Landmarks in the rise of Estonian nationalism were the compilation of the national epic, *Kalevipoeg*, published between 1857 and 1861, and the foundation of a collection of all kinds of popular traditions under the title of *Monumenta Estoniae antiquae* a little later. Similarly, the Latvians created their own epic, *Lacplesis*, and started a collection of popular songs which contributed to the awakening of a truly national spirit. This was further augmented among both of these small ethnic groups by the foundation of cultural societies and newspapers in the native languages, as well as by an interest in archaeological research reviving their prehistory, the only period in which they had been completely free.

Different in that respect was the Lithuanian national renaissance because here a proud medieval tradition of independence could be evoked. New, however, was the tendency to disregard the tradition of the Polish-Lithuanian Union which had resulted in a Polonization of the upper classes, and to base the new Lithuanian nationalism on ethnic and linguistic grounds. Writing in the Lithuanian language was making progress in spite of all restrictions imposed by the czarist regime. The first Lithuanian periodical, founded in Tilsit, East Prussia, in 1883 under the name of *Aušra* (Dawn), was regularly smuggled into the Russian-controlled country and its editor, Dr. Jonas Basanavičius, became the leader of a national movement which created secret Lithuanian schools and societies.

Even in the Lithuanian case there was, however, no clearly expressed political aim before the outbreak of the Russian Revolution in 1905. That revolution was primarily of a social and constitutional character. This was also the case among the non-Russian nationalities which first joined the movement with a view to replacing czarist absolutism by a parliamentary form of government. While among the Russian revolutionaries there were only differences among more or less radical parties, socialist and liberal, the socialist already divided into Mensheviks and Bolsheviks, the program of the various nationalities had a basically twofold aspect which recalled the role of the non-Germans in the Austrian Revolution of 1848. In all the various ethnic groups there were radical forces that were chiefly interested in a change of social conditions. But the nationalist leaders at once realized that a constitutional reform of the empire would be a unique occasion for obtaining equal rights at least in the field of cultural development. And the trend toward federalism which used to appear among all Russian revolutionaries, beginning with the Decembrists of 1825, seemed to favor the rising claims for national autonomy.

Autonomy could not satisfy the Poles, as the events of the preceding century had shown so many times, and the Polish Socialist Party of Piłsudski, decidedly aiming at full independence, was completely apart from the so-called "Social Democracy of the Kingdom of Poland and Lithuania" which put social revolution first. The National Democrats under Dmowski, however, considered it more realistic to work for autonomy as a preliminary step and to take advantage of the opportunities which the czar's October Manifesto and the creation of the Duma seemed to offer.

In that first Russian Parliament which opened on May 10, 1906, the Poles, along with other national groups, had indeed a fairly large representation. They continued to cooperate with the Russian liberals not only in the second but also in the third Duma in which the number of their deputies was greatly reduced and the representation of all other nationalities became insignificant. The failure of these latter can be explained not only by the repression of the whole revolutionary movement but also by the lack of clearly defined programs. Only in Finland, which claimed, of course, the re-establishment of her constitutional government, was that aim achieved in November, 1905. But even the Lithuanian Diet, which assembled in Wilno (Vilnius) at the beginning of the following month and which decidedly claimed an autonomous Lithuania with her own parliament, though federated with the other states of the former empire, received only vague promises from the local Russian authorities which were completely disregarded after the doom of the revolution. The social element definitely prevailed in the Ukrainian movement, and even more among the Latvians and Estonians, who like all other nationalities were hoping for some kind of autonomy and claimed it in the first Duma, but chiefly turned against the German landowners only to be ruthlessly repressed by Russian troops.

What the non-Russian nationalities gained through the 1905 Revolution was therefore very little and mainly of a temporary character. The most shocking restrictions as, for instance, the interdiction of Lithuanian publications printed in the Latin alphabet or the almost complete prohibition of publications in the Ukrainian language, were lifted, thus making possible some progress in the development of national culture. The edict of April, 1905, granting religious tolerance, but not for the Uniate church, was followed by the passing of many former Uniates from Orthodoxy to Catholicism of the Latin rite.

The Poles, though disappointed like all the others in their hopes for any autonomy, were at least permitted to open private schools in their own language under the auspices of a voluntary society. But when even that private organization was abolished at the end of 1907, this was a clear indication that the growing reaction which followed after the revolution would also turn against the most modest rights of the non-Russian nationalities. Among several other measures directed particularly against the Poles, the separation of the Chełm district from Congress Poland, where conditions were still somewhat better than in the rest of the empire, which had been announced in 1909 and was carried out three years later, was particularly resented.

At the same time the old program of Pan-Slavism was revived under the misleading name of "Neo-Slavism," which was to distinguish it from the earlier movement under an openly Russian leadership. Even now, however, there was no place for the Ukrainians in the Slavic community. And even the Poles, among whom Dmowski had favored the new conception, were soon completely disillusioned and ceased to participate in these Slavic congresses. Dmowski's own attitude can only be understood in the light of his conviction that Poland's main enemy was Germany, where indeed the anti-Polish policy of the Prussian government was reaching its climax. However, not only many Poles but also other Slavs, discouraged by Russian imperialism, were looking toward the third of the empires which had divided Poland and, in general, East Central Europe. This was the Habsburg monarchy where the problem of nationalities continued to be discussed in an entirely different spirit from that which prevailed in Russia after the interlude of 1905 and in spite of Russia's entente with the democratic powers of Western Europe.

THE NATIONALITIES PROBLEM IN THE HABSBURG MONARCHY

The whole history of Austria-Hungary from its constitution as a dual monarchy to its fall half a century later is the instructive story of a serious effort to solve the problem of a multinational state with an unusually complicated composition and structure, particularly after the occupation of Bosnia and Herzegovina in 1878. The annexation of these two provinces, thirty years later, though a natural consequence of the occupation and continued administration, provoked an-

other international crisis which once more disclosed the intimate connection between the internal nationalities problem and the foreign
policy of the monarchy.

In order to understand that connection, it must be remembered
that the numerous nationalities of Austria-Hungary were clearly
divided into two groups. The really important distinction is, however,
not that usually made between the so-called historic and nonhistoric
nationalities, but that between nations which in their entirety were
living within the boundaries of the monarchy, and fragments of nations whose larger part was outside these frontiers. As to the latter,
an additional distinction must be made between such minorities as
were attracted by an independent national state on the other side of
the border, as was the case of the Italians, Serbs, and Rumanians,
and those nations which had no state of their own at all, their major
part remaining under a foreign rule much more oppressive than that
of the Habsburgs. This was the case of the Poles and the Ukrainians.

The relatively most numerous group, the German Austrians or
Austrian Germans, could hardly be placed in any of these categories.
If their German character is emphasized, they would seem to be in a
situation analogous to that of the Italian, Serb, or Rumanian "irredenta." And there was indeed among them a certain number of Pan-
Germanists with a loyalty divided between Berlin and Vienna if not
influenced more by the former than by the latter. Conscious of a racial
and linguistic community and inspired by the tradition of the Holy
Roman Empire, they were disappointed at not belonging to that second purely German Empire which the Hohenzollerns were making
much more powerful than the empire of the Habsburgs where the
Germans had to share their influence with almost a dozen other
nationalities. But on the other hand, only by remaining in the Dual
Monarchy could these Austrian Germans continue to control these
other groups, all of which were economically and socially weaker than
the Germans and, according to the German interpretation, on a lower
cultural level. And only through the Austrian Germans could the
Habsburg monarchy be kept under the political influence, if not direction, of the new German Empire as its "brilliant second." Furthermore, there were many German-speaking Austrians who were indeed
first, if not exclusively, loyal subjects of the Habsburgs, who were
definitely opposed to the Prussian spirit which inspired the Reich of

the Hohenzollerns, who were devoted to the separate Austrian tradition and interested in what they considered their historic mission of unifying the Danubian region in cooperation with its non-German populations.

How far these German Austrians, practically a distinct nationality, would go in recognizing the equal rights of the non-German nationalities of Austria, that was another problematic question. In any event they had to recognize the equal rights guaranteed to the Hungarians in the Compromise of 1867, and it was only natural for them to do so, since the Hungarians, or strictly speaking, the Magyars of Hungary—just one-half of the kingdom's population—were next to the German Austrians most interested in the existence of the Dual Monarchy in which they enjoyed a privileged position. And since most of the Magyar leaders, fearful of Slavic influence, were also in favor of the alliance with the German Empire, their understanding with all Germans of Austria was one of the foundations of the whole policy of the monarchy, internal and external, irrespective of the claims of the German minority in Hungary and of occasional friction in the parliamentary delegations, chiefly on financial issues.

Even jointly, however, Germans and Magyars, about twenty-two millions, were inferior in number to the twenty-four million Slavs of the monarchy. And without even speaking of almost totally Slavic Bosnia-Herzegovina, in the Austrian part the Slavs constituted more than two-thirds of the population. Fully aware of the impossibility of keeping that Austrian part under the supremacy of the German minority which thanks to an unfair electoral law continued even after 1867, prime minister Count Edward Taaffe, of Irish descent, who was appointed to his office in 1879 and held it for fourteen years, decided to base his administration on the respect of nationality rights. He was supported by the Poles, who at least had the chance of free cultural life only in Austria, and who gradually developed the self-government of Galicia. He was also supported by most of the Czechs who under the Taaffe regime received numerous concessions. These included the opening of a Czech university in Prague in 1882 alongside the old one which had long since been Germanized. Along with all the other Slavic nationalities they profited from new regulations with regard to respect for their linguistic rights. The social progress made during these same years was to be implemented by a democratic reform of the electoral law.

But when that project was attacked by both conservatives and radicals, the Germans, who had always been opposed to the Taaffe ministry which as they said kept them in an "iron ring," reversed it at last. And it was only three years later that another prime minister, this time a Pole, Count Casimir Badeni, returned to the idea of similar reforms in the direction of both a strict enforcement of linguistic equality and a gradual extension of the right to vote. The following year, however, Badeni fell victim to German obstructionism in parliament and it was not until 1907 that universal equal suffrage was established in Austria.

Prime Minister Baron Beck who carried out that reform, as well as the emperor who approved it in spite of his conservative leanings, hoped that a larger representation of the Left, concerned with class interests, would reduce the friction among the various nationalities. But at the same time the representation of the non-German peoples was increased, and it soon became obvious that the lower classes too, including the peasant parties and to a certain extent even the Socialists, were animated by strong nationalist feelings which continued to create difficulties in the legislature, whether central or provincial, and in the administration. Even minor issues affecting the weakest of the various national groups aroused a great deal of excitement, a frequently quoted example being the dispute over the opening of a Slovene high school in the town of Celje (Cilli) in southern Styria.

Like most of the others, that province had an ethnically mixed population so that the autonomy of the various crownlands was no solution to the problem. Therefore, among the many projects of fundamental change which were supposed to put an end to all these conflicts, was also the idea of cultural autonomy for each individual person. This was favored by some Socialist leaders. Projects of territorial readjustment seemed to have more chances of success but encountered basic difficulties. First, in many cases there were different nationalities in one and the same territory, with German minorities scattered almost everywhere, sometimes in isolated islands. Among the conflicts between non-Germans, that between Poles and Ruthenians was the more intricate. There were many Poles even in the predominantly Ruthenian eastern part of Galicia, particularly in Lwów and other cities. The Ruthenians themselves were divided into Ukrainian nationalists and the so-called Old Ruthenians who considered themselves a branch of the Russian nation. Equally tense were the relations between Italians and Slavs—Slovenes or Croats—in the maritime provinces. But by far the greatest difficulty resulted from the position of Hungary in the dualistic system that was fixed in 1867.

After Deák's death in 1876, the trend toward Magyarization of all other nationalities of the kingdom became even stronger, and an electoral law, much less democratic than in Austria and quite unsatisfactory even when eventually reformed in 1913, gave these nationalities no chance for a fair representation in the Hungarian Parliament. Thus, for instance, the Slovaks remained not only separated from the Czechs but in a much less favorable position; such was the position of the Rumanians in Transylvania if compared with those of the Austrian Bukovina. Yet any change in the "Compromise" which would have ameliorated the conditions of the various nationalities in either part of the monarchy was excluded by the Magyars. Their Independence Party was claiming, on the contrary, additional concessions from the common ruler. Furthermore, even Croatia's autonomy was hardly respected, particularly during the long period when a Hungarian, Count Khuen-Héderváry, governed that kingdom as ban.

The controversies between Magyars and Croats were a special danger because they opened the whole Yugoslav question, certainly the most thorny aspect of the nationalities problem in the monarchy. In spite of the old rivalries which separated Catholic Croats and Orthodox Serbs, both speaking the same language, the movement toward Yugoslav unity, including also the Slovenes, was making progress, as evidenced in the Fiume Resolution of 1905. Yet some of these Yugoslavs were under Austria, facing either German or Italian antagonism in five different provinces. Others were under a joint Austro-Hungarian administration in Bosnia-Herzegovina. The Serbs of Hungary proper had special reasons to complain, and since even autonomous Croatia-Slavonia now had to suffer from Magyar penetration, there was among practically all these southern Slavs a dissatisfaction greater than among any other national group and an unrest which was increased by influences coming from the independent Yugoslav states of Serbia and Montenegro.

There appeared, therefore, among the politicians and writers who saw the necessity for a further federalization of the Habsburg monarchy, the bold idea of changing its dualistic into a trialistic structure which would give to the Yugoslav part a position equal to that of the Austrian and the Hungarian. However, such a solution, which was not unacceptable to the Germans since it would have reduced the number of Slavs in Austria, was always rejected by the Magyars as a threat to the territorial integrity of the kingdom of St. Stephen and to their favorable position in a partnership of two states only. Furthermore, such a concession to the Yugoslavs meant a revival of the Czech claims for a restoration of their historic statehood. And most important, even if trialism were adopted, the Yugoslav question was one of those which could not be completely solved within the limits of the Habsburg monarchy since Serbia and Montenegro obviously had no desire of being included.

On the contrary, their fear of Austro-Hungarian imperialism was greatly increased when in 1908 the inclusion of Bosnia-Herzegovina in the monarchy became final through the formal annexation of that territory. Therefore that step which changed little in the internal problems of the Habsburg realm had immediate repercussions in international relations and contributed to another of those European crises which threatened the peace of the Continent almost from the beginning of the twentieth century.

THE CRISIS OF 1908 AND THE BALKAN WARS OF 1912–1913

At the beginning of the twentieth century, the peace of Europe which, except in the Balkans, had not been disturbed since 1871, seemed so well established that wars in distant extra-European lands, in which some of the leading European powers were engaged, had no repercussions in Europe itself. This is even true for the most important of these wars, the Russo-Japanese, which in spite of the simultaneous revolution in Russia was not used by any of her neighbors to threaten her security in the West. On the contrary, a few months before peace was made with Japan at Portsmouth, New Hampshire, a Russian-German alliance was negotiated at Björkö, in the Baltic region, where Czar Nicholas II and Emperor Wilhelm II met on July 24, 1905.

If that treaty, which was a return to an old tradition, and, in view of the German-Austrian alliance, to the conception of the Three Emperors' League, never came into force, it was because it seemed incompatible with the earlier French-Russian alliance. This, in connection with the Anglo-French Entente of 1904, was to lead to the Triple Entente of France, Britain, and Russia which from 1907 opposed these three powers to the Triple Alliance of Germany, Austria-Hungary, and Italy. But even that alignment seemed no immediate threat to international peace but rather the establishment of a durable balance of power in Europe.

From 1905 onward, however, there followed a whole series of crises which made it quite clear that such a balance, precarious as usual, was no guaranty against clashes of conflicting interests among the great powers. Some of these issues, particularly the dangerous Morocco crises of 1905–1906, 1908–1909 (the Casablanca incident), and 1911, had little if anything to do with the real aspirations of the European peoples and certainly nothing with those of the peoples of East Central Europe. It was therefore only natural that Austria-Hungary, the only great power which had no colonial ambitions and instead had so many internal problems typical of the unsettled conditions in East Central Europe, avoided any direct entanglements in these problems, although the Habsburg monarchy remained faithful to the Triple Alliance. In general, Austro-Hungarian foreign policy remained cautious and well balanced so long as it was directed by Count Agenor Gołuchowski, a son of the Polish statesman of the same name who fifty years before had played such a constructive part in the internal politics of the monarchy.

But in 1906 Gołuchowski was replaced as foreign minister by Baron (later count) Alois von Aehrenthal, an ambitious diplomat who after long negotiations at the Buchlau conference of September, 1908, accepted a proposal of the equally ambitious Russian foreign minister Alexander Izvolsky. This proposal was strangely similar to that which preceded the occupation of Bosnia-Herzegovina. Now, forty years later, Russia offered Austria-Hungary her consent to the final annexation of these provinces on the condition that the Habsburg monarchy would in turn consent to opening the Straits to Russian warships. The whole delicate Eastern question was thus reopened. As usual, it affected not only the Ottoman Empire and all powers interested in its fate but also the non-Turkish peoples of the Balkan Peninsula, who were liberated only in part and looking for a final division of the European territories still held by Turkey.

This was, however, not the only reason why the announcement of the annexation of Bosnia-Herzegovina by Austria-Hungary, on the sixth of October of the same year, combined with the proclamation of Bulgaria's full independence under "Czar" or King Ferdinand I, provoked a particularly violent European crisis which this time created the greatest possible interest among all peoples of East Central Europe, especially the Slavs. Izvolsky complained that Aehrenthal made his announcement by surprise and without waiting for approval of the Russo-Austrian deal by the other powers which, as a matter of fact, opposed the opening of the Straits to Russia only. The latter therefore gained nothing and proved to be as indignant about Austria-Hungary's unilateral action as were France and Britain.

Nevertheless an open conflict was avoided, since the countries which were directly touched by the annexation felt obliged to recognize it. So did Turkey, still formally the sovereign of the two provinces but with little hope of ever regaining possession of them and therefore satisfied with financial compensation. Serbia resented that final incorporation of a territory with a predominantly Serbian population by Austria-Hungary even more than the occupation of 1878. Besides, under King Peter—a Karageorgevich who after the assassination of Alexander in 1903 had again replaced the Obrenovich dynasty—the Serbs had rather bad relations with Austria-Hungary. But even Serbia finally accepted the accomplished fact. In her note of March 31, 1909, she admitted that her rights had not been affected and she even promised to change her policy toward the Habsburg monarchy in a spirit of friendly neighborliness.

Serbia had to do this because Russia was at that moment not prepared to go to war. She was, however, aware that the czarist empire remained as resentful as herself, and more than ever before she regarded Russia as her only real friend and protector. She also looked for compensation in another direction, though Austria-Hungary was opposed to any further change of the status quo in the Balkans. But the lasting tension which resulted from the annexation crisis did not line up all the Slavic peoples of Europe against the Habsburg monarchy, which was supported by Germany. Not only was Bulgaria, which herself had profited from the crisis, now rather inclined toward the Triple Alliance to which her Rumanian neighbor had also formally adhered as early as 1883, but many of those Slavs who suffered from Russian domination and were better treated in Austria were preparing themselves for another struggle against czardom in case of an Austrian-Russian war which seemed to be only postponed. Such was the program of the Polish independence movement under Piłsudski, who started military preparations in Galicia. But even those Poles who continued to regard Austria's German ally as their main enemy, and in general all peoples who hoped for an improvement in their condition, saw a serious chance in any conflict among the empires which controlled East Central Europe.

The first conflict which broke out soon after the annexation crisis was another war against the Ottoman Empire which the liberated Balkan states, encouraged by Turkey's defeat in the Tripolitan War against Italy, started in October, 1912. All neighbors of what still was European Turkey, not only Serbia and Bulgaria—in a rather exceptional agreement—but also little Montenegro, a kingdom since 1910, which first declared war, and Greece, disappointed by the outcome of her isolated struggle with Turkey in 1897, were convinced that even without any assistance from the great powers they could completely free the Balkans from Turkish rule which after the revolution of the Young Turks in 1909 was even more nationalistic than under the corrupt regime of Sultan Abdul Hamid II.

The allies indeed made astonishing progress, including a victory of the Serbs near the place where medieval Serbia had fallen in 1389 and an advance of the Bulgarians almost to the gates of Constantinople, similar to that of their ancestors a thousand years before. The dream of retaking the capital of the Byzantine Empire, which also inspired the Greeks, did not come true, but in spite of a reorganization of their forces under Enver Bey, the Turks also lost the second phase of the first Balkan War. After an armistice and preliminary negotiations under the auspices of the great powers, in the treaty which was eventually signed in London, on May 30, 1913, they had to cede all territories west of a line drawn from Media on the Black Sea to Enos on the Aegean. In Europe this left them hardly more than Constantinople and the coast of the Straits.

But it remained to be decided how these territories would be divided among the victors. That problem, difficult in itself because the largest section, Macedonia, with her mixed population, had been a trouble spot for many years, was made even more intricate by big power interference. Not only was Bulgaria requested to cede part of Dobrudja to Rumania, which had remained neutral, but Austria-Hungary, opposed to an aggrandizement of Serbia to the Adriatic coast, pressed with Italy's support for the creation of an independent Albania under a German prince on a territory which she wanted to enlarge at the expense of the claims of Serbia and Montenegro.

When Serbia, in secret alliance with Greece, tried to get compensation in the part of Macedonia originally assigned to Bulgaria, that country, encouraged by the Macedonian Revolutionary Organization, attacked her former allies.

In the second Balkan war which thus started, Bulgaria also had to fight against the Rumanians and the Turks. In the Treaty of Bucharest, signed on August 10, 1913, Bulgaria lost even more of Dobrudja to Rumania, Adrianople to the Turks, and Macedonia to Serbia and Greece which received a common frontier. Although access to the Aegean Sea was left to them, the Bulgarians remained deeply resentful toward Russia, which seemed to favor the other side. But Serbia too felt humiliated and disappointed when, after a few more months of tension, which the London discussions of the great powers tried with little success to mitigate, the Austrian ultimatum of the 18th of October forced the Serbian army to evacuate what was declared to be Albanian territory.

What was deplorable in the final outcome of the two Balkan wars was not the attribution of this or that territory or the drafting in detail of the new frontiers. In ethnically mixed regions, these boundaries had to be based on compromise. In general, the restoration of almost the whole peninsula to the peoples of that region, constituted as independent states, including Albania, was a fair solution. But besides the renewed antagonism between Bulgaria and her neighbors, especially Serbia, the interference of the great powers, in disagreement among themselves, left general dissatisfaction behind and projected their rivalries into a part of Europe which after so many centuries of foreign domination and penetration was in an atmosphere of excitement even after complete liberation.

It seems, therefore, that the so-called European concert which was meeting in London contributed to creating a situation leading to much deeper conflicts in the future, even though it succeeded in localizing the conflicts of 1913. In particular, Austria-Hungary, without obtaining anything for herself, once more unnecessarily antagonized her Yugoslav neighbors who had so many sympathizers among their kinsmen within the boundaries of the Dual Monarchy. Even the creation of Albania was no unqualified success for that monarchy. Italy's interests in that new state, which was placed under the weak rule of Prince Wilhelm von Wied, added another element to the misunderstandings between the two minor partners in the Triple Alliance. And Rumania's association with that alliance became a mere fiction since she now entered into some kind of coalition with her allies in the Second Balkan War, all of them looking for protection toward the Triple Entente. The balance of power was therefore shifting toward the latter, and Austria-Hungary's dependence on Germany was dangerously increased.

THE ORIGINS OF WORLD WAR I IN EAST CENTRAL EUROPE

It is frequently stressed that both world wars started in East Central Europe, and the first one in particular in Serbia. This is, of course, correct so far as the formal and immediate origin of the conflict is concerned, but it requires two important qualifications if the whole background of war is to be envisaged and the real issue explained.

First, even in 1914 the basic unrest in East Central Europe was not limited to Serbia and the Serbs alone, or even to the Balkan peoples liberated from Turkish rule. The Serb or rather Yugoslav question was not only part of the Balkan problem but also of the general nationalities problem in the Danubian region which was controlled by the Habsburg monarchy. And the aspirations of the various peoples of that monarchy, who were much better off than fifty years before but all of whom were far from being completely satisfied, were again only part of the trend toward full national freedom which was becoming increasingly strong among the oppressed nationalities of the Russian Empire and also among the non-German minorities under Prussian rule.

On the other hand it is evident that nowhere was that trend of nationalism, directed against the well-established states and their power, leading to wars or even to new revolutions which could have resulted in foreign intervention and international, or more correctly, interstate, conflicts. In Prussia a revolution against the dominant German majority and the powerful German Empire was out of the question. In Russia a violent revolutionary movement had recently failed in spite of the empire's defeat in a foreign war and without leading to any other outside trouble. And neither in Austria nor even in Hungary was the dissatisfaction of any nationality great enough to lead to any outbreak in time of peace and so long as evolutionary reforms were in progress or at least remained possible.

This was also true for the particularly dissatisfied Yugoslavs of the Habsburg monarchy, including even the Orthodox Serbs. Therefore the fear of some elements in the army and bureaucracy that the nationalist agitation coming from the kingdom of Serbia would endanger the whole empire was hardly justified. That fear seemed, however, to receive an apparent justification when on the fateful day of June 28, 1914, the heir to the throne, Archduke Francis Ferdinand, was murdered in Sarajevo by a Serb nationalist from Bosnia as the result of a plot in which organizations and most probably even officials of Serbia proper were involved. Coming in the midst of a tension between the two states which had been greatly intensified by the events of the preceding year, that outrageous assassination necessarily provoked a dangerous diplomatic conflict, but a conflict which for both sides was rather a question of prestige than an issue of nationalism and which did not necessarily have to lead to a war and certainly not to a European or world war.

To make the first of these points quite clear, it must be recalled that the slain Archduke, far from being hostile to the Slavs in general— his morganatic wife assassinated at his side was of Czech origin— and even less to the Yugoslavs, was in favor of a trialistic reorganization of the monarchy and opposed to that Magyar supremacy which the Yugoslavs particularly resented. The issue, rather obscured by the Sarajevo crime, was whether the Yugoslav problem would be solved through another internal reform of the Habsburg Empire or under the leadership of the Karageorgevich kingdom. Many of the Yugoslavs outside Serbia, especially among the Catholic Croats, were rather in favor of the former solution.

If the Austro-Hungarian ultimatum and the rejection of the conciliatory Serb reply went far beyond legitimate claims for investigation and reparation, that truly imperialistic attitude toward a much smaller power was mainly caused by the certainty that such an attitude would have the full support of the allied German Empire which was the leading representative of the imperialistic conception in the western part of Europe. And if Serbia preferred to risk an invasion rather than to yield completely, as she had done in 1913, it was because this time she was sure to be supported by the whole might of Russian imperialism.

Russia gave that support not because of any interest in Serb nationalism but because she was fearful of losing her prestige among the Slav and Orthodox peoples. Influence among these peoples was indeed a valuable instrument of Russia's imperialistic policy. But that policy, closely associated with aggressive Russian nationalism, had so little appeal for smaller, even Slavic, peoples in the neighborhood of the empire and for the non-Russian nationalities kept within its boundaries that from the Russian point of view it was a great mistake to contribute in whatever degree to the outbreak of a war which, even as a Russian-Austrian war, could not be localized around Serbia or in the Balkans and which in consequence of the existing system of alliances, was to become a European war.

An even greater mistake was the unconsidered action of Austria-Hungary. The numerous nationalities which composed that empire, though not dissatisfied enough to disrupt the monarchy in time of peace, were not satisfied enough to obediently suffer the hardships of a war over an issue in which they were not really interested. Nor were they willing to fight against countries with which many of them were in sympathy—frequently against their own kinsmen—or to sacrifice themselves for an indispensable ally to whose policy most of them were completely opposed. In 1914 it was not easy to foresee that under such conditions the war, which lasted much longer than was expected, would lead to a complete disintegration of the monarchy which otherwise could have been avoided. But it was much easier to anticipate that in any case, even in the case of victory, that war, which was impossible without the backing of Germany's so much stronger military might, would result in a complete subordination of the Habsburg to the Hohenzollern Empire, intolerable to the non-German nationalities and therefore undoing all the achievements of the gradual reorganization of the Danubian monarchy in the direction of multinational federalism.

Without again discussing here the whole problem of Germany's war guilt—which was not exclusive but was certainly very heavy—or the question as to what extent Hohenzollern imperialism was identified with German nationalism, it must be recognized that Germany's chances in the war were much greater than those of the other empires. But her victory would have meant complete control of at least that *Mitteleuropa* which in the German interpretation also included the whole non-German East Central Europe, and therefore the eventual domination by the Germans of all nationalities of that region, on whatever side they might have been fighting or rather had been obliged to fight in the war. Here, however, another conclusion is even more important.

Whatever the evils of the frequently excessive nationalism of these comparatively small peoples of East Central Europe, whatever their own mistakes and their diplomatic rivalries amongst themselves, it was *not* that nationalism which was responsible for the end of the period of relative peace which Europe had enjoyed before 1914. On the contrary it was big-power imperialism, combined with the nationalism of the ruling nations in two of the empires, which after so many other crises, only precariously appeased, so intensified the crisis after the Sarajevo murder that a local conflict between one of the empires and one of the small national states evolved into a world war. The formal and immediate cause of that catastrophe and the whole issue of Serbia's independence was soon obliterated, becoming only one of the many unsettled questions of European and world politics which immediately appeared in the war aims of both sides.

The most delicate and controversial of these questions indeed appeared in East Central Europe, but the peoples of that region, after suffering most from all the shortcomings of the European order in the preceding century, now had to suffer more than any others, with the exception of Belgium and the occupied part of France, from a war of unprecedented horror fought to a large extent on their own soil. With the exception of the Balkan nations which had been freed before the outbreak of that war which they entered, one after the other and not without strong pressure from both sides, the peoples of East Central Europe had no initiative of their own, at least in the first phase of a war which, therefore, not without good reason though with misleading implications, is in some quarters called an imperialistic war. Even as far as the Austro-Hungarian and Russian empires are concerned, it was almost exclusively the part of their territories inhabited by non-German and non-Russian peoples which was a badly devastated battlefield, much larger than that on the Western front.

It was therefore just compensation that this time the peoples which at the beginning of the war were practically helpless under their foreign rulers were not deceived in their expectations that after the failure of their revolutions a European war would be a chance for liberation. The mere fact that the empires, with which they were incorporated and which for such a long time had cooperated, were now fighting each other, increased that chance, although the immediate consequence was much fratricidal fighting for those peoples which were subject to two or more of the hostile powers. At the same time this brought about great difficulty in deciding to which side these peoples should give their real sympathy. As usual, the case of the Poles was typical though not unique. In the course of the war Russia would cease to be an ally of the democracies of Western Europe, which the great American democracy would join instead. This was of course impossible to foresee at the beginning. Yet it was only then, in the third year, that the war turned into a struggle between imperialism, represented by Germany only, Austria-Hungary making desperate efforts for a separate peace, and national self-determination as the legitimate form of nationalism was now being called.

Although the idea of equal rights for all nations was used even before in the war propaganda of both sides, it was only in the case of the Poles that in the first month of the war efforts were already being made by both to win their sympathies by rather vague promises of liberation or autonomy and unification. Thus the same question, which through the partitions of old Poland had marked the beginning of a period more than one hundred years long, when the history of the submerged East Central European peoples was nothing but the resistance of their growing nationalism against imperialistic domination, was reopened at the very beginning of another period in which the national rights of almost all these peoples were to triumph at least temporarily. But even the Polish question, in spite of the formation of Polish legions under Joseph Piłsudski which as in the days of Napoleon fought for the freedom of their country in conjunction with foreign forces, made little progress until the very character of the war was basically altered.

PART VI

TWENTY YEARS OF FREEDOM

20

THE CONSEQUENCES OF WORLD WAR I

TOWARD NATIONAL SELF-DETERMINATION

In the study of contemporary history, beginning with World War I, East Central Europe is indeed no longer neglected but on the contrary it frequently receives special attention because the new Europe which emerged from the turmoil seemed particularly "new" in the East Central region. The facts are therefore sufficiently known but the interpretation usually suffers from a few misconceptions. The first of these results from insufficient knowledge of the earlier history of the whole area. Most of the so-called "new" states which reappeared after the European war had a long tradition going back to the Middle Ages and were divided among the neighboring empires only at later dates. Hence the idea of granting these nations the rights of self-determination was no artificial innovation at all but naturally developed in the course of the war as the only fair basis for a just peace.

It will, however, remain President Wilson's lasting merit that he gave clear expression to that idea which had been rather vaguely in the air, and that he requested, at least in principle, its universal application, whereas before it had been dependent on mere political expediency. At the beginning, each side, particularly among the empires in the eastern part of Europe, promised "liberation" only to those nationalities which were under the rule of an opponent. They continued, however, to consider the problems of the nationalities in their own countries a purely internal question where few if any concessions were envisaged.

The whole issue passed from the sphere of propaganda warfare to that of concrete realization as soon as foreign territories were occupied by one of the empires. When Russia invaded Austrian Galicia in the fall of 1914 and held most of it until the spring offensive of the Central Powers in the following year, she declared at least the eastern part of that province to be an old "Russian" land, ignoring, as usual, the very existence of a separate Ukrainian nation and limiting the Polish question to promises of self-government under the czar for what the Russians considered ethnographically purely Polish territories. When the Russians had to evacuate not only their temporary conquest but also precisely the purely Polish territories which they had possessed before the war, Germany and Austria-Hungary had in turn to decide how their equally undetermined promises were to be honored. After dividing the former kingdom of Poland, as it was created by the Congress of Vienna, into a German zone of occupation, which was badly exploited, and an Austro-Hungarian one where mostly Polish officials were used, the two emperors at last, on November 5, 1916, issued a proclamation announcing the re-establishment of an "independent" Polish state.

However, that new kingdom without a king was to be limited in its real independence by rather undefined military and economic ties with the "liberating" empires, and the whole problem of its frontiers was left in suspense. Germany never thought of giving up even the smallest part of Prussian Poland, but rather of a revision of the prewar frontier in her favor. Simultaneously Austria granted a larger degree of autonomy to Galicia, but that promise had the obvious implication that this province would remain outside the restored kingdom. The so-called Austro-Polish solution, that is, the connection of a Polish kingdom including Galicia with a reorganized, truly federalized Habsburg monarchy, was never seriously supported by Austria, hardly favored by an otherwise friendly Hungary which feared for the principle of dualism, and always opposed by Germany. The latter had no clear program as to the future of the Russian provinces east of Congress Poland, which were also occupied in the later part of 1915, approximately to the line of historic Poland's second partition. When they entered it, the Germans would call Wilno a Polish city, but they would also play off against the Poles those Lithuanians who were permitted to organize a national council in that same city. At the same time they would consider the possibility of uniting with the Hohenzollern Empire, under the appearance of autonomy, all the Baltic lands, including Lithuania.

So far as the planned kingdom of Poland was concerned, the Germans were disappointed that the mobilization which they announced there had no success at all, and that even the Polish legions which played a remarkable part in the offensive against Russia refused to serve under German control. The crisis which in July, 1917 led to the imprisonment of Piłsudski, whose partisans went underground in a "Polish Military Organization" (POW), was softened through the gradual formation of a Polish administration in the kingdom but it was not before October, 1917, that a Council of Regency, composed of three prominent Poles, was placed at the helm. This and other concessions of the occupying powers were, however, already influenced by a great change in the approach to the Polish problem which meantime had taken place in the allied camp.

Russia had, of course, immediately protested against the proclamation of an independent Poland by the German invaders, and the Western Allies, including France, in spite of her traditional sympathies for Poland, continued to recognize the Russian point of view that the Polish question was an internal problem of the empire of the czars where, however, even the discussions regarding Poland's autonomy after her reconquest were making no progress. On the contrary, the Allies became more and more interested in the nationalities of the Habsburg Empire. They were particularly interested in the Czechs, whose exiled leaders, Thomas G. Masaryk and Edward Beneš, were making very successful propaganda in the West in favor of a total disruption of that empire. The other peoples of the monarchy were also in a state of unrest, evidenced both at home in political trials, and in the Parliament when it was reopened in May, 1917, and abroad where representatives of these peoples participated in various congresses of "oppressed nationalities." The participation of Italy in the war (from May, 1915) and Rumania (from August, 1916), both of which claimed Austro-Hungarian territories on ethnic grounds, contributed to the decision to make the liberation of the various nationalities of the Dual Monarchy one of the allied war aims.

That point was therefore included in the peace conditions formulated by the Allies in January, 1917, in reply to President Wilson's appeal for peace negotiations. Insisting on a breakup not only of the Ottoman but also of the Habsburg Empire, the Coalition demanded the liberation of "Italians, Slavs, Rumanians, and Czechoslovaks from foreign domination," in addition to their initial claim for a restoration of the invaded countries, Belgium in the west, and Serbia and

Montenegro in the east. The general reference to "Slavs" in the enumeration of the nationalities of Austria-Hungary was rather confusing, since the Slavic Czechoslovaks were mentioned separately. It allowed the omission of those Slavs whose "liberation" Russia considered her exclusive business, and it avoided the name of Yugoslavs to which the Italians objected, opposed as they were to the union of the Croats and Slovenes with Serbia.

They were also opposed to a separate peace with Austria-Hungary which would have saved the monarchy and which was therefore the objective of the new emperor, Charles I. Soon after succeeding Francis Joseph I, who died on November 21, 1916, he started secret negotiations which continued through the first half of the following year but which had little chance of success because of the intimate connection of the Austro-Hungarian armed forces with the Germans in a close alliance which had many supporters among the military and political leaders of the monarchy. The internal nationality problems were hardly touched upon in these negotiations, both sides being more interested in the solution of the western issues. In the meantime, however, peace programs inspired by a real concern with the aspirations of the peoples, whether in the West where comparatively minor territorial changes regarding Alsace-Lorraine and the Italo-Austrian border were involved, or in the East where a basic political reconstruction was needed, were being prepared by President Wilson and Pope Benedict XV.

It is significant that in both these programs the first concrete application of the right of self-determination was recommended in the case of Poland. Already on January 22, 1917, when the President of the United States, still neutral, stressed the points on which in his opinion there was a general agreement, he declared that Poland should be both united, as promised by the Russians, and independent, as proclaimed by the Central empires. And in his message of the first of August of the same year, the Pope was particularly specific with regard to the restoration of the historic Polish Kingdom.

The Pope's suggestions were disregarded and he had no occasion to enter into further details. Wilson's position, however, was of paramount importance since it had become obvious that America's interference would decide the European War which was now turning into a real world war. Wilson's peace plan was concretely defined in his famous Fourteen Points of January 8, 1918. The general principles on which these points were based were explained in his address of the eleventh of February, and in some other speeches of the same year. Demanding that "the utmost satisfaction" should be given to "all well-defined national aspirations," he made it quite clear that in his opinion self-determination was not to be an absolute rule and ought to be applied "without introducing new or perpetuating old elements of discord and antagonism." Therefore the changes which he requested in the points dealing with individual countries or regions were rather moderate. Again it was only in the case of Poland that the erection of an independent state which had not existed in the prewar period was recommended with even more details. With regard to Austria-Hungary, whose place among the nations he wished to see "safeguarded and assured," Wilson's original program was limited to "the freest opportunity of autonomous development" for all her peoples, and similar words were used with reference to the non-Turkish nationalities still under Ottoman rule. The Balkan states already liberated in the preceding century were of course to be restored, like the occupied territories in Western Europe, and their relations were to be based upon both history and nationality.

As far as the eastern part of Europe was concerned, the questions affecting Russia were decisive. But except for the Polish question, which was dealt with separately, the longest of the Fourteen Points, dedicated to Russia, did not at all touch upon the problems of her nationalities. Instead, it stressed her right to the evacuation of all Russian territories and to "the independent determination of her own political development and national policy." In order to understand the careful restraint in suggesting the treatment of Russia, it must be remembered that the President's address was made in the midst of the Russian Revolution when the negotiations for a separate peace between the Soviets and the Central powers had just started.

Under such conditions, the fate of the various peoples which had been under czarist rule could hardly be determined by the Western Allies. In the Danubian monarchy a revolution much less violent and radical than the Russian broke out only at the very end of the war. But the disintegration of the Habsburg Empire was another internal process which created accomplished facts before the peace conference had met.

THE DISINTEGRATION OF THE RUSSIAN AND
AUSTRO-HUNGARIAN EMPIRES

In spite of the basic difference between the Russian and the Austro-Hungarian revolutions, they have at least one thing in common : they were made possible and to a large extent provoked by the failures of the two respective governments in the conduct of a war for which these governments were at least partly responsible. In Russia the realization of these failures came much earlier and therefore the fall of czardom came as early as March, 1917.

That change of regime was, however, not yet necessarily a disintegration of the empire. It is true that the overthrow of the government had been preceded by the loss of large territories, occupied by the enemy and unwilling ever to come back under Russian rule. But the very fact that a substantial part of the empire's non-Russian population was thus already separated from its main body, made the revolution of 1917, similar in this respect to that of 1905, primarily a struggle for constitutional reform and social change rather than an insurrection of oppressed nationalities.

Therefore the first of the two revolutions, which must be clearly distinguished in the Russian crisis of 1917, after establishing a truly democratic provisional government did not give sufficient attention to the nationalities problem. Only with regard to Poland did the new regime almost at once, on the thirtieth of March, make a formal declaration recognizing the right of the Polish people to the creation of an independent state. But at that moment the territory where the Poles "constitute a majority of the population," was already beyond Russia's control, and even then the new Poland was invited to join Russia in a "free military union." The Poles were no longer prepared, however, to accept any limitations of their independence. Complete independence was now the goal of the Finns, too. They were exasperated by the severe repressions that had taken place before 1917, while the provisional Russian government was merely prepared to restore Finland's autonomy. In July it rejected the bill of the Finnish Diet defining the terms under which the country should receive complete freedom.

At the same time serious difficulties arose from the unexpected development of a separatist movement among the Ukrainians who were by far the most numerous nationality which in its great majority still remained in the unoccupied part of the empire. Immediately after the outbreak of the March Revolution, the prominent historian, Michael Hrushevsky, who already as a professor in Lwów, Galicia, had greatly contributed to the rise of Ukrainian nationalism, was elected president of the Central Council (*Rada*) which the parties working for the Ukraine's independence set up as a provisional administrative body. At the beginning of April when a national convention was convoked in Kiev, that council at first claimed only the autonomy of the Ukraine which was formally proclaimed in the *Rada's* first "Universal" of the twenty-third of June. Although a general secretariat was created at the same time to serve as an executive organ, with Volodymir Vynnychenko as prime minister, the new state still seemed ready to enter into some kind of federation with Russia.

But the Russian provisional government was not prepared to accept such a federalization of the former empire, and it resented the fact that the Ukrainians, declaring their autonomy, had not waited for the approval of the central authorities. Even when those members of the government who were opposed to negotiations with the *Rada* resigned and Alexander Kerensky replaced Prince Lvov as prime minister, the agreement announced in the second "Universal" of the sixteenth of July did not work satisfactorily. Even the Kerensky regime confirmed the statute of Ukrainian self-government only with reservations, and mutual relations were still confused when on the fateful day of the sixth of November the Bolsheviks seized power and started the second Russian revolution of 1917.

The very next day the third "Universal" of the *Rada* declared the Ukraine a "Ukrainian People's Republic." And although only the fourth "Universal" of January 22, 1918, made it quite clear that this republic was to be a completely "independent, free, sovereign state," the idea of full independence not only for the Ukrainians but also for all nationalities of the former empire had already been officially approved by the Soviet regime on the fifteenth of November. It was then, soon after issuing their first decrees which gave all land to the peasants and promised the immediate conclusion of peace, that the Bolsheviks proclaimed the right of all nationalities to full self-determination, including the right of separating themselves from Russia. And in rapid sequence, one nation after the other took advantage of that right. The autonomous bodies which had been created after the first revolution in Estonia and Latvia declared these countries independent of Russia on the fifteenth and seventeenth of November, respectively, and so did the Finnish Diet on the sixth of December. Even the White Ruthenians or Byelorussians were ready for a similar decision.

One of the reasons why all these peoples were no longer satisfied with autonomy only but had decided upon complete independence was, in addition to the rapid progress of their national movements, the desire to avoid any connection with the Soviet form of government which after a brief democratic interlude was now established in Russia, enforcing its power through ruthless terror. But on the other hand, in spite of the apparent willingness of the Bolsheviks to recognize all these secessions, their policy was from the outset a serious threat to the real freedom of the new states. For they made their astonishing concession to non-Russian nationalism only in the hope that in each liberated nation the Communists would seize control, as they had done in Russia. If necessary, this was to be done with open or disguised Russian support and with a view to joining a future Soviet federation, thus replacing the democratic federation which the first revolution had tried to establish.

There was also, however, another danger which the barely organized new states along Russia's western border had to face. That danger, too, manifested itself in the form of an insincere recognition of their right of self-determination which was granted by Germany. It was under German occupation that the "independent" Kingdom of Poland continued to be organized and that the Lithuanian National Council (*Taryba*) could issue, on December 11, 1917, a first declaration of independence. But at the same time, Lithuania felt herself obliged to request Germany's "protection and assistance" for the restored state. The southern part of Latvia was also under German occupation and the German minorities of the remaining part and of Estonia were eager to establish ties with the German Empire. Even in distant Finland German help seemed necessary to check Russian penetration which was now in Communist form. Most important, however, was the fact that after accepting the Soviet peace proposal on the twenty-seventh of November and concluding an armistice on the fifth of December, representatives of the Central powers opened negotiations with the Soviet Delegation at Brest-Litovsk on the twenty-second of the same month. There both sides played the part of defender of the rights of self-determination with a view to bringing under their exclusive control the nationalities to which that right was to be granted.

None of these nationalities, not even the Poles who under the Council of Regency had formed a regular government with Jan Kucharzewski as prime minister, were admitted to the conference. The Ukrainians, whom the Germans wanted to play off against the Russians, were the only exception. A separate peace treaty was indeed signed with the Ukraine on February 9, 1918, the very day on which Kiev was taken by the Bolsheviks. In spite of that success and of Trotsky's attempt to end the war without concluding any formal peace, another German advance forced the Russians to accept German terms on the third of March. In addition to the Ukraine, Russia had to give up all territories east of a line running from a place north of Riga to the northwestern corner of the Ukraine, whose frontier was fixed only in the West. Thus not only Poland but also Lithuania and a part of Latvia were definitely lost, while the other part, as well as Estonia, was to be evacuated by the Russians, though they renounced their sovereignty there only in a supplementary treaty signed in Berlin on August 27, 1918. In the meantime the Germans, having been asked for assistance by the *Rada*, had occupied the Ukraine and established a puppet government under Hetman Paul Skoropadsky by the end of April. They also prepared the disguised annexation of the "liberated" Baltic lands. Even Lithuania, which on February 16, 1918, issued another, now unrestricted, declaration of independence, a few months later had to invite a German prince to become king, a similar invitation being addressed to a brother-in-law of Wilhelm II by the Finns. Russia also had to recognize the full independence of the Finns. Even earlier she had lost Bessarabia in the south, where at first an autonomous Moldavian republic had been formed. In January, 1918, this government invited Rumanian troops in and voted for union with that kingdom.

Though Rumania was also forced on May 7, 1918, to sign a separate peace with the Central powers which controlled the whole Balkan Peninsula except Greece, and was compelled to make territorial cessions to Austria-Hungary, the internal situation of the Habsburg monarchy was rapidly deteriorating. The last military successes made under German leadership interested the various nationalities much less than the increasing hardships of the long war and the aspirations toward a federalization of the empire which the government failed to satisfy. Already in May, 1917, not only Czech and Yugoslav but also Polish deputies presented a program in the Vienna Parliament which involved a basic reorganization of the empire. Even the most loyal among the Poles were alienated when at Brest-Litovsk a section of Congress Poland was attributed to the Ukraine. The Russian revolutions, especially the second, had little if any repercussions in Austria-Hungary, where even the Marxist Social Democrats were hostile to the Soviet system and where conditions were so much better than they had been in the czarist empire. Much greater was the influence of the activities of Slavic leaders working in exile among the Western powers, which in the course of 1918 granted recognition to Polish and Czechoslovakian national committees. The influence of President Wilson's peace program was also notable.

But since that program originally requested only autonomy for the nationalities of the Danubian monarchy, its existence could have been saved if Charles I had not waited until October 16, 1918, with the announcement that he would transform his empire into a federation, even then reserving the integrity of the kingdom of Hungary. This was only two days before Wilson's answer to the Austro-Hungarian armistice proposal in which he stressed the recognition of independent Czechoslovakia and Yugoslavia. In the course of the second half of October, in view of the complete military collapse of the Central Powers, in all non-German and non-Magyar parts of the monarchy national councils could take over without bloodshed or violence and proceed to the organization of the so-called successor states into which the Habsburg Empire was divided. Furthermore, even the vague promise of federalization had sufficed to make Hungary sever all her ties with Austria except for the personal union, which also ceased to exist when even the German part of Austria declared itself a republic.

EAST CENTRAL EUROPE AT THE PARIS PEACE CONFERENCE

When World War I ended on Armistice Day, November 11, 1918, the empires of the Romanovs, Habsburgs, and Hohenzollerns, which before the war dominated Central and Eastern Europe, with even the free Balkan states in their respective spheres of influence, no longer existed. This was deeply to affect the deliberations of the peace conference which opened in Paris on January 18, 1919. But there was a great difference between the complete disintegration of Russia and Austria-Hungary which followed the fall of their dynasties, and the position of Germany, the main enemy. Here, too, a last-minute revolution had replaced the emperor and all the other monarchs of the minor German states by a republican form of government. But that German Republic, more unified than the empire had been, continued to call itself a Reich, which, far from disintegrating, hoped to reduce as much as possible the territorial losses along its borders, the unavoidable consequence of the acceptance of Wilson's peace program.

It was obvious that in addition to Alsace-Lorraine, these cessions would have to include at least part of that large section of East Central Europe which had been attached to German West Central Europe through the partitions of Poland. Since, however, Wilson's thirteenth point demanded a Polish state, not in the historic boundaries before the partitions but on the territories "inhabited by indisputably Polish populations," the drafting of the new German-Polish frontier required long discussion. The Polish claims were presented to the five big powers, which alone made the decisions in territorial matters, by Roman Dmowski, the chairman of the delegation of Poland which was recognized as an allied power. The other delegate of Poland, the famous pianist, I. J. Paderewski, now prime minister and minister of foreign affairs, had shortly before the conference succeeded in establishing an agreement between the Polish National Committee presided over by Dmowski, the wartime representative of the Poles in the West, and Joseph Pilsudski, the first head of the Polish state, to whom the council of regency had handed over the power in Warsaw after Germany's collapse.

In addition to the Prussian share in the partitions, that is, the provinces of Poznania and West Prussia, the Polish claims also included those territories which came under Prussian domination before the partitions but had remained ethnically and linguistically Polish. These were Upper Silesia and the southern part of East Prussia. Drafting the treaty with Germany, the Big Five decided that plebiscites should be held in two sections of East Prussia. And revising their draft to meet the objections of the German delegation, they replaced their first decision to attribute Upper Silesia to Poland by that of holding another plebiscite there. This was done at the request of the British prime minister, Lloyd George, who also opposed the inclusion into Poland of the predominantly German city of Danzig. Therefore, already in the first draft of the treaty, not only minor frontier areas of Poznania and West Prussia were left to Germany in order to reduce the German minority in the new Poland, but also Danzig, Poland's historic port, which was indispensable for "a free and secure access to the sea" promised to Poland in the thirteenth point, was refused to her and declared a free city under the control of the League of Nations. Special rights were guaranteed to Poland, particularly in the port of Danzig, but that solution was to be a source of permanent friction. Serious troubles also resulted from the plebiscite in Upper Silesia, which was delayed until March, 1921. Since the big powers could not agree on the details of the division of that territory which proved necessary in view of the votes in the individual communes, the problem had to be settled by the League of Nations, which in the Geneva Convention of May 15, 1922, almost three years after the signing of the Versailles Treaty on July 28, 1919, carried out that division in the most objective and careful fashion.

Since the plebiscites in East Prussia, held in July, 1920, at the very moment of Poland's invasion by the Soviets, were in favor of Germany, that whole province, except the Memel region in the northeastern corner, which later went to Lithuania, remained part of the Reich. Such a German enclave east of the Polish province of Pomerania—called by German propaganda a "corridor"—was indeed a permanent threat to Poland's security. Doubtful from the economic and military point of view, the whole settlement of the Polish-German frontier problem—the only part of the Versailles Treaty which concerned East Central Europe—was made with the genuine desire to apply the principle of national self-determination as objectively as possible.

The other treaties prepared and signed at the Paris Peace Conference dealt almost exclusively with problems of East Central Europe. This was true of all of them except for the Treaty of Sèvres which was concluded with Turkey on August 10, 1920, but which was never ratified or enforced, and which was replaced by the Treaty of Lausanne on July 24, 1923. Only the determination of new Turkey's boundaries in Europe, which remained almost unchanged, and the demilitarization of both shores of the Straits, which with Constantinople remained in Turkey's possession in spite of the transfer of her capital to Asiatic Ankara, were of direct interest to East Central Europe. Comparatively small were the territorial changes made in the Treaty of Neuilly, signed on November 27, 1919, with Bulgaria, but that country deeply resented the loss of her access to the Aegean Sea by the cession of Western Thrace to Greece, besides minor cessions to Yugoslavia. Bulgaria had joined the Central powers with a view to regaining her losses of 1913, and now, after another defeat, she suffered an even greater disappointment.

With Albania also restored as an independent country, the situation in the Balkans underwent no basic changes. Fundamental were, on the contrary, the changes in the Danubian region made in the treaties with Austria, on September 10, 1919, at Saint-Germain, and with Hungary, on June 4, 1920, at Trianon, the delay of the latter being largely caused by the Communist seizure of Hungary which lasted from March to August, 1919. Both treaties were much more severe than that of Versailles, but it must be remembered that the most striking change, the replacement of the Habsburg monarchy by a group of completely independent states, had already taken place before any intervention of the peacemakers who therefore had only to fix the boundaries among these states.

Two of them, the new Austria and the new Hungary, were, however, considered a continuation of the former realm of an enemy state which had its share in the responsibilities for the war. Therefore they had to suffer from reparation and disarmament clauses which were to a large extent copied from the Versailles Treaty, as in the case of Bulgaria. In adjusting the principle of national self-determination to military, economic, or any other considerations, the peace conference was inclined to favor those successor states which were considered allies: Italy; the state of the Serbs, Croats, and Slovenes, which after the unification of all the Yugoslavs replaced Serbia and which was also enlarged by the incorporation of Montenegro; Rumania, which had re-entered the war on the allied side in the fall of 1918; and Czechoslovakia, exclusively created out of parts of prewar Austria and Hungary, but whose exiled leaders had succeeded in making her a cobelligerent. Poland was also partly a successor state of the Habsburg monarchy, but since her claims nowhere reached the prospective new boundaries of either Austria or Hungary, she was not interested in the treaties with these countries but only in the controversial problem of dividing among various successor states the territories which in these treaties were formally ceded to the big powers.

A special feature of the Saint-Germain settlement was the inter-diction against the new Austria's joining Germany. That interdiction, included in both the Versailles and the Saint-Germain treaties, might seem a violation of the right to self-determination, since "German Austria," as the new republic wanted to call itself, declared in the original draft of its constitution that it was part of the new federated Germany. But it is doubtful whether the *Anschluss*, as the inclusion of Austria in a greater Germany used to be called, which was favored by many Austrians under the first shock of the breakup of the old Austrian Empire, really was a lasting desire of the majority. Self-determination, the indisputable right to freedom from foreign rule, must not necessarily mean the union of all peoples of similar origin in one state. Finally, such an enlargement of German-controlled West Central Europe would have been some kind of German victory in defeat, dangerous not only for Western, but also particularly for East Central Europe which had just been restored to full freedom.

More questionable from the point of view of self-determination was the inclusion of more than three million Austrian Germans of the Sudeten region in the new Czechoslovakia, although geographically most of that region could hardly have been united with the Austrian republic. Smaller, but more difficult to justify, was the loss of part of German-speaking Tyrol to Italy. On the other hand, the frontier between Austria and the Serb-Croat-Slovene state was at least partly determined by a plebiscite which left to Austria even that southern part of Carinthia where the population was predominantly Slovene. A plebiscite was also eventually held in the Burgenland, the western part of Hungary, which because of its largely German-speaking popu-lation was transferred in the treaties from that country to Austria— a compensation for so many losses which was welcomed by the Aus-trians. Part of the contested region remained with Hungary as a result of the plebiscite.

It was only in the case of that controversy with her former asso-ciate that Hungary's new frontiers were determined by a plebiscite. The Hungarian delegation, when presenting its objections against the Trianon Treaty in an eloquent speech by Count Albert Apponyi, vainly requested such plebiscites in all cases where the historic bound-aries of Hungary, at the same time a geographical unit, were some-times pushed back far into the Hungarian Plain. As a matter of fact, the kingdom, as Hungary continued to call herself though now without a king, lost 71.4 per cent of its territory and about 60 per cent of its population, including three and one-half million Magyars, of whom about 1,800,000 lived in areas contiguous to what remained Hungarian.

Not only did the former autonomous kingdom of Croatia and Slavonia become part of the new Yugoslav state—a change which Hungary was ready to admit though by doing so she lost her access to the sea—but minor frontier regions of Hungary proper were also assigned to that state. The ethnically mixed Banat in southern Hungary was divided between Yugoslavia and Rumania, which in addition to the whole of Transylvania, with its Rumanian majority, also received a few purely Magyar districts, though not all that had been secretly promised to her before she entered the war. Another Rumanian gain, the Bucovina, had formerly been an Austrian province.

Hungary also lost the whole northern part of the kingdom, not only the land inhabited by the Slovaks, who were now united in one state with their near kin, the Czechs, but also the territory between Slovakia and Transylvania where the majority of the population was Ruthenian. For geographical reasons and because the fate of the Ruthenians or Ukrainians on the northern side of the Carpathians still seemed uncertain, this non-Magyar and Slavic part of Hungary was also attached to Czechoslovakia as an autonomous territory, the only case in the peace treaties where the idea of regional autonomy was formally introduced. The southern boundary of the Carpathian region included in the Czechoslovak state was partly extended as far as the upper Danube, another reason why the Treaty of Trianon created among the Hungarians a "revisionism" second only to that of the Germans.

THE DEFENSE AGAINST SOVIET RUSSIA

In spite of five peace treaties signed at various places in the Paris region, the conference of 1919–1920 left much business unfinished. Among the controversies regarding the repartition of formerly Austro-Hungarian territories, the Italo-Yugoslav dispute about the port of Fiume (Rjeka) caused the most serious crisis during the conference, and was not finally settled before 1924 when Italy annexed the city. The situation in East Central Europe was even more affected by the Polish-Czechoslovak dispute over Cieszyn (Těšín) in Austrian Silesia and three small frontier districts in former Hungary. The decision of the great powers on July 28, 1920, which rather favored Czechoslovakia, left much resentment in Poland, especially since it was made at the most critical moment of the Russian advance.

In general, however, it was the Russian problem which, being beyond the possibility of action at the Paris Conference, made the whole peace settlement incomplete. As a matter of fact the war lasted in Eastern Europe for two more years after the armistice in the West, and it was not concluded before the series of peace treaties which the border states, liberated from Russian rule, signed with the Soviet government in 1920 and 1921.

On November 13, 1918, immediately after Germany's collapse, the Bolsheviks, denouncing the Brest-Litovsk Treaty, invited all peoples of Central Europe to join a union of Soviet republics. Trying to enforce such a solution, the Russians advanced in the footsteps of the withdrawing and disintegrating German occupation forces. In spite of the civil war raging in Russia and of limited and hesitating intervention by the Western Allies, the Red Army already proved strong enough to seriously threaten all smaller neighbors. These extended from Finland and the Baltic states in the north, where Communist penetration created internal troubles that were exploited by the remaining German forces, to Rumania in the south, whose reannexation of Bessarabia was never recognized by the Russians and was sanctioned by the Allies only on October 28, 1920. The main drive of Soviet Russia was, however, directed against Poland, the gateway to the center of the Continent, which had already been invaded at the very beginning of 1919 when the Paris Conference was going to meet.

Since all attempts of the Western Allies to negotiate simultaneously with both the Bolsheviks and the counterrevolutionary forces in Russia, or with either of them, ultimately failed, the Conference felt unable to make any decision regarding the territories of the former Russian Empire. Even in the case of Poland, whose independence had been recognized by the last legitimate allied Russian government, it did not seem possible to fix her eastern frontier whose determination the Versailles Treaty left to a later decision of the great powers. At the Paris Conference only a provisional line was indicated on December 8, 1919, up to which Poland was authorized to establish her regular administration at once, her rights to territories east of that line, which corresponded to Russia's frontier after the third partition of Poland, being expressly reserved.

In these territories the fight against the Red Army was continuing. Pushing it gradually back, the Poles had on April 19, 1919, already liberated Wilno, which the Lithuanian government, withdrawing to Kaunas, had left under Soviet pressure at the end of 1918. Three days later Piłsudski, who favored a federal solution of Poland's relations with Lithuania, White Ruthenia, and the Ukraine, promised all peoples of the former grand duchy of Lithuania full self-determination through a vote which, however, had to be postponed until the end of the war. Particularly confused was the situation among the Ukrainians. In the formerly Russian territories, the national Ukrainian government which had retaken power after the defeat of the Germans was in a desperate struggle against Communist forces, while in Eastern Galicia the struggle between Ukrainians and Poles which had started after the fall of the Habsburg monarchy ended in June, 1919, with a Polish victory, but without any final decision of the Peace Conference as to the future of that territory.

A decisive turn in the Polish-Russian war seemed to come in the spring of 1920 after the failure of armistice negotiations. In the north where Estonia and Latvia had at last succeeded in liberating themselves from both Russian and German invaders, the Poles helped their Latvian neighbors to regain the region of Dünaburg (Daugavpils), and with the Ukrainian government of Petlyura on the twenty-first of April they concluded an agreement which left Eastern Galicia and Western Volhynia to Poland. Poland was to assist in liberating the Ukraine proper from Soviet rule and in creating an independent allied state there. On the eighth of May Polish and Ukrainian forces entered Kiev.

The Russians, however, reacted with two counteroffensives. One of these was on the northern, White Ruthenian sector of the front which, after being first stopped by the Poles, advanced in July under Tukhachevsky in the direction of Wilno. Another was in the south under Budenny. After retaking Kiev, this thrust soon entered Eastern Galicia but without reaching Lwów. On the twelfth of July the Soviets signed a peace treaty with the Lithuanians granting them the possession of Wilno, but with the reservation that the Red Army could use that region as a basis for its further advance toward Warsaw.

The day before, the British foreign secretary, Lord Curzon, sent a note to the Soviet government suggesting an armistice on conditions which the Polish prime minister, Władysław Grabski, after asking for Allied help at the Spa Conference, had accepted under Lloyd George's pressure. Both Polish and Russian forces would stop thirty miles west and east of the line drafted in Paris in December of the preceding year, and peace negotiations conducted in London would settle all controversial problems. Through an error, the armistice line, which in Galicia was to follow the actual front, was described in the note as leaving all of Eastern Galicia on the Russian side. But the so-called Curzon line, thus extended as far as the Carpathians, never came into force even as an armistice demarcation line since the Soviets rejected the British proposal.

Nevertheless the Poles did not receive the Allied help promised to them in that case, and only a few French officers under General Weygand came to Warsaw to assist the Polish general staff in organizing the defense of the country. At the very moment when the Bolsheviks were already at the gates of the capital, which was protected only by a small army of volunteers under General Stanisław Haller, and when a Communist puppet government was already prepared to take over, a bold strategic plan of Piłsudski turned the tide on the fifteenth of August. Through an attack from the south Piłsudski encircled the Russian forces which General Władysław Sikorski was pushing back north of Warsaw, and soon the Poles were again advancing on the whole front. Western Europe, which Tukhachevsky had hoped to reach by pushing through Poland, was saved. After another defeat in the Niemen region near Lida, a Soviet delegation came to Riga where first, on the twelfth of October, an armistice, and then, on March 18, 1921, a peace treaty, was signed.

It was signed by three independent Soviet republics: the Russian, White Ruthenian, and Ukrainian, thus creating the fiction that the latter two nations had reached their self-determination under native Communist regimes. This was a blow to their real national movements whose leaders now had to go into exile. Some White Ruthenian and Ukrainian minorities were left on the Polish side of the new border, a line of compromise which in the south corresponded to the agreement with Petlyura and in general followed the line of the second partition of Poland.

In the north the controversial problem of Wilno was left to an agreement between Poland and Lithuania, which unfortunately was never reached. After clashes between the armies of these two countries during the Polish advance, their conflict was brought before the League of Nations and an armistice was signed at Suwałki on October 7, 1920, leaving Wilno on the Lithuanian side of a line which was supposed to end the fighting on part of the front. Fearing that this would prejudice the fate of the city and her predominantly Polish population, Polish forces of local origin under General Żeligowski, advancing on another sector of the front, occupied Wilno two days later. Various solutions suggested by the League, which returned to the idea of a Polish-Lithuanian federation, were not accepted, a plebiscite proved too difficult to organize, and finally a diet assembled in Wilno in February, 1922, after elections held with the participation of 64 per cent of the population, voted almost unanimously in favor of an incorporation of the whole region with Poland. It was, however, only on March 15, 1923, that the conference of ambassadors of the great powers, recognizing the eastern frontier of Poland which was fixed at Riga, at the same time accepted a provisional demarcation line, which had left the Wilno region to Poland, as her boundary with Lithuania.

The protest of Lithuania which continued to consider herself in a state of war with Poland created serious tension between two liberated countries with so many common interests. But, in general, conditions in East Central Europe seemed at last settled, not only in the western and southern sector where the Paris Conference had planned the peace but also in the northeast where the non-Russian successor states of the former czarist empire had to defend themselves, almost exclusively by their own forces, against the Soviet form of Russian imperialism. Most of them succeeded in doing so, because after the Polish victory of 1920, the independence of the three small Baltic republics was also assured, as well as that of Finland which at last got her peace treaty with the Soviets in October of that year, almost simultaneously with the Riga armistice. Only White Ruthenia, now called Byelorussia, and the Ukraine were sovietized at the same time, and they soon had to experience that Communist control meant reunion with Russia in the U.S.S.R. which was created two years later. They were therefore left outside the new East Central Europe, the belt of free nations between that Communist federation under Russian leadership and a reduced but still powerful Germany.

In Eastern Europe, ruled from Moscow where the capital of Russia was retransferred from St. Petersburg (Petrograd, now called Leningrad), peace was also established in the fall of 1920. What remained of the non-Communist Russian forces, which never were in any real cooperation with those of the non-Russian nationalities, lost their last chance in the civil war when the Soviets made peace with the border states. These forces were evacuated from the Crimea, as the interventionist forces of the Western Allies in various parts of Russia had also been much earlier. The issue now was whether the new Russia would reconcile herself with her territorial losses and whether communism would give up its idea of westward expansion, or whether the U.S.S.R. would come to an understanding with Germany, directed against East Central Europe.

21

THE PEOPLES OF EAST CENTRAL EUROPE
BETWEEN THE WARS

RECORDS OF INDEPENDENCE

The liberation of the East Central European nations, which started in the Balkans in the nineteenth century, was not completed before 1918. It was challenged twenty years later. And since in the northern section the defense against Soviet Russia required two more years of hard struggle, while in the south the final peace with Turkey was only signed in 1923, not even a full score of years was granted to these nations to enjoy their independence in undisturbed constructive activities. Furthermore, during the last five years they were exposed to totalitarian pressure from both the west and the east. Without taking all this into consideration, the achievements of the liberated peoples during so short a period of independence are usually underestimated and their almost unavoidable failures and mistakes are overemphasized.

An additional difficulty which that group of nations had to face resulted from the fact that some of them had been treated in the peace settlement as former enemies so that their basic community of vital interests with the others was hard to realize for either side. Nevertheless, it seems most appropriate to review the internal development of all of them in a strictly geographical order.

(A) *Finland.* The Western world showed the most sympathetic understanding to Finland, and it was not only because of the reliability of that country in paying all foreign debts that such a sympathy was well deserved. In the peace treaty with Soviet Russia the Finns received access to the Arctic Ocean at Petsamo but gave up their claims to Eastern Karelia although the promised autonomy of that region had no likelihood of being respected under the Communist regime. After the settlement of a dispute with Sweden over the Åland Islands the following year, Finland concentrated on her internal problems.

A particularly urgent one was the historic antagonism between the Finnish and the Swedish populations. The Åland Islands were entirely Swedish-speaking, and though the decision of the League of Nations left them to Finland, that country had to grant them an autonomy which proved fully satisfactory. In the main part of the republic the Swedes were a small minority which, however, had occupied in the past, not only in the long centuries of Swedish rule, a position of cultural and economic supremacy which was resented by modern Finnish nationalism. Implementing the constitution of 1919, the language law of 1922 decided that all districts with a linguistic minority of more than 10 per cent would be considered bilingual in administration and education. That fair compromise worked very well. And when, in addition to the University of Helsinki, which now became completely Finnish, two new free universities were founded in the old capital, Åbo (Turku), one of them was Swedish. Both ethnic groups shared not only in the cultural but also in the equally remarkable economic and financial progress of the country which, while primarily agricultural, also successfully developed its industries, particularly timber, paper, and pulp.

Finland's deep-rooted democracy found expression in a sound constitution which was based upon her traditional institutions. It tried to combine the western European and American systems, and has remained basically unchanged since 1919. The only real difficulty came from a small Communist party which was so obviously under Russian influence that it was twice disbanded, first after the civil war and again in 1923, but only to reappear under other names, winning from eighteen to twenty-three seats in the Diet. When in 1929 the Communist youth movement started a violent propaganda campaign, a rightist reaction appeared among the rural population in the Lapua province. The repressive measures which the Lapua movement wanted to enforce were, however, rejected by the Social Democratic party, and though after the elections of 1930 the right had a small majority in the Diet and its leader, Peter Svinhufvud, was elected president (1931–1937), the Finnish people as a whole remained opposed to violence from either side. An abortive revolt of the Lapua movement ended, therefore, in its disappearance from Finnish politics; Communism, too, once more outlawed in 1930, lost all chances when the economic crisis, affecting Finland in connection with the world depression, was overcome in 1934.

Trade agreements were concluded with Britain and other western countries. The defense of the country was well insured under the Conscription Act of 1932. In close cooperation with the whole Scandinavian group of northern peoples, Finland enjoyed an undisturbed prosperity until the outbreak of World War II. In the last elections, held in 1939 before the war, the Patriotic People's party, the only one to show some antidemocratic inclinations, obtained only 4 per cent of the seats in the Diet, where the Socialist Democratic labor party held 42.5 per cent, and the Agrarians or small farmers, cooperating with the former after 1936, held 28 per cent.

Particularly remarkable was the development of the cooperative movement which by 1939 handled some 30 per cent of the total retail trade and almost one half of the internal grain trade. An agrarian reform which started at the very beginning of Finland's independence helped the renters of land to become independent landowners, and over a hundred thousand new holdings were established by 1935. The almost four millions of Finnish people were certainly among the happiest in Europe, where their country of more than 132,000 square miles was one of the largest. Though still sparsely populated, it had great possibilities for further progress.

(B) *Estonia.* Closest kin of the Finns, the Estonians, living on the other side of the Gulf of Finland, less than 1,200,000 in number, constituted one of the smallest European countries. Estonia is even smaller—with its little more than 18,000 square miles—than the other two Baltic republics with which it had so much in common. Like Latvia, where the analogies are particularly striking, Estonia really was a new state, but both proved equally successful in that first experience of independent national government.

Estonia, too, had her minorities problem, almost 10 per cent of the total population being German, Russian, or Jewish. But it was in that country that in 1925 an unusually liberal law of cultural autonomy granted to any minority group of more than 3,000 people the right to set up its own council for educational, cultural, and charitable matters. The Estonian majority, which in the past had never enjoyed full opportunity even in the cultural sphere, rapidly developed its whole intellectual life. The city of Tartu (formerly Dorpat), where the old German-Russian university now became a center of native culture, proved to be equally as important as the capital Tallin (Reval) with its old port. The numerically small but culturally prominent Ger-

man minority suffered only from a radical land reform which, however, was long overdue, since 58 per cent of the land had been in the
hands of landowners, mostly of German origin, whose average holding exceeded 5,300 acres.

In spite of the difficulties which resulted from the distribution of
those large estates to peasant landholders and tenants, and in spite of
reduced trade relations with the Russian hinterland, which were
replaced by intensified trade with Germany and Britain, Estonia,
with her well-balanced budget and careful management was showing
persistent progress in agriculture, commerce, and industry, thanks
also to her valuable oil shales. A foreign loan authorized by the
League of Nations made it possible to stabilize the currency on a
sound basis with all terms of the agreement strictly fulfilled.

The political life of the country started under a constitution of June
15, 1920, as thoroughly democratic and inspired by Western models
as in all the other liberated countries. The same critics who blame
some of these countries, including Estonia, for having later revised
their constitutions in an authoritarian sense have serious doubts
whether the Western party system was suited to local conditions. In
Estonia, where from the beginning the executive was strengthened by
making the prime minister at the same time president of the republic,
democracy, based upon a long list of guaranteed rights of all citizens,
could have worked very well. But in December, 1924, a small though
troublesome Communist group, which was inspired by Moscow, organized an open revolt that had to be suppressed by the army.

It was under the impression of that danger that a movement for
constitutional reform started. A group of ex-servicemen called "liberators" tried to enforce a change in the electoral system, a reduction
of the powers of Parliament and an extension of those of the president.
After being defeated in two earlier referendums, these rightists won
the elections of 1933 and under a new constitution Constantine Päts
assumed the presidency. But in March, 1934, Päts himself, alarmed
by the extreme trends among the "liberators," arrested many of their
leaders and soon proclaimed a cooperative system with a single government party.

The reforms of the following years resulted eventually, in 1938,
in a constitution which was at least a partial return to democracy,
with a bicameral assembly, as approved by the referendum of 1936.
The first chamber was to be freely elected, the other nominated by the

president, the corporations, and the churches. In April, 1938, Päts was re-elected president by a very large majority, and if more time had been granted to free Estonia, her latest constitutional experiment could have been truly instructive. Even so, when the new world crisis started, conditions seemed fairly settled, with the extremists of both right and left under control.

(C) *Latvia*. Similar were the developments in Latvia, from which Estonia was separated by a frontier that strictly followed the ethnographic boundary and was fixed by common agreement. In that southern, somewhat larger republic of 25,409 square miles, the majority of the population of more than a million and a half was of the Baltic race. But in addition to these Latvians, there were about 25 per cent of minorities which, in addition to Germans, Russians, and Jews, as in Estonia, also included White Ruthenian natives and Polish landowners in the province of Letgale, former Polish Livonia. In Latvia, too, the policy toward these minorities was in general tolerant, as also in the religious sphere where the Catholics of that predominantly Lutheran country had their archbishop in Riga.

That historic capital of Livonia now became a flourishing center of Latvian culture which, like the Estonian, had its first chance for free development. The old Institute of Technology was transformed into a large Latvian university. But the Germans who lost their social predominance through a radical land reform, just as in Estonia, could develop their cultural organizations, including the Herder Institute, which was practically a free university. Through the large attendance at schools of all grades illiteracy was greatly reduced, art and literature were encouraged on the basis of the old interest in native folklore and archaeology, and great efforts were made to promote intellectual relations with the Western countries. The same can be said about the economic development, though Soviet Russia made little use of the privileges granted to her in the great port of Riga. The Latvian merchant marine of some two hundred thousand tons contributed to trade relations with the West, especially Germany and Britain, as in Estonia, to which agricultural as well as the growing industrial products were exported.

In internal politics Latvia, too, went through a constitutional crisis similar to that in Estonia. The original constitution of 1922 went even further in assuring the supremacy of the legislature. This was a one-chamber parliament (Seima) in which, through a very liberal system of proportional elections, about twenty different parties were represented. Particularly strong was the opposition between the Nationalists, who wanted to check any possible Communist danger in advance, and who were supported by a strong military society of "civil guards," and the Social Democrats, who had their own armed organization under the name of "Workers' Sporting Club."

In order to avoid a violent clash between these two opposed camps, Prime Minister K. Ulmanis, the leader of the Peasant Party, dissolved parliament on May 15, 1934, forbade party activities, and with the support of the civil guards established some kind of dictatorship until in 1936 he was elected president and could proceed to a reform of the constitution. This was completed two years later through a "Law of Defense of the State." Just as in Estonia, the power of the executive, and especially that of the president, was greatly increased, and in addition to the Seima, a state council, based upon the conception of a corporate state, came into existence. That new body was composed of an economic council, with all professions organized in national chambers similar to the old guilds, and of a cultural council, with special representation for art and literature. Education and cooperative enterprises were to be systematically encouraged. That far-reaching reform had, however, no more time to prove its efficiency or to revive Latvian democracy than did the revised Estonian constitution of the same year.

(D) *Lithuania.* There are also some analogies between the two sister republics into which old Livonia was divided and the third of the three Baltic states, Lithuania. This country was somewhat smaller than Latvia, 21,553 square miles, but with a larger population of more than two million. These figures do not include the Wilno region which the Lithuanians continued to claim from Poland, but they do include the territory of Memel (*Klaipeda* in Lithuanian), the corner of East Prussia which the Versailles Treaty separated from Germany because of the predominantly Lithuanian population of the countryside but did not finally attribute to any other state. Even after the formal recognition of the new Lithuanian Republic by the Allies in January, 1921, that territory, with the city and port of Memel, Lithuania's only possible outlet to the sea, remained for two more years under Allied control with a French garrison and administration. The Germans of the city wanted the whole region to be made a free state similar to Danzig, but local Lithuanian organizations worked for a union with

Lithuania, and with the assistance of volunteers from the neighboring republic, seized the whole area between January 10 and 15, 1923, making it an autonomous unit within the Lithuanian state.

It was not before the eighth of May of the following year, however, that the Conference of Ambassadors in Paris, after an investigation on the spot by a commission of the League of Nations, finally recognized Lithuania's sovereignty over the Memel territory and in a special convention guaranteed its local autonomy. The solution was more favorable to Lithuania than was that of the similar Danzig problem to Poland, but even so it resulted in a permanent tension between the Lithuanian authorities and German parties and organizations in the city. After 1933 this tension was encouraged by the Nazi regime in Germany and soon resulted in a conspiracy and the trial of more than a hundred Nazi leaders in 1935.

The Memel problem, vital for Lithuania's trade relations, and the unsettled relations with Poland, both of which were to lead to serious crises on the eve of World War II, absorbed the attention of the Lithuanian government throughout the whole period of independence, but nevertheless the constructive achievements of these less than twenty years were as remarkable as in the other Baltic states. In spite of all that Lithuania had in common with both of them, and particularly with the Latvian neighbors of common race and similar language, conditions were different in at least two respects. Geographically, the new Lithuania had no common frontier with the Soviet Union, from which it was separated by Polish territory. Therefore there was less danger of Communist penetration than in Estonia and Latvia. Historically, Lithuania, though limited to her ethnic area, had a medieval tradition of independence in the large and powerful grand duchy, which the other two did not possess. Furthermore, the long centuries of union between that grand duchy and Poland had left lasting traces which were affected but not eliminated by the conflict between the two restored nations.

Instead of the German minority, so important in Estonia and Latvia but non-existent in Lithuania in spite of her common frontier with Germany, there was a Polish minority of similar importance in the cultural and social field. Exact figures are hardly available, however, since that minority, more numerous than the Russian or Jewish, was mostly composed of Polonized Lithuanians who were not recognized by official statistics as a separate group. Like the German Balts, these Polish or Polonized landowners suffered from the agrarian reform. Eager to eliminate the Polish cultural supremacy of the past, the new Lithuania based her culture on ethnic and linguistic grounds.

In that respect the independent republic proved eminently successful. In Kaunas, the *de facto* capital though the constitution continued to claim Vilnius (the Polish Wilno) as the historic capital, an entirely new Lithuanian university was founded at once. This developed into an outstanding cultural center. A number of other educational and scholarly institutions in the same flourishing city and in a few other places were also established. Literature and art, particularly painting and music, were making excellent progress, and a purely Lithuanian culture, prepared by the national revival in the preceding century, was at last definitely created. Equally remarkable was the economic progress which was facilitated by the establishment of the Bank of Lithuania and of a stabilized currency in 1922. Within ten years the volume of production had doubled, and though the country remained predominantly agrarian, there was a promising beginning of industrialization (textiles and timber) and foreign trade increased, particularly with Britain.

In cultural and economic development Lithuania could well compare with Estonia and Latvia, but the constitutional crisis was even more protracted. When the provisional constitution of October, 1918, was replaced by that of August 6, 1922, no basic changes were made in its strictly democratic character and the supremacy of the parliament (Seimas) was confirmed. There followed the usual controversies among the numerous parties, however, particularly between the nationalist Christian Democrats and the liberal and Socialist Left. In reaction against the liberal policy of Prime Minister Slezevicius, supported by the minorities, and alarmed by Communist propaganda, a group of officers dispersed the Seimas during the night of December 16–17, 1926. There followed the authoritarian regime of Anthony Smetona with increased powers as president of the republic. The dictatorial trend represented by Prime Minister Valdemaras with the aid of the "Iron Wolf" organization lasted, however, only until 1929 when that ambitious politician was finally driven out. But the new constitution of May 15, 1928, which made the president, chosen for a term of seven years by an electoral college, practically independent of the legislature, restricted the number of deputies, and created a state council as advisory organ, remained in force and served as the basis of the final constitution of May 12, 1938.

Without introducing the idea of the corporate state, as was done in Estonia and Latvia, Lithuania was also looking for some form of government intermediary between the full adoption of Western democracy and a stronger executive authority which seemed badly needed in the difficult conditions of East Central Europe. Therefore it is no wonder that the same issue also appeared simultaneously in the much larger but even more exposed Republic of Poland.

(E) *Poland.* Though much smaller than before the partitions, with her 150,000 square miles and a rapidly growing population which in 1939 reached 35 million, the new Poland was not only much larger than the Baltic States but was also in general by far the largest country in the restored East Central European region and the sixth largest state in Europe. It was one of those countries which without being among the great powers can hardly be called a small nation. As in the past, even more significant was her geographical position in the very center of the whole region where she was the only country having a common frontier with both Germany and the Soviet Union.

In 1918 the liberation found the nation in an extremely difficult situation not only because of the terrible devastation of almost the whole territory during the war but also because the three sections, which from the partitions had been under different foreign rulers and completely separated from one another, had first to be reintegrated. Even in the formerly Russian part, the largest, there was a great difference between the once autonomous largely industrialized Congress kingdom and the fragment of the eastern provinces of the ancient commonwealth which through the Riga Treaty came back to Poland in a very backward condition.

Although most of these eastern provinces remained outside the new Poland, she included a rather high percentage—more than 31 per cent—of non-Polish minorities. This proved a much more delicate problem than the reunification of Prussian, Austrian, and Russian Poland, which was achieved very rapidly. Among the minorities, the Jews, about 10 per cent, constituted a special question, as in some other countries of East Central Europe. Nowhere were they so numerous as in Poland. Partly religious, partly racial, the Jewish question in Poland was primarily economic because in some professions, especially in commerce, the Jews were of a much higher percentage than in the population at large. Anti-Semitism, which first appeared in the critical years of Poland's struggle for her frontiers, again increased toward the end of the independence period but never led to any legal discrimination. And since the number of the Lithuanian and Russian minorities was insignificant, the real issues were the German and the Ruthenian problem.

The German minority, less than one million and smaller than the Polish minority left in Germany and which was mostly scattered in the formerly Prussian section, was a serious danger, being highly developed culturally and economically and strongly influenced in its anti-Polish attitude by the neighboring Reich. The appeasement of that tension after the nonaggression treaty with Hitler proved completely fallacious. Much larger, about 13 per cent of the whole population, was the Ukrainian minority, which along with the White Ruthenians in the northeast (about 5 per cent, including those which at the census designated themselves merely as "local" peoples) inhabited the eastern provinces and in many districts constituted a majority. The Ukrainians were disappointed because not even in Galicia, where their nationalism was most highly developed, did they obtain the expected local autonomy or a university of their own. Especially around 1931 the terrorist action of some of their leaders created troubles which had to be severely repressed. In spite of that situation, which seemed to improve in the following years, the Ukrainians and to a lesser extent the White Ruthenians also shared in the cultural progress which was one of the distinctive features of the restored Polish Republic.

After a long interruption, Polish culture was again promoted by a national government. While the arts, letters, and sciences had succeeded in developing remarkably even under foreign rule, education now found entirely new possibilities which had been unknown before except in Austrian Galicia. To the two universities which existed there in Cracow and Lwów, were now added the re-Polonized University of Warsaw, soon to become the largest in the country, the reopened University of Wilno, and entirely new ones in Poznań and Lublin (Catholic). A whole Polish school system had to be created in the formerly Prussian and Russian sections, and illiteracy had to be eliminated in the latter. The progress made in that field was extraordinary.

So also were some of the achievements in economic life, particularly the creation of a great Polish port in what had been the small fishing village of Gdynia. Such a port was badly needed since that of Danzig proved insufficient and was handicapped by persistent friction with the administration of the Free City. Though Danzig also developed economically much more than before, when it had been one of the secondary ports of Prussia, Gdynia rapidly grew into the largest port of the whole Baltic region. The new Polish merchant fleet appeared on all the seas and also contributed to ever-closer relations with America.

Poland remained predominantly an agricultural country, the peasants making up 68 per cent of the population. Much attention was therefore given to land reform. The law of 1920, confirmed in 1925, limited the area to be held by any individual landowner to 180 hectares (to 300 in the eastern borderlands). In the application of that law, 734,000 new farms and holdings were created by 1938 so that only one-seventh of all arable land was still left to holders of more than 50 hectares (about 120 acres). Since, however, not even the complete carrying out of that reform could solve the problem of the landless rural population, great effort was made to create jobs and to increase production by the progress of industrialization. On the eve of World War II a central industrial district was being created in what seemed to be the safest part of the country in addition to the industrial centers of Warsaw and Łódź, the mining districts in Upper Silesia, and the oil fields in eastern Galicia. Financially, that whole development had been made possible by the stabilization of the currency in 1924–1925 under Prime Minister (and Minister of Finance) Władysław Grabski.

Grabski's cabinet was one of the most successful among those which followed one another, in frequent changes, during the first period of Poland's independence. This era was characterized by the supremacy of the Diet, the bicameral *Sejm*, and by the limitation of presidential power. For just like the other liberated countries, Poland started with a fully democratic form of government on the French model which was also influenced by her own historic tradition. As soon as peace was secured, these principles, already embodied in the provisional "little" constitution of 1919, were worked out in the constitution of March 17, 1921. In Poland too, however, there appeared a great number of parties which made it difficult to form a stable majority in the Diet. Therefore Piłsudski, made first marshal of Poland after the victory of 1920, first resigned from his position as head of the state in 1922, and later, in May, 1926, decided to interfere with a situation which in his opinion was also to affect the army and the security of the country. He forced the president, Stanisław Wojciechowski, and the cabinet of the peasant leader, Wincenty Witos, to resign, and until his death on May 12, 1935, he exercised full control of public affairs.

He had his coup legalized by the Diet, however, refused the presidency, to which at his suggestion Professor Ignacy Mościcki was elected (re-elected for another seven-year term in 1933), and was for most of the time formally in charge of military affairs only. But he insisted upon a constitutional reform which was prepared during the first years of the Piłsudski regime by a moderate group of his partisans and then carried out under strong pressure against the opposition in the Diet. In the absence of that opposition, the draft of the new constitution was approved in the session of January 26, 1934, and formally proclaimed on the twenty-third of April of the following year.

That second constitution of the new Poland concentrated the supreme power in the hands of the president of the republic who was supposed to coordinate the activities of the various branches of the government, including the legislature. The Diet and the Senate retained their legislative power, the right to control the cabinet and fix the budget, but the president, free to appoint and dismiss the ministers, was also given the right to convoke and dissolve Parliament. As in the past, the Diet was to be elected through universal, secret, equal, and direct suffrage, but an electoral law that supplemented the constitution limited the free selection of candidates and the influence of political parties. The "Non-Partisan Bloc of Cooperation with the Government" (BB), which had an absolute majority in the Diet, was dissolved and a "Camp of National Unity" (OZN) was created. But this failed to coordinate the political life of the country.

More important was the law which made Marshal Edward Rydz-Smigły, Piłsudski's successor as head of the army, "the second person in the state." As a matter of fact, neither he nor President Mościcki had any dictatorial ambitions and they were eager to promote the cooperation of all constructive forces in the country. The Communist movement, outlawed as a party, was very weak, and Fascist trends among youth organizations, both of supporters and of opponents of the regime, had very little political influence. But in view of Poland's increasingly dangerous situation between Soviet Russia and Nazi Germany, it was of vital and urgent importance to give all democratic parties, both of the nationalist right and of the left—peasant parties and Socialist—an opportunity to share in the responsibilities of government. The participation in the last prewar elections in 1939 was indeed much larger than in those of 1936, the first under the new constitution, and there was general agreement that at least the unsatisfactory electoral law ought to be revised. A return to a truly democratic form of government, though probably retaining an authority of the president greater than before 1926, was therefore a perspective of the nearest future when the international crisis interrupted free Poland's normal development.

(F) *Czechoslovakia.* Smaller than Poland but with her 54,207 square miles and more than fourteen million people also one of the medium-sized countries, Czechoslovakia was on the one hand a continuation of the once powerful kingdom of Bohemia, and on the other a new creation so far as the union of Czechs and Slovaks in one state was concerned. That union gave to the new republic the control of the whole northern part of the Danubian region and, through the autonomous Carpatho-Ruthenian territory, a common frontier with Rumania. But that same extension created intricate nationalities problems in Czechoslovakia, in addition to those which had existed in the land of the crown of St. Václav from the Middle Ages.

If Czechs and Slovaks are considered as one nation, then they indeed constituted a majority of two-thirds of the total population. Even so, the percentage of minorities was slightly larger than in Poland, chiefly because of the large number of Germans, almost three million and a half and nearly one-fourth of the total. These lived in compact groups in the Sudetenland along the northern and western frontier, and they were also scattered over most of the country, particularly in the cities. Also considerable was the number of Magyars, more than 720,000, and of Ukrainians, more than 570,000, and quite important was the number of Poles in Silesia though the statistics are very controversial. But the problem of the Germans who for centuries had occupied a leading position was the biggest issue. Their treatment, as well as that of the other minorities, was certainly not so ideal as T. G. Masaryk, the real founder and first president of the republic, wanted it to be. His collaborator and successor, Edward Beneš, for many years foreign minister, at the Peace Conference described his country as another Switzerland. Critics pointed out that this successor state of the Habsburg monarchy had inherited all its difficulties and shortcomings in the matter of nationalities. But though the Germans received no territorial autonomy, in general they had little to complain of after the initial troubles of readjustment to an entirely changed situation. Until the interference of Nazi propaganda from Germany, relations were improving to such an extent that German ministers participated in the government.

Both Czechs and Slovaks were now at last free from foreign rule. But the latter, who were opposed to any unification of the two closely related yet different peoples, hoped that the structure of their common state would be based upon the agreement signed on June 30, 1918, in Pittsburgh, Pennsylvania. That agreement promised Slovakia "her own administrative system, her own diet, and her own courts," with Slovak as the official language. Strictly carried out it would have made the republic a Czecho-Slovak (the hyphen also proved an object of controversy) federation, while in practice, since no Slovak Diet was created, there was only some kind of local self-government for the Slovaks in the state as a whole. But those who had met in Pittsburgh in the presence of Masaryk were Americans of Czech and Slovak descent who could not determine conditions in the liberated European country. The issue was never completely settled because the centralizing practices of the administration were strongly opposed by the Slovak Populist Party led by Father Andrej Hlinka. On the other hand, prominent statesmen of Slovak origin held high positions in the government: for instance, Dr. Milan Hodža who was prime minister during the critical years 1935–1938.

In spite of their serious reasons for dissatisfaction, the Slovaks for the first time enjoyed full freedom of national development. Their capital, Bratislava (the Pozsony of the Hungarian era), where a Slovak university was organized, became a cultural center second only to Prague itself and equal to Moravian Brno where another new university was founded after the liberation. In Prague the German university now occupied a secondary position, the Czech one being considered the real heir of the old foundation of Charles IV. Based upon a solid tradition, cultural progress in all fields was remarkable throughout the whole republic, including regions which, like Carpatho-Ruthenia, required a special effort in view of their backward conditions.

Much more industrialized than any other country of East Central Europe, Czechoslovakia had a basically sound economy, particularly after the currency reforms which were carefully planned in the years after the depression (1934–1936). With her intensive foreign trade she tried to play the role of a bridge between the West and the agricultural countries in the East. And in spite of an agrarian crisis which preceded the general depression, the redistribution of land through an agrarian reform which started right after the liberation proved to be a remarkable achievement from the social point of view. But it was not so much because of her social legislation, a field in which Poland was equally prominent, that Czechoslovakia was always considered a stronghold of democracy in East Central Europe. Decisive in that respect was the fact that during her twenty years of independence she did not make any constitutional changes similar to those which occurred in almost all the other countries of that region except Finland.

The Czechoslovak constitution, voted by the National Assembly on February 29, 1920, and based upon the principles of the provisional constitution of 1918, was strongly influenced by Masaryk's devotion to the American ideals of democracy but in its details it came nearer to the French model as in the other countries of East Central Europe. This is particularly evident in the limitation of the power of the president who was elected by both houses of Parliament for a term of seven years. Only two terms were permitted, but an exception was made for Masaryk who served until his resignation in 1935, with Beneš as foreign minister during that whole period of seventeen years. Their personal prestige was a safeguard against the rivalries of the political parties which were also very numerous in Czechoslovakia and which benefited from the principle of proportional representation.

The Social Democratic Party, which in the first elections of April, 1920, proved to be by far the strongest both among the Czechoslovak and the German parties, lost considerably in the elections of 1925. From that date the Agrarian Party was in the lead under Antonin Švehla who twice served as prime minister. But a majority could never be formed except through the cooperation of a group of parties, therefore the country always had a coalition government with a council of party leaders who tried to agree on a working compromise.

This system also worked fairly well under the presidency of Beneš who had, however, to face much more opposition, particularly among the Slovak Catholics who formed a party, the strongest in Slovakia and separate from the Czech Catholics. Fascist influence which appeared among the Slovak autonomists was quite negligible among the Czechs, only six Fascists being elected in 1935. Much more numerous were the Communists who after splitting off from the Social Democrats in 1921 got forty-one seats in the elections of 1925 and kept thirty in those of 1929 and 1935. The greatest danger came, however, from the German Nazis who in 1935, the last elections in independent Czechoslovakia, appeared as a new party called "Sudeten German." At once they got 56 per cent of all German votes and forty-four seats in Parliament, while all the other German parties either vanished entirely or became insignificant. The representation of the other national minorities was very small. But the Sudeten movement, under its local "Führer," Conrad Henlein, which later also attracted what remained of the other German parties, was to prove strong enough to create an internal crisis which served Hitler as a pretext for destroying Czechoslovakia.

(G) *Austria.* The origins of German nationalism in Czechoslovakia can be traced back to the Pan-German movement in the former Habsburg monarchy, after the fall of which the Germans of the "Sudetenland" wanted to join the new republic of "German Austria" and with her the German Reich. But this is by no means the only reason for including the new Austria in the survey of East Central European countries. The long and intimate association of the German-speaking part of the monarchy with the other lands of the Danubian region had left deeper traces than Austria's past participation in the Holy Roman Empire and in the German Confederation up to 1866. And since the peace treaties prohibited any union with the new Germany, continued cooperation with the other successor states of the Austro-Hungarian Empire would have been the best solution of the problem of Austria's survival. That survival of a small country, limited to 32,369 square miles and with a population of six and a half million, a third of which lived in the city of Vienna, was mainly an economic issue. In addition to the former imperial capital, now much too big for the new republic, the country chiefly consisted of Alpine mountain lands cut off from the provinces which in the past had been Austria's food reservoir and the consumers of her industrial products. Yet the restoration of even the economic unity of the Danubian region proved impossible in the tense conditions of the postwar years. Under the threat of the reparation clauses of the Saint-Germain Treaty, the financial situation of Austria, where inflation was making rapid progress, seemed desperate.

This was the main cause of the continuing movement in favor of union with Germany, particularly among the Social Democrats whose party was leading in the Weimar Republic and who at the outset were also the strongest party in Austria. But the Christian Social (Catholic) Party succeeded in giving the democratic constitution of October 1, 1920, a federal character, similar to that of the Swiss. This made Vienna, which was dominated by the Socialists, only one of the nine parts of the *Bund*. In the first elections held under that constitution the Socialists lost their majority. The Catholic Party, though not much stronger, with the small group of German nationalists who were sometimes in a key position, now assumed the direction of Austria's policy. Their prominent leader, Monsignor Ignaz Seipel, as federal chancellor from 1922, obtained the support of the League of Nations for the financial reform which through foreign loans saved the existence of the new republic and gave it a workable economic basis. Nevertheless he was violently opposed by the Socialists. He resigned in 1924 after being wounded in an attempt on his life. When he returned to power two years later, the political situation was even more critical and soon led to Socialist riots in Vienna in 1927. Seipel's successor, Chancellor Schober, wanted to conclude at least a customs union with Germany in 1930, but the other powers, considering this a first step to political unification, made such a solution impossible. There continued to be an internal struggle between the two leading Austrian parties, each of which had an armed organization at its disposal.

Under these conditions Chancellor Engelbert Dollfuss, a Catholic peasant leader who came to power in 1932, the following year decided to dissolve Parliament in which the exactly equal representation of Catholics and Socialists made any decision impossible. With the support of President Miklas he proceeded to a basic constitutional reform. The new Austrian constitution of May 1, 1934, had this in common with all the revised constitutions of the East Central European states, that it strengthened the executive at the expense of the legislature. More than any other constitution, it based the whole structure of the state, and of the various councils which were supposed to replace the former bicameral parliament, on the idea of corporations. Emphasizing the Christian character of the federal state, as the republic was now called, an effort was made to apply the solutions recommended in the papal encyclicals on social matters. And though the German character of the state was also stressed, this was merely a recognition of Austria's German culture. At the same time, developing the specifically Austrian features of that culture, attempts were made through the creation of a nonpartisan "Fatherland's Front" to promote some kind of Austrian nationalism that would be clearly distinct from the German.

Such a reinterpretation of Austria's historic mission would have facilitated cooperation with the other new states of the Danubian region, relations with which were indeed improving. But internally the Dollfuss administration had to fight on two different fronts. A few months before the proclamation of the new constitution, in February, 1934, the chancellor, not without the influence of the Austro-Fascist leader Prince Starhemberg, had crushed through violence what he suspected to be a Socialist conspiracy. Thus the whole Left was alienated at the very moment when the Austrian Nazis, a vociferous minority systematically encouraged by the Hitler regime in Germany, intensified their struggle against the new Austria.

In the revolution which they started in July of the same year, Dollfuss was murdered, but the brief civil war ended in a victory of the government which was supported by a mobilization of Italian forces at the border. The new chancellor, Dr. Kurt von Schuschnigg, a distinguished intellectual who was determined to defend Dollfuss' achievements, had to face even greater difficulties. Serious progress was made in developing Austria as an independent nation, and the economic situation was also improved through the tourist movement which continued to be notable. But without Dollfuss' great popularity, and unable to gain the confidence of the Left for a regime with a distinctly authoritarian character, Schuschnigg remained under the persistent attack of the Nazi partisans. Fully aware that their whole attitude was dictated by Hitler, and unable to get international assistance, the Austrian chancellor, after almost four years of courageous resistance, made a desperate attempt to appease the Führer by a visit to Berchtesgaden in February, 1938. Their dramatic meeting was to be not only the end of Austria's independence but also the beginning of a series of events that led directly to World War II.

German Austria, with its ambiguous character, was indeed the weakest element in the whole structure of East Central Europe between the two wars, although under her Catholic leaders she made a serious effort to integrate herself in the new state system of the Danubian region, breaking with any tradition of nationalistic German imperialism. In spite of ultimate failure, her existence as a small but independent country, ready to make valuable cultural contributions as in her imperial past, proved fully justified. It is highly significant that Austria's internal problems, particularly in the constitutional field, were so similar to those of the other East Central European peoples. She was also the only defeated country which seemed to become reconciled to the peace settlement after World War I.

(H) *Hungary.* Different in that respect was the policy of Austria's former partner in the Dual Monarchy. And strangely enough, while the Habsburgs, in spite of the genuine sympathy among the Catholics of Austria and their leaders, never had any chance for restoration in the country where their power originated, legitimism seemed so strong in the kingdom of Hungary that the last Habsburg emperor, Charles I, as king of Hungary Charles IV, made two disastrous attempts to regain at least the Hungarian part of his heritage, only to be exiled to Madeira where he died as early as 1921.

He and his partisans particularly resented the successful resistance of the former Austro-Hungarian admiral, Horthy, who ruled Hungary as regent pending the restoration of royal power. He reached that position, which he was to keep until the last phase of World War II, after the exceptionally painful internal crisis which Hungary alone among all the "new" states had to pass through immediately after World War I. The government of Count Michael Karolyi, the first government of a Hungary at last fully independent again after the dissolution of the Austro-Hungarian union, opened the door to a Communist revolution which exposed the country to the terror of the dictator Béla Kun and which ended with the humiliating occupation of Budapest by the Rumanians.

Under the impression of these events, there followed a violent Rightist reaction. After a short democratic interlude, Admiral Horthy, who had led the anti-Communist forces, was on March 1, 1920, made regent for life. His powers were increased in 1933 at the expense of Parliament which, however, never lost its traditional place in the life of the country. But this was no real guaranty of democratic government because the universal suffrage observed in the elections of 1920 (boycotted nevertheless by the Socialists) was replaced in 1922 by a new electoral law which not only reduced and restricted the electorate but in the countryside also returned to the open ballot. Only in the cities did the voting remain secret. This was done through a decree of Count Stephen Bethlen who was prime minister from 1921 to 1931. During this period of ten years he restored stability and legality to Hungary, but on a strictly conservative basis, after uniting the Christian National Party and the small Landowners' Party into a strong government bloc. The latter favored the project of land reform, and as a matter of fact 1,785,000 acres were taken from great landowners and used for the establishment of family dwellings and small holdings.

Hungary's frontiers, so drastically changed by the Trianon Treaty, created serious difficulties both in the cultural and in the economic fields. Along with the Magyar minorities in the successor states, Hungary lost important cultural centers, including two universities which had to be transferred to the cities of Pécs and Szeged in what was left of her prewar territory. Even on that reduced territory Hungary had about 10 per cent of minorities, but with the exception of more than half a million Germans, these were rather insignificant groups in what was now definitely a national state. On the contrary, the financial situation was alarming after the loss of the former sources of raw material and the main markets for Hungarian industry. But as in the case of Austria, the assistance of the League of Nations, which started in 1923, proved very helpful, and through a loan and reconstruction scheme the inflation was stopped and industrial production was in progress during the later twenties.

However, Hungary too was affected by the following world depression, and since the secret ballot in the cities went against Bethlen in the elections of 1931, he resigned. A year later the war minister, General Julius Gömbös was made prime minister, to remain in office until 1936. The new regime, less aristocratic, favorable to land reform, and even more opposed to Habsburg legitimism than Bethlen had been, was at the same time, however, more authoritarian and openly favored Fascist conceptions. Particularly alarming was the appearance of nationalist groups influenced by German naziism, which made progress under Gömbös' successors and in 1938 united in the "Arrow Cross" Party. And as in Austria, though opposed to those dangerous extremists of the Right, the government failed to cooperate even with moderate elements of the Left which were divided into the reorganized peasant party of the Small Landowners and the Social Democrats.

At the last moment before World War II, however, a notable improvement came about in Hungary's internal situation. The elections of May, 1939, were held under a new electoral law which granted wider franchises and also the secret ballot in the villages. Yet the government obtained a fair majority, although forty-three Nazis appeared in Parliament. The new prime minister, Count Paul Teleki, a distinguished scholar and statesman who had occupied that office for a short time before Bethlen, would have been well qualified to find a solution for the internal crisis if the international crisis which created a particularly hopeless situation for Hungary had not already set in. Hungary's case is typical of the close connection between the domestic problems of the East Central European nations and foreign politics, and for defeated Hungary it was harder than for any other country to combine her efforts toward reconstruction with a well-balanced conduct of external affairs.

(I) *Rumania*. Hungary's revisionism was chiefly directed against the three victorious states which, in addition to Austria, had gained territorially by the Trianon Treaty. Greatest were the gains of Rumania, and this therefore resulted in a violent antagonism between the two nations which the intricate problem of Transylvania had divided for so many centuries. But the "Greater Rumania" which emerged from World War I, with its area of 122,282 square miles which was more than twice as large as in 1914, and with a population three times larger, of almost eighteen million, also had to face Bulgarian revisionism. Furthermore, it was the only country in the Danubian and Balkan region which had a common frontier with the Soviet Union. This was another source of tension because of the dispute over Bessarabia.

But also from the internal point of view, the great extension of the prewar kingdom created very serious problems. Unification of old Moldavia and Wallachia with the new acquisitions was no easy task even with regard to the Rumanian population, which, in the former Hungarian and Austrian lands, had a different background and had been from time immemorial under Western influence. All Rumanians were indeed anxious to develop their relations with the West and proud of their Latin origin. But in the part of their country which from the later Middle Ages had been under the impact of the Ottoman Empire, the consequences of that suzerainty could not be completely obliterated in the first decades of full independence. This delicate problem explains various shortcomings of the new Rumania, although between the two world wars much progress was made in the direction of national unity. This was particularly true in the cultural field where the new Rumanian universities of Cluj, the capital of Transylvania, and Çernauti, the capital of the Bucovina, replacing the Hungarian and German institutions of the same cities, closely cooperated with the large University of Bucarest and that of Jassy in Moldavia. The great historian N. Iorga, at the same time a leading statesman, was the living symbol of that cultural revival which was uniting all Rumanians.

Much more intricate was the problem of minorities in the various territories that had been added to Rumania proper. Within its enlarged frontiers, the kingdom, formerly quite homogeneous, included almost 30 per cent (28.1, according to the official statistics) of minorities, divided into many different groups. Some of the groups were rather insignificant, but five of them presented difficult issues. By far the most numerous, and strongest in their opposition, were the Magyars, almost one and a half million, including the Szeklers in the southeastern corner of Transylvania which was now at the very center of the enlarged kingdom. Quite large—half a million—was also the Ukrainian minority along the eastern border, but this group was scarcely attracted by the Soviet Union. The Bulgarians, of whom there were about 350,000 in the mixed Dobrudja region, constituted a rather dangerous irredenta. The Jewish problem was also important, since the Jews numbered almost 5 per cent of the population. Anti-Semitism on cultural and even more so on economic grounds was increasing in connection with the political developments of the later interwar period.

In Rumania, the internal policy after World War I also started on an apparently democratic basis. Universal suffrage had already been introduced in 1918, land reform in favor of the numerous peasant population was inaugurated in 1920–1921, and the constitution was finally voted in 1923. The general opinion that Rumanian "royal parliamentarism" was particularly inadequate is not without exaggeration, but it is also true that much depended on the personality of the king. In spite of great economic difficulties and serious social tension between the rural and the urban population, conditions were rather satisfactory until the death of King Ferdinand I in 1927. Together with his British-born wife, Queen Mary, he had gained much popularity during and after the war. A few months later, the death of his closest collaborator, Prime Minister Ionel Bratianu, also ended the leading role of the Liberal Party, because in the following year his (Bratianu's) brother Vintila was replaced by the Transylvanian peasant leader, Juliu Maniu.

A few years before, his party had been united with the Peasant Party of the prewar kingdom into a National Peasant Party which was an important step toward closer cooperation of the various sections of the country. Although the peasant government did not fulfil the high hopes for a complete solution of the agrarian problem, democratic principles and minority rights were respected and foreign loans eased the economic situation. The change for the worse came not only with the consequences of the world-wide depression, but also with the return of Prince Carol, the exiled son of King Ferdinand, who in 1930 took the place of his own minor son, King Michael. Maniu, who facilitated this return in opposition to the Liberal Party which was hostile to Carol, lost his premiership before the end of the year. King Carol II, as he was called, disregarding his promises, governed for ten years with the ambitious aim of some kind of royal dictatorship.

In the midst of frequent cabinet crises and the disintegration of both the Peasant and the Liberal parties through court intrigues, there appeared an antidemocratic organization of extreme nationalists, the "Iron Guard." This group was first encouraged by the authorities, but soon it so alarmed the king himself that after the government defeat in the elections of December, 1937, he first chose as prime minister the leader of another rather small nationalistic group, and then the patriarch of the Rumanian Orthodox Church. In 1938 a plebiscite approved the new constitution which concentrated the power in the hands of the king and limited the role of parliament, which was elected on a corporative basis. Although Carol II thus finally alienated all democratic forces, at the same time he continued to repress the Fascist Iron Guard movement whose leaders were shot in November, 1938, under shocking circumstances. But in spite of a "Front of National Rebirth" organized by the king, the Iron Guard continued its subversive activity. By assassinating another premier, it created general confusion at the very moment when the outbreak of World War II made Rumania fully aware of her exposed situation between naziism, advancing from the West, and Russian communism. In the Rumanian case as in so many others, the desire to escape from both these dangers explains the desperate attempts to establish a really strong national government even by the most doubtful means.

(J) *Yugoslavia.* Less exposed seemed to be the situation of the other state which through the peace settlement after World War I developed from a small Balkan country into a medium-sized power that reached far into the Danubian region. The state, or kingdom—as it later used to be called—of the Serbs, Croats, and Slovenes, officially named Yugoslavia in connection with the basic reforms of 1929, was not as large as the new Rumania but its area of 96,134 square miles, inhabited by more than twelve million people, presented even more serious problems of national unity.

As in the case of Czechoslovakia, a clear distinction must be made between the question of national minorities, unavoidable in that part of Europe, and the issues raised by the relationship among the leading peoples which had joined one another to create a new common state. The total of real minorities was not particularly high, about 17 per cent, and there was among them such a variety, Magyars, Germans, Albanians, and others, scattered in various frontier regions, that none of these groups was really important. Certainly they were much less important than the Yugoslav minorities left under foreign rule, especially in Italy. But the Yugoslavs themselves consisted of three different peoples which in connection with the disintegration of the Habsburg monarchy decided to realize their old dream of uniting in an independent state of their own, but without all having the same conception of such a Yugoslavia.

For the Serbs, who by themselves constituted the larger half of all Yugoslavs, that state was to be, as a matter of fact, an enlarged Serbia. It was to have as a nucleus the kingdom which through its efforts and final victory in the Balkan wars and in World War I had made the unification possible, and which at the time of the peace settlement had already annexed Montenegro, the other formerly independent state created by the Serb people. Even there, in spite of the common ethnic and religious background, at least at the beginning, an opposition appeared against such an absorption. Confused, as always, was the situation in Macedonia, officially considered purely Serbian but with an autonomy movement influenced by partisans of Bulgaria. And the Serbs of Bosnia also felt themselves to be different from the others, not only for historical reasons but chiefly because 750,000 among them were Moslems. But the religious difference between the Orthodox majority of the Serbs and the exclusively Catholic Croats had even deeper consequences in spite of their common Christian heritage and almost identical languages. What separated them, however, was not only religion. Nowhere else in East Central Europe did the antagonism between Western and Eastern cultural trends prove stronger, even in the twentieth century. Furthermore, the idea of Croatia's state rights, preserved through more than eight centuries of union with Hungary, was now an equally effective obstacle to the centralization which the Serbs wanted to enforce.

If the position of the Slovenes, Catholics of Western culture just like the Croats, is considered, the importance of that last factor becomes apparent. That third and smallest branch of the Yugoslavs, less than one and a half million, which never had formed a separate body politic, resented Serb predominance much less. Furthermore, these two peoples, separated by the Croats, were not immediate neighbors. It was also important that the Slovenes, the least favorably treated of the nationalities of prewar Austria, now for the first time enjoyed full opportunity for cultural development, with their national university at last founded in Ljubljana. The Croats, who even under Hungarian supremacy had had their university and national academy in Zagreb, had nothing to gain in that respect. The cultural progress of all Serb populations which were formerly separated by political boundaries was of course greatly accelerated in the enlarged state. A university, though incomplete, was founded even in Skoplje, the capital of backward Macedonia.

From the economic point of view it was also Serbia which gained most, because after being refused any access to the sea for such a long time, she could now take advantage of the ports of the Dalmatian coast. The fact that one of them, Zadar (Zara), had been given to Italy at the peace table, and the fact that the even more important Croatian port of Rjeka (Fiume) was finally annexed by that power after years of irritating controversy, indeed affected but did not basically change the possibilities of new development which opened before the whole country. And since Serbs and Slovenes were both peasant peoples, while in Croatia the peasants, organized in a strong party, were now after a rather drastic land reform the main representation of the national movement, there was in the tripartite kingdom less social tension than in most of the other countries of East Central Europe.

The Karageorgevich dynasty, also of native peasant stock, was supposed to be a unifying force. But it was indeed much more popular in Serbia, where the family originated and which old King Peter I and his son Alexander, who succeeded him in 1921, had so bravely defended during the war. The real difficulties set in, however, when after a provisional administration in which Croat and Slovene leaders held key positions alongside Serb statesmen, a constituent assembly was elected in 1921. The fifty-four Communists, who won seats in connection with the postwar depression, were deprived of their mandates after the assassination of the minister of the interior by a Communist. The whole party, which was declared illegal, soon lost any influence it may have had. But there was a dangerous antagonism between Serb centralism, represented by the Radical Party under Nicholas Pashich, and the federalist trend, defended by the Croatian Peasant Party which got an overwhelming majority in Croatia and was ably directed by Stephen Radich. Under the influence of the former, the Constitution of St. Vitus Day (*Vidovdan*) established a centralized administration, which was therefore opposed by the Croats from the outset, notwithstanding the democratic freedoms and the proportional representation in parliament which as elsewhere favored the coexistence of numerous parties.

The situation became critical when Radich, once in prison, once in the government, allied in 1927 with federalist elements among the Serbs, was shot with two of his followers by a deputy from Montenegro when speaking in Parliament on June 20, 1928. When the new leader of the Croatian Peasant Party, Dr. Vladko Machek, requested the division of the country into federal units with full self-government, the king reacted by establishing his own dictatorship on January 9, 1929. He hoped to save the unity of the kingdom by a centralism that would no longer be Serb but truly Yugoslav. It was then that the state was officially called "Yugoslavia," with a division into nine provinces (*banovinas*) under royal governors, which corresponded to geographical rather than to historic or ethnic units. The new constitution of 1931 seemed to be a return to democracy, but the system of elections greatly reduced the role of all opposition parties.

When Alexander I was assassinated in Marseilles on October 9, 1934, his brother, Prince Paul, became chief regent because of the young age of his son, Peter II. There was no change in the system of government, though there was less systematic leadership. The antagonism between Serbs and Croats seemed to continue indefinitely, and Machek was twice arrested. But the elections of 1938, where the Croats and the Serb opposition jointly got a majority, forced the new prime minister, D. Cvetkovich, to enter into negotiations with Dr. Machek. In spite of great difficulties from both sides, this resulted in the agreement (*sporazum*) of August 26, 1939, which created an autonomous Croatia, comprising more than one-fourth of the whole kingdom, a first step in the direction of federalization and also of really restoring democratic freedoms with secret ballot and free party activities. Dr. Machek entered the government as vice-premier, and Yugoslavia seemed to have solved her main problems at last, when only a few days later the outbreak of World War II created entirely new dangers.

(K) *Bulgaria.* Strictly speaking, the unity of all Yugoslavs, that is Southern Slavs, also ought to include the Bulgarians. But after the Second Balkan War and because of Bulgaria's position in World War I, the antagonism between Serbs and Bulgarians was deeper than ever. Bulgaria, one of the defeated countries, was in an entirely different situation. Reduced to less than 40,000 square miles and to a population of about six million which included almost no minorities except about 800,000 Moslems, most of them of Turkish race, Bulgaria had no problems of unification to face, being rather absorbed by her revisionistic tendencies. The social structure of that predominantly peasant nation was also quite homogeneous so that the main difficulty of its internal life resulted from the readjustment after two successive defeats and from the tension between revolutionary nationalism, inspired by the Macedonians who were particularly opposed to the peace settlement, and those who wanted to make a serious effort at reconstruction.

The start seemed rather favorable. Young King Boris III, who immediately after the armistice succeeded his badly discredited father, Ferdinand, who was forced to abdicate, did his best to promote a truly democratic government in agreement with the real interests of the country. In the elections of August, 1919, the Agrarian Party received such a huge majority that its leader, Alexander Stambolisky, a violent opponent of the wartime regime, could rule as prime minister for almost four years. His policy was so exclusively in favor of the peasant class, however, both in internal and foreign affairs where he planned the cooperation of Eastern European countries governed by peasant parties, that his persistent struggle with the opposition ended on June 9, 1923, with his assassination by a Macedonian revolutionary.

There followed a reaction which failed to put an end to political murders and Communist plots. The crisis reached its climax in April, 1925, when after several attempts on the king's life, a bomb exploded at the funeral of an assassinated general in the Cathedral of Sofia, killing and wounding several hundred people. The Communist Party was now outlawed, but there remained the endless troubles created by the Macedonian Revolutionary Organization and its nationalist sympathizers in Bulgaria. These persisted until in an effort to improve relations with the neighbors and to restore order in the country, military leaders and a new political group which tried to unite urban and rural elements succeeded in establishing a barely disguised dictatorship under Prime Minister Georgiev in May, 1934.

It was the king who tried to return to parliamentary government after replacing the military by civilian leaders. He issued a new electoral law which was supposed to eliminate the influence of the rivaling parties but which made possible the representation of the opposition. Parliament met again in 1938, though as a merely consultative body. Another coup prepared by the Macedonian terrorists failed, and the few Communist members were expelled from Parliament, so that on the eve of World War II there was an apparent stabilization in Bulgaria under a regime which tried to curb all extremists.

If, nevertheless, the situation was worse in Bulgaria than in almost all the other countries of East Central Europe, it was to a large extent the consequence of a foreign policy which had left her isolated in the Balkans. In spite of efforts at reconciliation with Yugoslavia and at developing the nation culturally and economically, Bulgaria had not yet succeeded in a complete reorientation of her external and internal politics when a new European crisis once more confronted her with a hard decision.

(L) *Albania.* The position of Albania, the smallest and least developed Balkan nation, was also unusually difficult. She had been restored after World War I in boundaries that were established after long troubles, which left her a territory of little more than 10,000 square miles and a population of less than one million. Even so, there was among the Albanians an entirely isolated racial and linguistic group, a great religious diversity which included both Orthodox and Catholic Christians and Moslems.

It was a Moslem leader who in that country, proud of a long tradition of fighting the Turks, played the most important role after the meeting of the National Assembly at the end of 1918 and the withdrawal of the Italian occupation forces in August, 1920. Ahmed Bey Zogu was first minister of the interior, then, in 1922, prime minister. Though expelled two years later when an Orthodox bishop, Fan Noli, exercised a decisive influence, he returned at Christmas, 1924, and one month later was elected president of the republic. He was, however, convinced that Albania was hardly prepared for a democratic form of government, and on September 1, 1928, was proclaimed King Zogu I.

The services which he rendered to his country were very real and under his leadership much progress was achieved. Albania was pacified and modernized, not only in the material field, by improving communications, developing the cities—the capital, Tirana, and the ports of Valona and Durazzo—and creating an important oil industry, but also by a codification of law in a progressive spirit and by educational and literary activities which contributed to the rise of national consciousness. Occasional uprisings of an undisciplined population which objected to some badly needed reforms had to be crushed, but gradually the opposition was reduced and conditions seemed to stabilize.

There remained, however, the danger of Italian influence which the king first hoped to use in order to get much needed financial assistance. In the treaty of 1926 he even admitted Italy's right to intervene in Albanian affairs if requested. Later, Zogu tried to check that interference, rejecting the project of a customs union and closing Italian schools. A compromise seemed to be possible in the later thirties. In 1938 the king married a Hungarian lady whose mother was an American, and an heir was born to him. But the next year, in the midst of rather promising developments, Albania quite unex-

pectedly became one of the first victims of unprovoked aggression
which reintroduced foreign rule into the Balkans and at the same time
made her a threat to her Greek neighbor.

(M) *Greece.* In spite of her undecided attitude which continued
almost to the end of World War I, and thanks to the skill of the liberal leader Eleutherios Venizelos who represented her at the Peace
Conference, Greece was treated as an allied power and greatly enlarged by the Sèvres Treaty. But in order to secure all her gains,
Greece had to enter another war against the new Turkey of Mustafa
Kemal, which ended in her defeat and in the disappointments of the
Treaty of Lausanne. Even when peace was at last restored, almost
five years later than in the West, exhausted Greece had to face the
tremendous problem of an exchange of population. As a matter of
fact, this mitigated the strained relations with Turkey, but mainly at
the expense of the Greeks who had to resettle about 1,400,000
refugees. The dream of imperial expansion in the direction of Constantinople and Asia Minor came to an end, and Greece's position
was so weakened even in the Aegean Sea that Italy could refuse the
promised cession of the Dodecanese Islands. Far from restoring the
power of Byzantium, the new Greece remained one of the smaller
Balkan states with less than 50,000 square miles and a population of
around seven million.

Furthermore, after the war an internal conflict remained between
the Liberals, who favored a republican form of government, and the
Royalists, who in 1920 restored King Constantine to power. He had
been expelled by the Allies during World War I and in spite of his
failure in the war with Turkey and his abdication in 1922, the
Royalists gave him his son George II as successor. But early the following year the young king had to leave Greece, where a republic was
proclaimed in March, 1924. A new constitution, drafted after the
French model, which left to the president much less power than was
formerly held by the king, was ratified in 1927. The twelve years of
republican government were not unsuccessful. The big refugee problem was largely solved, economic conditions were improved with the
assistance of Greek immigrants in the United States, industrialization
and irrigation works made progress, and intellectual life flourished
both in Athens and in the new university center at Salonika.

As elsewhere, the main trouble was political rivalry between the
parties, especially the Liberals and the Populists, as the Royalists were

now called. The latter were so strong that the republicans themselves occasionally had to resort to dictatorial methods against the coalition of their opponents led by Panagis Tsaldaris. In such a situation even the small and insignificant Communist Party could play a dangerous part. When the Populists received a majority in the elections of 1933, and the Liberals reacted by staging another military revolt, a plebiscite decided for a restoration of the monarchy and George II returned in 1935.

In spite of a general trend toward reconciliation and the king's desire to maintain a parliamentary government, the equal strength of the two main parties, with fifteen Communists keeping the balance in a house of three hundred, led to the appointment in 1936 of a nonparty government under General Joannes Metaxas who suspended the constitution and dissolved Parliament. Even his dictatorial regime, with which the king identified himself, was not without constructive achievements. Taking advantage of the general improvement of the economic situation, both agricultural and industrial production were increased, foreign trade was developed, and a program of social reforms inaugurated. But lacking popular support, Metaxas had to disregard the proud tradition of Greek democracy and meet with at least passive opposition, particularly among the intellectuals. Therefore Greece, too, was in a difficult internal situation when the growing external danger required the unity of all national forces.

The mere fact that in spite of these internal divisions Greek resistance proved particularly heroic—though practically hopeless—when her freedom and independence were challenged, is an eloquent answer to all exaggerated criticisms which are being made with regard to the general records not only of Greece but also of all the countries of East Central Europe in the period between the two world wars.

The analogies in the records of these countries, so different in many respects, are indeed striking. In all of them, including the smallest and weakest and even those who suffered from recent defeats, truly astonishing progress was made in the economic and, what is frequently entirely overlooked, in the cultural field. Even quite recently liberated nationalities, which never before had been fully independent and self-governing, developed very rapidly and under the most difficult circumstances into real nations, thus giving ample evidence that for them, too, independence was the normal condition of life. In spite of the controversies between some of the new or enlarged and reorganized states, which were almost unavoidable in view of the involved frontier problems, in the whole period when they were left alone by the big powers there was not a single war in the whole region and the individual nations were busy with their internal problems, with social and constitutional reforms.

Social reforms were progressing everywhere in the right direction. If their goal was fully achieved in exceptional cases only, and if improvement was seemingly too slow in many cases, the shortness of time must be taken into consideration in order to evaluate the results of such a promising evolution, which in any case was much more desirable than violent revolutionary upheavals. In that field as in all others, the greatest difficulty came from the constitutional crises which developed almost simultaneously in practically all East Central European countries and which are usually pointed to as evidence of their failure in establishing truly democratic forms of government. In that respect the analogies in their parallel development are indeed highly significant.

Immediately after the peace settlement, all countries of East Central Europe wanted to start their restored or reorganized life on a democratic basis, following the pattern of Western Europe, particularly of the French Republic. Such a desire was natural not only as a reaction against the forms of government which had been forced upon most of them in the preceding period of history but also as a return to the earlier democratic traditions of many of them and as the best possible way of joining what seemed to be the general trend in the postwar world.

This being so, it is of course legitimate to ask why, with only two exceptions, these same nations found it necessary to change their constitutions after a few years and to look for forms of government characterized by a strong executive, sometimes definitely authoritarian, influenced by the conception of the corporate state, although in no case really Fascist in the usual sense.

It is misleading to say that democracy did not work in East Central Europe. In addition to the old parliamentary tradition of some countries in that region, the achievements of the democratic regimes in the first years after the war would contradict such an interpretation. It is also inaccurate to consider the turn of the following years as something exceptional which happened only in the East Central European countries. On the contrary, it was precisely the constitutional development in neighboring states which influenced them decisively. That happened, not because of any appeal which the totalitarian regimes, apparently so successful in other parts of Europe, could possibly have among the freedom-loving peoples which found themselves surrounded by communism, fascism, and naziism, but because of the danger threatening them in their exposed geographical positions, a danger so often experienced in the past in the time of despotic, aggressive empires which preceded the contemporary totalitarian systems. It proved an illusion that a form of government intermediary between those systems and plain democracy would be a guaranty of security. But it is difficult to blame the statesmen who tried such a solution for having been alarmed by shortcomings of the democratic system which raised similar apprehensions even in safer parts of the world.

It certainly was a mistake to choose at the beginning what seemed to be the most liberal and progressive among the various forms of democratic government, with presidential power extremely limited and intricate proportional systems of elections. When extremists from either Right or Left tried to take advantage of such situations, a limitation of democracy would seem to be the only chance for saving its basic elements from completely antidemocratic pressures. But it is remarkable that there usually followed a trend toward gradually restoring the curtailed democratic freedoms, a trend which, however, was drastically interrupted by the totalitarian aggression which it was impossible to avoid.

That this really was impossible is evidenced by the two countries of East Central Europe which are rightly praised for never changing their democratic institutions and yet were among the first to be attacked: Czechoslovakia by naziism, Finland by communism. Neither in their case nor in the others where democracy went through more or less acute crises in the brief independence period can the general record of that period be questioned merely because all these countries, whatever their constitutional development had been, were not strong enough to defend their freedom against overwhelming forces. What all of them needed for continuing their peaceful activities was a more favorable international situation which their foreign policy tried in vain to improve, frequently in joint efforts which are therefore best examined from a general point of view. But before doing so, the entirely different position of two more individual nations must be explained.

THE UKRAINIANS AND WHITE RUTHENIANS IN THE
SOVIET UNION

In contradistinction to the thirteen free and independent countries which freely developed between Sweden, Germany, and Italy on the one hand and the Soviet Union on the other hand, two nations of the same region, which also hoped to gain their independence as democratic national states, were included in the U.S.S.R. and again placed under Russian supremacy. These were the Ukrainians and the White Ruthenians or Byelorussians.

Parts of both nations were included in the frontiers of Poland, some of the Ukrainians in Czechoslovakia and Rumania also, and a few of the White Ruthenians in Latvia. But after the final peace settlement the great majority of both found themselves in Soviet republics which at first were supposed to be independent but under Communist regimes strictly controlled by Moscow. This control was easy to establish in the comparatively small Byelorussian Republic where national consciousness was less developed and where, after the overthrow of a short-lived democratic government, a local Soviet regime had already been proclaimed on February 10, 1919. This regime at once declared in favor of federation with Russia and less than one year later, on January 16, 1920, it concluded a close military and economic alliance with Moscow. But in the much larger Ukraine too, the Ukrainian Communist Party, under leaders such as Manuilsky and Rakovsky who were not Ukrainians at all, completely subordinated the "independent" republic, whose first capital was Kharkov, near the Russian border, to Soviet Russia. On December 28, 1920, during the peace negotiations with Poland in Riga, a treaty of alliance was signed between the Ukrainian and the Russian Soviet republics. This treaty provided for joint People's Commissariats within the framework of the Russian government which was now enlarged by the inclusion of Ukrainian representatives.

After the Peace of Riga the idea of a real federal union of all Soviet republics, already prepared on June 1, 1919, by the establishment of a preparatory commission, made rapid progress under Russian pressure and in connection with the almost complete exhaustion of the Ukraine by war, revolution, drought, and typhus. The R.S.F.S.R. (Russian Soviet Federal Socialist Republic), overwhelmingly larger in area and population than all the other Communist republics including those in Transcaucasia and Central Asia, was of course the nucleus of the union. It was to this government that more and more power was gradually transferred by the allied republics, including the right to represent them in foreign relations, as happened in the Ukraine at the Genoa Conference in April, 1922. Finally, on the thirtieth of December of that same year, a "treaty of amalgamation" united the R.S.F.S.R., the Ukraine, Byelorussia, and the Transcaucasian Soviet Federation (already established on March 12, 1922, by Armenia, Azerbaijan, and Georgia) "into a single federal state."

As first conceived and ratified in 1923, the union was so strongly centralized that in the final text of the first constitution of the U.S.S.R., of January 30, 1924, some apparent concessions had to be made to the susceptibilities of the non-Russian nationalities. The "right of secession" granted to all union republics in Article 4 was, however, a mere fiction, subordinated to the right of the working class to consolidate its power. And though the sovereignty of the individual republics was restricted by Article 3, "only in respect of matters referred to the competence of the Union," the constitution transferred so much real power to the central "All Union Commissariats" in Moscow that very little was left to the local administration. In addition to the Soviet of the union, in which delegates of the Russian Republic had of course a tremendous majority, the Soviet of Nationalities was established as a second chamber. There the union republics, and even the autonomous units within these republics (mainly within the R.S.F.S.R.), had equal representation but that chamber had to deal chiefly with the settlement of nationalities problems.

As to these problems, the basic principle, repeatedly stressed by Lenin and Stalin (the official specialist in that matter) was freedom in form but identity in content, a formula which recognized the right of each nationality to the use of its language and its folk customs, but on condition that the whole political, economic, and cultural development of all of them would strictly follow the Communist pattern. And since it was the Communist Party, one for the whole union and dominated by the Russian majority, which really governed the federation, any constitutional guaranties based on a division of power between the union and the individual republics was to remain merely formal.

The predominance of the R.S.F.S.R. remained overwhelming even after the creation of additional union republics in Central Asia. One of these, the Kazakh S.S.R. which was established in 1936, received a territory of more than one million square miles but which was very sparsely populated (about six million inhabitants). The two Soviet republics at the western border of the union were the largest in population, but even the Ukraine with its thirty-five million people was in that respect only one-third of the Russian republic. Its area, although consisting of almost 200,000 square miles was insignificant in comparison with the six and a half million square miles of Russia. Furthermore, there was a considerable Russian minority among the inhabitants of the Ukrainian Republic.

Yet it was Ukrainian nationalism which constituted the most serious difficulty for the nationalities policy of the Soviet Union, and it was in the Ukraine that this policy showed the most amazing fluctuations. During the first years of the Communist regime, Ukrainian language and culture were officially promoted. Kiev, again made the capital of the republic, developed into an important intellectual center with its Ukrainian academy and university. But when, in spite of these formal concessions, communism did not make sufficient progress, as an antithesis there came a policy of standardization and unification under Moscow which was even more ruthless than that under the czars. The first Five Year Plan, which was set afoot in 1928, was an opportunity to bring to the old and new industrial centers of the Ukraine a large number of workers from Russia. Russian was reintroduced as a second language in all schools, and repressions were organized against both intellectual leaders accused of reactionary nationalism and peasants opposed to the collectivization of agriculture.

Arrests, trials, and deportations, including that of old Professor Michael Hrushevsky who died in exile a broken man, were disorganizing the national life of the Ukrainian people, while the so-called political famine of 1932–1933 threatened its very existence. It is impossible to strictly evaluate the number of those who, in addition to the millions transferred to remote areas of the Soviet Union, died of starvation because of the economic policy of the government which tried to conceal that artificial famine from the outside world and did not permit any foreign relief action. The victims were replaced by non-Ukrainians, mostly Russians, who to a large extent changed the national structure of the republic.

No such violent measures were needed in the much smaller Byelorussian S.S.R., with only about 60,000 square miles and eight million people. Here, too, native language and culture were encouraged, at least at the outset, and an intellectual center was created in the capital, Minsk, with its Byelorussian university. But since national consciousness was less developed here than in the Ukraine, and since organized resistance against communism was even more difficult, the essence of that new, formally Byelorussian culture could be decisively influenced by Moscow. Like the Ukrainians, the White Ruthenians also had less real liberty in their Soviet republics than in neighboring Poland where even as minorities they could organize politically without any imposed ideology.

In the Soviet Union the trend toward centralization, growing in connection with the progress of economic planning, was evidenced in the new constitution of 1936 through a novel distribution of power which transferred even more matters to the Union Commissariats or placed local activities under federal direction. It was no real compensation that a change in the composition of the Soviet of Nationalities deprived the R.S.F.S.R. of its majority in that body, whose role became more and more reduced to that of a platform of discussion for the non-Russian nationalities. Even that change favored the non-Slavic peoples rather than the Ukrainians and White Ruthenians. These in general, despite their comparatively large number and higher level of development, were regarded as only two of the countless ethnic groups (sometimes figures of about 180 are given) which are officially distinguished in what is really a new Russian Empire with a Communist regime. The protection of all their Union Republics, Autonomous Republics, Regions, and Districts by the 1936 constitution is a fiction similar to that which gave to some articles of that constitution appearances of a return to democracy, while the purges which started about the same time made Stalin's dictatorship even more absolute.

Under that dictatorship and under a new system of Russification, more efficient and more subtle than the czar's, the Ukrainians and White Ruthenians, tied up with all the nationalities of the Eurasian subcontinent, were cut off from East Central Europe and from the Western community of nations. Left within the boundaries of the U.S.S.R., they were, in spite of their situation at the western fringe of the Soviet Union, practically forgotten by the Western world which continued to call the whole federation Russia as in the past. East Central Europe was once more reduced to the territories which Russia had not succeeded in attaching to her empire or to its new ideology.

No more than the federal conceptions of the Pan-Slavists did the new Soviet federalism guarantee to the non-Russians of that empire a normal, free development which in Stalinist terminology was called national mysticism.

That terminology, however, did not fail to produce a certain impression in the Western world which was left under the illusion that the Soviet Union alone had solved the problem of the coexistence of numerous racial and linguistic groups in one body politic and had created an unusually successful form of federalism. In both respects the Russian-controlled, Communist Eastern Europe seemed to be in advance of East Central Europe, where in spite of a large-scale application of self-determination, each of the "new" independent nation-states had its own more or less acute minorities problems and where no federalism facilitated economic cooperation at least. It is therefore important to remember that the free nations of East Central Europe, as members of the League of Nations which the U.S.S.R. violently opposed for many years and joined only in 1934, had opportunities for solving their difficulties and especially for entering into regional agreements. Again only lack of time and totalitarian pressure from both sides prevented these prospects from developing fully.

22

INTERNATIONAL RELATIONS BETWEEN
THE WARS

EAST CENTRAL EUROPE IN THE LEAGUE OF NATIONS

It was in the obvious interest of the liberated nations of East Central Europe that President Wilson's program of self-determination was combined with a project of international organization which materialized in the League of Nations. Such a league, which guaranteed the independence and territorial integrity of all member states great or small, was welcomed by those countries which in the past had seen these rights so frequently violated and even completely refused to them. Furthermore, in the opinion of the peacemakers, the League was to provide a solution for all those problems which had not been adequately settled in the various treaties, and such problems were particularly numerous in East Central Europe, that basically reorganized part of the continent.

On the other hand, however, the new, restored, or enlarged states of that region were so concerned with their urgent national issues, at least at the beginning, that even those of them who were represented at the Peace Conference and in the drafting of the Covenant could not give sufficient attention to the general questions which were involved. They also resented the privileged position of the big powers, first in the Commission which worked out the organization of the League, and then in the League's Council. Only one of the nonpermanent seats could be attributed to the countries of East Central Europe, Greece being chosen as their first representative, thanks to the prestige of Venizelos. And Poland's disappointment at the solution of the Danzig problem did not make her favorable to the idea of having to share with the League the limited power given to her in an area which she had hoped to obtain without restriction.

Poland, too, was the first country which was obliged to sign, simultaneously with the Versailles Treaty of June 28, 1919, a special treaty with the great powers whose main provisions dealt with the rights of her minorities, racial, linguistic, or religious, which were placed under the guaranty of the League. The resentment caused by that treaty was directed not against the provisions themselves, since Poland was ready to include even more extensive rights for all minorities in her national constitution, but against the international interference with that delicate matter. In the case of Poland, the interference of her neighbors with the religious minorities problem on the eve of the partitions was indeed a painful recollection. Though now a similar interference was entrusted to an international body, the Council of the League, the fact that this international protection of minorities was not made universal was resented as a discrimination not only by Poland but also by the other "new" states, Czechoslovakia, Rumania, Yugoslavia, and Greece, which had to sign similar treaties. Among the defeated nations, only the small countries, but not Germany, also had to accept these obligations regarding minorities in their respective peace treaties.

The apprehension raised by the system of minorities protection also proved justified for another reason. Originally that new system was introduced mainly for assuring protection to the large Jewish minorities in East Central Europe. When extended to all other groups, however, it was soon used and misused in favor of the German minorities that were scattered all over that same region. And it served the German Reich as a weapon for creating trouble in the countries concerned and for supporting the German groups in their opposition against the states to which they now belonged. However, that danger became apparent only after Germany's admission into the League, which did not take place until after the admission of all the states of East Central Europe.

In addition to the five of them which as Allied powers were among the original members of the League, the new Republic of Finland, restored Albania, and two of the former enemies, Austria and Bulgaria, were admitted by the first Assembly in December, 1920. On that same occasion all nations which had formerly been under Russian rule asked for such admission, but their applications were rejected by a large majority which, except in the case of Finland, did not consider their situation sufficiently stabilized and which doubted whether or not the League would be able to safeguard the newly proclaimed independence of these countries. These apprehensions proved correct with regard to the Ukraine as well as the distant Transcaucasian republics, but Estonia, Latvia, and Lithuania were admitted by the second Assembly of the League in September, 1921, having in the meantime received *de jure* recognition by all powers. The admission of Hungary was delayed until the next year because of the unsettled Burgenland question. All these new members, as far as they had not signed treaties that included the protection of minorities, had to sign declarations in that matter (Finland only with respect to the Åland Islands) on the occasion of their admission, making these international guaranties a general rule in East Central Europe. Reciprocal guaranties in favor of the minorities on both sides of the border were included only in the Riga Treaty and in the Geneva Convention regarding Upper Silesia.

Besides that minorities problem, the countries of East Central Europe had many other occasions, much more numerous than in the case of any other nations, to use the machinery of the League. Some of these issues resulted from territorial controversies connected with the establishment of the new boundaries but were neither definitely settled nor touched on at all by the Paris Peace Conference. They were brought before the League's Council under Article 11 of the Covenant as threats to international peace. The League was successful in the question of the Åland Islands and of Upper Silesia, and though the Wilno problem could not be settled in Geneva, the Council's action contributed greatly to avoiding an armed conflict in that matter.

The League also contributed to the settlement of a few minor controversies regarding the frontiers of Albania and the Polish-Czechoslovak border, and successfully settled two rather dangerous incidents in the Balkans. Particularly difficult to deal with was the Greek-Italian dispute in 1923 because one of the great powers was involved and had already taken military action by bombarding and occupying the island of Corfu. Though Italy wanted to keep the whole affair in the hands of the Conference of Ambassadors, the suggestions of the Council of the League were followed in substance and Corfu was restored to Greece. In 1925 a clash also occurred, this time between Greek and Bulgarian forces, but in that dispute between two small countries the League was able to act with noteworthy efficiency and to avoid any serious trouble.

The activity of the so-called technical organizations of the League, which as a whole was much more successful than its purely political action, proved particularly helpful to the war-torn countries of East Central Europe. Immediately after the war, the Health Organization stopped the typhus epidemic which was spreading westward from Russia, and in the economic and financial field, in addition to the reconstruction of Austria and Hungary, assistance through international loans was given to Greece, Bulgaria, Estonia, and to the Free City of Danzig.

The East Central European countries were, however, most interested in the League's efforts to create a system of collective security through mutual guaranties against aggression which would be more efficient than those provided for in the Covenant. High hopes were raised at the Assembly of 1924 when the Geneva Protocol was drafted, giving a clear definition of aggression and promising joint action against a country that would refuse a peaceful settlement by arbitration. Edward Beneš from Czechoslovakia was very active in preparing that agreement, and among the other East Central European powers, Poland, through her foreign minister, Count Alexander Skrzyński, gave special support to the project.

The protocol was abandoned, however, chiefly because of Britain's opposition, and the Locarno agreement, which was negotiated the next year outside the League, proved to be a substitute that was very unsatisfactory to Germany's eastern neighbors. Poland was particularly alarmed by the prospect that Germany, invited to join the League with great power privileges, would have a permanent seat in the Council. Therefore she claimed a similar privilege for herself. In 1926, however, she accepted a compromise. This was a so-called semipermanent seat through the right of re-election. At the same time the number of nonpermanent seats was increased to eleven so that two more countries from East Central Europe were always practically certain to be chosen for a period of three years. And although there were frequent clashes in the Council between the German and Polish representatives, the new Polish foreign minister, August Zaleski, was also a strong supporter of the League.

It was the Polish delegation which at the Assembly of 1927 made a proposal to outlaw war and thus prepared public opinion for the Briand-Kellogg Pact which was signed in Paris on August 28, 1928, and condemned recourse to war for the solution of international controversies. And it was that same delegation which actively participated in the Disarmament Conference of 1932 and submitted a project of "moral disarmament" that would make the material limitation and reduction of armaments easier to accept.

The failure of that Conference and, in general, of the League's efforts to combine arbitration, security, and disarmament according to the French formula, was a special disappointment to the countries of East Central Europe. It was only then that most of them turned to bilateral agreements with the most threatening neighbors in order to find other ways to secure their independence and security. Poland, particularly endangered in her position between Germany and Russia, completed that change in her policy under Foreign Minister Joseph Beck who also declared in 1934 that his country would not consider herself bound by the minorities treaty so long as the whole system was not extended to all countries.

It was indeed difficult for the smaller nations of East Central Europe to have any confidence in collective security when that security was to be assured by pacts among the big powers, negotiated outside the League, or when the Soviet Union, admitted to the League in September, 1934 almost simultaneously with Germany's withdrawal, suddenly appeared as a champion of the Geneva institution, once so violently opposed, and of a collective security system. The League's failure to stop aggression in Manchuria and Ethiopia made it easy to foresee that she would be powerless also against totalitarian forces turning against East Central Europe. And when at the last Assembly in December, 1939, the League condemned at least one of the acts of aggression by excluding Soviet Russia, it was too late. Too many aggressions had already been tolerated to save a peace settlement which had lasted twenty years but which already in the thirties could not be saved by mere confidence in the League of Nations.

TOWARD REGIONAL FEDERATIONS

Article 21 of the League's Covenant encouraged the conclusion of regional agreements. Nowhere was there a greater need for such agreements than in East Central Europe where about a dozen independent states, most of them rather small and none of them a great power, had so many common interests to develop and so many common dangers to face. Contrary to widespread opinion, it was *not* the creation or restoration of these states, misleadingly called a "Balkanization" of Europe, which was a source of trouble and difficulties.

The liberation movement which in the nineteenth century had started in the Balkans and which after World War I included the whole area between Germany and Russia, was an act of justice and a natural process based upon historical traditions as well as modern aspirations which at last received satisfaction. On the contrary, it was because that liberation had been so long delayed and continued to be challenged by imperialistic neighbors who considered the independence of so many "new" states merely a provisional solution that the adjustment and stabilization of the peace settlement proved such a delicate task and required the organized cooperation of all the interested nations.

In an area where it was impossible to draft frontiers which would strictly correspond to ethnic divisions and satisfy all economic requirements, none of these nations could remain in isolation. The trend toward federalism which had been so significant in earlier periods of their history reappeared as soon as they regained their freedom. There had never been any federal union or even any looser system of cooperation comprising all of them. Therefore, it was natural that in the period between the two world wars more than one regional agreement was planned in the East Central European area. Each of them developed only gradually in the direction of a real federation or at least confederation, without having the necessary time for reaching that goal. As usual in the history of the whole area, the Baltic, Danubian, and Balkan regions had to be distinguished, without there being, however, precise dividing lines between them. In all three cases regional conferences or bilateral treaties were leading to ententes, with the creation of permanent organs as the next step.

The Baltic conferences began as early as 1919 and at the outset included all five states of East Central Europe which had access to and a vital interest in the Baltic. Not only the three small specifically Baltic republics were represented, but also Finland in the north and Poland in the south, which latter seemed to lead the movement. But for that very reason the Polish-Lithuanian conflict proved a serious obstacle to such general Baltic cooperation. From 1921 onward Lithuania no longer participated in these conferences, to the regret of her closest neighbor, Latvia, which did not want to take sides in the conflict and yet was particularly interested in the whole scheme. It was her able foreign minister, S. Meierovics, who at the Baltic Conference of four states held in Warsaw in March, 1922, suggested joint action by these states in Geneva, and at the conference of February, 1924, advocated the formal constitution of a Baltic League.

Particularly successful seemed the next Baltic Conference which in January, 1925, met in Helsinki, where all four states signed treaties of conciliation and arbitration and decided to set up interstate commissions of conciliation. But it soon became apparent that Finland, host to that conference, was hesitating to continue her cooperation because she did not want to become involved in any possible conflicts between the other Baltic states and the Soviet Union. Hoping that her security would be better guaranteed by a rapprochement with the Scandinavian countries, Finland definitely turned in that direction in the following years. In 1933 she joined the so-called Oslo Agreement which had been concluded three years before between the Scandinavian kingdoms and the western neutrals, the Netherlands, Belgium, and Luxemburg. Particularly close remained Finland's cooperation with the Scandinavian group, including Iceland, as was evidenced by the economic agreement of 1934 and the regular conferences of foreign ministers.

Estonia and Latvia, allied with each other from 1924, continued to have very friendly relations with Poland but eventually proved more interested in establishing closer ties with the third small Baltic country, Lithuania, with which they formed a Baltic Entente in 1934. This was much more limited than the regional agreement which had originally been planned, but apparently it was safer from entanglements in big-power politics. When the big neighbors decided to interfere with the Baltic situation, the security of the three allies of course proved to be an illusion. But their cooperation, inadequate in a European crisis, gave valuable results in the last years of peace and in the framework of the League of Nations.

In the Danubian area some kind of regional cooperation seemed particularly desirable in view of the breakup of the Habsburg monarchy which had united the Danubian lands for such a long time. But all projects for a Danubian federation were regarded with suspicion by those who feared a restoration of the defunct monarchy even in a disguised form. The antagonism between the two groups of successor states, the victors and the vanquished, made impossible an agreement including all of them. It was, therefore, only among the three countries which had benefited from the peace settlement and which feared its revision, which Hungary so strongly requested, that the so-called

Little Entente created a close cooperation which was an important element of general European politics between the two wars.

The entente was based upon three treaties : between Czechoslovakia and Yugoslavia, of August 14, 1920; Czechoslovakia and Rumania, of April 23, 1921; and finally Rumania and Yugoslavia, of June 7, 1921. Czechoslovak initiative, particularly that of Dr. Beneš, was evident, but prominent statesmen of the other two countries were also deeply interested in an agreement which was to guarantee all three against a possible Habsburg restoration, and especially against "an unprovoked attack on the part of Hungary," to which the Yugoslav-Rumanian treaty also added the danger of a similar attack by Bulgaria.

Much more important than these original provisions against dangers which were illusory so long as no great power supported the revisionist movement, was the positive cooperation of at least three Danubian countries which jointly defended the peace settlement and helped to consolidate it at numerous international conferences within and outside the League of Nations. The relations of the Little Entente with Austria soon improved to such an extent that the group participated in the rehabilitation of that country. To a certain extent, financial assistance to Hungary was also favored, although her political relations with the Little Entente always remained tense.

On May 21, 1929, that entente received an organic structure by an agreement which made the renewal of the three alliances automatic at the end of each five-year period and by a tripartite treaty for the peaceful settlement of all possible disputes through arbitration and conciliation. The necessity for such closer ties became evident in the midst of the world depression and even more so after Hitler's coming to power. Therefore on February 16, 1933, the Little Entente was virtually transformed into a diplomatic confederation with a permanent council of the three foreign ministers or their delegates and a joint secretariat, including a permanent branch office in Geneva. The new organization, whose objectives now went much beyond the limited, rather one-sided scope of the first alliances, seemed quite efficient in the international discussions of the next two or three years, but proved helpless when the great crisis started in 1938. The last meeting of the Little Entente Council, on the twenty-first of August, of that year, when a belated attempt was made to come to an agreement with Hungary, could not save Czechoslovakia from German aggression, Yugoslavia being already chiefly concerned with changes in the Mediterranean and Rumania with the danger from the Soviet Union.

In the early days of the Little Entente, two possible extensions had been considered—north and south of the Danubian region. On March 3, 1921, Poland concluded an alliance with Rumania, but even when her relations with Czechoslovakia improved in 1923–1925, she had no interest in joining an entente that was primarily directed against her traditional Hungarian friends. Greece had indeed a common interest with her Yugoslav neighbor and with Rumania in opposing Bulgarian revisionism, but instead of her joining the Little Entente, the two southern members of the latter, being at the same time Balkan countries, participated in the creation of another regional agreement in the Balkan Peninsula.

There, as in the Baltic region, the movement was going back to earlier projects of Balkan federalism and started in 1930. The first conferences included all six Balkan states, not only the three allied powers but also Albania and the former enemies, Bulgaria and Turkey. The relations between Greece and Turkey improved so much that both countries signed a treaty of alliance and mutual guaranty on September 14, 1933. But it proved impossible to come to a full agreement with Bulgaria or even with Albania, so that the Balkan Pact, which after many preliminary projects was signed in Athens on February 9, 1934, included only Greece, Yugoslavia, Rumania, and Turkey. In the fall of the same year, which can be considered the climax of the whole movement toward regional federalism, that pact was implemented at a meeting in Ankara by a statute of organization which provided the Balkan Entente, like the Little Entente, with a permanent council of foreign ministers and also with an advisory economic council.

In the Balkans, as in the Danubian region, a last-minute effort was made in the summer of 1938 to include in the mutual understanding the country which seemed the greatest obstacle to unity, in that case Bulgaria. But like the Little Entente, the Balkan Entente was also a guaranty against aggression only on the part of a small state of the region which was supposed to be better organized. There were no obligations of joint action against an aggression coming from a great power outside the Balkans, and yet here too this was the real danger which the smaller countries, even all together, were unable to prevent.

RELATIONS WITH WESTERN EUROPE

Since neither the world-wide League of Nations, with strictly limited powers, nor regional agreements which needed time to develop and could hardly build up sufficient strength, were a guaranty of East Central Europe's regained freedom, all the nations of that area were looking for support from the West. There they hoped to find the assistance of great powers which, being of a democratic character and having no common frontier with any country of East Central Europe, were no threat to the independence of these nations and had already been allies of some of them in World War I.

The United States of America, particularly distant but interested in the problems of East Central Europe because of the origin of many of its citizens, had proved especially favorable to the self-determination of all peoples of that region. But since America neither ratified the peace treaties nor joined the League, but instead entered into a period of isolationism, there remained only France and Britain, Italy being a rather dangerous neighbor, particularly after the establishment of the Fascist regime in 1922.

At the Peace Conference France had already supported those countries which would help her to check Germany from the east and replace her prewar alliance with Russia, at the same time checking the advance of bolshevism. It was also French culture which, as in the past, attracted all East Central Europe, and her constitution served as a model for the new constitutions in that region. But precisely that many-sided cooperation with France which in most countries east of Germany had deep historic roots was an obstacle to equally close relations with Britain. She was less interested in East Central Europe and considered French influence there a further step to French predominance on the whole Continent, of which she was traditionally afraid.

It was Poland, with her old friendship for France, which in the years of the peace settlement had already had special difficulties with Britain, and after the war was the first to definitely join the French camp. The close French-Polish military alliance, signed on February 19, 1921, was for many years to remain the cornerstone of Poland's foreign policy and the most concrete guaranty of her independence and integrity. But although the first formal alliance between France and one of the Little Entente states, Czechoslovakia, was not concluded before January 25, 1924, that whole entente was from the outset as close to France as was Poland, and together with the latter constituted a solid area of French influence in East Central Europe. That situation found its expression time and again in Geneva and in the most important international conferences, such as that of Genoa in 1922. The agreements which France concluded with Rumania in 1926, and with Yugoslavia the following year, seemed to round up and to stabilize that French "sphere of influence" in the main part of East Central Europe.

It must be pointed out, however, that French influence was never any real limitation on the full independence of her smaller allies in the east, and that the cooperation between what then was the strongest military power of the Continent, and four states which taken together seemed at least equally strong, far from being any danger to the peace of Europe was its best possible guaranty.

Such an additional guaranty had become particularly necessary after the Locarno agreements of October, 1925. Although both Poland and Czechoslovakia participated in that conference, these eastern neighbors of Germany did not receive the same guaranties of security and integrity as were given to her western neighbors. The arbitration treaties which Germany signed with the two eastern republics were no recognition of their western boundaries, which were not guaranteed by Britain and Italy as were the frontiers of France and Belgium. In view of this dangerous distinction between peace in the west and peace in the east, it was of great importance that France had concluded treaties of mutual assistance with Poland and Czechoslovakia at Locarno. These were to supplement the earlier alliances and be a safeguard against any German aggression.

It so happened, however, that contrary to the high hopes raised in Western Europe by the Locarno Pact and Germany's subsequent entrance into the League of Nations, contrary also to the atmosphere of confidence which the Pact of Paris of 1928 was supposed to create, even France herself could not feel entirely secure from a Germany which was so rapidly recovering from her defeat, was able to play off Britain and Italy against France, never was really disarmed and only claimed the disarmament of all others, and where the Nazi movement was making rapid progress.

Under these conditions France became less interested in her eastern alliances in the last years of the Weimar Republic, propagated the rather utopian plan of a European Union, and after Hitler's seizure of power was not prepared to accept the Polish proposal for preventive action. Instead, a few months later on July 15, 1933, she joined the Four Power Pact with Britain, Italy, and Germany. This was a return to the obsolete and dangerous idea of a control of Europe by the great powers only which had been suggested by Mussolini but which was violently opposed by the countries of East Central Europe, particularly Poland and the Little Entente.

After the failure of that project, France, looking for stronger support in the east, returned to another prewar conception which was dangerous for all countries between Germany and the Soviet Union—alliance with Russia. After concluding a trade agreement with Russia on January 11, 1934, as a first step, the French foreign minister, Louis Barthou, suggested a so-called Eastern Locarno, a pact of mutual guaranty in which the Soviet Union and Germany as well as the smaller nations of East Central Europe would participate. When this plan, too, rejected by Germany, regarded with suspicion by Poland, and never clearly defined, had to be abandoned, on May 2, 1935, France did indeed sign a mutual assistance treaty with Russia after sponsoring her admission into the League. But she delayed its ratification and her example was followed only by Czechoslovakia which also allied herself with the Soviet Union on May sixteenth of the same year.

That policy offered Hitler a pretext for denouncing first, in March, 1935, the disarmament obligations of Germany, and a year later, the Locarno Treaties by militarily reoccupying the Rhineland. In spite of her nonaggression pact with Germany, Poland informed France that, faithful to her earlier commitments, she would join in the repression of that challenge. But in view of Britain's negative attitude, France, too, merely limited herself to futile protests in the League's Council and nothing was done about it. Under these circumstances the countries of East Central Europe, no longer confident of the support of the Western democracies and threatened by all three totalitarian powers at once, also followed a policy of appeasement. Being in a particularly difficult position between Germany and the Soviet Union, and in view of the cooling off of her relations with France, Poland tried to take advantage of the breathing space which the nonaggression pact with Hitler seemed to guarantee for ten years. In the Danubian and Balkan region, however, it was Italian influence which was in progress.

Yugoslavia, whose relations with France had also suffered through the assassination of her king in Marseilles on October 9, 1934, and unwilling to join her Czechoslovak ally in the rapprochement with the Soviet Union which she had never recognized, considered it best for her security to promote friendly relations with her Italian neighbor in spite of all the controversies of the past. Italy also tried to supplant the old French sympathies in Rumania, and had a special chance in those countries of East Central Europe which were in the revisionist camp and outside the French system of alliances. This was not only in Austria but also in Hungary, and particularly in Bulgaria whose young king had married a daughter of the king of Italy in 1930 and had a son and heir by her in 1937. Convinced, furthermore, that Albania could always serve as a basis for action in one way or another, Italy was stronger in South Eastern Europe than ever before.

The constitutional changes in almost all East Central European countries which also facilitated closer relations with Fascist Italy had little, if any, connection with the decline of French influence. But the frequent internal crises in the Third Republic seemed to be one more argument in favor of more authoritarian forms of government and confirmed all critics of full democracy and parliamentary supremacy in their opinions. And in France herself the conviction was growing that her far-reaching commitments in East Central Europe, which the renewed ties with Russia had not made at all easier, were beyond her actual forces, both military and financial, which had been so overestimated in the years after her great victory of 1918.

Great Britain, whose rivalry with France, largely caused by that very overestimation, had been from the beginning one of the main causes of unrest in postwar Europe, continued to give little attention or support to the small countries in the distant and little-known eastern part of the continent which she always considered a possible source of trouble. The stabilization of that "new" Europe which after all survived even the great economic depression certainly impressed British opinion, particularly in the case of Poland, with whom, as with the smaller Baltic countries, maritime trade relations were developing on an ever larger scale. But there always remained the fear that in case of a serious political crisis any of these countries could be an obstacle to that appeasement of the dictators which continued to seem desirable and possible. And since faraway America seemed even less interested in that troublesome part of the world which was divided by so many rather strange frontiers, the Anglo-Saxon democracies were even less prepared than France to meet the growing danger to European and world peace which was once more rising in East Central Europe. They were not even sufficiently convinced and aware that it was not the countries of that region themselves but exclusively Germany and Russia which were responsible for "the gathering storm."

THE GERMAN AND RUSSIAN DANGER

The war of 1914–1917 had interrupted the long tradition of German-Russian cooperation, and though the Soviet government made a separate peace which gave Germany a last chance of victory in the West, the harsh terms of the Brest-Litovsk Treaty left deep resentment among the Russians. When, however, the victory of the Western Allies and the following peace settlement left Russia with practically the same territorial losses (except in the case of the Ukraine), and when a belt of free East Central European countries was created between Germany and Russia at the expense of both of them, it was only natural that both were equally opposed to that solution. Their common feeling of frustration resulted in a solidarity and in a desire to resume their former cooperation with a view to regaining their lost areas of expansion, and even the difference of their regimes seemed no insurmountable obstacle. Although the Communists had little chance during the brief German revolution, and although most of the Germans were afraid of bolshevism, many of them rather welcomed the successes of the Red Army during the invasion of Poland in 1920. And when the *cordon sanitaire* between Germany and Russia—as both of them called the zone of liberated nations—was definitely re-established and the "new" states could no longer be called *Säsonstaaten,*

EAST CENTRAL EUROPE BETWEEN THE TWO WORLD WARS

(Map opp.)

——————— Frontiers of the region

–·–·–·–·–· National boundaries

✦✦✦✦✦✦✦✦✦ Dividing line between the German and the Russian "spheres of influence" established in 1939

the two powers which remained great powers, though outside the League of Nations, were equally eager to come to an understanding directed against the restored East Central Europe.

An excellent opportunity for negotiating such an agreement was offered them in 1922 when at Lloyd George's suggestion it was decided to invite both Germany and the Soviet Union to the Genoa Conference. Fully justified proved the alarm of Poland, the main object of their hostility, and of the Little Entente which was also a check to German influence formerly so strong in the Danubian Monarchy and to Russian advance in the direction of the Balkans. For the only result of the futile attempt to reintegrate the two big outsiders in the European state system was the treaty which these two concluded on April 16, 1922, at Rapallo, near Genoa, where the conference was making so little progress.

Apparently the Rapallo Treaty was nothing but a normalization of German-Russian relations, indispensable since the Treaty of Brest-Litovsk was abrogated, and a basis for the resumption of economic intercourse. But its political implications were obvious and remained a basis of renewed cooperation independent of internal changes in either country as well as an open threat against the nations which separated the two partners. The apprehensions of these nations were confirmed when, just before leaving for the Locarno Conference in October, 1925, Chancellor Gustav Stresemann signed another apparently innocuous agreement with the Soviet Union. A few months after Locarno, in April, 1926, when Germany's admission to the League encountered some difficulties, this was implemented by a formal nonaggression treaty which included provisions that Germany, when a member of the League, would not participate in any possible sanctions against Russia.

The time was not yet ripe, however, for an aggression by either of them, directed against the countries of East Central Europe. Although Stresemann openly showed his hostility against Poland when raising in the League's Council the question of German minorities, and though he hoped that Germany's membership in the League would facilitate a revision of her eastern frontier, such a revision was openly requested only by German propaganda. And the Soviet Union, then engaged in its first Five Year Plan, concluded another series of treaties with her western neighbors which seemed to imply a definite acceptance of Russia's new boundaries. The first of these treaties was a protocol signed in Moscow on February 5, 1929, by the delegates of Estonia, Latvia, Poland, Rumania, and the Soviet Union, whereby it was decided that the provisions of the Paris Pact of August 28, 1928, outlawing war, would come into force without delay between the contracting parties as soon as ratified by their respective legislatures and without waiting for the entry into force of the Paris Treaty as such. Even more important, because more specific, was the nonaggression treaty which the Soviet Union concluded with Poland on July 25, 1932, because reference was made to the Riga Treaty of 1921 as the basis of relations between both countries. And while Russia avoided a collective pact of that kind, with all her neighbors acting jointly, on July 3, 1933, she signed the London Convention with not only Estonia, Latvia, Poland, and Rumania but also with her Asiatic neighbors, Turkey, Persia, and Afghanistan, giving the clearest possible definition of "the aggressor in an international conflict," "in order to obviate any pretext" for threatening the independence, integrity, and free internal development of any state.

That excellent definition, supplementing the Briand-Kellogg Pact of 1928 which was once more quoted, had been suggested by Maksim Litvinov, the same foreign commissar of the Soviet Union, who at the Disarmament Conference in Geneva, also referred to in the London Convention, had closely cooperated with the German delegates, claiming an obviously impossible immediate and total disarmament of all countries. Such a decision would have left East Central Europe and its possible allies defenseless against the clandestine armament of Germany, the forces of the U.S.S.R. which were beyond any control, and the tremendous war potential of both of them. But the community of interest which was behind that propaganda move seemed to disappear when on January 31, 1933, Hitler at last succeeded in gaining full control of Germany, not only because the Nazi Party had risen in violent opposition against communism but even more so because of the foreign policy outlined in *Mein Kampf*.

In Hitler's public program of action, German expansion, independent of any question of regime or political ideology, was advocated as a historic necessity both in the West and in the East. But even the threat to France was less emphasized than that against the Slavic peoples and particularly Russia, from the Ukraine to the Urals, a region which was described as a field of German conquest. Since Hitler wanted to avoid a simultaneous war on two fronts, however, the question remained open in which direction he would move first. And in the case of aggression in the East, the fact that Germany was no longer Russia's immediate neighbor raised another problem. Would Hitler's Third Reich first attack the countries between Germany and Russia or try to induce them to join in an aggression against the Soviet Union? If the first alternative were chosen, a return to the traditional cooperation with Russia would be desirable but only as a temporary expedient. Similarly, any alliance against Russia with one or more countries of East Central Europe would be only temporary and a step toward their inclusion in the German *Lebensraum* which was a prerequisite to any further expansion in the eastern direction.

Among the countries equally threatened by both alternatives, Poland was the most important and at the same time the most directly exposed. But she was also the most fully aware of the simultaneous danger threatening from the Russian side, and was therefore suspicious of the sudden interest of the Soviet Union in collective security and anxious to keep a well-balanced position between the two totalitarian powers. In the opinion of Joseph Beck, Polish foreign minister since the fall of 1932, this dangerous game was the only possible course to choose as long as the Western democracies persisted in their policy of appeasement. He therefore seized the opportunity offered to Poland when Hitler, contrary to all expectations, declared himself in favor of an improvement in German-Polish relations and on January 26, 1934, a nonaggression pact between the two countries was signed for ten years. But Poland avoided any further commitment which would have been contrary to her earlier international obligations and in the same year, on the fifth of May, extended her nonaggression pact with Russia, originally concluded for three years only, until the end of 1945, with automatic prolongation for further periods of two years.

German-Polish relations seemed indeed better than ever before. Satisfied with Hitler's promise that Polish rights in Danzig would be respected, Poland did not oppose the nazification of the internal administration of the Free City, and on November 5, 1937, signed an additional agreement which was supposed to ease the persistent tension in the matter of minorities. This was already after the crisis of 1936, provoked by the Rhineland remilitarization, when Poland's second offer to stop Hitler through a joint action received no attention. But even then the Polish government consistently rejected all proposals or suggestions for joining a German action against Russia, which were secretly made whenever a Nazi dignitary visited Warsaw. Nevertheless an impression of solidarity of both countries in international affairs was created, since both of them, though for different reasons, rejected the conception of an Eastern Locarno. Soon after Germany's withdrawal from the League of Nations, Poland also seemed to lose her interest in that institution and did not ask for re-election to the Council in 1935.

It was not Poland alone, however, which was in a delicate position. Realizing the difficulty of at once starting the main drive in the eastern direction, whether with Poland or against her, Germany, along with Italy who was soon to be her Axis partner, was again trying to extend her influence in what had formerly been the closely allied Habsburg monarchy, particularly in Hungary and Yugoslavia. At the same time Hitler prepared the conquest through local Nazi movements of the two immediate neighbors in the southeast, Austria and Czechoslovakia. That these were only first steps in the destruction of all East Central Europe was not sufficiently realized in Poland. Similarly the other countries of that region and also those of Western Europe failed to understand that Poland's attempts to remain equally independent of Nazi Germany's and Soviet Russia's influence were of importance not only for herself but for the whole group of nations between the two prospective aggressors, all of which would come under the control of one of them if Poland should fall.

This was not an exceptional situation. On the contrary, the pressure from two sides was unfortunately the normal condition of East Central Europe throughout the whole course of history. The liberation of that whole region after World War I could have changed the destiny of its peoples if they had shown more solidarity, if German and Russian power had not been so quickly reborn under particularly aggressive totalitarian regimes, and if the system of international organization, inseparable from lasting self-determination in one of the most exposed regions of the world, had worked more satisfactorily. The Western democracies which had created, but not sufficiently supported, that system failed to replace it in time by at least individually supporting their natural allies in the East, and therefore their passive attitude in the successive crises of 1938 made all that they did in 1939 too little and too late.

PART VII

DURING AND AFTER WORLD WAR II

23

HITLER'S WAR

THE FIRST AGGRESSIONS

World War II, which was to be followed by a long period of "no war, no peace," not concluded even until the present day, was also preceded by a similar though shorter period in which, without actual fighting, a whole series of aggressions was committed against various countries of East Central Europe. And since the actual war also started in that region of Europe, as in 1914, the importance of all these countries for universal history became more evident than ever before. Though in World War I that importance was more and more realized and was seriously taken into consideration when peace was made, this time exactly the opposite happened. Therefore, though it would be too early to write any definitive history of a world-wide conflict not yet ended by any real peace settlement, it is high time to recall how from the beginning the peoples of East Central Europe, without being in any way responsible for the new catastrophe, were and still are its main victims.

The first totalitarian aggression was directed against Austria. Her chancellor, Kurt von Schuschnigg, realized on his return from his visit to Berchtesgaden on February 12, 1938, that this attempt to appease Hitler had been a mistake. Though abandoned by the Western powers, he decided to hold a plebiscite which would demonstrate that in spite of Nazi agitation the majority of the Austrians wanted to remain an independent country. When it became obvious that Hitler would prevent such a plebiscite by force, Schuschnigg resigned in order to avoid hopeless fighting. He was replaced by the Nazi, Seyss-Inquart, who on March 12, 1938, invited German troops to occupy Austria. On the following day the *Anschluss* was proclaimed, contrary to the peace treaties. It appeared to be not a federation of Austria with Germany, but the complete absorption of the former as a German province which was soon to be called "Ostmark" and divided into seven *Reichsgaue*. Immediately a violent persecution also set in, not only of the Jews but also of all Austrians who were faithful to their tradition, including Schuschnigg himself. He was at once arrested.

That brutal annexation which was passively accepted by the Western powers was not only a first violation of the territorial status of Europe as established after World War I, not only a hard blow for the Austrian people, but also a threat to all other countries of East Central Europe. Hungary and Yugoslavia were now Germany's immediate neighbors, and Czechoslovakia, encircled on three sides, was naturally chosen as next victim.

After the seizure of Austria hardly one month had passed when the leader of the Sudeten Germans, Conrad Henlein, was called to Berlin. On his return on the twenty-fourth of April, he announced at Karlsbad the request for the creation of an autonomous German province within the Czechoslovak Republic. The bargaining which now started between the German minority directed from Berlin and the Czechoslovak government, the latter quite insufficiently backed by the Western democracies, almost led to an outbreak of hostilities at the end of May and was not at all facilitated by the August mission of Lord Runciman, a friend of British Prime Minister Neville Chamberlain, who became convinced that the very liberal concessions offered by Czechoslovakia were inadequate. And so they were, but only because what the Nazis really wanted was the complete separation of the Sudeten territory and its incorporation into Germany. This was openly announced to Chamberlain when on the fifteenth of September, alarmed by Hitler's threats, he visited the dictator in Berchtesgaden. Under British and French pressure, President Beneš even accepted that solution, but when Chamberlain returned to Germany on the twenty-second of September and informed Hitler of that agreement at the Godesberg conference, the Führer rejected all proposals of a gradual transfer and demanded the immediate occupation of the Sudetenland by Germany.

After a few days of imminent war danger it was decided, at Mussolini's suggestion, to hold a four-power conference in Munich. There, on the twenty-ninth of September, an agreement was reached without any participation by Czechoslovakia. She was merely notified of it the next day. Hitler's only concession was that the territory which he wanted to annex was to be occupied progressively during the first week of October. Czechoslovakia lost over 10,000 square miles of territory with a population of 3,600,000, including 800,000 Czechs. At the same time that meant the loss of her natural boundaries, of her only defensible fortifications, and of three-quarters of her industrial resources. Furthermore, Beneš felt obliged to resign, and the new president, Emil Hacha, together with his new government, was forced to reorientate the whole policy of the mutilated country toward close cooperation with Germany.

The Soviet Union resented the fact that it was not invited to the Munich Conference, but the only action which it took in favor of the victim was a warning addressed to Poland on the twenty-third of September, that the Polish-Russian nonaggression pact would be denounced if Poland violated the Czechoslovak frontier. Poland had indeed declared that since all minority territories were to be separated from Czechoslovakia, she would claim the part of the Teschen (Cieszyn, Těšín) region which in spite of its predominantly Polish population had been attributed to Czechoslovakia in 1920. These Polish and similar Hungarian claims were mentioned at Godesberg and Munich where, however, neither of these neighbors of Czechoslovakia was represented. As to the Czechoslovak-Hungarian dispute, it was arbitrated by Germany and Italy which on the second of November, in Vienna, gave Hungary 4,200 square miles with more than a million people. The day before, Czechoslovakia handed over to Poland the small frontier district, 800 square miles with a population of 230,000 (many of them Poles, the statistics are highly controversial), which that country had requested in an ultimatum presented the day after Munich.

To raise that minor issue at that very moment was, of course, most unfortunate, and in spite of all the arguments in favor of the claims of Poland, harmed that country in foreign public opinion. An equally bad impression had been produced earlier in the same year when, a few days after the annexation of Austria, Poland sent an ultimatum to Lithuania which the latter accepted on the nineteenth of March. But that ultimatum, provoked by a frontier incident in which a Polish soldier had been killed, asked exclusively for the establishment of normal diplomatic relations which Lithuania had refused since the conflict of 1920 and which now contributed at once to a notable improvement of the general relations between the two countries. Both in the Lithuanian and in the Czechoslovakian case, Poland acted so abruptly because, alarmed by Germany's advance, she wanted to strengthen her own position in anticipation of Hitler's next move.

That his next aggression would be directed against Poland, had already become apparent in the month after Munich. A first clash almost occurred when Poland occupied the important railway junction of Oderberg (Bogumin, near Teschen), which Germany had claimed for herself. On the twenty-fourth of October Foreign Minister von Ribbentrop for the first time presented to the Polish ambassador the German "suggestions" regarding the return of the Free City of Danzig to the Reich and an extraterritorial railroad and highway through the Polish "corridor." Poland's reaction to these claims, which threatened to cut her off from the Baltic, was of course negative, and although the growing tension was concealed through diplomatic visits of Beck in Berchtesgaden and Ribbentrop in Warsaw, relations became even worse when in the course of these last apparently friendly conversations Poland once more rejected all suggestions to join in an aggression against Russia.

Therefore Hitler finally decided to start his great eastward drive by the destruction of Poland. But in order to have the best possible chance for a speedy victory, he first prepared her encirclement by two actions, one in the south against what remained of Czechoslovakia, the other in the north against Lithuania. The former, by far the more important, was facilitated by the federal structure which had also been imposed on the republic soon after Munich. Under strong pressure the autonomous government of Slovakia, headed by Monsignor Tiso, after a vote of the Slovak parliament for complete independence, on March 14, 1939, placed the new state under Germany's protection. At the same time President Hacha was summoned to Berlin and early in the morning of the fifteenth of March was forced to sign a document creating the "Protectorate of Bohemia and Moravia" which was at once occupied by German troops though the fiction of a separate government was maintained. German forces also received the right to enter Slovakia, and only Carpatho-Ruthenia, which also proclaimed its independence, was retaken by Hungary which thus obtained a common frontier with Poland, something that was desired by both countries.

From the point of view of Poland's security, however, this was very small compensation for the creation of a German front in the southwest, and only a few days after the partition of Czechoslovakia, on the twenty-second of March, Lithuania had to accept a German ultimatum forcing her to return Memel (Klaipeda) and its territory to the Reich. She thus lost her only port, while Germany's position was strengthened in East Prussia, another important strategic basis for the invasion of Poland.

Hitler's breaking of the Munich agreement shocked Britain to such an extent that when Hitler made public his claims regarding Danzig and the "corridor"—obviously a first step to destroy Poland after Czechoslovakia—Chamberlain offered Poland, on the thirtieth of March, a guaranty of her independence which on the sixth of April, during Beck's visit to London, was converted into a mutual guaranty supplementing the French-Polish alliance. On the eighteenth of April British and French guaranties against aggression were also given to Rumania and Greece. Greece was particularly threatened, since Mussolini, encouraged by the successes of Hitler with whom he was soon to conclude a "Pact of Steel," had invaded Albania on the seventh of April, forcing that country to accept the King of Italy as her king also.

But the belated action of the Western powers failed to stop Hitler. On the contrary, on the twenty-eighth of April, he denounced his nonaggression treaty with Poland, which should have remained in force for five more years, and was already encouraged to continue his preparation for war by the suggestions for improving German-Russian relations which the Soviet ambassador in Berlin started making on the seventeenth of April.

On that same day the Soviet Union, in reply to a British proposal that Russia, too, give a guaranty of assistance to any neighbor expressing such a desire, suggested a mutual assistance pact with all states between the Baltic and the Black Sea. But in the protracted negotiations between the Western powers and Russia, where on the third of May Litvinov was replaced as commissar for foreign affairs by V. Molotov, it soon became apparent that the Soviet Union demanded as a price the right to occupy the Baltic states and eastern Poland militarily. The reluctance of these countries to accept any Russian assistance under such conditions was only too justified, and while discussing such a "grand alliance" against Hitler, Russia was making good progress in her negotiations with Germany which led to the Nonaggression Treaty of the twenty-third of August during Ribbentrop's visit in Moscow.

THE INVASION OF POLAND AND HER WAR RECORD

The Nazi-Soviet Pact made it immediately clear that in spite of all peace efforts, including those of Pope Pius XII and President Roosevelt, and of a belated British mediation between Germany and Poland, war had become unavoidable and that there was a serious danger that Poland would be invaded from two sides. Therefore when Britain signed on the twenty-fifth of August, her final Agreement of Mutual Assistance with Poland it was specified in a secret protocol that immediate "support and assistance" were to be given only against Germany. But we know today that the German-Russian treaty was also accompanied by a secret protocol which outlined in advance the partition of Poland and all the rest of East Central Europe into "spheres of influence" of the two partners. Poland was to be "rearranged" along a line following the Narew, Vistula, and San rivers, thus bringing the Soviet Union as far as the eastern suburbs of Warsaw. Furthermore, Finland, Estonia, Latvia, and Rumanian Bessarabia were placed in the Russian sphere of influence, while Germany claimed only Lithuania and declared her disinterestedness in South East Europe.

Germany's invasion of Poland on the morning of September 1, 1939, without declaration of war and after a last-minute compromise proposal which was not even directly communicated to the Polish government within a reasonable time, met with the first resistance ever put up against Hitler. But Britain and France declared war upon the aggressor only on the third of September and even then found it impossible to give their ally any substantial assistance. Poland therefore stood alone during seventeen days of blitzkrieg and ruthless air bombardment by overwhelming forces, experienced for the first time by any nation. Then, on the seventeenth of September she was informed by the Soviet government that the Red Army was crossing her eastern frontier to "protect the population of Western Ukraine and Western White Ruthenia." The Soviet note announcing that stab in the back was well timed through continuous negotiations with the Nazis. Although it pretended that the Polish state, its government, and its capital had already ceased to exist, nevertheless fierce resistance against the Germans continued for more than two weeks. Warsaw in particular surrendered on September 27 only after a heroic defense and savage destruction by the *Luftwaffe*.

The next day another German-Russian treaty of friendship which determined the new boundary on the partitioned territory "of the former Polish state" was signed in Moscow. For in the meantime it had been decided at Stalin's personal suggestion that it would be "wrong to leave an independent Polish rump state" which "in the future might create friction between Germany and the Soviet Union" and that a slight change in the original delimitation of their respective spheres of national interests would be desirable. The German share in the partition of Poland was enlarged to include almost one-half of the country to the Bug River, but as explained in another secret protocol Lithuania was now placed in the Russian sphere of influence with only a slight boundary modification in favor of Germany.

It was soon to become apparent what those assignments meant for Lithuania, to which the Wilno region was to be attributed, and also what they meant for the other Baltic countries. But immediately Poland had to face the two vital problems of assuring her continued existence as an independent allied state under a constitutional government and of organizing underground resistance in the occupied country in close connection with the legal authorities in exile. When President Mościcki, together with his cabinet, crossed the border into Rumania where all were interned, he resigned. In agreement with the provisions of the constitution, he designated Władysław Raczkiewicz, a former president of the senate, as his successor. Raczkiewicz was then in Paris, where he appointed a new government with General Władysław Sikorski as prime minister and minister of war. They agreed that the constitution of 1935, which could not be revised in wartime, would be applied, following democratic principles, and the famous artist and patriot, I. J. Paderewski, was elected president of a national council which acted as a parliament in exile.

In France, where the Polish authorities received an exterritorial residence at Angers, General Sikorski immediately organized a new Polish army. This was joined by many soldiers who after crossing the frontier of their country escaped from internment in Rumania or Hungary. Therefore numerous Polish forces could fight as allies in Norway during the Narvik expedition and in the defense of France when she, too, was invaded by the Germans in the spring of 1940. After the French capitulation, these Polish forces refused to surrender. Except those interned in Switzerland, they were at once transferred to Britain. There, too, the president of the republic and the

Polish government were received as representatives of an allied power and could continue their political activities. When Britain otherwise stood alone, Polish forces, mainly stationed in Scotland, joined the defense organization and many Polish pilots played an outstanding part in the air battle over London.

At the same time contact was established with the occupied country. The Germans divided their share in the new partition of Poland into two parts: all that had been Prussian before 1914 and moreover a large strip of territory beyond that old border was incorporated with the Reich; the rest was called "General Government" without even the name of Poland and placed under the administration of the Nazi leader Hans Frank. The invaders found no one who would cooperate with them, as in the other occupied countries, and therefore the persecution of everything Polish was particularly violent. It was most systematic in the annexed section from which millions of Poles were deported under inhuman conditions to the "General Government." There, also, executions, internment in concentration camps, and deportation for forced labor were to break the spirit of Poland. Cultural and educational activities were prohibited, and not only the Jews, who were exterminated in masses, but also the Catholic clergy and the intellectual leaders served as the main targets.

From the outset, however, there was a well-organized resistance movement which gradually developed into a real underground state acting on secret instructions from London and in turn making known to the exiled government the political aspirations of the suffering nation. These were worked out by an underground parliament with representatives from the four leading democratic parties and were discussed in a widely distributed clandestine press. The executive, under a delegate appointed by the London government, directed the sabotage activities against the occupying forces and Polish courts continued to function secretly.

The eastern part of Poland was for twenty-one months under Russian occupation and exposed to an equally violent sovietization. Already on October 22, 1939, elections under the Soviet system, prepared for by mass arrests and executions, were held and the delegates to the local Soviets were forced to apply for incorporation into the Soviet Union, the southern part of the invaded territory being annexed by the Ukrainian and the northern part by the Byelorussian Soviet Republic. There followed mass deportations to distant parts of the

U.S.S.R. which continued throughout the whole occupation period and under the most appalling conditions. It is impossible to determine the number of victims, including women and children separated from their families, and besides the particularly persecuted Poles, many Jews as well as Ukrainian leaders also. But the number certainly exceeded one and a half million, all of whom were used as forced labor under conditions of starvation and utmost misery.

In spite of that terrible experience and with a view to liberating these peoples, the exiled Polish government immediately after Hitler's invasion of Russia on June 22, 1941, decided to enter into negotiations with the new ally of the democracies. Not without British pressure, did the government sign in London, on the thirtieth of July, a treaty with the Soviet Union which declared "that the Soviet-German treaties of 1939 relative to territorial changes in Poland have lost their validity." It was not specified that the frontier of 1921 was hereby restored, and the liberation of the deported Polish citizens and prisoners of war was called an "amnesty." But in any case, the treaty was a formal recognition of the Polish government in exile by Soviet Russia, which also consented to the formation of a Polish army on the territory of the U.S.S.R.

When, however, General Sikorski came to Moscow and on the fourth of December signed a declaration of friendship and collaboration with Stalin, the Soviets were already organizing the so-called Union of Polish Patriots there. This was a Communist-controlled group which the Soviets intended to oppose to the legal Polish government. The formation of an army from the Poles of the Soviet Union, who were liberated only in small part, also encountered serious difficulties, particularly because no information could be obtained as to the fate of about fifteen thousand missing officers, and because there started immediately controversies about the citizenship of all those born in eastern Poland, which Russia continued to claim, at least as far as the so-called Curzon line of 1920.

The Polish army in Russia under General Anders finally had to be transferred through Iran to the Near East. It later distinguished itself in the North African campaign, and especially in the Allied invasion of Italy, taking the stronghold of Monte Cassino in May, 1944, liberating Ancona and Bologna, and fighting there under British supreme command until the end of the war. During all these years the reorganized Polish air force and what remained of the Polish navy also cooperated with the Allies, and two Polish divisions from Britain participated in the invasion of the Continent and the liberation of Belgium and Holland.

At the same time the resistance movement inside Poland, which had been completely occupied by the Germans since the summer of 1941, was intensified. On August 1, 1944, a large-scale insurrection broke out in Warsaw under General Bór-Komorowski, only to be crushed after sixty-two days of street fighting and to end in the total destruction of the city. That insurrection received no help from the Russians, who had already reached the other side of the Vistula. Even Allied assistance by the air was seriously handicapped because on April 25, 1943, the Soviet Union, already pushing back the German invasion, had broken off relations with the Polish Government and was preparing to force a Communist regime upon Poland as soon as the Germans were driven out of that country. Therefore in spite of her brilliant war record on the Allied side, Poland was already facing "defeat in victory."

THE FATE OF THE BALTIC AND DANUBIAN REGIONS

The fate which Poland suffered in September, 1939, had immediate repercussions in the whole Baltic region and was also soon to affect the situation of South Eastern Europe, only briefly touched on in the original Nazi-Soviet agreement.

The day after the final fixation of their respective "spheres of influence," when Poland seemed liquidated and partitioned, the Soviet government started its negotiations with the Baltic republics, requesting each of them individually to send delegates to Moscow and there to sign "mutual assistance pacts." These included granting the Soviets military, naval, and air bases on their territories. Estonia did it at once on the twenty-ninth of September, Latvia on the fifth of October, and Lithuania on the tenth of October, the latter receiving Wilno with its environs, which had been taken from Poland, as a compensation. Red Army forces moved into the territories of the three small countries, occupying the bases assigned to them, but Molotov protested against any suspicion that the independence of these republics would not be respected. It seemed to be to the advantage of Estonia and Latvia that Hitler agreed with Stalin as to the transfer of their German minorities to the Reich.

Finland, too, after some delay, sent representatives to Moscow, but feeling stronger than the other three, hesitated to accept the conditions of the proposed agreement. In protracted negotiations which lasted more than a month, the Finns proved ready to make concessions regarding the change of the frontier which Russia wanted to move farther away from Leningrad, but they refused the lease of the island and port of Hangö (Hanko) at the entrance of the Gulf of Finland, feeling that this would mean the control of their whole southern coast by Russia. Soon after the failure of these negotiations and the return of the Finnish delegation on the thirteenth of November, and after a border incident, Russia unilaterally denounced the nonaggression pact concluded with Finland in 1934, and two days later, on November 30, 1939, started the war by air raids on several cities, including Helsinki. The creation of a Communist puppet government for Finland seemed to indicate that the ultimate goal was the forceful inclusion of that country into the Soviet Union.

The aggression against Finland, however, met with unexpectedly strong resistance under the old national hero, Marshal C. G. Mannerheim. It shocked public opinion all over the world to such an extent that after the expulsion of the U.S.S.R. from the League of Nations on the fourteenth of December, and after a thirty-million-dollar loan had been granted to Finland by the United States, France and England decided to give her military support. But the chief difficulty was that the Scandinavian countries, particularly Sweden, having been formally warned by Germany which supported her Russian partner, were afraid to permit these auxiliary forces to cross their territory, although they were themselves in sympathy with Finland. Except for a few volunteers, no help reached her on time, and when the Russian invasion at last made serious progress in February, the Finns felt obliged to use a Swedish intermediary for peace negotiations which led to the Moscow Treaty of March 12, 1940.

The terms were much harsher than Russia's original demands. In addition to the lease of Hangö, Finland had to cede much more territory on the Karelian Isthmus, including the city of Vyborg (Viipuri) and in general lost 10 per cent of her territory, from which most of the population emigrated to what remained free. The mutilated nation at least saved its independence, though Moscow was to use the treaty for frequent interference with the internal questions of Finland.

The three other Baltic republics, in spite of their submission to all Russian claims were less fortunate. Prepared by their partial military occupation and by interferences under various pretexts, their annexation by the Soviet Union was decided as soon as Germany's sweeping successes in the West made Russia desire some additional compensation in the East. Under the pretext that the three small countries had made a secret military alliance directed against the U.S.S.R., their representatives were again summoned to Moscow but only to receive ultimatums, Lithuania on the fourteenth of June, and Latvia and Estonia two days later, which requested the formation of new governments "friendly" to the Soviets and the admission of an unlimited number of Red Army forces.

Under the strongest pressure, with all non-Communist parties outlawed, fake elections were held in all three countries by these new Communist-controlled governments, which gave these government majorities of almost 100 per cent. On the thirty-first of July delegations consisting of twenty members from each of the three so-elected parliaments came to Moscow to ask for the admission of their respective countries as republics of the U.S.S.R. On the third, fifth, and sixth of August, Lithuania, Latvia, and Estonia were thus "accepted" by the Supreme Soviet. Already before these fateful dates which marked the end of their independence through annexations which the United States of America never recognized, nationalization of property and the amalgamation of the former national forces with the Red Army had begun. Now, under new constitutions that strictly followed the Soviet pattern, a reign of terror set in. This was directed against all "nationalists," former political leaders, and religious and cultural organizations. It was to destroy all the achievements of twenty years of freedom and to reduce the populations of these small nations through mass deportations. In Lithuania alone about 50,000 people were transferred with customary ruthlessness during the one year of Russian occupation.

Opposed by strong underground movements, these persecutions were intensified when the German invasion of the Soviet Union became imminent. It was even feared that the whole native population, which was considered unreliable, would be transplanted to distant parts of Russia. Uprisings took place on that occasion, but as a matter of fact the three unhappy peoples only changed their totalitarian masters for a few years.

The three Baltic states were named the fourteenth, fifteenth, and sixteenth Soviet Republics, because before their formal establishment two others had been added to the eleven which existed before World War II. One of these was the Karelo-Finnish Republic, an area of 77,000 square miles along the new Finnish border with a population of 600,000, which was created when the idea of Sovietizing Finland herself had to be given up. The rather artificial formation of that republic as a permanent organization of Communist Finnish forces remained an indication that further projects directed against any independent Finnish state could be resumed at any time.

The creation of a Moldavian Soviet Republic out of the Rumanian-speaking part of Bessarabia, that province of imperial Russia which the U.S.S.R. never formally ceded to Rumania and claimed for her sphere of influence in the agreement with Hitler, had a somewhat similar significance. The implementation of that claim was to be another compensation, parallel to that in the Baltic region, which the Soviet government obtained without difficulty soon after the fall of France. On June 27, 1940, Rumania had to accept the Russian ultimatum which demanded the immediate cession not only of Bessarabia but also of the northern part of the Bucovina, with a partly Ukrainian population.

That territory, an integral part of historic Moldavia, had never belonged to Russia and was not mentioned in the agreement with Hitler. Therefore that extension of the Russian gains, small as it was, created one of those minor frictions in Nazi-Soviet relations which occurred time and again during the twenty-two months of cooperation between the two aggressors. Nevertheless Germany, which at about the same time renounced the strip of Lithuanian territory that was promised to her in 1939, not only advised Rumania to yield but also forced that country to make territorial concessions to her other neighbors. After renouncing the Anglo-French guaranty on the first of July Rumania had to send representatives to a conference of the Axis powers in Vienna where it was decided on the thirtieth of August that the northern part of Transylvania, which was arbitrarily cut in two, would be returned to Hungary. And a week later the southern part of Dobrudja had to be ceded to Bulgaria. King Carol abdicated in favor of his minor son, Michael, who became king for the second time, but the real power went to General Antonescu who established a dictatorial regime with the support of the Iron Guard.

Amidst the anarchy which followed, even Professor Iorga, Rumania's most distinguished national leader, was murdered. The country was now sufficiently weakened to submit to further pressure. Together with Hungary and Slovakia, the Tripartite Pact of September twenty-seventh concluded by Germany, Italy, and Japan, was signed by Rumania at the end of November. Rumania thus joined those Danubian countries which were already completely dominated by Hitler, and the German "sphere of influence" reached the Balkans.

Originally Hitler had not favored the idea of extending the war to South Eastern Europe, in which he pretended to be less interested. But in addition to the strengthening of the German position in the Danubian countries, another unexpected development alarmed both the opponents of the Axis and the Soviet Union. On the twenty-eighth of October Mussolini, not satisfied with his last-minute share in the victory over France and anxious for gains as spectacular as those of his major partner, decided to attack Greece. After the usual ultimatum, which was rejected by Prime Minister Metaxas, Mussolini invaded that country from the springboard which Italy had held in Albania since the spring of the preceding year.

As in the case of the Russian aggression against Finland, the resistance of the much smaller victim proved to be much stronger than could be anticipated, and by December the Italian forces were even pushed back into Albanian territory. It was easy to foresee, however, that Hitler would sooner or later come to the rescue of the allied dictator. Therefore Stalin sent Molotov to Berlin, where in long conversations with Hitler on the twelfth and thirteenth of November, he tried to find out what Germany's intentions really were. In spite of an apparently cordial farewell, these discussions clearly demonstrated how difficult it was to divide the whole of East Central Europe, whose situation was reviewed in detail, between the Nazi and Soviet empires. It was particularly significant that Ribbentrop tried to divert Russia's attention from that region by offering her another sphere of influence in faraway Iran and India. But Moscow's reply made it equally clear that the Soviet Union remained primarily interested in the area that lies to the west of her: from Finland, where she opposed the presence of German troops in transit to and from occupied Norway, to the Straits, which reappeared as one of the traditional goals of Russia's expansion. The rivalry revealed in connection with these last Nazi-Soviet negotiations in Berlin was to lead to the break between the two big powers, each of which wanted to control all of East Central Europe. But the date of Hitler's turn against Russia, planned for May, 1941, depended on the timetable of his conquest of the Balkans which he decided to complete first.

HITLER'S CONQUEST OF THE BALKANS

In order to reach Greece, at the southern tip of the Balkan Peninsula, where Italy's failures required a swift intervention of Germany in advance of Britain's, Hitler's forces had to have a free passage through the countries in the center of the peninsula. It proved comparatively easy to include among the Nazi satellites that same Bulgaria which, during the Berlin conversations, Russia had claimed as an indispensable link in her own security zone. Using as an argument the support given to Bulgaria in the question of Dobrudja and also the promise to support her claims to Macedonia, Germany induced King Boris to adhere, on March 1, 1941, to that same Tripartite Pact which the Danubian countries had signed before and German troops could at once enter Bulgaria as a gateway to Greece.

Much more important, however, was the direct passage through Yugoslavia. Therefore strong pressure was put upon the regent, Prince Paul, and the Cvetkovich government to follow the Bulgarian example. On the 25th of March, a Yugoslav delegation led by the prime minister really came to Vienna to sign the Tripartite Pact. Though the concessions requested from Yugoslavia with a view to facilitating Germany's access into Greece were apparently rather limited, the country fully realized the implications of such a decision and reacted two days later by overthrowing the government. Young King Peter II assumed full power in place of his uncle the regent, and General Simovich, a hero of World War I, became prime minister, with the Croat leader Dr. Machek as vice-premier.

Although the new regime took no anti-German action and on the fifth of April, merely concluded a nonaggression pact with the Soviet Union, formally still in friendly relations with Germany, the change in the Yugoslav attitude was well understood in Berlin. The next day one of the sudden aggressions that were typical of World War II took place. Notifying the Soviet government that Germany only wanted to expel the British from Greece and that she had no interest in the Balkans, the Nazis started the war by a violent air raid which destroyed most of Belgrade, and invaded Yugoslavia from Hungary, Rumania, and Bulgaria. The first of these neighboring countries had quite recently, on December 12, 1940, concluded a treaty of friendship with Yugoslavia, so that the enforced cooperation in that act of aggression drove Prime Minister Count Teleki to suicide and made his country even more dependent on Germany.

In twelve days most of Yugoslavia seemed to be conquered so that on the twenty-ninth of August a puppet government under General Milan Nedich could replace the legal authorities, viz., the king and the exiled government in London. But that puppet regime was for Serbia only. In cooperation with Italy, the Germans at once proceeded to a partition of what was supposed to be left of Yugoslavia after the annexations of large frontier regions by Germany, Italy, Hungary, and Bulgaria. Playing off all national and regional movements which in the past had resented Serb supremacy, the independence of not only Croatia but also of Montenegro was proclaimed on the tenth of April and the twelfth of July, respectively. Both countries were placed under Italian protection, however, and on the eighteenth of May a nephew of the king of Italy, the duke of Spoleto, accepted the royal crown of Croatia, leaving the real power in the hands of a local German-sponsored "leader," Ante Pavelich. Worst was the fate of Slovenia which was completely divided, the main part, along with Dalmatia, being annexed by Italy. But it soon became apparent that in spite of all these arbitrary arrangements and the stirring up of Croats against Serbs, the spirit of Yugoslavia was far from broken.

On the contrary, in no other Axis-occupied country, except Poland, was the resistance movement stronger, with the difference that in the inaccessible mountains of Yugoslavia the struggle against the invaders could be even more successful. It was not limited to underground activities but was organized as continuous guerilla warfare which never permitted the enemy really to conquer all the country. That resistance also found a remarkable leader in the person of General Draja Mihailovich who remained in close contact with the royal government in London as its minister of war.

There appeared, however, in Yugoslavia, earlier than in Poland where the role of the Communists in the underground movement was insignificant, a serious danger of Communist penetration in spite of the great distance from Russia. Of course, as in the other occupied countries, there could be no Communist resistance so long as Germany was in cooperation with the Soviet Union. Contrary to the last-minute treaty, the latter even broke off relations with the Yugoslav government as soon as the German invasion proved successful. But when Russia herself was in turn invaded, and the Communists everywhere turned against the Nazis, or rather against the Fascists, as they preferred to call them, it was in Yugoslavia that a strong "liberation" movement under Communist control appeared first by the end of 1942. The mostly Serb "Chetniks" of General Mihailovich were now opposed by the "Partisans" led by a formerly unknown Croat Communist trained in Moscow, Josip Broz, who became famous under the name of Tito.

The unhappy country thus became the scene of a three-cornered conflict among the German occupants (who exercised the most ruthless terror), the followers of Mihailovich (loyal to the government in exile), and the followers of Tito (who were loyal to Moscow). This situation was to last until the end of the war. In spite of their obligations toward the legitimate government, the Western Allies, misled by Communist propaganda which branded Mihailovich a collaborator, gradually transferred their assistance from the heroic general to the Partisans. In November, 1943, the latter set up a provisional revolutionary government at Jajce, in the mountains of Bosnia. Under the name of "Anti-Fascist Council for National Liberation," with a federalist program, this was supposed to attract the non-Serb elements.

The exiled king too made a concession to these elements by appointing a Croat and former ban of Croatia, Dr. Ivan Subasich, as prime minister. The following summer Subasich met Tito in the still-occupied country and negotiated an agreement with him, as a result of which Mihailovich was dismissed from his post. That policy of appeasement, under Allied pressure, was to prove as disastrous as all similar steps in the relations with totalitarian forces.

While Yugoslavia thus suffered from both these forces, Nazi-Fascist and Communist, Greece, too, after so courageously resisting the Italian invasion, succumbed to the Germans. The Nazi forces attacking from Bulgaria, cut off the Greeks fighting in Albania from those who tried in vain to stop the overwhelmingly strong new enemy in the center of the country near historic Thermopylae. British support came too late, and by the end of April, 1940, the Greek mainland was conquered. The king and the government retired to the island of

Crete where the resistance continued for another month with British help. It was finally broken by German paratroopers. The Greek government, like so many others, was transferred to London, but in the later phase of the war it moved to Cairo to be nearer at the time of liberation.

That liberation was prepared also in Greece by an uninterrupted resistance movement which harassed the German, Italian, and Bulgarian occupation forces, unafraid of their usual terror and the inhuman exploitation of the miserable country. Unfortunately, here too there was a dangerous division into rightist and leftist liberation movements. Both controlled considerable guerilla forces, the former loyal to the exiled government, the latter not only opposed to the monarchy and to the prewar regime but also more and more subject to Communist infiltration. That division was, of course, fomented by the invaders. But in September, 1944, unity seemed to be established, both movements recognizing the government in exile and cooperating with the British as soon as they reappeared in Greece the following month.

For almost three years, however, all the Balkans were under Hitler's control, directly or indirectly through his Italian partner, a control which became exclusively German after Italy's surrender and the fall of fascism in the summer of 1943. Only the small area near the Straits remained free. This was a part of Turkey which was in sympathy with the Allies but which, in spite of her mutual assistance pacts with Britain and France, remained neutral almost to the end of the war. One of the reasons for her cautious attitude was the fact that Turkey's dangerous neighbor in Asia, the Soviet Union, found itself on the Allied side through the final break with Hitler and the invasion that he launched on June 22, 1941.

That invasion had been delayed for at least several weeks because of the unexpected resistance which Hitler met with in Yugoslavia and which in turn delayed the conquest of Greece. Thus Yugoslavia and her legitimate government rendered the Soviet Union a great service by frustrating Germany's chance to defeat Russia before the coming of winter. On the other hand, the complete control of both the Danubian and the Balkan regions facilitated the concentration of almost all the land forces of the Reich on the eastern front. Out of Hitler's newly gained satellites in these regions only Bulgaria, where Russian sympathies were always considerable, refused to declare war upon the

Soviet Union. Both Hungary and Rumania, in spite of their old rivalry which the recent partition of Transylvania could not possibly settle, fought side by side with the Germans against Russia, Rumania with the hope of regaining at least her recent eastern losses if not more territory in the southern Ukraine.

With similar hopes, and after four days of having her neutrality violated by Russian bombing, Finland also re-entered the war against the Soviet Union. Without concluding any agreement with Germany, she officially declared time and again that hers was a separate war, defensive as in 1939–1940 and conducted with the exclusive aim of again obtaining a frontier that would guarantee a minimum of security. The territories which Russia had annexed in the period of her cooperation with Germany, under the pretext of protecting the security of her gigantic empire, proved of little strategic importance. Not only the area taken away from Finland but also the Baltic republics and the eastern half of Poland were lost very quickly in the first weeks of the war against Hitler, and it was only when the Soviet Union was attacked on its prewar territory that its peoples were able to oppose the invader with that fierce resistance which raised the well-deserved admiration of the world. Even so, Byelorussia and the Ukraine were temporarily lost in their entirety, while comparatively small areas of Russia proper were occupied. Thus the whole of East Central Europe which Germany and Russia had planned to partition was for about two years in the hands of Germany alone.

24

STALIN'S PEACE

FROM NAZI OCCUPATION TO SOVIET "LIBERATION"

The main reason for the break between Hitler and Stalin was the impossibility of agreeing on a lasting division of East Central Europe between Germany and Russia, both more imperialistic than ever before. It was not the ideological differences between the two most radical forms of totalitarianism. Therefore the claim of the German dictator that he was leading a crusade against communism did not convince anybody. The cruel treatment which the invaders inflicted upon the peoples in the occupied part of the Soviet Union excluded any chance of cooperation with anti-Communist and anti-Russian Ukrainians and White Ruthenians. Even the Lithuanians, Latvians, and Estonians, who had hoped to liberate themselves on the occasion of the German invasion and who tried to form provisional national governments, were completely disappointed. They were placed under the German administration of the so-called *Ostland* which treated them so harshly, trying to mobilize all their resources in the interest of the occupants, that active and passive underground resistance were organized and secret committees for liberation were created.

As everywhere else, that resistance was encouraged by the firm belief that Hitler could not possibly win the war, since his hopes of crushing the Soviet Union in another blitzkrieg had failed, and since in that same decisive year of 1941 the United States had joined the Allies. Even before formally entering the war after Pearl Harbor, America cooperated in preparing "a better future for the world . . . after the final destruction of the Nazi tyranny," as was declared in the Atlantic Charter which President Roosevelt, together with British Prime Minister Winston Churchill, signed on August 14, 1941.

For the peoples of East Central Europe, all of whom were enslaved by the Nazis at the time, that joint declaration had an appeal similar to that of Wilson's peace program in World War I. Less specific than the Fourteen Points, the Atlantic Charter included, however, the solemn promise that "sovereign rights and self-government" would be "restored to those who have been forcibly deprived of them." In full agreement with that promise, the exiled governments of those allied nations which Germany had deprived of their sovereign rights and self-government were admitted to sign, on January 1, 1942, in Washington, the United Nations Declarations which reaffirmed the principles of the Atlantic Charter. The governments in exile of the allied countries of East Central Europe at the same time were making a constructive contribution to the common peace program by preparing a federal system. This was based upon the plan of a confederation which had already been announced on November 11, 1940, by the Polish government and the Czechoslovak government, the latter reorganized in London with Edward Beneš again assuming the presidency, and on a similar Greek-Yugoslav agreement of January 15, 1942. Close cooperation of both groups in a federal system open to the other countries of East Central Europe was included in that project of postwar organization which was to be placed within the framework of the international organization of the United Nations.

The Soviet government also signed the United Nations Declaration and thus adhered implicitly to the Atlantic Charter, including its first article in which the signatories promised to "seek no aggrandizement, territorial or other." But according to the Russian interpretation, that engagement did not refer to those "aggrandizements" which the Soviet Union had gained before the drafting of the Atlantic Charter, in the years of cooperation with Nazi Germany. The claim to Eastern Poland, the three Baltic republics, and parts of Finland and Rumania was therefore never abandoned. Furthermore, the Soviet government was definitely opposed to any federation or confederation among the western neighbors of the Soviet Union, and they practically forced the Czechoslovak government to discontinue its negotiations with the Polish government in that matter. Even more than the Greek and Yugoslav governments in exile, that of Poland was considered insufficiently "friendly" to Russia because it was not prepared to yield to Russia's territorial claims.

But since Britain and particularly the United States also still hesitated to recognize these claims, another pretext had to be found before the formal break with that government. That first Russian blow to Allied unity, delivered on April 25, 1943, was motivated by the fact that the Polish government had requested an investigation by the International Red Cross into the murder of many thousands of Polish officers, prisoners of war taken by the Russians in 1939, whose disappearance the Soviet government had failed to explain for almost two years and whose bodies were now discovered by the Germans in a mass grave in the Katyn forest near Smolensk. Although the Polish government in exile did not accept in advance the German version which was later substantiated by ample evidence, namely, that the victims had been executed by the Russians, the U.S.S.R. considered the very claim to an impartial investigation "a treacherous blow to the Soviet Union," a pressure exerted "in accord with Hitler" for the purpose "of wresting territorial concessions" from the Soviet republics.

After severing relations with the legitimate government of Poland which on the sixth of July of the same year, 1943, lost Prime Minister and Commander in Chief General Sikorski in an airplane crash, Soviet Russia openly opposed to that government the small group of Polish Communists which continued to function in Moscow as the "Union of Polish Patriots." Contact was established with the few Communists inside occupied Poland in order to create in that country, as in Yugoslavia, a division in the resistance movement. In the Polish case it was particularly obvious that as soon as the Red Army in its victorious advance after Stalingrad could reach the territory of that allied country, the "liberators," instead of restoring "sovereignty and self-government," would simply replace German by Russian occupation, make impossible the return of the national government, and force upon the population a Communist-controlled regime.

The other two big powers, Britain and America, were not unaware of that danger which was a challenge to the principles of the Atlantic Charter. But their main immediate objective was, of course, winning the war, a truly global conflict in which the fate of Poland—the initial issue—had long since ceased to be of decisive importance. And Russia's continued cooperation was essential. Furthermore, the Western democracies were under a twofold illusion. They failed to realize in time that Russia's policy toward Poland was only part of a general pattern to be applied in all countries of East Central Europe, allied or not. And as far as Poland was concerned, they believed that the Soviet Union could be appeased and the independence of even that country saved if the requested territorial changes were admitted.

These changes did not seem unreasonable to Western statesmen, who were quite superficially informed on Polish problems, since Russia no longer claimed the Ribbentrop line of 1939 but the Curzon line of 1920 which was a little more favorable to Poland and which had been misinterpreted as having been the Allied decision at the Paris Peace Conference regarding Poland's eastern boundary. Therefore, although the Anglo-Saxon powers, and especially the United States, wanted to postpone all boundary problems until the end of the war, Stalin persuaded Roosevelt and Churchill at the Teheran Conference, at the end of November, 1943, that the Polish-Soviet frontier had to be agreed upon at once in view of the imminent penetration of the Red Army into the territory under dispute. He obtained the secret consent of the other two Allied leaders to the Curzon line.

As a matter of fact, when in their sweeping advance the Russians occupied the eastern half of prewar Poland as in 1939, they rapidly liquidated the forces of the Polish home army which went into the open and cooperated in the fight against the Germans. They then treated that area as an integral part of the Soviet Union. The Western Allies now persuaded Sikorski's successor as prime minister of Poland, Stanisław Mikołajczyk, to go to Moscow. Churchill exercised a particularly strong pressure upon him to accept the Russian demands. These were, however, not at all exclusively territorial. After crossing the Curzon line, the Russians transformed the "Union of Polish Patriots" into a "Polish Committee of National Liberation" which, together with a so-called "National Council" presided over by the Communist agent Bolesław Bierut, was established in Lublin, the first "liberated" city in what the Soviet Union recognized to be Polish territory. There, on July 22, 1944, these Russian puppets issued a manifesto taking over the power in the country. Therefore it was with the representatives of that Committee, and not only with the Russians, that Mikołajczyk had to negotiate when he arrived in Moscow a few days later, facing the demand for the creation of a new Polish government with strong Communist participation.

Under these circumstances the Poles received no credit for the Warsaw uprisings in August and September which had been partly provoked by Russian broadcasts. Instead they were left completely to the mercy of the Nazis. When in October, after the Warsaw tragedy, Mikołajczyk returned to Moscow, the pressure exercised upon him was so strong that he was prepared to yield. He failed, however, to persuade the president and the majority of the government in exile, resigned as prime minister, and was replaced on the twenty-ninth of November by a former underground leader, the Socialist Thomas Arciszewski. And while the Soviet Union on January 1, 1945, recognized the Lublin Committee as the "Provisional Government of Poland" which soon was established in Warsaw, Britain and the United States ceased to support Poland's legitimate authorities in exile, though formally they still recognized them.

In the meantime, however, it had become obvious that the Russians wanted to control not only Poland. Delaying their offensive on the Polish front, they advanced all the more rapidly in the direction of the Danubian countries and the Balkans where they had always opposed an invasion by the Western Allies who hoped in vain to share some kind of influence in South Eastern Europe with the Russians. The Red Army first conquered Rumania which surrendered on the twenty-third of August and two days later declared war upon Germany after the overthrow of the Antonescu regime by King Michael. Bulgaria wanted to surrender to the Western Allies, but on the fifth of September the Soviet Union declared war upon that country, which had avoided breaking with Russia, and through this fictitious conflict succeeded in conquering Bulgaria and forcing surrender terms upon her after a state of war which had lasted only four days.

The occupation of Rumania and Bulgaria was immediately followed by the Russian advance into Yugoslavia, Hungary, and the Carpatho-Ukraine, the latter a part of prewar Czechoslovakia. In the first of these countries Russian control was particularly easy to establish, since the Tito-Subasich agreement in August had already opened the door to the supremacy of the Communist leader who practically ignored the king and helped the Russians to enter Belgrade in the middle of September. King Peter's last-minute decision to dismiss Prime Minister Subasich, which was made at the end of 1944, was simply disregarded. In Hungary the regent, Admiral Horthy, who on the fifteenth of October had tried to save the country by surrendering to the Allies, was overthrown by adherents of the Nazi alliance. But before Budapest was finally taken by the Russians in February, 1945, a new government set up under Russian auspices in Debrecen accepted the armistice terms of the Soviet Union on the twentieth of January and declared war upon Germany. Last among the countries of East Central Europe, Czechoslovakia as a whole was to be freed from the Germans. But though the Soviet Union had promised in the 1943 treaty with the Czechoslovak government in exile to restore the pre-Munich boundaries, it was already resolved to annex Carpatho-Ruthenia.

YALTA

This was the situation in East Central Europe when another wartime conference of the Big Three met at Yalta in the Crimea from February 4 to 12, 1945. This proved to be the real peace conference after World War II, which was by then practically decided, at least in Europe. A few weeks before Yalta, a last desperate counter-offensive of the Germans in the West had created the misleading impression that their power to resist was still considerable. Incorrect military information on the situation in the Far East was responsible for the conviction that in order to defeat Japan in a war which might last for a long time, Russia's cooperation was sorely needed. This was the main reason why Churchill and Roosevelt (who probably paid with his life for the tremendous effort a sick man made in flying to the Crimea) considered it necessary to make another series of concessions to Stalin. Stalin too made concessions, more apparent than real, on some points, but he was adamant as far as the basic issues in East Central Europe and the secret decisions affecting China were concerned.

One of Stalin's concessions was a promise of full cooperation in setting up the United Nations Organization. He also accepted limitation of the number of votes of the Soviet Republics in the Assembly to three instead of sixteen. In addition to the U.S.S.R. as a whole, votes were promised and really given to Byelorussia and the Ukraine at the San Francisco Conference. The choice of these two republics was in close connection with the privilege of autonomy in foreign affairs and defense granted to them in agreement with the amendment of the Soviet Constitution of February 2, 1944, which made possible such a concession to individual Union Republics under the general supervision of the central authorities. In both cases the Ukraine and Byelorussia were singled out because they had particularly suffered under Nazi occupation and had made a special contribution to the war effort. These arguments were indeed fully justified. Next to the Russian, they were also the most populous and (with the exception of Kazakhstan) the largest of the Soviet republics. Culturally, they were more highly developed than any of the others except the three Baltic countries, whose reannexation after the expulsion of the Germans was tacitly admitted in the peace settlement. But the privileges granted, not indeed to the White Ruthenian and Ukrainian peoples but to their imposed Communist leaders, could serve in turn as an argument that inclusion in the Soviet Union was compatible with a high degree of self-government, in order to justify further annexations in East Central Europe.

As a matter of fact, in all the countries of that region which the Red Army had occupied, there was a widespread fear that the next step would be a forced inclusion into the Soviet Union, thus indefinitely increasing the number of the sixteen Union Republics. That the Russian claims neither at the end of the war nor in the following years went as far as that was received with some feeling of relief and made easier the acceptance of the Yalta decisions even in their Russian interpretation.

Easiest to accept and even welcome, in spite of some initial doubts on the part of President Roosevelt, seemed the section of the Yalta decisions which was entitled "Declaration on Liberated Europe." But though quoting the Atlantic Charter, the Big Three announced that in any country "where in their judgment conditions require," they would "jointly assist" the people concerned to establish internal peace, to form "interim governmental authorities broadly representative of all democratic elements," and to hold free elections. Such interference with the internal problems of any nation, even of allies who were put on the same level as "former Axis satellites," was left to the decision of the three signatories of the Yalta agreement, including the totalitarian Soviet Union, of course, which thus received the right to determine what were the "democratic elements" in the liberated countries. And though the planned interferences were supposed to be "joint responsibilities" of all three powers, it was easy to anticipate that in practice all would depend on the question which of the three had liberated and militarily occupied the given country.

In contradistinction to Western Europe, liberated by the truly democratic Anglo-Saxon powers and therefore left free from any arbitrary interference with unavoidable internal difficulties of its peoples, almost all East Central Europe was being occupied by the Red Army and was therefore at the mercy of the Soviet Union, without any guaranties for the Western Allies that they would really be consulted and permitted to share in the discharge of the promised "assistance." That danger had already become obvious at Yalta in two concrete cases which seemed particularly urgent, when the internal problems of allied nations, not represented at the conference at all, were decided by the Big Three exactly as the Soviet Union, which was in control of both counties, wanted it to be done.

The case of Poland was discussed at length but the question of her eastern boundary, which was taken up first, was not at all an internal problem. It was a dispute between Poland and the Soviet Union, which in the absence of Poland was decided in favor of the Soviet Union, the host to the conference. President Roosevelt wanted to save at least the city of Lwów and her only oil fields for Poland. His appeal to Stalin's generosity was made in vain. The Curzon line, as interpreted by the Russians, was fixed as Poland's eastern frontier at once, while the "substantial" compensation which the again partitioned country was to receive from Germany was left undetermined and was supposed to "await the peace conference."

More involved and therefore subject to controversial interpretation was the decision regarding Poland's government. Her president and legal government, the wartime ally still recognized by all powers except Russia, was not even mentioned. The "provisional government now functioning in Poland," that is, the former Lublin Committee sponsored by the Soviet Union, was to be "reorganized on a broader democratic basis." This was indeed not the formation of an entirely new government, as the Anglo-Saxon powers wanted it, but merely an enlargement of the Communist-controlled group without any indication as to how many "democratic leaders from Poland itself and from abroad" should be included. Their choice was not left to the Polish people but to a commission composed of Mr. Molotov and of the American and British ambassadors to the Soviet Union, who would "consult" in Moscow some Polish leaders chosen by them, but again with the tacit exclusion of the legal authorities of the Republic. The "reorganized" Provisional Government was pledged to hold "free and unfettered elections," but without any fixed date or guaranties of control, and it was to be recognized by America and Britain as soon as formed, without waiting for the result of the elections.

Not having thus "restored" but destroyed the sovereign rights of allied Poland, the Yalta Conference, without much discussion, did practically the same with allied Yugoslavia. It began by "recommending to Marshal Tito and Dr. Subasich," without any reference to the king and the government in exile, that they form a new government based on their agreement. In that case, too, the idea of extending the Communist-controlled bodies, in Yugoslavia the "Anti-Fascist Assembly of National Liberation," by including members of the last parliament, was put forward. It was added that the legislative acts of that assembly should be ratified by a "Constituent Assembly," but how and when the constituent assembly should be elected was left open.

In Yugoslavia, Tito was so strong already that King Peter transferred his power to a regency, anticipating the abolition of the monarchy by the Communist dictator whose regime, with Subasich as a mere figurehead, was now universally recognized and already represented at the San Francisco Conference. But at that conference, which opened on the twenty-fifth of April and, soon after Germany's unconditional surrender of the seventh of May, set up the United Nations Organization, Poland, the first nation to oppose Hitler and therefore the nucleus around which the United Nations had gradually been formed, was not represented at all. The Yalta agreement, rejected by the legitimate Polish government, simply failed to work from the outset.

Before President Roosevelt's death on the twelfth of April, it had already become apparent, to his disappointment, that the Soviet Union hardly respected and differently interpreted the Yalta "compromise," as the President himself called that agreement in his report to Congress. He did not live to hear Molotov's announcement at the very beginning of the San Francisco Conference that the Polish underground leaders, invited to the negotiations regarding the formation of a new government, had been arrested by the Russians and brought to Moscow not for consultation but for trial. In spite of the indignation first raised by that announcement, Harry Hopkins was sent to Stalin one month later and the Russian list of Polish democratic leaders to be heard by the Molotov Commission was approved by America and Britain, with only the addition of Mr. Mikołajczyk who, contrary to the attitude of the government in exile of which he was no longer a member, accepted the invitation of the Commission. During the trial of the sixteen underground leaders who received prison terms as reward for their resistance against the Nazis, the sixteen members of the Provisional Government created and sponsored by the Soviets accepted participation of five democratic Poles in the "Government of National Unity." One of them refused, while Mr. Mikołajczyk was made second vice-premier. On July 5, 1945, America and Britain recognized that settlement and withdrew recognition from the legal Polish government.

Four weeks later, at the Potsdam Conference of the Big Three, it was declared that that government no longer existed. After hearing representatives of the regime now established in Warsaw, it was decided that the eastern part of Germany, to the Oder-Neisse line, would not be part of the Soviet zone of occupation but would be placed "under the administration of the Polish State." Since the transfer to the West of the German population of these territories was authorized at the same time, that decision could be interpreted only as the delimination of Poland's territorial compensation in the north and west which had been promised at Yalta. Again, however, the reservation was made that the new German-Polish frontier would be finally determined at the peace settlement, while the Russian annexation of part of East Prussia, together with Königsberg, was at once approved by the other two big powers.

BEHIND THE CURTAIN

It took a long time before the West realized that the new Poland, much smaller than before the war in spite of the formerly German territories that had been acquired at Potsdam, together with almost all the other countries of East Central Europe, was left behind a dividing line which Mr. Churchill, himself partly responsible for that solution, now called an "Iron Curtain," although it was quite easy to see what was going on behind that line.

The last joint action of the Western powers and Russia was the laborious drafting of peace treaties with Hitler's satellites, all of them —except Italy—in East Central Europe, which was achieved between the twenty-fifth of April and the fifteenth of October at another Paris Peace Conference, very different from that of 1919. This time the most important peace treaty, which would again have been that with Germany, was postponed indefinitely, like that with Japan, in view of the obvious impossibility of agreeing with Russia as to the future of the main enemies in the war. Also delayed was the conclusion of peace with Austria, which during the war had been promised the treatment of a liberated victim of Hitler's first aggression, and which after victory remained, like Germany, divided into four zones of occupation, with a division of Vienna even more complicated than that of Berlin. For the Russians also wanted to keep that country, closely associated indeed with East Central Europe, under their control, even after the eventual signature of a treaty with the new Austrian government to which really free elections had given a truly democratic character.

Among the remaining treaties, the only ones which under such conditions could be signed in Paris on February 10, 1947, the one with Italy greatly reduced the territory of that country which had been defeated in World War II, in favor of Yugoslavia which had to yield to most Italian claims after their common victory in World War I. Now not only Fiume (Rjeka), then the main object of controversy, but also the whole Istrian Peninsula, Dalmatian Zara (Zadar) in the south and most of Venezia Giulia (the province of Gorizia) in the north, were transferred to Tito's Yugoslavia. This move was strongly supported by the Soviet Union. The predominantly Italian city of Trieste, also claimed by Yugoslavia, was to be made a Free Territory. It proved even more difficult to organize this, however, than the Free City of Danzig after World War I.

With the exception of the Italo-Yugoslav frontier, the territorial settlement in the Danubian and Balkan region was to a large extent a return to the much criticized boundaries of the 1919–1920 peace treaties. Again Hungary lost what Hitler had restored to her in 1939–1940 at the expense of Czechoslovakia and Rumania. But Czechoslovakia did not regain Carpatho-Ruthenia, which she formally ceded to the Soviet Union on June 29, 1945, and Rumania did regain the whole of Transylvania but not her losses to the Soviet Union and Bulgaria. The treaty with Finland was even harsher than that imposed on that country in 1940. She now also lost to the Soviet Union her access to the Arctic Sea at Petsamo. She had to pay her powerful neighbor the same tremendous amount of reparations—three hundred million dollars—which was claimed from Rumania and Hungary.

The treaty with Finland did not have to promise the withdrawal of occupation troops because that country, after concluding an armistice with the Soviet Union on September 19, 1944, was not occupied by the Red Army. And in spite of the economic clauses of the treaty which made Finland heavily dependent upon Russia, she had to suffer much less political interference than any other country of East Central Europe and was permitted to again enjoy a democratic form of government, having to observe a very cautious attitude, however, in the field of foreign relations. Such comparative respect for Finland's sovereignty and self-government, at least for the time being, can be explained by the fact that as in the past the main drive of Russia's expansion was not in the direction of the Scandinavian region, with which Finland remained more closely associated than with East Central Europe, but in the direction of the center and the south of the Continent.

In the south, at least as far as the shores of the Mediterranean were concerned, again as in the past that drive met the decided opposition of Britain and now of the United States too. And this not only explains why Russia hesitated to press her traditional claims regarding the Straits, which Turkey was determined to defend with Western backing, but also the situation of Greece which, like Finland in the north, remained exceptionally free from Russian and Communist domination. Liberated by British troops, the Greeks, too, in 1946 could hold free elections supervised by the Western powers. These elections showed a rightist majority as well as a plebiscite in favor of the return of King George II who after his death in 1947 was succeeded by his brother Paul. After failing to seize power through violence, the Communist minority in the country could continue guerilla warfare, particularly in the northern border regions. This delayed sorely needed postwar reconstruction because the guerilla fighters were supported from the Communist-controlled neighboring states.

From the very moment of Red Army occupation, the whole of East Central Europe between Finland and Greece was indeed Communist controlled. This was true not only of the Baltic countries, which like Byelorussia and the Ukraine were again considered Soviet Republics and had to suffer once more the most violent terror and mass deportations, amounting to a gradual genocide of these small nations, but also of the remaining seven countries which were supposed to be restored to independence. The fate of the former allies, Poland, Czechoslovakia, and Yugoslavia, of the ex-enemies, Hungary, Rumania, and Bulgaria, and that of Albania, submerged by the Italian conquest on the eve of the war, was strangely analogous. One of the few differences in their respective situations resulted from the fact that under the pretext of protecting the communications lines with the Russian zones of occupation in Germany and Austria, strong Red Army forces were to remain indefinitely in Poland as well as in Hungary and Rumania, which otherwise should have been evacuated ninety days after the coming into force of the peace treaties.

There were also differences in the timetable of the sovietization which in all these countries was steadily progressing on Moscow's orders, the promise of consultation or joint action with the Western powers broken everywhere immediately after Yalta. Since comparatively free elections like those held in Czechoslovakia and Hungary did not give the Communists a needed majority, the elections in Poland, to whose complete control Russia attached a special importance as in the past, were delayed until January 19, 1947. They were then prepared and held under such pressure that the only important opposition group, the Peasant Party, was reduced to an insignificant number of seats in the Diet and could be completely excluded from the government. Its leader, Mr. Mikołajczyk, decided to escape from the country in the fall of the same year. One year later the Socialists were forced to merge with the Communists, and on November 7, 1949, the last appearances of Poland's independence were dropped, when at the "request" of Communist President Bierut the Soviet Marshal Constantine Rokossovsky was made commander in chief of the Polish army, minister of defense, and the real master of the country.

Under these circumstances it proved to be of the highest importance that Poland alone among all the countries "behind the curtain" continued to have her free and legitimate government in exile which still is recognized by at least some powers, including the Vatican. From London it remains in contact with Poles all over the world. Before he died in 1947, President Raczkiewicz constitutionally designated the former foreign minister, August Zaleski, as his successor, and the National Council or Parliament in Exile was reopened in 1949.

King Michael of Rumania, who first was forced by the Russians to appoint a Communist government and who on December 31, 1947, had to abdicate, while a reign of terror liquidated all democratic opposition in the country, also went into exile, along with King Peter of Yugoslavia. In Bulgaria mass executions started at once after the occupation by the Red Army, and culminated in the death of the peasant leader Petkov in 1947. A year before the monarchy had been abolished, though King Boris who died during the war, probably a victim of the Nazis, had left a minor son, Simeon II. Equally easy proved to be the establishment of a Communist dictatorship in Albania under the partisan leader Enver Hoxha.

A similar "People's Democracy," as these regimes were everywhere called, could be forced upon the Hungarians only gradually. The royal tradition, here more than nine hundred years old, was abolished at once. But the truly democratic party of the Small Landholders first gained a decisive majority in Parliament so that the most ruthless pressure with the usual arrests and trials was necessary until its leader Ferenc Nagy was forced to go into exile. He was replaced as premier by the Communist Matyas Rákosi, whose regime became notorious through the persecution and trial of Cardinal Mindszenty, sentenced to life imprisonment on February 8, 1949—a symbol of the resistance of the Catholic Church against Communist tyranny.

Those who hoped that Czechoslovakia with her uninterrupted democratic tradition and consistently pro-Russian policy would remain comparatively free were disillusioned when on February 25, 1948, a Communist coup also enslaved that country. President Beneš, who had returned from exile immediately after a liberation to which the American forces, though already approaching Prague from the West, were not permitted to contribute decisively, now had to resign, as after Munich. He died soon after and was replaced by Communist Klement Gottwald. Jan Masaryk, the son of the founder of the republic and Beneš' closest collaborator, holding the office of foreign minister to the last moment, was either killed or committed suicide.

Russia continued to oppose any federations among her satellites, even after bringing them under complete Communist control. Only bilateral treaties among them were permitted to supplement the treaties of close alliance and cooperation which each of them had to conclude with Moscow. Their policies were, however, coordinated under the strict supervision of both Russia and the Communist party by the creation of the Communist Information Bureau (Cominform) in September, 1947. This now took the place of the famous Comintern, the Communist International, which was formally dissolved in 1943. But the following year, 1948, there nevertheless occurred a surprising split in the apparently well-consolidated camp of Russian satellites in East Central Europe. Tito decided to oppose Russian interference and Cominform control and to make Yugoslavia independent.

The local dictator who had started out as a tool of Russia, and whose regime had been particularly ruthless from the beginning, as evidenced by the execution of General Mihailovich and the subsequent trial of Archbishop Stepinac, the Primate of Croatia, remained, however, a Communist who pretended to follow Lenin's doctrine more faithfully than Stalin. It would therefore be a dangerous illusion to believe that the Western democracies can find in Tito a reliable ally, and that the freedom-loving individualistic peoples of Yugoslavia now enjoy real liberty in their internal life. There is no liberty behind the barbed wire which separates East Central Europe, abandoned to Communism, from the democratic world.

EAST CENTRAL EUROPE AND AMERICA

In the desperate situation after World War II, the peoples of East Central Europe are looking toward the United States of America, which contributed so much to their liberation after World War I and which, by contributing so decisively to the fall of Hitler, hoped to liberate them again. If that second liberation within the lifetime of the same generation did not succeed, it was because Soviet Russia, too weak to conquer East Central Europe in the confused situation after 1918, was not only strong enough to do so in the even more chaotic conditions after 1945 but in that critical year still enjoyed the confidence of the United States which did not yet know its most powerful ally sufficiently well or Russia's earlier role in the history of East Central Europe.

Even less well known in America was East Central Europe itself. The historic tradition of the close association of that whole region with the Western world had been concealed by the hostility of the immediate western neighbor, Germany, which always tried to create the impression that she was the last bulwark of the West and that east of her there was nothing but a semi-Asiatic region of transition, destined to be controlled by either Germany or Russia.

Even in the times of their greatness and freedom, the friendly relations of the East Central European peoples with the West had been almost exclusively with the Latin West, particularly with France. Similar relations with the Anglo-Saxon world were slow to develop. First of these, of course, were with England. It was not before the Wilsonian era that intimate relations were established with the United States, since in the earlier phase of America's independence most of East Central Europe was under the neighboring empires. But in addition to the well-known participation of a few Polish leaders in the American War for Independence, there was, from the colonial period and particularly through the emigration movement of the nineteenth century, a participation of large masses of people from all East Central European countries in the rise and development of the United States. Their descendants, so numerous among the Americans of today, have of course a special interest in their respective countries of origin, whose cultural tradition, badly distorted under the present regimes, has the best chance of survival on American soil.

But East Central Europe is important for all Americans whatever their origin may be. As a world power, the United States has an interest in the whole world, and especially in those regions where peace has been frequently threatened in the past and may be threatened again in the future, and where the American principles of freedom and justice for all are disregarded. If this is true for all continents and for peoples of any race, even if their culture is completely alien to the American, it is even more evident in a case where at least one hundred millions of Europeans—one hundred and fifty if the Ukrainians and White Ruthenians are included—all of them united with the Americans by the most intimate bonds of religion, race, and culture, could be a stronghold of peace at the very frontier of Western civilization.

The tragic fate of these peoples, claimed by the East but only to be absorbed and dominated by old Russian imperialism and modern totalitarianism in its Communist form, frequently rejected by a West that is artificially limited to the Anglo-Saxon, Romance, and Germanic peoples, ought to be a matter of serious concern for America, not only for reasons of principle but also because her own vital interests are directly affected. This was realized, though only for a short time, toward the end and in the aftermath of World War I. It was quite insufficiently realized at the beginning of World War II which shocked America deeply only from the moment when Western Europe was invaded and the British Empire endangered. And at the end of that war the great mistake was made of practically abandoning East Central Europe while theoretically assuming heavy responsibilities there without securing ways and means of carrying them out.

There reappeared, therefore, a situation, familiar to those who look upon all history from the point of view of the nineteenth century, where Russia with her strictly controlled sphere of influence once more became a direct neighbor of Germany. This means a permanent pressure exercised upon the Western world with Germany as last line of defense, and a chance for the Germans, defeated at such a heavy price, to play the decisive role in the rivalry between West and East which divides Europe and the world.

For the nations between Germany and Russia, this simply means a death sentence which at the same time would deprive America of a whole group of potential allies. Allies many of them have been in a recent past, and all of them would like to be in the future, after their terrible experiences of the present. They have been deeply impressed by American aid, official and private, in their tremendous task of postwar reconstruction, although their actual Russian masters did not permit them to participate in the Marshall Plan. They have been neither convinced by anti-American propaganda nor discouraged by the real failures of American diplomacy. They are aware that if the United States and the other Western powers continue to have diplomatic relations with their foreign imposed masters, who misrepresent them in the United Nations if they do not walk out at Russia's order, it is because they would otherwise be entirely cut off from the free world. And they are more eager than ever before to join that world in the spirit of their own democratic tradition and cultural heritage.

How that could be achieved is not a question for the historian to answer. But history clearly shows the foundations for such a process, which had been laid in the Middle Ages, which were developed in the Renaissance at least by those peoples of East Central Europe which were still free, and which survived the crises of modern times that temporarily deprived all of them of freedom. Since the democratic Christian West ceased to be limited to Western Europe and received America as a partner and eventually as a leader, the chances for such cooperation of East Central Europe with that West were greatly improved, although in the twenty years of freedom granted to that region between the two world wars no sufficient advantage was taken of these new possibilities. But such a chance can reappear again under circumstances that are still impossible to foresee. Then a new era might be inaugurated for all those who today suffer in East Central Europe, or at least for their descendants, because for the first time in history they would belong to the same great community, not only with Western Europe but also with America.

BIBLIOGRAPHY

I. General

This bibliography, which is limited to books in English, French, and German, does not include any publications on general European history, although in some of them, especially in a few recent works, for instance in J. L. La Monte, *The World of the Middle Ages* (New York, 1949), or C. E. Black and E. C. Helmreich, *Twentieth Century Europe* (New York, 1950), a serious effort has been made to give the countries of East Central Europe more attention than before. The only book which tries to cover the history of all these countries, along with that of Russia and Turkey, is *Central-Eastern Europe,* by J. C. Roucek and associates (New York, 1946). This volume, however, considers chiefly the contemporary period. For those nations of East Central Europe which are Slavic, the historical chapters of *A Handbook of Slavic Studies* (Cambridge, Mass., 1949), edited by L. Strakhovsky, with excellent bibliographies, are of basic importance. Among other publications dealing with the general background of Slavic culture, the following are particularly valuable:

BRÜCKNER, A. *Der Eintritt der Slaven in die Weltgeschichte.* Berlin, 1909.
CROSS, S. H. *Slavic Culture Through the Ages.* Cambridge, Mass., 1948.
LÉGER, L. *Les anciennes civilisations slaves.* Paris, 1921.
MOUSSET, A. *The World of the Slavs.* New York, 1951.
NIEDERLE, L. *Manuel de l'antiquité slave.* 2 vols. Paris, 1923, 1926.
ŠAFAŘIK, P. J. *Slavische Altertümer.* 2 vols. Leipzig, 1843, 1844.

Among the general histories of individual nations or regions, the following might be mentioned:

A. FOR THE BALTIC REGION

BILMANIS, A. *Baltic Essays.* Washington, D. C., 1945.
———. *History of Latvia.* Princeton, 1951.
CHASE, TH. G. *The Story of Lithuania.* New York, 1946.
JURGELA, C. R. *History of the Lithuanian Nation.* New York, 1948.
SOMMER, W. *Geschichte Finnlands.* München, 1938.
VITOLS, H. *La mer baltique et les États baltes.* Paris, 1935.

B. FOR POLAND

Cambridge History of Poland from the Origins to Sobieski (1696). Cambridge, 1950.
Cambridge History of Poland from Augustus II to Pilsudski (1637–1935). Cambridge, 1941.

There is a new edition [handwritten]

478   BIBLIOGRAPHY

DYBOSKI, R. *Poland in World Civilization.* New York, 1950.
HALECKI, O. *A History of Poland.* New York, 1943.   *1955* [handwritten]
KUTRZEBA, H. *Grundriss der polnischen Verfassungsgeschichte.* Berlin, 1912.
LEDNICKI, W. *Life and Culture of Poland.* New York, 1944.
ROSE, W. J. *Poland—Old and New.* London, 1948.
WOJCIECHOWSKI, Z. (ed.). *Poland's Place in Europe.* Poznań, 1947.
ŻÓŁTOWSKI, A. *Border of Europe—A Study of the Polish Eastern Provinces.*
    London, 1950.

                    C. FOR THE UKRAINE

ALLEN, W. E. D. *The Ukraine: A History.* Cambridge, 1940.
CHAMBERLIN, W. H. *The Ukraine: A Submerged Nation.* New York, 1944.
DOROSHENKO, D. *History of the Ukraine.* Edmonton, 1939.
HRUSHEVSKY, M. *A History of the Ukraine.* New York, 1941.
MANNING, C. *The Story of the Ukraine.* New York, 1947.
SMOLKA, ST. *Die reussiche Welt.* Wien, 1916.

                  D. FOR CZECHOSLOVAKIA

KROFTA, K. *A Short History of Czechoslovakia.* New York, 1934.
———. *Das Deutschtum in der tschechoslowakischen Geschichte.* Prague, 1934.
LUETZOW, C. F. *Bohemia.* New York, 1939.
SETON-WATSON, R. W. *A History of the Czechs and Slovaks.* London, 1943.
THOMSON, S. H. *Czechoslovakia in European History.* Princeton, 1943.
WISKEMANN, E. *Czechs and Germans.* New York, 1938.   *53* [handwritten]

                    E. FOR HUNGARY

DOMANOVSZKY, A. *Die Geschichte Ungarns.* München, 1923.
KOSÁRY, D. G. *A History of Hungary.* New York, 1941.
LUKINICH, I. *A History of Hungary.* Budapest, 1937.
SZEKFÜ, J. *Der Staat Ungarn.* Berlin, 1918.
TELEKI, P. *The Evolution of Hungary and Its Place in Europe.* New York, 1923.

Lengyel, E. 1000 Years of Hungary, " " 1958 [handwritten]

                  F. FOR THE BALKAN REGION

FORBES, N., *et al. The Balkans: A History of Bulgaria, Serbia, Greece, Rumania,*
    and Turkey. Oxford, 1915.
IORGA, N. *Histoire des États balkaniques jusqu'à 1924.* Paris, 1925.
RISTELHUBER, R. *Histoire des peuples balkaniques.* Paris, 1950.
SCHEVILL, F., and GEWEHR, W. M. *A History of the Balkan Peninsula.* New York,
    1933.
STADTMÜLLER, G. *Geschichte Südosteuropas.* München, 1950 (including the Danu-
    bian region).

                    G. FOR RUMANIA

IORGA, N. *A History of Roumania.* New York, 1926.
———. *Histoire des Roumains et de la romanité orientale.* 5 vols. Bucarest, 1937.
———. *La place des Roumains dans l'histoire universelle.* 2 vols. Bucarest, 1935.
SETON-WATSON, R. W. *History of the Rumanians.* Cambridge, 1934.

H. FOR YUGOSLAVIA

GOPCEVIĆ, J. *Geschichte von Montenegro und Albanien*. Gotha, 1914.
KLAIĆ, V. *Geschichte Bosniens*. Leipzig, 1885.
LOUČAR, D. *The Slovenes—A Social History*. Cleveland, 1939.
ŠIŠIĆ, F. *Geschichte der Kroaten*. Zagreb, 1917.
TEMPERLEY, H. *History of Serbia*. London, 1917.
VOJNOVIĆ, L. *Histoire de Dalmatie*. 2 vols. Paris, 1934.

I. FOR BULGARIA

ANTONOFF, V. *Bulgarien vom Beginn seines staatlichen Bestehens bis auf unsere Zeit, 679–1917*. Berlin, 1917.
SLATARSKI, V. N., and HANEFF, N. *Geschichte der Bulgaren*. 2 vols. Leipzig, 1917–1918.
SONGEON, G. *Histoire de la Bulgarie des origines jusqu'à nos jours, 485–1913*. Paris, 1913.

J. FOR GREECE

FINLAY, G. *A History of Greece*. 7 vols. Oxford, 1877.
HERTZBERG, G. F. *Geschichte Griechenlands*. 2 vols. Gotha, 1876–1879.

II. MEDIEVAL BACKGROUND AND ORIGIN

For this and the following two sections, to the end of the eighteenth century, the monographs in Western languages are rather scarce. Therefore no classification according to countries or regions has seemed advisable. In the medieval section, a few books which include the Renaissance period have been listed.

BACHMAN, A. *Geschichte Böhmens bis 1526*. 2 vols. Gotha, 1899–1905.
DVORNIK, F. *The Making of Central and Eastern Europe*. London, 1949.
———. *Les légendes de Constantin et Methodius vues de Byzance*. Prague, 1933.
———. *Les Slaves, Byzance et Rome au IXe siècle*. Paris, 1926.
GIESEBRECHT, H. L. Th. *Wendische Geschichten aus den Jahren 780–1182*. 3 vols. Berlin, 1843.
GRÜNHAGEN, C. *Geschichte Schlesiens*. 2 vols. Gotha, 1884–1886.
HÓMAN, B. *King Stephen the Saint*. Budapest, 1938.
JIREČEK, C. *Geschichte der Serben*. 2 vols. to 1571. Gotha, 1911, 1918.
KOSTRZEWSKI, J. *Les origines de la civilisation polonaise. Préhistoire-protohistoire*. Paris, 1949.
PALACKY, F. *Geschichte von Böhmen*. 5 vols. to 1526. Prague, 1864–1867.
RUNCIMAN, S. *History of the First Bulgarian Empire*. London, 1930.
TOTORAITIS, J. *Die Litauer unter König Mindowe*. Freiburg, 1905.
VERNADSKY, G. *Ancient Russia*. New Haven, 1944.
———. *Kievan Russia*. New Haven, 1948.
WERUNSKY, E. *Geschichte Kaiser Karl IV und seiner Zeit*. 4 vols. Innsbruck, 1880–1892.
WOJCIECHOWSKI, Z. *L'État polonais du moyen âge. Histoire des institutions*. Paris, 1949.
———. *Mieszko I and the Rise of the Polish State*. Toruń, 1936.

III. Renaissance Developments

Bellée, H. *Polen und die römische Kurie 1414–1424.* Berlin, 1914.
Berga, A. *Pierre Skarga.* Paris, 1916.
Berzeviczy, A. *Béatrice d'Aragon, reine de Hongrie.* 2 vols. Paris, 1911–1912.
Caro, J. *Geschichte Polens.* vols. 3–5 1386–1506. Gotha, 1865–1888.
Champion, P. *Henri de Valois, roi de Pologne.* Paris, 1946.
Denis, E. *Huss et la guerre des Hussites.* Paris, 1878.
Etienne Batory, roi de Pologne, prince de Transylvanie. Cracovie, 1935.
Fox, P. *The Reformation in Poland.* Baltimore, 1926.
Fraknói, W. *Mathias Hunyady.* Budapest, 1890.
Halecki, O. *Das Nationalitätenproblem im alten Polen.* Kraków, 1916.
————. *The Crusade of Varna.* New York, 1943.
Kellogg, Ch. *Jadwiga, Poland's Great Queen.* New York, 1931.
Likowski, E. *Die Kirchenunion von Brest-Litovsk.* Freiburg, 1900.
Luetzow, C. F. *The Life and Time of Master John Hus.* New York, 1909.
————. *The Hussite Wars.* New York, 1914.
Morawski, C. *Histoire de l'université de Cracovie.* 2 vols. Cracovie, 1903.
Nieborowski, P. *Der Deutsche Orden und Polen.* Breslau, 1924.
Noailles, Marquis de. *Henri de Valois et la Pologne.* Paris, 1867.
Pfitzner, J. *Grossfürst Vitold von Litauen als Staatsmann.* Brünn, 1930.
Spinka, M. *John Hus and the Czech Reform.* Chicago, 1941.
Uebersberger, H. *Österreich und Russland: I (1488–1605).* Wien, 1906.
Wilbur, E. M. *A History of Unitarianism.* Cambridge, Mass., 1945.
Wotschke, Th. *Geschichte der Reformation in Polen.* Leipzig, 1911.
Zivier, E. *Neuere Geschichte Polens: I (1506–1572).* Gotha, 1915.

IV. Seventeenth and Eighteenth Centuries

Askenazy, S. *Danzig and Poland.* London, 1930.
Bain, N. *The Last King of Poland and His Contemporaries.* New York, 1903.
Bretholz, B. *Neuere Geschichte Böhmens.* Gotha, 1920.
Denis, E. *La fin de l'indépendance bohême.* 2 vols. Paris, 1890.
————. *La Bohême depuis la Montagne Blanche.* 2 vols. Paris, 1930.
Forst-Battaglia, O. *Jan Sobieski, König von Polen.* Einsiedeln, 1946.
————. *Stanislaw August Poniatowski.* Berlin, 1927.
Hadrovics, L. *L'Église serbe sous la domination turque.* Paris, 1947.
Haiman, W. *Kosciuszko in the American Revolution.* New York, 1943.
————. *Kosciuszko, Leader and Exile.* New York, 1946.
Hajek, A. *Bulgarien unter der Türkenherrschaft.* Berlin, 1925.
Kerner, R. J. *Bohemia in the Eighteenth Century.* New York, 1932.
Konopczynski, W. *Le Liberum Veto.* Paris, 1930.
Lord, R. H. *The Second Partition of Poland.* Cambridge, Mass., 1915.
Marczali, H. *Hungaria in the Eighteenth Century.* Cambridge, 1910.
Martel, A. *La langue polonaise dans les pays ruthènes, 1569–1667.* Lille, 1935.
Morton, J. B. *John Sobieski, King of Poland.* London, 1932.
Rose, W. G. *Stanislaw Konarski.* London, 1929.
Sobieski, W. *Der Kampf um die Ostsee.* Leipzig, 1933.
Spinka, M. *John Amos Comenius.* Chicago, 1943.
Vernadsky, G. *Bohdan, Hetman of Ukraine.* New Haven, 1941.

V. Nationalism Versus Imperialism: 1795–1914

Ancel, J. *La Macédoine, son évolution contemporaine.* Paris, 1930.
————. *L'unité de la politique bulgare, 1870–1919.* Paris, 1919.
Askenazy, S. *Napoléon et la Pologne.* Paris, 1903.

————. *Prince Joseph Poniatowski.* London, n.d.

AUERBACH, B. *Les races et les nationalités en Autriche-Hongrie.* Paris, 1917.

BERNHARD, L. *Das polnische Gemeinwesen im deutschen Staat.* Leipzig, 1910.

BLACK, C. E. *The Establishment of Constitutional Government in Bulgaria.* Princeton, 1943.

BOGIČEVIĆ, M. *Die auswärtige Politik Serbiens, 1903–1904.* 3 vols. Berlin, 1931.

CHACONAS, S. G. *Adamantios Korais: A Study in Greek Nationalism.* New York, 1942.

CLINE, M. A. *The American Attitude Towards the Greek War of Independence.* Georgia, 1930.

CRAWLEY, C. W. *The Question of Greek Independence, 1821–1833.* New York, 1931.

DENTON, W. *Montenegro, Its People and Their History.* London, 1877.

DMOWSKI, R. *La question polonaise.* Paris, 1909.

DRIAULT, E., and LHERITIER, M. *Histoire diplomatique de la Grèce.* 5 vols. Paris, 1925–1926.

EISENMANN, L. *Le compromis austro-hongrois de 1867.* Paris, 1904.

FELDMAN, W. *Geschichte der politischen Ideen in Polen seit dessen Teilungen.* Leipzig, 1917.

FISCHEL, A. *Der Panslavismus bis zum Weltkrieg.* Stuttgart, 1919.

GEWEHR, W. M. *The Rise of Nationalism in the Balkans.* New York, 1931.

HAJEK, A. *Bulgariens Befreiung und staatliche Entwicklung unter seinen ersten Fürsten.* Berlin, 1939.

HANDELSMAN, M. *Les idées françaises et la mentalité politique de la Pologne au XIXe siècle.* Paris, 1927.

————. *Czartoryski, Nicholas Ier et la question du Proche Orient.* Paris, 1934.

HELMREICH, E. C. *Diplomacy of the Balkan Wars, 1912–1913.* Cambridge, Mass., 1938.

HENRY, R. *Le Congrès slave de Prague en 1848.* Paris, 1903.

HYDE, A. M. *A Diplomatic History of Bulgaria, 1870–1886.* Urbana, 1931.

JAKŠIĆ, J. *L'Europe et la résurrection de la Serbie, 1804–1834.* Paris, 1917.

JÁSZI, O. *The Dissolution of the Habsburg Monarchy.* Chicago, 1929.

KALTCHAS, N. *Introduction to the Constitutional History of Modern Greece.* New York, 1940.

KANN, R. A. *The Multinational Empire: Nationalism and National Reform in the Habsburg Monarchy, 1848–1918.* 2 vols. New York, 1950.

KRASIŃSKI, V. *Panslavism and Germanism.* London, 1848.

LAMBERT, M. *Die deutsche Polenpolitik, 1772–1914.* Berlin, 1920.

LISICKI, H. *Le Marquis Wielopolski.* 2 vols. Vienna, 1880.

MAY, A. J. *The Hapsburg Monarchy 1867–1914.* Cambridge, Mass., 1951.

MILLER, W. *The Ottoman Empire and Its Successors, 1801–1936.* New York, 1936.

MORISON, W. A. *The Revolt of the Serbs Against the Turks, 1804–1813.* New York, 1942.

NINČIĆ, M. *La crise bosniaque 1908–1909 et les puissances européennes.* 2 vols. Paris, 1937.

POPOVICI, A. *Die Vereinigten Staaten von Gross-Österreich.* Leipzig, 1906.

RADOSLAVOV, V. *Bulgarien und die Weltkrise.* Berlin, 1923.

ROBINSON, V. *Albania's Road to Freedom.* New York, 1942.

ROSE, W. J. *The Rise of Polish Democracy.* London, 1944.

ROYAL INSTITUTE OF INTERNATIONAL AFFAIRS. *Nationalism.* New York, 1939.

SCHMITT, B. E. *The Annexation of Bosnia.* New York, 1937.

SETON-WATSON, R. W. *Racial Problems in Hungary.* London, 1908.

————. *The Rise of Nationalism in the Balkans.* New York, 1918.

————. *The Southern Slav Question in the Habsburg Monarchy.* London, 1911.

SOKOLNICKI, M. *Les origines de l'émigration polonaise en France.* Paris, 1931.

STAVRIANOS, L. S. *Balkan Federation.* Northampton, 1944.

STOJANOVIC, M. *The Great Powers and the Balkans, 1875–1878.* Cambridge, 1939.

STEED, H. W. *The Habsburg Monarchy.* New York, 1919.
SZAROTA, M. *Die letzten Tage der Republik Krakau.* Breslau, 1911.
TAYLOR, A. J. P. *The Habsburg Monarchy, 1815–1948.* New York, 1949.
TIMS, R. W. *Germanizing Prussian Poland.* New York, 1941.
VOJNOVIC, L. *Dalmatia and the Yugoslav Movement.* New York, 1913.
VOSHNJAK, B. *A Bulwark Against Germany: The Slovenes.* New York, 1919.
WEILL, G. *L'Europe du XIXe siècle et l'idée de nationalité.* Paris, 1938.
WUORINEN, J. H. *Nationalism in Modern Finland.* New York, 1931.

VI. CONTEMPORARY HISTORY: FROM WORLD WAR I

In contradistinction to the earlier periods, the recent developments in East Central Europe up to the present are discussed in numerous books published in Western languages and listed in various bibliographies. The comprehensive sections on Central Europe, Eastern Europe, and the Balkan Area in *Foreign Affairs Bibliography 1919–1932*, by W. L. Langer and H. F. Armstrong (New York, 1933) and *Foreign Affairs Bibliography 1932–1942*, by R. G. Woolbert (New York, 1945), include publications in all languages. Therefore only a limited number of books which seem particularly useful have been selected here.

A. GENERAL PROBLEMS

BASCH, A. *The Danubian Basin and the German Economic Sphere.* New York, 1943.
GRAHAM, M. W. *The New Governments of Central Europe.* New York, 1924.
——. *The New Governments of Eastern Europe.* New York, 1927.
KROFTA, K. *Les nouveaux états dans l'Europe centrale.* Paris, 1930.
LHERITIER, M. *L'Europe orientale à l'époque contemporaine.* Paris, 1938.
MACARTNEY, C. A. *National States and National Minorities.* London, 1934.
MITRANY, D. *The Effects of the War in South-Eastern Europe.* New York, 1936.
NEWMAN, B. *The New Europe.* New York, 1943.
POSVOLSKY, L. *Economic Nationalism of the Danubian States.* New York, 1928.
SETON-WATSON, H. *Eastern Europe Between the Wars: 1918–1941.* Cambridge, 1945.
TEMPERLEY, H. W. W. (ed.) *A History of the Peace Conference of Paris.* 6 vols. London, 1921–1924.
WHEELER-BENNETT, J. W. *The Forgotten Peace—Brest Litovsk 1918.* New York, 1939.

B. THE BALTIC COUNTRIES

BILMANIS, A. *The Baltic States and the Baltic Sea.* Washington, D. C., 1943.
——. *Latvia and Her Baltic Neighbors.* Washington, D. C., 1942.
——. *Latvia in the Making.* Riga, 1928.
GRAHAM, M. W. *The Diplomatic Recognition of the Border States.* 3 vols. Berkeley, 1935–1941.
HANNULA, J. O. *Finland's War of Independence.* London, 1939.
HARRISON, E. G. *Lithuania, Past and Present.* New York, 1922.
HEUMANN, G. *Aspects juridiques de l'indépendance estonienne.* Paris, 1938.
JACKSON, J. H. *Finland.* New York, 1940.
——. *Estonia.* New York, 1941.
MONTFORT, H. DE. *Les nouveaux États de la Baltique.* Paris, 1933.
PICK, T. W. *The Baltic Nations: Estonia, Latvia, Lithuania.* London, 1945.

PUSTA, K. R. *The Soviet Union and the Baltic States.* New York, 1942.
REDDAWAY, W. F. *Problems of the Baltic.* London, 1940.
ROYAL INSTITUTE OF INTERNATIONAL AFFAIRS. *The Baltic States.* London, 1938.

C. POLAND

BLOCISZEWSKI, J. *La restauration de la Pologne et la diplomatie européenne.* Paris, 1927.
BREGMAN, A. *La politique de la Pologne dans la Société des Nations.* Paris, 1932.
BUELL, R. L. *Poland: Key to Europe.* New York, 1939.
BURKE, E. R. *The Polish Policy of the Central Powers During the World War.* Chicago, 1936.
DYBOSKI, R. *Poland.* London, 1933.
FISHER, H. H. *America and the New Poland.* New York, 1938.
MACHRAY, R. *The Poland of Pilsudski.* New York, 1936.
MODZELEWSKI, J. (ed.). *La Pologne de 1919 à 1939.* 3 vols. Neuchatel, 1945–1947.
PHILIPP, CH. *Paderewski.* New York, 1934.
PILSUDSKI, J. *L'année 1920.* Paris, 1929.
Problèmes politiques de la Pologne contemporaine. 4 vols. Paris, 1931–1933.
ROSE, W. J. *The Drama of Upper Silesia.* London, 1936.
SCHMITT, B. E. (ed.). *Poland.* Berkeley, 1945.
ZWEIG, F. *Poland Between Two Wars: A Critical Study of Economic and Social Changes.* London, 1944.

D. UKRAINE

BORSCHAK, E. *L'Ukraine à la Conférence de la Paix.* Paris, 1938.
CHOULGINE, A. *L'Ukraine contre Moscou.* Paris, 1935.
MANNING, C. *Twentieth Century Ukraine.* New York, 1951.

E. AUSTRIA AND HUNGARY

ALMOND, N., and LUTZ, R. H. *The Treaty of Saint-Germain.* Stanford, 1935.
BALL, M. M. *Postwar German-Austrian Relations: The Anschluss Movement, 1918–1936.* Stanford, 1937.
DEAK, F. *Hungary at the Paris Peace Conference.* New York, 1942.
FUCHS, M. *Showdown in Vienna: The Death of Austria.* New York, 1939.
MACARTNEY, C. A. *Hungary and Her Successors.* New York, 1937.
SCHUSCHNIGG, K. *My Austria.* New York, 1938.
———. *Austrian Requiem.* New York, 1947.

F. THE LITTLE ENTENTE COUNTRIES

BAERLEIN, H. *The Birth of Yugoslavia.* 2 vols. London, 1922.
BEARD, CH., and RADIN, G. *The Balkan Pivot: Yugoslavia.* New York, 1929.
BENEŠ, E. *My War Memoirs.* Boston, 1928.
ČAPEK, K. *President Masaryk Tells His Story.* New York, 1935.
CODRESCU, F. *La Petite Entente.* 2 vols. Paris, 1932.
CRANE, J. O. *The Little Entente.* New York, 1931.
HAUMANT, E. *La formation de la Yougoslavie.* Paris, 1930.
KERNER, R. J. (ed.). *Czechoslovakia: Twenty Years of Independence.* Berkeley, 1940.
———. *Yugoslavia.* Berkeley, 1949.
KYBAL, V. *Les origines diplomatiques de l'État tchécoslovaque.* Paris, 1929.
MASARYK, TH. G. *The Making of a State.* London, 1927.

MACHRAY, R. *The Struggle for the Danube and the Little Entente 1929–1938.* London, 1938.
MARKOVICH, L. *La politique extérieure de la Yougoslavie.* Paris, 1935.
ROUCEK, J. S. *Contemporary Rumania and Her Problems.* Hanford, 1932.
TEXTOR, L. E. *Land Reform in Czechoslovakia.* London, 1923.

G. THE BALKAN COUNTRIES

ABBOTT, G. F. *Greece and the Allies 1914–1922.* London, 1922.
ALASTOS, D. *Venizelos.* London, 1942.
ARMSTRONG, H. F. *The New Balkans.* New York, 1926.
GENEV, G. P. *Bulgaria and the Treaty of Neuilly.* Sofia, 1935.
GESHKOFF, T. I. *Balkan Union.* New York, 1940.
KERNER, R. F., and HOWARD, H. N. *The Balkan Conferences and the Balkan Entente 1930–1935.* Berkeley, 1936.
MILLER, W. *The Balkans.* London, 1923.
———. *Greece.* New York, 1928.
POSVOLSKY, E. *Bulgaria's Economic Position.* Washington, D.C., 1930.
ROUCEK, J. C. *The Politics of the Balkans.* New York, 1939.
ROYAL INSTITUTE OF INTERNATIONAL AFFAIRS. *South Eastern Europe.* London, 1939.
STICKNEY, E. P. *South Albania and North Epirus in European International Affairs 1912–1923.* Stanford, 1926.
SWIRE, J. *Albania: The Rise of a Kingdom.* London, 1929.
———. *King Zog's Albania.* London, 1937.

H. WORLD WAR II AND AFTER

ANDERS, W. *An Army in Exile.* New York, 1950.
BOR-KOMOROWSKI, T. *The Secret Army.* London, 1950.
CIECHANOWSKI, J. *Defeat in Victory.* New York, 1946.
FOTICH, C. *The War We Lost.* New York, 1948.
FURLAN, B. *Fighting Yugoslavia.* New York, 1943.
GAFENCU, G. *The Last Days of Europe.* New York, 1948.
———. *Préliminaires de la guerre à l'Est.* Paris, 1945.
GRANT, D. H. *A German Protectorate.* London, 1942.
GROSS, F. *Crossroad of Two Continents: A Democratic Federation of East Central Europe.* New York, 1945.
GYORGY, A. *Governments of Danubian Europe.* New York, 1949.
HANC, J. *Tornado Across Eastern Europe.* New York, 1942.
HODŽA, M. *Federation in Central Europe.* New York, 1942.
KARSKI, J. *The Story of a Secret State.* New York, 1944.
KORBEL, J. *Tito's Communism.* Denver, 1951.
LANE, A. B. *I Saw Poland Betrayed.* New York, 1948.
MAC EOIN, G. *The Communist War on Religion.* New York, 1951.
MARTIN, D. *Ally Betrayal: The Uncensored Story of Tito and Mihailovich.* New York, 1946.
MIKOLAJCZYK, S. *The Rape of Poland.* New York, 1943.
NAGY, F. *The Struggle Behind the Iron Curtain.* New York, 1948.
NOEL, L. *L'aggression allemande contre la Pologne.* Paris, 1946.
SETON-WATSON, H. *The Eastern European Revolution.* New York, 1951.
WUORINEN, J. H. (ed.). *Finland and World War II, 1939–1944.* New York, 1948.

INDEX